LIBRARIES NI
WITHDRAWN FROM STOCK

Scotch-Irish Merchants in Colonial America

The Flaxseed Trade and Emigration from Ireland, 1718–1775

LIBRARIES NI
WITHDRAWN FROM STOCK

RICHARD K. MacMASTER

D1338956

ULSTER HISTORICAL FOUNDATION

For Eve

"We clamb the hill thegither."

Ulster Historical Foundation is pleased to acknowledge support for this publication from The Scotch-Irish Society of U.S.A.

COVER ILLUSTRATION:
View of the Long Wharf and Part of the Harbor of Boston in New England America (1889.0032.000A). Courtesy of the Bostonian Society.

First published 2009, reprinted 2013
by Ulster Historical Foundation
www.ancestryireland.com
www.booksireland.org.uk

Except as otherwise permitted under the Copyright, Designs and Patents Act 1988, this publication may only be reproduced, stored or transmitted in any form or by any means with the prior permission in writing of the publisher or, in the case of reprographic reproduction, in accordance with the terms of a licence issued by The Copyright Licensing Agency. Enquiries concerning reproduction outside those terms should be sent to the publisher.

© Richard K. MacMaster

ISBN: 978-1-903688-78-6

Printed by Sprint Print
Design and typesetting by FPM Publishing

CONTENTS

Abbreviations

CCCH   Cumberland County Court House (Carlisle, Pennsylvania)

HSP   Historical Society of Pennsylvania (Philadelphia, Pennsylvania)

HSYC   Historical Society of York County (York, Pennsylvania)

LC   Library of Congress

LCCH   Lancaster County Court House (Lancaster, Pennsylvania)

LCHS   Lancaster County Historical Society (Lancaster, Pennsylvania)

PHS   Presbyterian Historical Society (Philadelphia, Pennsylvania)

PMHB *Pennsylvania Magazine of History and Biography*

PRONI Public Record Office of Northern Ireland

PSA   Pennsylvania State Archives (Harrisburg, Pennsylvania)

Acknowledgements

I FIRST THOUGHT OF WRITING THIS BOOK fifteen years ago, but it would have been a very different book. During an academic year spent in Belfast in 1995–6 with support from a British Council Research Fellowship, I was researching eighteenth-century emigration from Ulster to the North American Colonies. My aim was to take R. J. Dickson's classic study *Ulster Emigration to Colonial America 1718–1775* through the next generation before the Napoleonic Wars interrupted the pattern. The men who went out to America in the 1780s to represent firms in Belfast and Derry caught my attention more and more and especially the Scotch-Irish merchants who linked Belfast with Baltimore. As I began to observe the complexity of their business connections, it was also evident that these transatlantic networks were functioning from the earliest days of emigration and that the passenger trade could not be separated from Ulster's flaxseed imports and linen exports. To tell that story I temporarily set aside my notes and photocopied documents from the years after the American Revolution and plunged into the business world of the earlier eighteenth century.

The Pennsylvania Historical and Museum Commission made it possible for me to explore the commercial links between "Philadelphia Merchants, Backcountry Shopkeepers and 'Town-Building Fever' in the Lower Susquehanna Valley, 1755–1775" as a scholar in residence at the Pennsylvania State Archives.

Several chapters had an initial airing at academic conferences, including the Ulster-American Heritage Symposium, the Scotch-Irish Identity Symposium, the Irish Atlantic Conference at the

College of Charleston and conferences of the Pennsylvania Historical Association and the British Group for Early American History, where helpful comments led to extensive rethinking and rewriting.

While the final version reflects the author's interpretation of the sources and he alone must be held accountable for omissions and tangential rabbit trails, the gathering of historical information is inevitably a corporate enterprise. I am indebted to a great many friends and colleagues who freely shared their knowledge, notably Jean Agnew, Bill Crawford, John McCabe, Robert McClure, and Brian Trainor who introduced me to unsuspected sources in Belfast and Dublin. William Roulston has been an outstanding editor as well. A common enterprise in helping the Ulster-American Folk Park in Omagh, Co. Tyrone tell the emigration story brought me the friendship and valuable insights of John Gilmour, Denis Macneice, Phil Mowat, Graeme Kirkham, Marianne Wokeck, Michael Montgomery, Anita Puckett, Patrick Griffin, Katharine Brown, Ken Keller, Warren Hofstra, and Kerby Miller who each contributed some of their insight into eighteenth-century America to this book. I am also grateful to Judith Ridner, Michelle Mormul, David Mitchell and Thomas Truxes for helpful suggestions. June Lloyd, then librarian of the Historical Society of York County, Pennsylvania directed me to the James Fullton papers in her custody. Tom Ryan, Ginger Shelley, Heather Tennies, and the other staff at the Lancaster County Historical Society made my visits there both pleasant and profitable, as did the staff of the Pennsylvania State Archives, the Historical Society of Pennsylvania, and the Presbyterian Historical Society.

I would be remiss not to include the many members of the library staff at the University of Florida as well. Research would be impossible without the help of interlibrary loan librarians. I am particularly indebted to Janice Kaylor and the University of Florida interlibrary loan staff who never failed to find the most obscure title I requested.

RICHARD K. MacMASTER

Introduction

IN THE COURSE OF THE EIGHTEENTH CENTURY migration from Europe and Africa shaped the emerging consciousness and culture of the American Colonies. Whether free, bond servant, or slave, migrants brought skills and folkways from their motherlands, contributing to the agricultural and commercial development as well as to the peopling of North America. Emigrants from Ulster, the northern province of Ireland, did all of this and more. Ulster exported an economy.

That economy centred on the production of linen cloth, which began in a small way in the seventeenth century. An act of the English Parliament in 1696 gave impetus to Ulster's nascent linen industry by admitting Irish linens on favourable terms to the English market. In 1705 the English Parliament opened the American Colonies to linen produced in Ireland. This market would expand to absorb a larger and larger percentage of Ulster's ever-increasing production. W. H. Crawford succinctly described the integration of every facet of Ulster life into the linen economy. In the eighteenth century the domestic linen industry expanded so rapidly across the province that annual exports increased from less than a million to forty million yards of cloth. Flax was grown on every small farm, prepared and spun into linen yarn and woven into webs of cloth by families in their own homes, and sold in linen markets in towns to the linen drapers and bleachers who finished the linens and marketed them in Dublin or in Britain.

> As linen transactions were conducted in coin, money percolated throughout Ulster society so that in time many families

managed to get their feet on to the property ladder and Ulster
became noted for the density of its family farms.[1]

Within a few years linen transformed the Ulster landscape. By the
1720s flax growing and linen weaving replaced food crops as the
staples of Ulster agriculture. Attitudes changed with full integration
into a market-oriented economy. Landowners and tenants alike saw
land as a commodity to be sold or mortgaged to raise capital.[2]
Belfast and Londonderry emerged from obscurity shipping surplus
farm produce and attracted a new breed of overseas merchants.
Commercial networks quickly developed, linking the port towns
with the linen market towns and with a wider Atlantic world.

Farmers growing flax for fibre which they would weave into cloth
tended their crops from sowing to harvest differently than if they
were growing flax for seed. The same plant would produce both
fibre and seed but the quality of both would suffer, so it made sense
to buy the best available seed each planting season.[3] In the early
stages of its development, Ulster's burgeoning linen industry
depended on flaxseed imported from the Baltic. By the 1730s, as
linen exports to America soared to new highs, merchants began
importing American flaxseed. The British Parliament permitted
shipment of flaxseed and other colonial produce to Ireland in 1731
and stimulated the trade with a bounty payment on flaxseed from
1733. American seed soon came to supply the entire Ulster market.

The cultivation of flax for seed made rural communities in
Pennsylvania, New York and New England integral to the Ulster
economy. American flaxseed provided the essential first step in the
linen-making process and the flaxseed export financed the sales of
Irish linen that made the British North American colonies the
largest market for linen cloth woven in Ulster. The men who managed this transatlantic commerce as merchants in New York,
Philadelphia, or Baltimore were invariably members of the mercantile families of Belfast, Londonderry, or Newry who shipped them
linen and other dry goods and sent them orders for flaxseed or flour
or proposals for a ship to be built. Credit moved seamlessly across
the ocean and through the American partner's own networks into
the backcountry, making it possible for inland shopkeepers to stock
the latest fashions in British and Irish textiles and for the city merchants to invest in ironworks, town lots and wilderness acreage.

The flaxseed ships consigned to these American merchants by their Ulster correspondents carried passengers, redemptioners and servants on their outward voyage. This passenger trade was an increasingly important part of their business and the Belfast and Londonderry newspapers always had advertisements offering passage to America. Emigration took off redundant weavers and their families when there was a downturn in the linen industry. Farmer-weavers could meet the costs of emigration by selling their leases of land as well as their livestock and farming implements. Poorer weavers and cotters financed their crossing by depending on family or friends in America to pay their passage or by selling their labour as servants.

With land a commodity and a major source of capital in Ulster and America, the chain of credit extended from London to the backcountry in facilitating movement of people as well as goods. Having investments of their own in western lands, flaxseed merchants on both sides of the Atlantic sometimes offered land for sale to incoming migrants and at other times worked with land agents to recruit settlers.

It was of course as part of a larger British Atlantic world that the burgeoning Ulster economy reached the port cities and the inland towns of the American colonies. Acts of the Westminster Parliament facilitated and channelled every aspect of the trade, adding bounties and subsidies as an incentive. The Dublin Parliament supplied its own encouragement and direction through the Linen Board and its policies. Within this context emigrants from Ulster, whether Philadelphia merchants, backcountry shopkeepers, or farmers on the frontiers of Virginia or North Carolina, forged their own identity. Were they British, Irish, or Scotch-Irish or simply Americans shaped by the culture and economy of their native province? What was the heritage they brought with them to this new land?

Notes

1   W. H. Crawford, *The Impact of the Domestic Linen Industry in Ulster*
      (Belfast, 2005), 2.
2   Patrick Griffin, *The People With No Name: Ireland's Ulster-Scots,
      America's Scots-Irish, and the Creation of a British Atlantic World, 1689–
      1764* (Princeton, NJ, 2001), 28–30. W. H. Crawford, "Landlord-Tenant
      Relations in Ulster, 1609–1820," *Irish Economic and Social History, 2*
      (1975).
3   Adrienne D. Hood, "Flax Seed, Fibre and Cloth: Pennsylvania's Domestic
      Linen Manufacture and its Irish Connection, 1700–1830," in Brenda
      Collins and Philip Ollerenshaw, eds, *The European Linen Industry in
      Historical Perspective* (Oxford, 2003), 148.

1
"Novel Traffics"

Emigrants

In August 1718 Robert McCausland, agent for the Hon. William Conolly's estates in County Londonderry, reported a number of tenants leaving that summer for New England. Ten families from the Manor of Limavady had already gone and five more were about to go. In the Grocers' Proportion nine families were gone and five more were going. All of them sold their leases and improvements they had made on the property to others, exercising the Ulster tenant right, and, McCausland added, there were "Many More Just Now upon Terms of Selling their Land."[1] McCausland witnessed the beginning of large-scale emigration from Ulster to North America, a movement that would in time have significant impact on the societies of both Ireland and the American Colonies. That impact would not be limited to the families who emigrated. Sons and grandsons of Col. Robert McCausland of Fruit Hill would be merchants and ship-owners in Londonderry and command some of the ships that carried flaxseed and emigrants across the Atlantic.

Those families from the Conolly estates between Limavady and Londonderry were not the only ones who chose to emigrate that summer from Ulster. A long drought the year before caused crop failures across the province at a time when many leases expired and some landlords decided to raise the rent. This was particularly true in the London Companies' estates in County Londonderry. At the Plantation of Ulster a century earlier the Crown made extensive grants to the City of London Companies, nearly the whole of present County Londonderry with the port towns of Derry (renamed

Londonderry) on Lough Foyle and Coleraine on the Bann, to encourage them to develop their estates with British settlers. In 1613 they divided the tract into twelve parts – termed the Clothworkers, Drapers, Fishmongers, Goldsmiths, Grocers, Haberdashers, Ironmongers, Mercers, Merchant Taylors, Salters, Skinners, and Vintners Proportions – and set up the Irish Society to manage it. The London Companies found it was to their advantage to lease each proportion as a whole and collect the annual rent from a single tenant.[2] William Conolly, reputedly the richest man in Ireland, bought the Manor of Limavady from the heirs of the original grantee, but he held the lands of the Grocers' Proportion under a long-term lease from the Grocers' Company.

The Clothworkers held a similar estate near Coleraine, which they leased in its entirety to the Jackson family. When the leases by which some individual farmers held their land expired in May 1717, the Jacksons increased the annual rent each one owed. In some cases they doubled and even trebled what each had formerly paid. The Rev. James McGregor, Presbyterian minister of Aghadowey in the Clothworkers estate, encouraged his congregation to seek new homes in America and sailed with them from Coleraine on the *William and Mary*, bound for Boston. Joseph Marriott talked with some of them and reported to the Clothworkers in August 1718 that "one reason they give for their going is the raising of the rent of the land to such a high rate that they cannot support their families thereon with the greatest industry."[3] Land agents who knew the importance of continuing reliable tenants on their farms cautioned against rack-renting and advised giving additional time to pay their rent. Pressing them too hard cost the landlord dearly, for when tenants left, rent rolls dropped.[4]

A similar story was told on the Mercers' Proportion. John McMullan, the chief tenant, died in 1716 leaving a tangle of legal and financial problems. He had mortgaged some of his property to James Wilson, who took over the entire estate and attempted to make it pay. Arrears of rents due to Wilson, and the arrears of payments due to the Mercers, grew to considerable proportions in three years and, beginning in 1718, many tenants emigrated to America. Kilrea and vicinity were seriously affected by emigration and even in the 1730s much of the Mercers' Proportion lay waste and unworked.[5]

Although historians have focused on the migration from the Londonderry Plantation, the 1718–19 exodus drew from every part of Ulster with reports of large numbers leaving north Down, Fermanagh, and Monaghan. In every case, rigorous collection of rents and tithes was the reason given.[6] Numbers of other emigrants left the Ballymoney neighbourhood in north Antrim, taking shipping from nearby Coleraine. Several families, Balls, Blairs, Caldwells, and others came from the single townland of Ballywattick.[7]

The Rev. James Woodside, a Presbyterian minister, led another group of one hundred who sailed for Boston in the *Maccalum* and arrived there from Londonderry in September. Other tenants and even freeholders realized what they could from their land and farming stock and chartered ships for America. Extant Boston port records listed the *William and Elizabeth* from Londonderry, the *William and Mary* from Coleraine, the *Maccalum* and the *Mary and Elizabeth* from Londonderry, each with a hundred passengers.[8] In addition, The *Boston News Letter* reported five other ships entered from Ireland that summer, including the *Robert* and the *William* from Coleraine and the *Mary and Anne* and the *Dolphin* from Dublin with servants.[9] R. J. Dickson, historian of Ulster emigration, concluded that "approximately one thousand north Irish people disembarked from ten vessels at Boston in 1718."[10] Massachusetts authorities had anticipated a still larger number from Ulster after receiving a petition the year before from a great many Presbyterian ministers interested in removing to New England.[11]

So many left from one townland in County Londonderry that Robert McCausland had no doubt the landlord "Cannot Get in his Rents."[12] The departure of so many Protestant families caused consternation in some quarters, but Conolly's agent did not share that view. McCausland, an Ulster-Scot himself, knew there would be no stopping them. He told Conolly, "Releating to the peoples Going for New England and South Carolina I am Satisfied that if they were hindered ... by any order from ye Govermt it wod Make them ye fonder to go." His sole concern was "to Oblidge those Rougs who goes off to pay there just Debts: And then Let all goe when they please, who are Inclined to goe."[13]

The exodus from Ulster began a few years earlier and continued unabated for a year or two, some choosing New England, others Pennsylvania or South Carolina. Robert McCausland's brother-in-law, Belfast merchant Robert Wilson chartered the ship *Hanover* in August 1717 for "a voyage to Boston or New-York or Charles Town in South Carolina" and a year later chartered the *Friendship* to sail "to Charles Town in South Carolina."[14] In 1718 Wilson carried a petition to the Presbyterian Synod of Ulster from emigrants on board a ship in Belfast Lough bound for South Carolina for a minister to go with them.[15] Jonathan Dickinson wrote from Philadelphia in October 1717 that "from ye north of Ireland many hundreds" had arrived "in aboute four months." In October 1719 he reported "This summer we have had 12 or 13 sayle of ships from the North of Ireland with a swarm of people."[16] At least one ship brought a hundred passengers from Londonderry to New York in 1718.[17] The *Boston News Letter* reported eleven ships, most with passengers, from Belfast, Dublin, and Londonderry in the summer and autumn of 1719.[18] As many as 7,000 emigrants may have left Ulster in 1717–19.[19]

Emigration to the American Colonies was an established fact after that. The tide might ebb or be at flood in different years, but it would never stop flowing. R. J. Dickson wrote that

> For the first time, thousands of north Irish people had success-
> fully transplanted themselves across the Atlantic and had
> shown the tens of thousands of relations and friends they left
> behind in the Bann and Foyle valleys that, for ordinary people
> like themselves, life in America was a practical alternative to
> life in Ireland.

The significance of 1718, then, was that "the flood gates of emigration were opened for the first time as an outlet for the distressed and discontented."[20]

This alternative was never merely theoretical. The compact geography and small population of Ulster meant that virtually everyone knew someone who had gone to America. This would be especially true in the close-knit Presbyterian community. While eighteenth-century German migrants, both to North America and to Eastern Europe, may have been more numerous, the much greater extent of German-speaking territory and the much larger population made the impact at home much less than in Ulster. Even in the Rhineland, the area of heaviest emigration, families leaving for Pennsylvania or Hungary caused only an occasional stir. In Ulster, emigration was part of the ordinary rhythm of life.[21]

The first wave of emigration may have taken merchants and ship-owners by surprise. Families sailing to New England had to make do with whatever shipping was available. The ships that carried passengers to Boston were small, even by 1718 standards. The *Maccalum* of 70 tons brought 100 passengers from Londonderry as did the *Mary and Elizabeth* of only 45 tons. The *William and Mary* which carried the McGregor party from Coleraine displaced just 30 tons. They were not ships one would select for a long voyage, given a choice. By the following season merchants offered more adequate shipping. In contrast to the small craft of 1718, the *Globe* of Dublin was advertised as "Ready to sail for New England, a good Ship of 160 Tons of 2 Decks with several Cabbins, on purpose for whole Families with Locks Keys and other agreeable conveniences fitt for the Voyage."[22] James Arbuckle, a Belfast merchant, and William Hutchinson, merchant of Dublin, chartered the *Prince Frederick* of Whitehaven, "about 180 Tuns," to "Sail for Boston in New England about the 15 of March" 1719 and advertised "that if any Person or Persons have a mind to Transport themselves or Family's, to the aforesaid place, they may be accommodated on Reasonable Terms." They also welcomed any who "have a mind to engage themselves as Servants for a Term of Years."[23] Accommodations for passengers improved over time on some larger ships, particularly with the adoption of a rule-of-thumb on the number who could be comfortably taken on a transatlantic voyage. Captain James Nicholson of the *Freedom* of Whitehaven, for instance, pledged "to take no more on Board than one Man for a Ton, the Ships Crew included."[24] The idea that the number of passengers should correlate with the ship's tonnage was a commonplace in published advertisements. The *Phoenix* of 120 tons, for example, would "take no more than 80 passengers."[25]

With little direct trade between the Colonies and Ulster ports, merchants in the passenger trade and would-be emigrants often had to find a ship whose captain was in search of a freight for an

American port. Few Belfast or Derry shipmasters would have looked in that direction and there were few of them. Even in the famine year of 1729, when emigration increased greatly, vessels arriving from the American Colonies with provisions provided much of the shipping needed to take emigrants across the Atlantic. An exasperated agent in County Donegal complained to the absentee landlord that "There's a ship now lying at Killybegs belonging to New England yt has indented with as Many passengers as she can carry" and other tenants had arranged for a different ship to come for them "in the Spring."[26]

Emigration from Ulster had continued through the 1720s. Crop failures in 1728 brought another massive flow of emigrants enroute to America.[27] A Dublin paper reported:

> We hear from some Parts of the North of this Kingdom, that Oatmeal is so scarce, that tis risen to 12 sh[illings] per hundred Weight, and tis feared, that if there is not a speedy stop put to the Exportation of our Corn, that the Nation in general will suffer very much.[28]

Another Dublin editor wrote of "The repeated Accounts of the great Misery and Hardships endur'd by the Distress'd Inhabitants of the North part of this Kingdom."[29] Failure of the wheat crop forced many to "feed so much on the Potatoes, as almost to deprive themselves of either food or seed of that kind, for future Seasons."[30] The price of wheaten bread and oatmeal soared, "and almost every kind of Food is dear in proportion."[31] With hunger stalking the province, many were ready to emigrate. Robert Gamble, a merchant in Londonderry, wrote in July 1729:

> There is gone and to go this Summer from this Port Twenty-five Sail of Ships, who carry each, from One Hundred and twenty, to One hundred and forty Passengers to America; there are many more going from Belfast, and the Ports near Colrain, besides great Numbers from Dublin, Newry, and round the Coast.[32]

Dublin papers advertised at least a dozen ships for Philadelphia in the summer of 1729.[33] Nearly all newspaper advertisements promised that passengers would not be stinted of rations on the passage. Those for Whitehaven ships claimed they carried plenty of provisions for the voyage because they would proceed from Philadelphia to the West Indies.[34]

Customs officials reported 925 passengers and 220 servants landed at Philadelphia between Christmas 1728 and Christmas 1729 and "In New-Castle Government have been landed about 4,500 Passengers & Servants, chiefly from Ireland."[35] New Castle, Delaware, below Philadelphia on Delaware Bay, siphoned off a high percentage of passengers from ships intended for Philadelphia. No records survive from the customs house there. A second contemporary record of "Passengers and Servants imported from Ireland" put the figure for 1729 at 1,865 for Philadelphia and 3,790 at New Castle."[36] New Castle, Delaware, and Philadelphia were the primary destinations, but not all emigrant ships landed there. The *Martha and Elizabeth* from Londonderry with 170 passengers had to put into New York harbour because the Delaware was frozen over.[37]

It is difficult, well nigh impossible, to identify these passengers and servants by the ports from which they embarked. The bulk of the passengers came from Ulster ports but there was no newspaper to report northern sailings. Dublin newspapers listed ten ships cleared out from that port for Philadelphia in 1729. Two sailed originally from Whitehaven, two from Waterford, one from Irvine in Scotland, and one from London. Four ships cleared for Madeira and Philadelphia, among them the *Prince Frederick* and *Phoenix* that both advertised for passengers and servants.[38] They were evidently bringing wine as well as dry goods to the American metropolis. The *Elizabeth* sailed "with 220 Servants and Passengers," but none of the later newspaper reports of Dublin sailings mentioned passengers.[39] Four of these ships, however, did advertise for passengers and servants.[40] Dublin Quaker merchants with connections in both Philadelphia and Whitehaven dominated the trade in both paying passengers and indentured servants. They favoured ships from Whitehaven with Quaker captains.[41] The collieries around Whitehaven had long supplied Dublin's coal, which became their major market, so there were strong commercial ties between the two ports based on the coal trade.[42] This famine emigration did not continue long. Robert Macky, a London merchant with interests in both Irish and American trade, wrote in April 1730 that food was again cheap in Ireland and few people would be going to America that season.[43]

Emigration on this large scale had a marked impact on the commercial life of Ulster. Without established patterns of trade between Ulster and American ports, there were no regular sailings for the Colonies, no competing ship-owners to offer the best accommodations for passengers. To find shipping to carry so many people across the Atlantic in 1717–19 strained the resources of Londonderry, Coleraine, Belfast, and even of Dublin, since the Irish ports had relatively little transatlantic trade. In the much heavier volume of emigration in 1728–9, a writer in the *Pennsylvania Gazette* observed that "the People, earnest to be gone, being oblig-'d to take up with any Vessel that will go; and 'tis like frequently with such as have before been only Coasters, because they cannot always get those that have been us'd to long Voyages, or to come to these Parts of the World."[44] The number of passengers reported for individual ships during this season was high, invariably more than 100 on each vessel, suggesting overcrowding.

Not a few tragedies occurred because ships were too small to carry adequate provisions. The "near 200" passengers on the *Mary* from Londonderry to Philadelphia were "so Straitened for Provisions, that Each one had but a Pound and a half of Bread, per Week, for 6 Weeks before" and "there was then on Board, for them all, but one Barrel of Oatmeal and one Tierce of Beef."[45] The *Jenny Galley* of Dublin, chartered to take 200 passengers and servants from Londonderry to New Castle on Delaware, sailed in July 1729. Captain Richard Murphy soon "brought the Passengers to short Allowance." They sighted the American coast after two months at sea, but Murphy refused to take his ship to New Castle as agreed. The passengers mutinied and the first mate brought the *Jenny Galley* into New York.[46] Another brig landed passengers from Ireland at New Castle in January 1730. "They had been Two and twenty Weeks at Sea, and had thrown seventy-five People overboard which died by the Way."[47] But no voyage equalled in horror that of the *Katharine*, which sailed from Londonderry in August 1728 with 123 passengers and sailors. Tossed about by storms and contrary winds, the *Katharine* had insufficient water for a crossing of more than ordinary length. Captain Hugh Davey died in October. His death may have doomed the ship. His son and thirteen other survivors brought the ship back to Ireland after more than five months at sea, running her aground on the coast of Mayo. By that time 109 of the passengers and crew were dead. Hugh Davey, Jr. reported the disaster to his uncles, Samuel Davey, merchant in Londonderry, and William Delap, merchant in Dublin.[48]

Merchants

Arranging passage for a family of emigrants was just one among the many things that engaged a merchant or shipowner. It was impossible to specialize in the passenger trade or even in commerce with the American Colonies. He had to keep his hand in a wide variety of import and export trades simply to survive. The Irish economy was essentially stagnant in the first two decades of the eighteenth century, although the steadily increasing production of linen and the equally steady expansion of flax growing to meet the needs of the linen industry gave it new life. By the end of the 1720s linen accounted for fully a quarter of the total value of exports from Ireland.[49] Belfast merchant James Arbuckle and his partner Daniel Mussenden were among the first to venture into the American passenger trade, when as joint owners of the ship *Friendship* of Belfast, they chartered her in August 1718 to Robert Wilson, another Belfast merchant, for a voyage "to Charles Town in South Carolina or any other port in America," returning to Belfast by way of Britain or Holland.[50] The *Friendship* had made earlier transatlantic voyages, e.g. bringing sugar, cotton, and other West Indian products from Antigua.[51] Arbuckle advertised for passengers and servants when he chartered a Whitehaven ship to take emigrants to Boston early the next year.[52] But his interest in trade with America was only one of many commercial enterprises. Like most Belfast merchants and traders, Arbuckle did not specialise in any one branch of commerce and, like them, he was well-connected. His wife Priscilla was a daughter of John Black, one of Belfast's more important merchants. Her brothers did business on a large scale in Cadiz, Bordeaux, and London. Two other brothers-in-law, William and Robert Moore, were merchants in Barbados.[53] Arbuckle always had close ties with Whitehaven, too, especially with the Lutwidge family, even before his son married merchant Walter Lutwidge's daughter. Overextended and deeply in debt to his brother-in-law in Bordeaux, James Arbuckle died in 1740 "in more debts than he had assets to pay with."[54]

Daniel Mussenden was more successful in business, and, typical of his time, traded with the Baltic and Northern Europe, the American Colonies, including the West Indies, England and Scotland, dealing in wine, salt, linen, and coal, among other things.[55] Early Belfast adventures to America often proved unprofitable. Isaac Macartney dispatched the *Laurel* first to Newfoundland with provisions for the fisheries and from thence to Virginia for tobacco. Arriving in the Chesapeake too late to load a cargo of tobacco, *Laurel* had to lay over seven months to take on a partial cargo and suffered more delay at Portsmouth waiting for a convoy to take her to Liverpool. Macartney urged his fellow owners to cut their losses and sell her to James Arbuckle for a bargain price.[56] At the beginning of the eighteenth century merchants in Belfast and Londonderry dealt almost exclusively with provisions, shipping beef, butter, salmon, oatmeal, and importing sugar, tobacco, and wine by way of England. Some beef went to the West Indies and grain and oatmeal to Scandinavia. Improvements in linen manufacture led to an expanded market for textiles from Ulster, especially in the mainland Colonies, but not to an increased demand for direct trade with America.[57]

Seventeenth-century Navigation Acts, in fact, wrought havoc with the commerce of the Kingdom of Ireland. Under the first Navigation Acts in 1660, Irish ports were open to colonial sugar and tobacco, but the direct exportation of manufactured goods to the American colonies could only be through English ports. English merchants resisted Ireland's status under the 1660 act as a place to which colonial goods could be sent directly and urged Parliament to close this loophole.[58] The Staple Act of 1663 limited exports from Irish ports to servants, horses, and "Victuals of the Growth or Production of Ireland" and required merchants in the Kingdom of Ireland to import colonial produce through England.[59] There was an exception. Until the further tightening up of the Navigation Acts in 1685 unrefined sugar could be imported directly into Ireland from the Caribbean and Belfast had a good share of the trade. This exception was eliminated in 1685 and thereafter tobacco and sugar intended for the Irish market had to be imported through Whitehaven, Liverpool, Bristol or other English ports and only then shipped to Ireland.[60] Under further pressure from English merchants, the Navigation Act of 1696 forbade all direct imports from the colonies and brought legal two-way trade to an end.[61] Once all colonial goods passed through England, Dublin's proportion of the traffic in sugar rose dramatically at the expense of other Irish ports.[62]

In adopting the Navigation Acts and in subsequent legislation regulating trade the Englis Parliament frequently responded to pressure from special interests in England. The lawmakers had no intention of crippling the economies of Ireland or the Colonies, but wanted to protect the staples of English commerce and eliminate direct competition. Cattle breeders in northern and western England, for instance, complained that Irish exports of live cattle made their trade unprofitable. Parliament responded by excluding Irish cattle altogether in 1665. Instead, Irish grazers were encouraged to ship beef in barrels, butter, tallow, and hides to England, the Continent, and the American Colonies.[63] The case was much the same with wool. Beginning in 1662 English legislation encouraged the export of raw wool and discouraged the export of Irish woollen cloth, but by the 1680s Irish woollens were beginning to compete in English markets and by the 1690s Irish serges were undercutting English serges in the Dutch market.[64] It was not this limited competition that spurred the English Parliament to action. Long wool from Ireland was essential for the serges woven in Devonshire and southwest England. Intensive lobbying by Exeter merchants resulted in the act of 1698 that forbade the export of Irish wool or woollen cloth except to England and Wales and levied a duty on Irish woollens equivalent to a prohibition.[65] Linen manufacturing, which complimented the English emphasis on woollens, would take the place of the Irish woollen industry. By the end of the century Parliament had passed acts to exclude Irish woollens and to encourage the manufacture and export of linen. Irish linen could enter England duty free, but its direct export to the Colonies was still forbidden.[66] This prohibition was only lifted in 1705.[67] Dutch and German linens were generally of a different quality from Irish linens and did not necessarily compete with each other; they were nevertheless heavily taxed when imported into England to encourage linen production in Ireland.

Dublin and Whitehaven

Dublin commerce largely met the needs of the capital and its hinterland for imported goods.[68] "One of the effects of the navigation acts was to quicken the shift of trade from the periphery to the centre … [and] to strengthen the position of Dublin, which already dominated exports from England."[69] By the end of the seventeenth century a considerable, and expanding, group of Ulster merchants settled in Dublin, virtually all Presbyterians and members of the Capel Street congregation. Alexander Mitchell from Glenarm, County Antrim, was among those trading with Belfast; his brother Hugh Mitchell was already established at Cork.[70] Dublin's almost complete dependence on Cumbrian coal for household fuel was a fact of life throughout the eighteenth century.[71] Whitehaven coal topped the list in demand and price; Workington and Saltcoats coal followed, with coal from Ballycastle on the North Antrim coast the lowest rated.[72] This was good news for the collieries on the Cumbrian coast of northwestern England and for the ship-owners of Whitehaven and Workington.

By the last years of the seventeenth century Whitehaven and Workington dominated the Irish market.[73] Although Dublin took the great majority of their output, the west Cumbrian mines also supplied the needs of Ulster. In 1715–16, for example, vessels came from Belfast, Londonderry, Newry, Killyleagh, Downpatrick, Bangor and Carlingford to load coal at Whitehaven.[74] Once the coal trade to Ireland was established, Whitehaven merchants and ship-owners looked for other profitable ventures to employ their ships and turned to the West Indies, the Chesapeake Colonies, and the Baltic. They became the carriers for the products of Ireland. As Belfast and Dublin ventures to the Caribbean and the Chesapeake became less frequent, little Whitehaven, across the Irish Sea on the Cumbrian coast, began sending ships to Virginia and the West

Indies.[75] Whitehaven's colonial trade was heavily weighted in favor of tobacco. Its links with Belfast and Dublin provided a ready source of goods, especially linen, for sale in America and its proximity to Scotland allowed Scottish merchants to freight Whitehaven ships for trade in Maryland and Virginia tobacco otherwise closed to them before the Act of Union in 1707.[76] Once landed at a Cumbrian port, tobacco could be legally shipped to Ireland or Scotland. In 1709–10, for instance, Whitehaven supplied not only tobacco, but sugar and other colonial produce to Belfast, Londonderry, Coleraine and Glenarm, although one Belfast-owned vessel carried tobacco from Glasgow.[77] Whitehaven captains routinely called in at Belfast or Dublin on their voyage to Maryland or Virginia to take on linen and servants. The increasing production of high quality linen in Ulster provided a valuable item in their cargoes.[78] When in 1696 the British government removed the tax on Irish linens shipped to England, many English dealers began to buy Ulster cloth because it was cheaper than Dutch and German linens. This growing market greatly stimulated linen weaving across the Irish Sea.[79] Dublin was also important for the servant trade. For instance, Joseph How, one of Whitehaven's principal merchants in the tobacco trade, instructed his factors to load 40 or 50 gallons of brandy in Dublin "and also if to be had without delay take in four or Six men Servants," since "Servants not only get ready Tobacco but engages substantial planters for their whole Crops."[80]

The Linen Trade Begins

Improving landlords seem to have recognized the potential of linen weaving and encouraged their tenants with prizes for the best woven webs and gifts of spinning wheels and looms. A fragmentary account of a linen exhibition and prize giving at Strabane, County Tyrone, under the patronage of the Earl of Abercorn, is dated October 17, 1700. The letter writer proposed that it be made an annual event.[81] It was only in 1705 that British policy reversed and with passage of the Linen Act opened the colonial market to linens sent directly from Ireland.[82] This ushered in a new opportunity for trade with the American Colonies and a new beginning for Belfast and other Ulster ports. Jean Agnew concluded that "the lifting of restrictions on the direct export of linen to the colonies contributed to the development of Belfast as a major international port, and for the Belfast merchants it meant that they were on the threshold of a new era in which they had a high quality non-perishable product for which there was a steady demand."[83]

The new era was not immediately evident. Belfast shipping news, as reported in the *Dublin Gazette* in 1709–10, included eight ships entering from Whitehaven with sugar, tobacco, or merchant's goods, five from Glasgow with tobacco and merchandise, and four from Liverpool with salt. Not many ships were bound to or from the American Colonies. Two English ships stopped at Belfast on their way across the Atlantic, one to Virginia, the other to South Carolina, and a Whitehaven ship and two registered at Liverpool all laden with Virginia tobacco put into Belfast Lough on their homeward voyage.[84] Among the few Belfast ships were the *Friendship*, returning from Antigua with sugar and cotton, and from Glasgow with tobacco, the *Upton* sailing for Ostend with butter and hides, the *Supply* bringing sugar from Whitehaven, and the *Endeavour*, *Rose*, and *Jane and Sarah*, taking yarn to Liverpool and returning with salt, tobacco and hops.[85]

Linen trade with the American Colonies was evidently insufficient of itself to make Belfast and Londonderry commercial centres with fleets of ships in transatlantic crossings. Most Ulster linen was shipped to America by London merchants in English ships. Linen manufacture was concentrated in Ulster, particularly the eastern counties of Antrim, Down, and Armagh, but as much as 90% of the linen made there went to England, mainly through the port of Dublin.[86] This was because the Ulster linen industry was conducted on a cash basis. The bleachers and linen drapers who bought linen at local markets paid the weavers in full for each piece they purchased. Since they could not afford to be out of pocket until the cloth was finally sold in London, they sent it to Dublin to merchants there who then sold the linen in England or overseas. The Dublin factors sold the linen on commission for the Ulster bleachers, but advanced them the cash they needed to make their spring and summer purchases at the brown linen markets.[87]

Flaxseed

Flaxseed was the missing ingredient, the *sine qua non* for the rise of the northern ports. Initially, Irish linen weavers worked with flax imported from Holland because too little flax was grown in Ireland to supply their needs. In 1707 the Flaxseed Bounty Act allowed a bounty of five shillings on every hogshead of imported seed to encourage the production of flax in Ireland. Seed had to be imported because the flax was pulled, ripped up roots and all, so that no part of the stem was lost and the fibers in the stem were as long as possible. Pulling the lint was no easy task and took a strong man. This had to be done before the plant went to seed. It was possible to get seed as well as fiber from the same plant, but the quality would suffer, and the cultivation of flax for seed and for fiber was different from the initial sowing.[88] The Linen Board, created by the Irish Parliament in 1711, further subsidized the flax growers by importing and distributing flaxseed.[89] "Being determined to give Encouragement for the raising large Quantities of Flax in this Kingdom," the "Trustees of the Linnen Manufacture" offered five bushels of foreign seed for every acre contracted to be sown in flax.[90] From the first the Board also paid bounties and premiums for high quality linen, supplied wheels and looms, and made grants for bleach greens and manufactories.[91]

There was still ample room for private enterprise. Isaac McCartney, one of Belfast's long-established merchants, advertised in 1718:

> There being a very considerable vent for Holland Lintseed imported into Belfast this Year, several hundred Hogsheads more than in former Years, Isaac McCartney Merchant in said Place being informed that the Country would still want to Sow their Ground prepared; did for Encouragement of said Trade Write to his Friend in Holland for 80 Hogsheads of fresh Seed, and 200 Firkens of black Seed, which said McCartney has Account from his Friend is Loaded and believes has been 8 Days at Sea.[92]

The amount imported by the Linen Board rose steadily each year. This was in addition to what merchants imported on their own account. The Board ordered 500 hogsheads of foreign flaxseed in

1726.[93] In 1729 they imported 3,000 barrels (equivalent to 1,500 hogsheads) and in 1730 2,000 hogsheads. Their 1731 importation amounted to 3,000 hogsheads.[94] People, "including some of Rank and Condition," sold the flaxseed given them on the open market.[95] The Board eventually required recipients to return twice as much seed as they first received. They were to deliver the flaxseed to Thomas Jolly in Dublin, Isaac McCartney, Esq. in Belfast, Joseph Burchess in Armagh, or Robert Boyle in Cavan, an indication of the concentration of flax growing in Ulster.[96]

Advertisements for sale of flaxseed by merchants are few in the early eighteenth. Thomas Strettel and James Usher in Dublin and Thomas Fletcher in Lurgan, for example, advertised "Just imported, Choice good and new Flax-Seed."[97] But there was obviously a large private importation of flaxseed and, in times of dearth in the domestic crop, of flax. Following the short supply in 1731, a Dublin paper reported: "By the vast quantities of Flax lately imported into this Kingdom, it is sold in the Country Markets, almost as cheap as ever it was, notwithstanding the bad Crop of Flax that was last year."[98]

Before 1731 the flaxseed planted by Ulster farmers came exclusively from the Baltic by way of Holland, as did imported flax. There was a great scarcity of flaxseed in the Baltic in 1723, for instance, and the Trustees of the Linen Manufacture advised farmers on how to save some of their seed for the next year.[99] They did not suggest an alternate source of seed. Baltic or "Holland" flaxseed had a deserved reputation as the best available and commanded the highest prices, so it continued to be imported throughout the eighteenth century. But within the framework of the Navigation Acts and subsequent legislation regulating trade, it made little sense to exclude American seed from the Irish market. "Holland's most important trading asset was its control of Baltic products, including flax, which it manufactured into linen and sold throughout the world."[100] Importing flax and flaxseed from Holland could be construed as subsidizing the competition while seed from the American Colonies would foster trade within the Empire.

In 1731 the Board of Trade and Plantations proposed opening Irish ports to colonial produce except for sugar, tobacco and a few other enumerated articles and Parliament promptly enacted legislation to this effect.[101] American flaxseed could now be imported directly into Ireland. The opening of the American flaxseed trade corresponded with a spurt of growth in the Ulster linen manufacture: in 1735 Ireland exported two and a half million more yards of linen than it had in 1730.[102] For the next two years the Flaxseed Bounty Act discriminated against American seed in favor of Holland flaxseed; Parliament amended the act in 1733 to allow the same bounty on flaxseed from the American Colonies. As a result, only a third of the average of 5,660 hogsheads of flaxseed imported each year in 1732–5 came from America. By the end of the decade the annual import of flaxseed had nearly doubled, averaging 10,720 hogsheads a year, and American flaxseed made up eighty percent of the seed shipped to Irish ports.[103] Between March 1734 and March 1735, the first full year of the bounty, Philadelphia alone exported 978 hogsheads and 392 tierces of flaxseed, all of it to Ireland.[104]

By 1735 the pattern of ships arriving at New Castle and Philadelphia from Belfast and Londonderry with passengers and redemptioners in September and October and sailing for home with flaxseed in the winter months was already established. Between March 1735 and March 1736 fourteen ships entered the port of Philadelphia from Ireland and twenty-three ships cleared for Irish ports.[105] The customs officer at New York reported four ships cleared for Belfast, evidently with flaxseed, in December 1735 and January 1736.[106] Flaxseed and emigrants set the rhythm of transatlantic trade between the northern ports and the American Colonies and began a new commercial relationship that demanded the oversight of capable merchants on both sides of the ocean.

Ships bringing flaxseed, flour and other products to Belfast and Londonderry provided the means for families and individuals in Ulster to sail for New Castle and Philadelphia every summer. Passenger trade complimented the flaxseed trade, giving ship-owners a profitable return voyage to Delaware Bay. The convergence of these forces changed Ulster commerce and required Scotch-Irish merchants in the major American ports to carry it out. At home, too, the transformation was remarkable enough. As L. M. Cullen noted, the real, if temporary, decline of Belfast and other Ulster ports from the late seventeenth century on "halted only when novel traffics – flaxseed and emigrants – gave it a new dynamism in the 1730s."[107]

Notes

1   Robert McCausland, "List of Persons gon & going to N England," August
    24, 1718 (Conolly Papers, T2825/C. PRONI). Cf. Richard K. MacMaster,
    "Emigrants to New England from the Conolly Estates, 1718," *Journal of
    Scotch-Irish Studies*, 1(2000), 18–23.

2   James Stevens Curl, *The Londonderry Plantation 1609–1914* (Chichester,
    Sussex, 1986), 37–8. Philip S. Robinson, *The Plantation of Ulster* (New
    York, 1984), 162, 209. "The letting to a single chief tenant relieved the
    Companies of direct control, and saved much time, trouble, and expense."
    Curl, *Londonderry Plantation*, 130, 158.

3   R. J. Dickson, *Ulster Emigration to Colonial America 1718–1775* (London,
    1966, reprinted Belfast, 1996), 29.

4   Patrick Griffin, *The People With No Name: Ireland's Ulster Scots, America's Scots
    Irish, and the Creation of a British Atlantic World 1689–1764* (Princeton, NJ,
    2001), 75–8.

5   Curl, *Londonderry Plantation*, 131.

6   Graeme Kirkham, "Ulster Emigration to North America, 1680–1720" in
    Tyler Blethen and Curtis Wood, eds., *Ulster and North America:
    Transatlantic Perspectives on the Scotch-Irish* (Tuscaloosa, AL, 1997), 84.

7   Catherine Ball to Mrs. McBeth, May 15, 1769, in John Caldwell,
    "Particulars of History of a North County Irish Family," 4, 15
    (T/3541/5/3, PRONI).

8   Dickson, *Ulster Emigration*, 21–3.

9   *Boston News Letter*, June 30, 1718, August 4, 1718, August 11, 1718.

10 Dickson, *Ulster Emigration*, 23.

11 H. J. Ford, *The Scotch-Irish in America* (Princeton, NJ, 1915), 190–93.

12 McCausland identified the landowner as Mr. Cary. Edward Carey leased the
    Skinners Proportion, south of Conolly's estates in the vicinity of Dungiven,
    County Londonderry. Curl, *Londonderry Plantation,* 294. Another Mr.
    Cary, had a freehold estate in Coolafinny near Muff, County Londonderry.
    Alan Rogers, *A Twice-Born Village Muff (Eglinton) Co. Londonderry*
    (Londonderry, 1984), 5.

13 Robert McCausland to His Excellence Ld. Justice Conolly, November 13, 1718
    (T2825/C, PRONI).

14 Charter Party, August 17, 1717, August 19, 1718 (Mussenden Papers,
    D/354/363, /369, PRONI).

15 Kirkham, "Ulster Emigration," 92.

16 Wayland F. Dunaway, *The Scotch-Irish of Colonial Pennsylvania* (Chapel Hill,
    NC, 1944), 34.

17 *Boston News Letter*, October 27, 1718. Richard C. Morris, ed., *Select Cases of
    the Mayor's Court of New York City 1674–1784* (Washington, DC, 1935,
    reprinted Millwood, NY, 1975), 684–7.

18 *Boston News Letter*, July 20, 1719, August 17, 1719, August 24, 1719,
    September 7, 1719, September 28, 1719, October 19, 1719, November 9,
    1719.

19 Kirkham, "Ulster Emigration," 96.

20 Dickson, *Ulster Emigration*, 24.

21   I am indebted to Professor Marianne Wokeck for this insight.
22   *Dickson's Dublin Intelligence*, January 6, 1718/19, February 21, 1718/19, May 23, 1719.
23   *Thomas Hume's Dublin Courant*, February 10, 1718/19.
24   *Dublin Weekly Journal*, February 28, 1729/30.
25   *Faulkner's Dublin Journal*, June 3, 1729.
26   James Hamilton to Alexander Murray, Feb. 4, 1728/29 (Murray of Broughton Papers, D/2860/12/21, PRONI).
27   E. E. R. Evans, "The 'Strange Humours' That Drove the Scotch-Irish to America, 1729," *William and Mary Quarterly*, 3rd ser., 12(1955), 113–23.
28   *Dublin Weekly Journal*, December 8, 1728.
29   *Dublin Intelligence*, January 28, 1728/29.
30   *Dublin Intelligence*, March 22, 1728/29.
31   *Dublin Intelligence*, March 29, 1729.
32   *Pennsylvania Gazette*, November 20, 1729.
33   *Faulkner's Dublin Journal*, May 24, 1729, June 3, 1729, June 14, 1729, June 17, 1729, July 26, 1729, August 5, 1729.
34   The *Prince Frederick* of Whitehaven, John Lutwidge, Commander, would "proceed from the above Place to the West Indies and other Places before her return Home." *Faulkner's Dublin Journal*, June 14, 1729.
35   *Pennsylvania Gazette*, January 13, 1729/30.
36   Marianne Wokeck, *Trade in Strangers: The Beginnings of Mass Migration to North America* (State College, PA, 1999), 169–70.
37   *Dublin Intelligence*, February 15, 1728/29.
38   *Dublin Gazette*, April 12, 1729 through September 6, 1729.
39   *Dublin Gazette*, April 12, 1729.
40   They were the *Prince Frederick* (*Dublin Weekly Journal*, June 14, 1729, *Dublin Gazette*, July 11, 1729), the *Joseph and Benjamin* (*Dublin Weekly Journal*, June 17, 1729, *Dublin Gazette*, July 8, 1729), *Sizargh* (*Dublin Weekly Journal*, May 24, 1729, *Dublin Gazette*, August 28, 1729), and *Phoenix* (*Dublin Weekly Journal*, June 3, 1729, *Dublin Gazette*, August 22, 1729).
41   Audrey Lockhart, "Quakers and Emigration from Ireland to the North American Colonies," *Quaker History*, 77(1988), 83–6.
42   J. V. Beckett, *Coal and Tobacco: The Lowthers and the Economic Development of West Cumberland* (Cambridge, 1981), 85–6.
43   Robert Macky to James Patton, April 7, 1730 (Preston Papers, 1QQ2, Draper Collection, Historical Society of Wisconsin, Madison, WI).
44   *Pennsylvania Gazette*, November 20, 1729.
45   *Dublin Intelligence*, February 8, 1728/29.
46   *New York Gazette*, October 6, 1729, October 27, 1729.
47   *Pennsylvania Gazette*, February 19, 1730.
48   *New York Gazette*, May 26, 1729.
49   L. E. Cochran, *Scottish Trade with Ireland in the Eighteenth Century* (Edinburgh, 1985), 9.
50   Charter Party, August 18, 1718 (Mussenden Papers, D/354/369, PRONI).
51   *Dublin Gazette*, September 5, 1710.
52   *Thomas Hume's Dublin Courant*, February 10, 1718/19.
53   Jean Agnew, *Belfast Merchant Families in the Seventeenth Century* (Dublin,

1996), 189, 211.

54   Walter Lutwidge to Robert Legg, July 20, 1740 (Lutwidge Letter Book, I, 298, Cumbria Record Office, Whitehaven, England).

55   A. P. W. Malcolmson, "Introduction to the Mussenden Papers." (D/354, PRONI).

56   Agnew, *Belfast Merchant Families*, 137–8.

57   Agnew, *Belfast Merchant Families*, 105–08.

58   Denis O'Hearn, *The Atlantic economy, Britain, the United States and Ireland* (Manchester, 2001), 46.

59   Charles M. Andrews, *The Colonial Period of American History* (New Haven, CN, 1938, 1964), 108–10, 125–6. Thomas M. Truxes, *Irish-American Trade 1660–1783* (Cambridge, 1988), 8–9.

60   Agnew, *Belfast Merchant Families*, 118–20.

61   Agnew, *Belfast Merchant Families*, 122. Truxes, *Irish-American Trade*, 10.

62   L. M. Cullen, *An Economic History of Ireland Since 1660* (London, 1972), 37–9.

63   O'Hearn, *Atlantic economy*, 53–7.

64   G. D. Ramsay, *The English Woollen Industry, 1500–1750* (London, 1982), 66.

65   W. G. Hoskins, *Industry, Trade and People in Exeter 1688–1800* (Manchester, 1935), 33–5.

66   O'Hearn, *Atlantic economy*, 62–7.

67   Adrienne D. Hood, "Flax Seed, Fibre and Cloth: Pennsylvania's Domestic Linen Manufacture and Its Irish Connection, 1700–1830," in Brenda Collins and Philip Ollerenshaw, eds., *The European Linen Industry in Historical Perspective* (Oxford, 2003), 146.

68   David Dickson, "The Place of Dublin in the Eighteenth-Century Irish Economy" in T. M. Devine and L. M. Cullen, eds., *Ireland and Scotland 1600–1850 Parallels and Contrasts in Economic and Social Development* (Edinburgh, 1983), 178.

69   L. M. Cullen, "Merchant Communities Overseas, the Navigation Acts, and Irish and Scottish Responses," in L. M. Cullen and T. C. Smout, eds., *Comparative Aspects of Scottish and Irish Economic and Social History* (Edinburgh, 1976), 172.

70   Agnew, *Belfast Merchant Families*, 182–5.

71   Dickson, "The Place of Dublin," 178.

72   *Dublin Courant*, March 3, 1721/22.

73   Beckett, *Coal and Tobacco*, 39–40.

74   Beckett, *Coal and Tobacco*, 98.

75   Daniel Hay, *Whitehaven, A Short History* (Whitehaven, 1966), 27.

76   Beckett, *Coal and Tobacco*, 103–05.

77   *Dublin Gazette*, October 18, 1709, January 21, 1709/10, May 9, 1710, September 19, 1710, October 10, 1710.

78   *Dublin Gazette*, February 21, 1709/10, February 28, 1709/10.

79   W. H. Crawford, *Domestic Industry in Ireland: The Experience of the Linen Industry* (Dublin, 1972), 1–2.

80   Richard K. MacMaster, "Instructions to a Tobacco Factor, 1725," *Maryland*

Historial Magazine, 63(1968), 172–8.

81 Letter to the Earl of Abercorn, Strabane, October 17, 1700 (Abercorn Papers, D623/A/2/1, PRONI).

82 Truxes, *Irish-American Trade*, 13.

83 Agnew, *Belfast Merchant Families*, 126.

84 *Dublin Gazette*, January 21, 1709/10, February 28, 1709/10, September 5, 1710, November 28, 1710.

85 *Dublin Gazette*, October 18, 1709, November 1, 1709, February 28, 1709/10, September 5, 1710, September 26, 1710, November 4, 1710.

86 Cullen, *Economic History of Ireland*, 59.

87 Crawford, *Domestic Industry in Ireland*, 4. Dickson, "The Place of Dublin," 183.

88 Hood, "Flax Seed," 148. Walter S. Barker, "Flax: The Fiber and the Seed, A Study in Agricultural Contrasts," *Quarterly Journal of Economics*, 31(1917), 500–29.

89 H. D. Gribbon, "The Irish Linen Board 1711–1828," in L. M. Cullen and T. C. Smout, *Comparative Aspects of Scottish and Irish Economic History* (Edinburgh, 1977), 77–87.

90 *Dublin Courant*, November 23, 1723.

91 John W. McConaghy, "Thomas Greer of Dungannon 1724–1808: Quaker Linen Merchant," Ph.D. diss., Queens University Belfast (1979), 6–7.

92 *Pue's Occurrences* (Dublin), April 26, 1718.

93 *Faulkner's Dublin Journal*, November 15, 1726

94 *Faulkner's Dublin Journal*, December 6, 1729, August 4, 1730. *Dublin Gazette*, September 14, 1731.

95 *Faulkner's Dublin Journal*, October 10, 1730.

96 *Pue's Occurrences*, January 22, 1733/4.

97 *Faulkner's Dublin Journal*, March 18, 1731/2.

98 *Faulkner's Dublin Journal*, February 8, 1731/2.

99 *Dublin Courant*, June 23, 1723.

100 O'Hearn, *Atlantic economy*, 68.

101 Andrews, *Colonial Period of American History*, 142.

102 Conrad Gill, *The Rise of the Irish Linen Industry* (Oxford, 1925), 10.

103 Truxes, *Irish-American Trade*, 194–5.

104 *Pennsylvania Gazette*, March 27, 1735.

105 *Pennsylvania Gazette*, April 8, 1736.

106 *Pennsylvania Gazette*, December 11, 1735, January 22, 1736, January 29, 1736.

107 Cullen, "Merchant Communities Overseas", 172.

2

Scowbanckers and Redemptioners

IN THE SUMMER OF 1735 JAMES COULTER sailed from Belfast on the *John and Margaret* bound for New Castle and Philadelphia. Coulter, who was originally from Banbridge, County Down, was on his way home to Pennsylvania, where his wife and two young children awaited him at his plantation on Pequea Creek in Lancaster County. He never reached America, dying at sea. Captain Archibald McSparran of the *John and Margaret* landed Coulter's goods at New Castle, where his executors came to inventory them and bring them up to Lancaster County. They recorded "the true value of the goods of James Coulter who departed this Life at Sea about the -- of august 1735" as "six Servant men at 18 pounds a peas," "two Servants Maids 29 pounds," and "one Servant Maid 12 pounds." They also appraised "Six Score parts of Linin Cloth" and "other Smal goods." (A second inventory the following April listed the usual household goods and farm implements as well as six bonds to secure debts due to him.) James Coulter's home in the lower Susquehanna valley was on the Pennsylvania frontier. Was Coulter a backcountry shopkeeper or chapman or simply bringing his money to America in a readily saleable form? Whatever the case, he was typical of both Ulster merchants and emigrants who dealt on a larger or smaller scale in linen and servants.[1]

Coulter would have purchased his linens in the brown linen market at Banbridge and from local bleachers.[2] But Irish linens generally reached the Colonies by way of dry goods merchants in England or through linen factors in Dublin. As linen production in Ulster steadily increased, Dublin became more dominant in the export of linens both to England for resale and directly to the

Colonies. In the first decades of the eighteenth century Belfast and Derry did not lag far behind the capital in direct exports. Dublin shipped an average of 39,420 yards to the Plantations in 1710–15 as compared with 35,870 yards from Belfast and Londonderry. The average for 1720–25 showed Dublin's share increasing to 56,890 and the two northern ports dropping to 30,710. The figures for 1730–35 indicate that Dublin shipped an average of 111,720 yards to the Colonies each year and Belfast and Derry together only 9,790 yards.[3] Impressive as these figures are, they represent only a tenth of the Irish linen sent to America in those same years, since most linen exports passed through England.

With the large emigration in 1728 came the first entrepreneurs who would find opportunity in the commercial world of the Colonies by selling Irish linen. Some of the earliest settled in Pennsylvania. A few emigrants brought a stock of goods with them or, like James Coulter, returned home to select goods to sell. Thomas Campbell, "lately arrived from Ireland," advertised rugs, blankets, coarse and fine linen, and hardware for sale in Philadelphia.[4] For others, a few pieces of linen and other dry goods offered a profitable sideline. Goods "lately imported from Ireland by John Walby, School Master, and to be sold at his house" consisted of various sorts of white and brown linen, "Stockens, white & Colour'd Threads."[5] Others were shopkeepers with good trade connections in Ireland. Thomas Hatton, who represented Abel Strettel, a Quaker merchant of Dublin, offered "Sundry Sorts of Linnen Goods" all of them "lately imported from Dublin" at his store in Market Street, Philadelphia.[6] Hatton was later associated in business in Philadelphia with James Mackey and with Samuel Carsan.

Another sort of businessman emerged on the frontier, the chapman or peddler. The goods sold by a Scotch-Irish chapman were designed to appeal to the pioneer farmer and more especially his wife. Samuel Shaw, who died in 1743, instructed his executors to sell "the merchant goods" as well as his horse and saddle, so a list was made of them, including from five to eighteen yards of cloth identified as "Checker," "Killimanco," Muslin, "Kellico," linen, and blue linen. His inventory also included three handkerchiefs, "three hangchirchefs of other sort," eight clasp knives, another "one dussin of Clasp Knives," six razors, three knives and forks, five inkhorns, plus "nine brace Inkhorns," five pair of worsted stockings,

eight worsted caps, laces and tapes, combs, four silk laces, garter-
ing, ribbon, five pair of buckles, and "some Little small goods." The
total value was less than £20 but Shaw held bonds, notes and book
debts amounting to £160.[7]

Scotch-Irish peddlers may have carried linens made by their
countrymen in the Pennsylvania backcountry as well as linen
brought over from Ireland, according to Samuel Powel, a Quaker
merchant in Philadelphia. He wrote in 1743 that

> a vast deal of linen and woolen is made within the Province;
> so much linen by the back Irish inhabitants that they not only
> hawk a great deal frequently about both town and county, but
> they carry considerable quantities away to the Eastward by
> land, quite away as far as Rhode Island.[8]

There were certainly peddlers aplenty from the Chesapeake to
New England. Dr. Alexander Hamilton dined with "one Boyd, a
Scotch-Irish pedlar" in Stonington, Connecticut in 1744. "This
pedlar told me he had been some time agoe att Annapolis
[Maryland] att some horse races" and also in Philadelphia.[9]

Some merchants, such as James Beekman in New York, had
extensive dealings in the 1740s and 1750s with peddlers like
Robert Gregg who took linens that did not sell in the city to rural
communities in the Hudson Valley.[10] Peddlers' wares were not limited to linens, of course. Archibald McCurdy was stopping at a tavern in Earltown (now New Holland) in Lancaster County,
Pennsylvania, when he was robbed of "hardware, table knives and
forks, clasp knives, buckles," and £50 in cash.[11]

Men like James Coulter or Thomas Campbell could bring some
linen with them on an Atlantic crossing, but to offer the range of
choices demanded by Thomas Hatton's customers required a settled correspondence with a linen draper in Dublin or Belfast or
more likely London or Liverpool. A connection with Ulster linen
drapers or bleachers gave a dry goods merchant no special advantage. He would do as well with the sort of London house that had
connections with many suppliers and could assemble the variety of
stock – woollens, linens, haberdashery, shoes, and hardware – needed. Although dry goods merchants often dealt with many different

manufacturers, it was cheaper and less risky to ship everything from London.[12]

Linens woven in Ulster were generally taken to Dublin and then shipped to Liverpool. John Henderson of Belfast, for example, imported New York flaxseed from Gerard Beekman and sent him four bales of Irish linens through Hollyday and Dunbar of Liverpool.[13] The advantage of shipping linens from Ulster to an English house to then be shipped to the Colonies came from the bounty introduced in 1743 to make British and Irish linens more competitive with German linens. Although transportation costs leeched out some of the profit, a bounty of a penny and a half on every yard made it worthwhile.[14] Much linen thus reached the Colonies through Dublin middlemen and Liverpool or other English ports, but Ulster merchants who ordered flaxseed often sent linen direct to their American correspondents. A merchant like Gerard Beekman would normally remit two-thirds of the proceeds from linen sales in flaxseed. Merchants charged a commission for selling linen and other dry goods. Beekman mentioned 7.5% for remittances in cash and 10% for flaxseed.[15]

For the merchant in Belfast or Londonderry, a shipment of linen would be used to pay for produce already received from America or to generate cash to buy it on the spot. Eighteenth-century merchants normally sent goods to fill an order from a business associate or correspondent or as a remittance for goods shipped by him. Where a merchant had no connection or wanted to begin one, he could ship goods consigned to a firm recommended by an associate with the request that they sell to the best advantage. Failing this, the goods could be consigned to the ship's captain or to the supercargo, who was usually a part-owner or agent for the merchant. The amount of linen shipped from Ulster ports or carried in the baggage of Ulster emigrants was enough to flood the market, especially in years of heavy emigration. Small dealers tended to undercut both the American linen weavers and the dry goods merchants who imported Irish linens from London or Liverpool. A Philadelphia merchant explained to his English correspondent in 1730 that certain kinds of linen "are become the greatest drug we have which is also occasioned by vast quantities of linen from Ireland." Another Philadelphian explained his inability to move linens consigned him "from the great importation of all sorts of linen much cheaper from the North Ireland."[16]

Although trade in linen, servants, and flaxseed tended over time to concentrate in the hands of merchants who specialized in one or the other, there was always scope for enterprising individuals like James Coulter. A dry goods merchant in New York complained that linens "are Dull and plenty, for the pedlars and Scowbanckers from Ireland Carry them Dayly along Street and offer them for sale at a very Cheap Rate."[17] These scowbanckers were also flaxseed buyers, dealing with the masters of vessels that brought seed from New England and Long Island to New York. The same New York merchant told his Dublin correspondent:

> You may thank a set of people called Scowbanckers that comes from your parts that seed has run so high this two years past. Our town is full of them and there is scarce a vessell comes along the wharffs but there is Immediately a half Dozen of them aboard bidding against each other. I would recommend to you not to countance them at any time or to suffer any of them ever to come over in a Vessell of yours.[18]

Philadelphia had its share of small flaxseed buyers. Davey and Carsan had difficulty in finding freight for a ship to Londonderry until "some aplications made to us by Sundry Pedling Chaps" completed the flaxseed cargo.[19] Such folk left few records, although they persisted in all colonial markets. Only the chance of an unpaid bill preserved a notice of "William Graham, or Grimes, an Irish pedlar," who "goes over to Ireland every fall, with flaxseed &c., and returns in the spring with servants and goods, generally taking shipping and landing at New Castle, and is said to be worth money."[20]

Established merchants, like Davey and Carsan, sometimes found scowbanckers useful as a source of flaxseed needed to complete a shipment in a season when it was scarce as it was in 1749. Samuel Carsan wrote from New Castle:

> I was Informed before I Left Philada. that one John Gillis who goes passenger in the Snow *City of Derry* was Inclinable to sell 85 hhds of Seed that he has aboard which I was Determin'd to Ship upon your acct. This was my Errand down but he alter'd

his resolution & Intends holdg them himself. Seed in the memory of man was never so scarce nor so high. it sells now at 12/– per Bus[hel]& hardly to be gott. I don't suppose there will be Ship'd from here & at [New] York four thousand hhds.[21]

Men like John Gillis and James Coulter are shadowy figures in this transatlantic commerce. Needing cash to buy flaxseed, they may have kept the price of Irish linens low and, as Thomas Truxes suggested, undercut any market for domestic linen.[22] But simply by making regular ocean crossings and being as familiar with the Philadelphia or New York markets for linen, servants, and colonial produce as they were with the brown-linen markets of Ulster, they were a source of information for emigrants and shopkeepers alike. While mercantile firms had their own channels to send letters to overseas correspondents, scowbanckers likely brought letters and bits of news with them. Recruiting servants and redemptioners at markets and hiring fairs in Ulster, these men played a role like that of the German "newlanders" in promoting emigration to the Colonies as a land of opportunity.[23]

Redemptioners and Servants

The servant trade began with large-scale emigration from Ulster, if not earlier. In August 1718 John Paterson agreed with Samuel Gordon, "Master of A Certain Ship or Vessel Called the *Hart* then Riding at Anchor in the harbour of Londonderry in Ireland and then bound on A Voyage to some part of America as the Majority of Passengers should Vote," to take as passengers Paterson and twenty servants whom he would recruit and who would be indentured to him, paying £5 sterling within fifteen days of arrival in America for each one's passage. Paterson had the option of paying £4 Irish before the *Hart* sailed, a considerably smaller sum, so he evidently expected to sell the servants' time to raise the passage money. The *Hart* landed at New York in October, with Paterson and his servants all sick and unable to work because of inadequate food on the voyage, obliging him to lay out "great sums of Money for his own and their Maintainance Nursing keeping and looking after them in their sickness."[24]

Servants came consigned to a New York merchant. Between 1728 and 1732, eight boatloads of indentured servants arrived at New York, seven from Ireland and one from England.[25] John and Joseph Reade, established New York merchants, handled many of these ships in the servant trade. They advertised men and women servants from Dublin on the *Happy Return* in 1728.[26] The next year the snow *Eagle* brought 55 men and women servants from Dublin, consigned to William Walton and John and Joseph Reade.[27] Other "Irish Men, Women and Boys, Servants," came on the ship *George and John* from Dublin. Captain Anthony Adamson and Samuel Moore, supercargo, sold their indentures, advertising that "They will take either Flower or Wheat as Pay."[28]

The Irish servant trade was not a significant commerce for New York merchants in the 1730s. Garret Van Horne imported Irish linen and about 50 servants from Dublin every year in his sloop *Garret* and he nearly had the trade to himself. New York was evidently not nearly as good a market for Irish servants as Philadelphia. The few vessels that brought Irish servants tried both markets. A Boston brig *Benjamin and Hannah*, for example, brought 25 servants from Cork in June 1732 and entered ten days later from Philadelphia with fifteen. She returned to Philadelphia later in the season, entering from New Castle on Delaware, with passengers. New York merchant Justus Bosch, on the other hand, imported 57 servants from Dublin in September 1732 in his schooner.[29]

Philadelphia emerged early as the primary market for servants from Ireland. Irish indentured servants accounted for two-thirds of the servants landed there between Christmas 1728 and Christmas 1729 but there were only 220 of them. The low figure reflected a temporary shift away from Philadelphia because in 1729 the Pennsylvania Assembly laid a tax of twenty shillings a head on all Irish servants imported into the province. At the same time, "In New Castle Government [Delaware] have been landed about 4500 Passengers & Servants, chiefly from Ireland."[30] This meant that four of every five persons coming to the Delaware Valley from Ireland in 1729 came ashore at New Castle. The greater number were, of course, emigrants who paid their own passage. New Castle had real advantages over Philadelphia for incoming passengers from

Ulster as it offered a shorter and more direct route to the Scotch-Irish settlements in Chester and Lancaster counties and, later on, across the Susquehanna River.[31]

James Coulter's nine servants, as well as his linen and other "smal things," were landed at New Castle in Delaware to avoid paying the duty on Irish servants. For Coulter or his heirs this would have entailed a payment of £9 on servants with a total value of £149 less the cost of their passage and provisions. It is no surprise that the Pennsylvania levy diverted the flow of servants away from Philadelphia.[32] A ship from Ireland with 200 servants arrived soon after the law took effect and landed the servants across the Delaware river at Burlington and Trenton in New Jersey to avoid paying the duty. Four more ships with passengers and servants were then at New Castle.[33]

The demand for Irish servants generally outpaced the supply. Labour was always scarce in the Colonies and this made for a brisk market for servants. The numbers who came on any one vessel were generally few, and there was no dearth of buyers for men and boys. Irish women and girls made up only a small percentage of the servants who were indentured in the Philadelphia Mayor's Court in 1745–6, presumably because shippers knew there was little demand for them in America. Most indentures were for four years and the buyer paid from £12 to £14 Pennsylvania currency, depending on the servant's aptitude for work and general health. Although newspaper advertisements sometimes included a list of skilled trades at which these servants were proficient, even those men and boys without any skills sold readily.[34]

Both Irish servants and linen were staples in transatlantic commerce and Dublin was equally central to the servant trade as to the linen trade. Cork and all of the northern ports sent servants across the Atlantic, but Dublin was the major shipping point for Irish servants as Bristol was for English servants. Seven out of eight advertisements offering newly-arrived Irish servants published in the *Pennsylvania Gazette* in 1738, for instance, mentioned they had come on a ship from Dublin. This meant, of course, that the majority of servants came from southern Ireland.

Servants were indentured before the mayor of the port of embarkation, usually to a merchant there or to the ship's captain.

This indenture, specifying a certain number of years they would serve, would be sold in an American port and officially registered there. Servants were thus a commodity, shipped by a merchant in Dublin or elsewhere and consigned to his correspondent in Philadelphia or New York. Established local merchants usually managed the sale of servants in northern cities, although ship's captains sometimes took care of finding purchasers for the times of servants and redemptioners. Belfast merchant Daniel Mussenden, for instance, shipped 32 servants to Philadelphia on the *Bruerton* of Liverpool in 1729; the ship's captain posted bond to sell their time and remit the proceeds.[35]

Some servants arrived in the autumn, as the flaxseed ships came in, but most came in the spring and early summer. German servants and redemptioners arrived in large numbers in September and October, depressing the market for Irish servants in Philadelphia.[36] This will explain why the servant trade concentrated on Dublin and secondarily Cork and Sligo with the Ulster ports a distant third. Servants and redemptioners did sail from Belfast, Londonderry and Newry in the flaxseed ships, but the servant trade generally followed a different calendar. Newspaper advertisements indicate many Philadelphia merchants had at least some interest in the servant trade. In the 1730s only a few of them had direct ties with Ireland. William Harper, a Philadelphia merchant from Londonderry, was in partnership with William Kirkpatrick of Londonderry and Hugh White and William Finley of Dublin in the ship *Happy Return* from 1737.[37] He advertised Irish servants as well as dry goods.

> Just arrived from Ireland in the Ship *Young Rebecca*, David Sterling, Commander, A Parcel of Likely Men and Women Servants, Whose Times are to be disposed of by William Harper.[38]

Notices in the *Pennsylvania Gazette* in 1738 offered servants for sale from eight ships, including men and women "fit for Town or Country Work" by James Mackey, another Derryman, and Thomas Hatton.[39] Six advertisements in 1739 called attention to servants from Ireland and England whose indentures could be bought.[40] In each of these years half were English servants, the other half Irish, all but two on ships sailing from Dublin. The famine year of 1740 saw a marked increase in the number of Philadelphia ships carrying grain and other provisions to Ireland and returning from a southern Irish port, but only six ships brought servants who were offered for sale in the newspaper in 1740. Four of them sailed from Cork, and two from Bristol, England. There was certainly a shift away from Dublin to Cork, which was in the region most affected by hunger. Three of the four advertisements for servants from Cork indicated that they were all males. The two ships from Bristol, on the other hand, brought "English and Welch Servant Men, Boys, and Women." Ulster-born flaxseed merchants Hugh Davey and Samuel Carsan offered "a Parcel of likely Men and Women Servants," imported in the Ship *Mary Ann* from Belfast, as well as "a great Variety of White and Check Linnens, Sail Canvas, Lead, earthen Ware, Smith's Coal, and fine Salt." The *Friendship* brought "several likely Tradesmen & Husbandmen, Servants, all young," the *Debby* "young Servant Men," and the *Prince of Orange* "Servant Men," all of them from Cork. All of these ships arrived in the flaxseed season, a poor time for the sale of servants, and all six loaded flaxseed and flour for their return voyage. It is likely that the flaxseed ships put in at Cork to take on servants in their outward voyage.[41] The snow *Mary Ann*, consigned to Davey and Carsan, had a singularly unlucky crossing from Belfast "with 190 Servants, Passengers, &c." They spent twelve weeks on the Atlantic and "were almost all starv'd, having then but two days Provision on Board." Twenty died on the voyage and the rest were sick when *Mary Ann* put into New York harbour for emergency supplies before going on to Philadelphia.[42]

Was there a spike in emigration and, in particular, emigration of indentured servants as a result of the hungry year of 1740? A severe winter in 1739–40 destroyed crops and left famine conditions in many parts of Ireland that continued into 1741. The price of bread in Dublin peaked in April 1741 at its highest level for the century, but by September food prices were again close to normal. Dickson minimized its impact on Ulster emigration, which, he believed, was confined to the single year 1740.[43] Based on *Pennsylvania Gazette* reports of the arrival of 20 ships from southern Irish ports in 1740 and 31 ships in 1741, a number never again equalled, together with eleven each year from northern ports, Wokeck suggested a record emigration from southern Ireland of 648 in 1740 and 993 in 1741 and a more normal 450 each year from Ulster landing at Philadelphia. She estimated the total number of immigrants, when figures are adjusted to include New Castle on the Delaware, at 1,649 in 1740 and 2,085 in 1741, of whom she judged two-thirds were indentured servants.[44]

Could the market for servants absorb such large numbers? Newspaper advertisements for servants may be a sign of a slow market, just as advertisements for freights may well indicate an overcapacity of shipping in the flaxseed season. With four notices of Irish servants in the *Pennsylvania Gazette* in 1740 and only three in 1741, the servant trade would seem to be at its normal volume. The snow *Penguin* brought servants from Cork in July 1741 and sailed for Dublin and Newry in October. The *Prince of Orange* returned in November from Dublin with servants. Agents for another of the flaxseed fleet, the ship *William and James*, "from and for Belfast," advertised for freights home and added that "There are several Redemptioners and Servants on board said Vessel."[45]

The following year, when just seven ships entered from southern Irish ports, there were the same number of advertisements for servants. In 1742 the *Friendship* again brought servants from Cork. Davey and Carsan advertised servants from the *Ann and Mary*, which entered from New Castle on Delaware. We might infer from another advertisement that the *Linen Draper* brought servants from Dublin.[46] Although the Dublin newspapers carried frequent notices of ships leaving that port, the only voyage for Philadelphia in 1740 or 1741 that Audrey Lockhart found was the *Catherine*, sailing with linen cloth and 120 passengers in June 1741. This was Davey and Carsan's ship, which cleared customs for Sligo and Londonderry in November.[47]

The record of indentures registered by the Mayor of Philadelphia between October 1745 and October 1746 permits analysis of the servant trade at that time and place.[48] By comparing the Mayor's Court record with the shipping news published in the *Pennsylvania Gazette* significant patterns of this branch of commerce are evident. In the course of that year indentures were registered for servants who came to Philadelphia in 29 different ships. A dozen sailed from Londonderry, six from Dublin, two from Cork, two from Liverpool and Belfast, two from Liverpool and Londonderry, and one directly from Liverpool, with one each from Belfast and Larne, from Coleraine, from Newry, and from Newcastle on Tyne. Although vessels from Ulster ports (20 of 29) comprised more than half of those that brought servants, ships from Dublin brought the largest numbers. Of the 570 servants on the registry, 240 came from Dublin, 108 from Londonderry, and 73 from Cork, with a scattering from Newry, Belfast, and English ports. Only those who imported servants from Dublin advertised them for sale in the newspaper, perhaps because they had a larger number to sell than those to whom other ships were consigned.

The Mayor's Court recorded indentures for 52 servants on the snow *George*, arriving from Dublin in September 1745, and 63 on her return to Philadelphia in August 1746.[49] The snow *Dublin's Pride* brought 56 servants in April 1746 and the brigantine *Rebecca* came with 39 in September 1746.[50] The ship *Delaware* from Cork brought 47 of the servants indented by the Mayor of Philadelphia and 26 of them came from the same port on the snow *City of Cork*.[51] The ship *Bolton* from Liverpool and Dublin brought 30 servants. Captain Edward Dowers advertised "a Parcel of likely Men Servants" as well as "good Cheshire and Gloucester cheese, and a Neat Assortment of Irish Linnens" to be sold at his house in Water Street.[52]

Ships from Ulster ports are represented by far fewer individuals among those named in the Philadelphia register. The snow *Martha* brought 26 servants from Londonderry, the largest number from that port. The ship *Catherine* from Londonderry and the snow *Chester* from Newry each accounted for 24 servants. Other Londonderry ships came with only a few servants: the snow *Happy Return* brought eleven on one voyage and fourteen on her next; the brig *William* came with eleven, the ship *William and Mary* had nine; five servants from the ship *La Pomone*, three from the brig *Nancy*, and just one on the ship *Rundell* are on the list. Only two servants were registered from the ship *Woodstock* and the snow *John*, also from Londonderry. The snow *George* brought thirteen servants from Newry. The brig *Sally* from Coleraine carried three. The brig *Carolina* from Liverpool and Belfast only four.[53]

The Philadelphia servant trade became more specialized and concentrated in the hands of a few firms, although other merchants found a shipload of servants a ready source of cash to remedy a temporary shortfall or when dry goods glutted the market.[54] By 1745 the servant trade was in the hands of a dozen Philadelphia firms, many of them with direct links to Ireland. Israel Pemberton, an eminent Quaker merchant and political leader, had the 56 servants on the *Dublin's Prize* consigned to him.[55] Robert Wakely managed the affairs of the snow *George* and the large number of servants imported on her in 1745 and 1746. He also dealt in Irish linens.[56] The other snow *George*, belonging to Newry, and the brig *Sally* from Coleraine were both consigned to John Erwin, who advertised that he had "several Sorts of Irish Linnens, Sheetings and Diapers" for sale.[57] Thomas Robinson, another dry goods merchant and Erwin's sometime partner, also dealt in servants.[58] The servants on the *Kouli Khan* were consigned to Alexander Lang, an Ulster-born flaxseed and dry goods merchant.[59] The snow *Chester*, owned by Thomas Walker, William Blair, and Caleb Copeland of Philadelphia, and commanded by George Blair, was entrusted to business partners Captain William Blair and David McIlvaine. Similarly the *William and Mary*, owned and commanded by Captain William Blair, was consigned to Blair and McIlvaine.[60]

The firm of Redmond Conyngham and Theophilus Gardner represented nearly all the ships arriving from Londonderry with servants, the ship *Woodstock*, the snow *John*, the snow *Happy Return*, the ship *Catherine*, the snow *Martha*, the ship *Belinda*, the ship *La Pomone*, and the brigantine *Nancy*. The number of servants on most of these vessels made this a negligible, if not burdensome, part of Conyngham and Gardner's business, but it indicates the extent to which the firm came to dominate trade from Londonderry and the servant trade in particular. Davey and Carsan were the agents for the *William*, owned by William Hogg of Londonderry, selling her cargo of servants, linen, gunpowder, and coal, and freighting her for the return voyage with flour, wheat, wheel pieces, barrel staves, and pig iron as well as flaxseed. Not all the servants and redemptioners were sold in Philadelphia; some were evidently taken into the backcountry for sale there. Davey and Carsan could not supply a final account of servant sales from the *William* in 1745 until June of the following year, since three of the servants "were sold back in the country" and Davey and Carsan reported they "have not learned what they sold for."[61]

Redemptioners

Passengers gave little trouble and are rarely mentioned in mercantile correspondence. Redemptioners were a somewhat different article. They were passengers who came up short in the cost of their passage and signed an indenture as a surety for its payment. Unlike servants who remained on shipboard until sold, redemptioners could go ashore and travel freely around the province seeking friends or relations to help with the passage money. James Mackey, a merchant in Front Street, Philadelphia, freighted ships from Londonderry with flaxseed and other produce. The ship *Hopewell*, the snow *Frodsham*, and the brigantine *Lawson* arrived from Londonderry in September 1735 with the first flaxseed fleet.[62] Each brought passengers and redemptioners. Mackey gave notice to

> Persons who came over Passengers or Servants upon Redemption, in the Ship *Hopewell*, Anthony Faucet, Master; in the Brigt. *Lawson*, Benj. Lowes, Master; and in the Snow *Frodsham*, James Aspinal, Master, that if they do not appear and pay or cause to be paid, the several Sums for which they indented, to James Mackey, Merchant in Philadelphia, within twenty Days from the Date hereof, they will be prosecuted as the Law directs.[63]

Redemptioners were always a troublesome business. Five years later Mackey was still trying to collect passage money.

> This is to desire Thomas Smiley, George Caldwell, Henry Robinson, and James Henderson, who came Passengers from Ireland with Capt. James Aspinall, in the Snow *Frodsham*, in the Year 1735, that they would immediately pay the respective Sums for which they stand engaged, to James Mackey of Philadelphia, or they may expect to be arrested.[64]

Others found redemptioners equally daunting. Hugh Davey and Samuel Carsan, partners in a Philadelphia mercantile house, reported to Nathaniel Alexander of Londonderry that "Sundry redemptioners per the *William* on her last voyage have absolutly reffused to pay one Shilling & are Screen'd by two Raskly Justices of the Peace in Chester County ... who say they are not obliged to Either pay or Serve."[65] They could do no better for Ninian Boggs of Londonderry "Concerning the outstanding Debetts on the Redemptioners, one shilling of which we presume neither we nor he will Ever be able to Colect."[66]

Where the ship's captain was responsible for the passage money owed by absconding redemptioners, he had to rely on business associates in America to collect after he sailed for home. Robert Hogg of Londonderry asked those who owed him "in Redemption or other ways" to pay William Shaw in New Castle or James Mackey in Philadelphia. Shaw threatened, in behalf of another client, that "such as were on Redemption if they do not pay directly, will be sold as Servants without any longer Forbearance."[67]

The profit in the servant trade depended on a quick turnover on both sides of the Atlantic, since servants had to be fed, clothed and housed while waiting for a ship to leave an Irish port or while remaining unsold in a colonial port. These costs had to be deducted from the apparent profit of from £9 to £21 Pennsylvania currency over the actual cost of a transatlantic passage. Davey and Carsan explained to Joseph Fade of Dublin, who consigned servants to them, the heavy charges they were obliged to pay.[68] Even when buyers appeared in a short time, they often wanted long credit.[69] Servants, nevertheless, sold well enough to encourage Philadelphia merchants to recommend to their Ulster correspondents sending them a number of indentured servants.[70] Only a few flaxseed merchants, notably Conyngham and Gardner, later Conyngham and Nesbitt, and John Erwin ventured into the servant trade on their own account at this time.[71]

Notes

1   Lancaster County Wills, A–1, 23 (LCCH). Inventory, October 28, 1735, Inventory, April 1736, and Accounts, March 24, 1740 (LCHS).

2   His brother Joseph Coulter of Banbridge and friend John Pettigrew were entrusted in his will with his business in the Kingdom of Ireland.

3   R. C. Nash, "Irish Atlantic Trade in the Seventeenth and Eighteenth Century," *William and Mary Quarterly*, 3rd ser., 42(1985), 337, 349. Truxes, *Irish-American Trade*, 184.

4   Campbell was still in business in 1747. *Pennsylvania Gazette*, January 21, 1728/29, October 15, 1747.

5   *Pennsylvania Gazette*, March 13, 1728/29.

6   *Pennsylvania Gazette*, February 11, 1728/29, May 22, 1729. Hatton had for sale, among other things, sheetings of various sizes, Irish Hollands, Hackabucks, Fine Diapers, shirting cloth of various sizes, buckrams, topsail canvas, bed tickings, shoe tickings, silk tickings for jackets and breeches, chequer'd and strip'd linen.

7   Samuel Shaw, Inventory, May 23, 1743 (LCHS). His will is in Lancaster Will Book, A–1–79 (LCCH).

8   Samuel Powel, Jr. to David Barclay and Son, London, June 16, 1743 (Powel Letterbook, HSP, as quoted in Anne Bezanson, Robert D. Gray and Miriam Hussey, *Prices in Colonial Pennsylvania* (Philadelphia, 1935), 267).

9   Note that Hamilton, a Scot, described Boyd as "Scotch-Irish." Carl Bridenbaugh, ed., *Gentleman's Progress: The Itinerarium of Dr. Alexander Hamilton, 1744* (Chapel Hill, NC, 1948), 160.

10 Philip L. White, *The Beekmans of New York in Politics and Commerce 1647–1877* (New York, 1956), 356.

11 *Pennsylvania Gazette*, October 31, 1751.

12 John Smail, *Merchants, Markets and Manufacture: The English Wool Textile Industry in the Eighteenth Century* (London, 1999), 77–8.

13 Gerard G. Beekman to John Henderson, September 28, 1758, in Philip L. White, ed., *The Beekman Mercantile Papers* (New York, 1956), I, 332.

14 Jane Gray, *Spinning the Threads of Uneven Development: Gender and Industrialization in Ireland during the Long Eighteenth Century* (Lanham, MD, 2005), 24.

15 Gerard G. Beekman to Adam Schoales, February 14, 1752, to Alexander Ogilby, February 18, 1752, in *Beekman Mercantile Papers*, I, 139.

16 Bezanson *et al.*, *Prices in Colonial Pennsylvania*, 267.

17 Gerard G. Beekman to Cunningham [Conyngham] and Gardner, November 18, 1750, in *Beekman Mercantile Papers*, I, 133.

18 Gerard G. Beekman to Matthew Henderson, December 4, 1750, in *Beekman Mercantile Papers*, I, 136.

19 Davey and Carsan to William Hogg, November 26, 1746 (Davey and Carsan Letterbook, LC).

20 *Pennsylvania Chronicle*, February 28, 1768.

21 Samuel Carsan to "Dear Robin" [Robert Barclay], November 30, 1749 (Davey and Carsan Letter Book, LC). Carsan's conjecture was close to the mark.

Only 3,719 hogsheads of American flaxseed reached Irish ports in 1750. Truxes, *Irish-American Trade*, 284.

22   Truxes, *Irish-American Trade*, 131.

23   On the newlanders, see Wokeck, *Trade in Strangers*, 31–4.

24   The *Hart* brought 100 passengers. *Boston News Letter*, October 27, 1718. Richard B. Morris, ed., *Select Cases of the Mayor's Court of New York City, 1674–1784* (Washington, DC, 1935), 684–7.

25   Joyce D. Goodfriend, B*efore the Melting Pot: Society and Culture in Colonial New York City 1664–1730* (Princeton, NJ, 1992), 135.

26   *New York Gazette*, June 10, 1728.

27   *New York Gazette*, April 28, 1729.

28   *New York Gazette*, June 24, 1728.

29   Naval Officers Returns, Port of New York (CO/5/114/111, PRO, Reel 46, British MSS, Manuscript Division, LC). *Pennsylvania Gazette*, August 28, 1732.

30   *Statutes at Large of Pennsylvania* (Harrisburg, PA, 1896), 4 (1724–44), 135–40. *Pennsylvania Gazette*, January 13, 1730.

31   For the historical researcher New Castle has serious disadvantages since no record of ships arriving there or their passengers has survived, either in customs records or newspaper summary.

32   Wokeck, *Trade in Strangers*, 176.

33   *New York Gazette*, August 4, 1729.

34   Truxes, *Irish-American Trade*, 138. Wokeck, *Trade in Strangers*, 210–11.

35   John Fowler, master of the *Bruerton*, Belfast, May 29, 1729 (Mussenden Papers, D/354/477 PRONI).

36   Wokeck, *Trade in Strangers*, 210–11.

37   "Ship Registers for the Port of Philadelphia," *PMHB*, XXIII (1899), 501.

38   *Pennsylvania Gazette*, July 27, 1738, June 28, 1739, January 1, 1741.

39   *Pennsylvania Gazette*, April 20, May 4, June 21, August 3, August 17, August 31, September 4, 1738.

40   *Pennsylvania Gazette*, May 3, May 31, June 14, June 21, June 28, July 12, 1739.

41   *Pennsylvania Gazette*, September 11, September 25, November 6, November 27, December 4, 1740.

42   *Pennsylvania Gazette*, September 25, 1740, October 9, 1740.

43   Dickson, *Ulster Emigration*, 52.

44   Wokeck, *Trade in Strangers*, 172–5, 180.

45   *Pennsylvania Gazette*, July 9, 1741, October 29, 1741, November 5, 1741.

46   *Pennsylvania Gazette*, April 22, 1742, May 13, 1742, May 20, 1742, December 21, 1742.

47   Lockhart, "Quakers and Emigration from Ireland", 185. *Pennsylvania Gazette*, November 5, 1741.

48   George W. Neible, comp., "Servants and Apprentices Bound and Assigned Before James Hamilton, Mayor of Philadelphia, 1745," *PMHB*, XXX (1906), 348–52, 427–36, XXXI (1907), 83–102, 195–206, 351–67, 461–73, XXXII (1908), 88–103, 237–49, 351–70.

49   The snow *George*, Nathaniel Ambler, master, arrived from Dublin with men and women servants (*Pennsylvania Gazette*, September 26, 1745) and

returned with "Servants, Labourers and Tradesmen." (*Pennsylvania Gazette*, August 14, 1746.) A second snow *George*, Francis Boggs, master, brought passengers and servants from Newry. (*Pennsylvania Gazette*, October 10, 1745, November 7, 1745.)

50 *Pennsylvania Gazette*, April 24, 1746, September 18, 1746.

51 *Pennsylvania Gazette*, November 14, 1745, June 19, 1746.

52 Among them were three who mentioned their homes as Liverpool, Antrim, and Kildare. *Pennsylvania Gazette*, October 10, 1745.

53 It must be remembered that these ships would have disembarked passengers at New Castle, Delaware.

54 Sharon V. Salinger, *"To Serve Well and Faithfully": Labor and Indentured Servants in Pennsylvania, 1682–1800* (Cambridge, 1987), 75–7. Truxes, *Irish-American Trade*, 133.

55 *Pennsylvania Gazette*, April 24, 1746.

56 *Pennsylvania Gazette*, October 29, 1741, September 26, 1745, October 24, 1745, August 14, 1746.

57 *Pennsylvania Gazette*, November 7, 1745.

58 *Pennsylvania Gazette*, May 16, 1745.

59 This ship was named for Shah Nadir, called Kouli Khan, an Afghan ruler. *Pennsylvania Gazette*, February 2, 1744.

60 Neible, comp., "Servants and Apprentices," *PMHB*, 32(1908), 248.

61 Davey and Carsan to William Hogg, November 10, 1745, November 25, 1745, December 31, 1745, June 24, 1746, November 26, 1746, December 5, 1746 (Davey and Carsan Letterbook, LC).

62 *Pennsylvania Gazette*, September 4, 1735, September 11, 1735.

63 *Pennsylvania Gazette*, January 6, 1735/6.

64 *Pennsylvania Gazette*, June 5, 1740.

65 Davey and Carsan to Nathaniel Alexander, July 24, 1746 (Davey and Carsan Letterbook, LC).

66 Davey and Carsan to Mrs. Mary Boggs, November 28, 1749 (Davey and Carsan Letterbook, LC).

67 *Pennsylvania Gazette*, January 31, 1738, April 21, 1738.

68 Davey and Carsan to Joseph Fade, May 20, 1746 (Davey and Carsan Letterbook, LC).

69 Davey and Carsan to William Hogg, December 8, 1746 (Davey and Carsan Letterbook, LC).

70 Davey and Carsan to Samuel Ewing, March 28, 1748, Hugh Davey to Joseph Davey, December 16, 1749 (Davey and Carsan Letterbook, LC).

71 *Pennsylvania Gazette*, June 8, 1749, June 14, 1749, May 10, 1750, June 21, 1750, November 29, 1750, May 30, 1751, July 11, 1751, August 8, 1751.

3
The Flaxseed Trade Begins

BY 1735 THE FIRST MERCHANTS FROM Ulster had begun establishing themselves in New York, Philadelphia and other colonial ports. Like the scowbanckers, they sold Irish linen, dealt in servants and bought flaxseed to send home. It was a matter of scale. They were able to fill large orders for flaxseed, flour, rum, and other commodities and to find freights for the ships that brought passengers, redemptioners and servants from Ulster. They supplied shop keepers and chapmen and peddlers with dry goods and collected country produce. Their own imports eventually were on a scale large enough to allow them to tell their correspondents in Ireland and England what goods would suit their market. Some of them may have started as seed buyers and linen peddlers, but they were soon on their way to much greater things. Neither the linen trade nor the servant trade dictated the presence of Ulstermen in the commercial centres of Philadelphia, New York, or any of the lesser American ports. That was a function of the flaxseed business.

Flaxseed and emigrants were two sides of the same commercial coin by 1735–6, as a singular ruling by George Macartney, Collector of Customs for the Port of Belfast, demonstrated. Macartney determined that "woollen blankets or bedclothes carried on board by or for the use of all or any passengers and servants" would violate the Act of Parliament forbidding shipment of Irish woollens to the Colonies. The masters of nine ships ready to sail for New Castle, Philadelphia, and New York in April 1736 immediately sent a petition to Macartney asking him to change his mind. They had "arrived with their several ships at the Port of Belfast laden with wheat, flaxseed, and other goods and merchandises from America" and for the return voyage had "contracted with several persons in this kingdom who are inclined to go as passengers and servants to America." The nine captains complained that Macartney's ruling came when their "ships are fitted out and them several passengers and servants in readiness to ship themselves with their goods on board the several ships for which they contracted respectively."[1] Macartney evidently relented as their ships arrived in the Delaware that year with emigrants and cleared later in the season for Belfast with flaxseed and flour from Philadelphia and New York.[2]

What was behind this strange decision by the Collector of Customs? Captain James Stewart, one of the shipmasters involved, complained to Thomas Penn, the Proprietor of Pennsylvania, that it was part of a campaign by landlords to discourage emigration by creating difficulties for "the poor people who are flying from the oppression of landlords and tithes (as they term it) to several parts of America." They attempted to secure an absolute prohibition of emigration by an act of the Irish Parliament in March 1736. Aware that it would be disallowed by the British Parliament, their only recourse was to bend existing laws to achieve the desired result. One of their manoeuvres was to charge the owners and masters of ships bound to the Colonies who advertised "their willingness to agree with the passengers" with illegally "encouraging his Majesty's subjects" to go abroad. When these cases came on at Carrickfergus assizes, the judge dismissed all the charges. It was then that Macartney thought of "a more hellish contrivance," forbidding "the poor people to carry their old bedclothes with them, although ever so old, under pretence of an Act of the British Parliament." Landlords may have had reason to fear the loss of a good many Protestant tenants. Stewart told Penn that, at the time he wrote, ten ships and more than 1,700 people were in distress, unable to sail for America.[3]

New York and the Flaxseed Trade

With the passage in 1731 of an act allowing direct importation of American flaxseed to Ireland and another two years later extending the bounty on imported flaxseed to seed from the American Colonies, trade between North American and Irish ports increased dramatically. Possibly the first ship to sail from the American Colonies with a cargo of flaxseed was the snow *Elizabeth and Catharine* of New York, which cleared for Belfast and Glasgow on December 8, 1731, with 606 casks of flaxseed, a cask of snuff, and 5,000 staves. She was owned by New York City merchants John McEvers and Cornelius Van Horne. The *Elizabeth and Catharine* made a second voyage in December 1732, with flaxseed and lumber, returning in September 1733, with salt from the Isle of May in the Azores. She sailed for Belfast again and returned to New York in July 1734, with a cargo of Madeira wine and salt. After another voyage to Belfast with flaxseed, she arrived at New York in July 1735 from Belfast and the Isle of May with Irish linen and salt.[4]

McEvers and Van Horne did not have the flaxseed trade to themselves even in its earliest days. Other New York merchants entered the flaxseed trade at the same time. John Blake's schooner *Lamb* sailed from New York the same day in 1731 as the *Elizabeth and Catharine* with 228 casks of flaxseed and 2,000 staves, bound for an unspecified port in Great Britain. A year later, in December 1732, the *Lamb* sailed for Dublin with flaxseed and returned the next summer from Belfast with Irish linens. In the last week of 1732, Jonathan Groesbeeck dispatched his brig *Thomas* with 408 flaxseed casks and Justus Bosch loaded 146 casks on the schooner *Ann and Eliza*, which he owned in partnership with her master Alexander Phoenix. George Montgomerie's brig *Eglinton* completed New York's first flaxseed fleet when she sailed for Ireland in January 1733, with 197 casks of flaxseed. On her homeward voyage, *Eglinton* brought linen and passengers from Belfast to Philadelphia, entering customs there in September, since New Castle and Philadelphia were the preferred destinations for the passenger trade.[5]

The new flaxseed trade drew in several Belfast merchants who would continue for many years to import seed and send passengers and servants to the American Colonies. Daniel Mussenden and John Gregg, two of Belfast's most prominent merchants, both imported flaxseed in 1733, and possibly earlier, through John McEvers of New York.[6] Daniel Mussenden, merchant and ship-owner, had interests in the American passenger trade from the first wave of emigration in 1717–18. Mussenden was also interested in the servant trade early on.[7] According to his later newspaper advertisements, Mussenden sold American and Dutch flaxseed, Swedish iron, German honey, Kentish hops and English malt at his store on High Street in Belfast.[8] Many of these goods came in his own ships. For example, Mussenden sent the *Isaac* to Stockholm for iron in 1726 and to Charleston, South Carolina in 1734, bringing home molasses, pitch, rice, rum and sugar. He chartered other ships for voyages to Bremen and Hamburg for flaxseed and linens.[9] Mussenden was also involved in the wine trade, the salt trade, the linen industry, and a colliery in County Tyrone. In addition, he acted as a private banker, before organizing Belfast's first bank in 1754.[10] Daniel Mussenden retired from business to his country home at Larchfield, County Down in 1758.[11] He died five years later, "one of Belfast's principal merchants."[12]

John Gregg came to Belfast from Scotland in 1715 when he was 22 years old and entered business as a merchant in the linen and provisions trade. He owned a beetling mill and bleach green in Shankill and a flaxseed warehouse on North Street. Gregg would continue as a major figure in Belfast enterprises for nearly sixty years and found a family who would be prominent in business circles for a much longer time. Although overshadowed to some degree in his latter years by his enterprising sons, especially Thomas Greg, and by his own bankruptcy in 1773, John Gregg, "Merchant, Slaughterer and Dealer," was still a person of consequence when he died in 1783 at the age of ninety.[13] Because of his Belfast connections, John McEvers and his partners were among the first New Yorkers in the flaxseed trade. McEvers arrived in New York in 1716, evidently with money in his pocket, setting up as a merchant specializing in Irish linens and other dry goods and speculating in New Jersey land. He married Catharine Van Horne in 1722, linking him to an important New York mercantile family. The Van Hornes traded to Madeira, the West Indies, England and Holland and owned at least six vessels and shares in others. McEvers purchased a pew in Anglican Trinity Church in 1724 and served as a vestryman from 1726 to his death in 1751.[14]

McEvers and his brother-in-law Cornelius Van Horne owned the

Elizabeth and Catharine on which they shipped flaxseed each year to Belfast. Their preference was for their Belfast correspondents to ship them linens to the value of the flaxseed. When her cargo was landed in Belfast in February 1735, Mussenden and Gregg reported that "the market was glutted with seed from Holland & America" and remained dull.[15] They sold 78 barrels in March and April, nevertheless, and more seed the next month.[16] In June they reported "a great deal of flaxseed coming in unexpectedly," but demand was also great and in July they wrote that the flaxseed on the *Elizabeth and Catharine* had "sold beyond our expectation." As for remitting the value of the seed, however, they were "obliged by reason of the glut to put it into good hands without fixing a time of payment, but our customers don't expect to be asked before the first of November."[17]

American flaxseed did not immediately find favour with Ulster farmers. One Irish seed buyer complained in a Philadelphia paper that "a considerable Part of your Flax-Seed is found not to grow by Reason that many Persons do rott the Flax before they Thresh the seed." The newspaper explained how the seed should be processed. This was published in 1732, reflecting on one of the first shipments.[18] There were still other hurdles to overcome. Americans had not yet learned how to properly clean and pack flaxseed for export. Mussenden and Gregg reported that the flaxseed sent them from New York was "cleaner than any we had before from your port; [but] it does not yet come up to the cleanliness of the Dutch seed, which it must do if your trade continues."[19] Farmers and storekeepers brought seed to market carelessly packed with grit, twigs and leaves in it; cleaning flaxseed to saleable quality was a continuing concern of individual merchants and the local authorities. In time, merchants in the Colonies built complex machinery to clean their seed. The City of Philadelphia adopted an ordinance in 1738 to prevent frauds and abuses in the measuring of flaxseed.[20]

Still other problems arose early in the trade for merchants on both sides of the ocean. Like all commodities, the price of flaxseed varied from day to day according to market demand. The shipper could easily pay more for seed in New York or Philadelphia than the market would bear in Ireland, where markets might be oversupplied by the time the American seed arrived. Hence the recurrent concern about scowbanckers bidding up the price of raw flaxseed. On the other side of the Atlantic, merchants could not know what a cargo of flaxseed would realize until the last cask was sold; even then customers expected long credit, buying seed in February or March and paying for it in November or December, after they harvested and sold their flax. Merchants in Belfast and Derry normally remitted the proceeds to the colonial merchant in linens or in bills drawn on a London correspondent. American merchants often found linen assortments overpriced or unsuited to their specific market, thus difficult to convert into cash. Bills were normally discounted and involved long delays.

John McEvers and Company shipped staves and plank as well as flaxseed to Belfast. In return, Mussenden and Gregg sent linens, which were already on board the *Elizabeth and Catharine*, when they dispatched her in 1735 to New York by way of the Isle of May.[21] A few Ulster importers sent their own ships to New York for flaxseed. John Gordon, an important Belfast merchant who dealt among other things in "Riga and American flaxseed," sent his brig *Grace and Molly* to New York in 1735 with a cargo of linen; she returned early in 1736 with flaxseed, staves, and grain. Ninian Boggs of Londonderry brought his New England-built snow *Sarah* to New York with linens in 1738 and sailed for Belfast with 399 casks of flaxseed. Noteworthy by their absence, in contrast with Philadelphia, are passengers. The 120-ton ship *William* of Londonderry, owned by Alderman William Hogg, brought 106 paying passengers and their baggage along with a cargo of linen when she arrived at New York in September 1739. *William* was the only arrival with passengers in the entire decade.[22]

After a number of exploratory "adventures to Ireland" by different merchants, New York's flaxseed trade settled into direct trade with Belfast and Dublin. The ship *Amsterdam* and the *Prince Frederick* regularly sailed to Belfast with flaxseed cargoes. Other New Yorkers, notably Garret Van Horne and the Waltons, concentrated on Dublin, exporting flaxseed and barrel staves and importing Irish linen and indentured servants.[23] McEvers and the Van Hornes continued to take a major share in New York's flaxseed trade. McEvers shipped seed to Mussenden in Belfast and occasionally bought seed for Davey and Carsan, his correspondents in

Philadelphia, through the 1740s.[24] In 1749 Gerard G. Beekman reported "Mr. Cornelius Vanhorne and Paul Richards has ordered for Shipping 3000" hogsheads of flaxseed and "Messrs. McEvers, Joseph Hayne & Clarkson has orders for 3000 more," an amount equivalent to all that would come to market that season.[25] Beekman and his uncle Cornelius Van Horne shipped seed to Archibald Cunningham at Londonderry as well as to Newry and Belfast in the 1740s.[26]

Naval Officers' Returns provide an accurate record of New York's flaxseed trade. In 1739 a dozen vessels carried 4,333 casks of flaxseed to Irish ports, 1,996 to Dublin, 1,621 to Belfast, 411 to Londonderry, and 305 to "Ireland." Nine vessels from New York brought 2,602 casks of flaxseed in 1740, 778 to Dublin, 365 to Belfast, and 1,459 to "Ireland." Flaxseed shipments in 1741 were calculated both in casks, as before, and in hogsheads. On board the first five vessels to sail were 793 hogsheads of seed for Dublin, 708 hogsheads for Belfast, and 313 hogsheads directed to "Ireland," as well as 643 casks to Belfast and 347 casks to Dublin.[27]

New York profited from the new trade, with vessels for Irish ports rising steadily from two in 1734 to sixteen in 1739, making Ireland a more common destination than ports in Great Britain, and New York would continue to ship seed grown in New England, Long Island, and northern New Jersey. Sailings from the Port of New York by 1750 reflected the importance of flaxseed. In that year, with eleven ships cleared for Irish ports, Belfast and Newry each accounted for four, Londonderry one, and Dublin one. Of fourteen sailings in 1751 four were to Dublin, three each to Belfast and Derry, two to Newry, and one to Cork. The same pattern persisted in 1752, with fifteen sailings, five to Belfast, three to Londonderry, two to Newry, two to Dublin, one to Coleraine, and one to Sligo. Each year's sailings, regardless of destination, are concentrated between the end of October and early February, indicating they were all part of the flaxseed fleet.[28]

The uneven impact of the burgeoning flaxseed trade was demonstrated by Francis James from shipping news in colonial newspapers. Sailings from Boston to Irish ports, declining from eight in 1732, two in 1742, and three in 1752, were negligible, especially in comparison with an average of thirty ships a year cleared from

Boston for English ports. New York had been the first to enter the flaxseed trade, but Philadelphia emerged almost immediately as the hub of this commerce with a steadily increasing number of ships cleared for Belfast, Coleraine, Dublin, Londonderry or Newry each year, most with flaxseed, 15 in 1732, 28 in 1742, and 51 in 1752.[29]

Bound for Philadelphia

Philadelphia's flaxseed trade began in a small way as soon as the British Parliament opened Irish ports to American produce. Reese Meredith, a Philadelphia merchant, advertised for flaxseed in 1732 in the *American Weekly Mercury* but an article on the same page of the newspaper criticized Pennsylvania shippers for sending seed that would not grow, which had to refer to flaxseed shipped in the 1731 season or earlier.[30] Philadelphia's trade with Ireland in the eighteenth century did not exceed 10% of the number or the tonnage of vessels sailing to and from the port, although, as early as 1737, John Reynell wrote that shipping flaxseed to Ireland "is grown a very considerable branch of trade here."[31] But the predominance of Philadelphia in the passenger trade, as the most common destination for emigrant ships, reflected both "the popularity of colonial Pennsylvania for Irish emigrants and the strength of the commercial ties that linked the Delaware Valley with much of Ireland." It was the flaxseed trade, the most important commercial link between Ireland and the North American colonies, that "established the importance of the middle colonies" as a destination and "largely determined the rhythm of the seasonal sailing patterns" for emigrant ships.[32] And early on Philadelphia drew a community of Ulster-born merchants who specialized in this trade and, as dry goods importers, built up significant backcountry networks, especially with their fellow countrymen.

The number of vessels arriving at Philadelphia and clearing for Irish ports can be roughly calculated from the shipping news and advertisements in the *Pennsylvania Gazette*. But the number of sailings to Irish ports does not tell the whole story, since by the 1730s Philadelphia merchants were engaged in the provisions trade with Cork and the servant trade with Dublin. All fifteen ships cleared for Irish ports in 1732 were in fact sailing to either Cork or Dublin.

The rise of the flaxseed trade is reflected in the sudden increase in ships entering from Belfast and Londonderry and *returning* there. Only one or two ships entered from Belfast each year from 1729 through 1733 and all of them cleared customs for Glasgow, Dublin, or Cork.[33]

The first sailing of a vessel bound from Philadelphia to any port in Ulster to be reported in the *Pennsylvania Gazette* was the brig *Warren* cleared for Belfast in October 1733.[34] In contrast, two ships, the brigs *Friend* and *William*, arrived at Philadelphia in 1734 from Londonderry and returned there and two others, the snows *Charming Molly* and *Brunswick*, entered from Belfast. Their arrival and their departure for Belfast and Derry coincided with what would thereafter be the season for flaxseed ships.[35] That year near-ly 10,000 bushels of flaxseed were shipped from Philadelphia.[36]

The official Philadelphia Customs House report indicated that 14 vessels entered from Ireland and 23 cleared for Irish ports between March 25, 1735 and March 25, 1736.[37] The snow *Charming Molly* entered at Philadelphia in August 1735 from New Castle on Delaware, but originally from Belfast.[38] She was the first of the flaxseed ships to arrive that year, all of them with passengers. September brought a ship from Carrickfergus and four from Londonderry. Two more Derry ships and one from Belfast came in October. These ships brought both passengers and servants.[39] At least four of the Londonderry vessels were consigned to James Mackey, a merchant in Front Street, who was himself from Derry and regularly advertised Irish linens. Mackey owned the snow *Thomas and Jane* in partnership with Alderman William Hogg and Patrick McKinsey of Londonderry. William and Robert Hogg of Londonderry were joint owners of the ships *Mary and Jane* and *St. Stephen*, both New England built.[40] The ship *Catherine* cleared for Derry at the end of November and the rest followed before ice closed the Delaware to shipping. The port of New York was ice free and two ships sailed thence for Belfast in January 1736. Their tim-ing is indicative that they were returning with flaxseed for the spring planting.[41] Nine of these ships, having off-loaded flaxseed, flour and wheat at Belfast, took on passengers and servants for the return voyage, as mentioned earlier.

The next season there were more. The *Catherine* and the *Mary and Jane,* both from Derry, came in August 1736. In September ships from Belfast, Coleraine, Carlingford, and Dublin and three from Londonderry entered. Two more Derry ships came in October, as did four from Carrickfergus, four from Dublin, three from Belfast, and one from Cork. Altogether there were twenty ships entered from ports in the north of Ireland, ten from Londonderry, four each from Belfast and Carrickfergus, one from Coleraine and one from Carlingford.[42] With this new commerce Ulster-born merchants came to the fore. Unlike New York where, apart from John McEvers, long-established Dutch and Huguenot families initially dominated the flaxseed trade, Philadelphia provided scope for merchants who were themselves emigrants from Ulster, men like James Mackey, Hugh Davey, Samuel Carsan, Alexander Lang, and Redmond Conyngham. With their associates in Belfast and Londonderry, they made Philadelphia the hub of commerce in flaxseed and emigrants.

The flaxseed trade forged strong links between Philadelphia and northern Irish ports. Londonderry merchants took an early interest in developing the passenger trade and flaxseed trade with Philadelphia, but ships cleared customs at Philadelphia for Belfast, Coleraine, and Newry as well. In 1739 the *Pennsylvania Gazette* reported a dozen ships leaving for Dublin, five to Cork, five to Londonderry, and two to Newry. The last seven were certainly flaxseed ships, as were two of those cleared to Dublin, making nine in all. Samuel Powel wrote enthusiastically in September 1739 that flaxseed had "become a great branch of trade in a very few years" and that he anticipated "there will be exported from this Province only at least 40,000 bushels this fall for Ireland."[43]

The 1740 flaxseed season saw seven sailings to Dublin, seven to Londonderry, three to Belfast, three to Newry, and one to Coleraine, in all 21 flaxseed ships. In 1741 there were three sailings to Dublin in flaxseed season, seven to Derry, five to Belfast, three to Newry, and two to Coleraine, a total of 20 vessels.[44] By 1742 references to "the flaxseed ships" are common. In that year, only one ship cleared for Dublin, seven to Londonderry, two to Belfast, three to Newry, and two to Coleraine, fourteen in all. In the 1743 season five vessels sailed for Dublin, seven to Londonderry, two to Newry, and one to Coleraine, a total of fifteen. Five ships cleared for Derry,

three to Belfast, two to Newry, and one to Dublin comprised altogether eleven ships in the 1744 flaxseed fleet. In 1745 sailings for
Dublin accounted for two of the flaxseed ships, while seven cleared
for Londonderry, three for Belfast, and one for Newry. During
many of these years the *Pennsylvania Gazette* reported ten or eleven
arrivals from ports in Ulster, and as few as four in 1742 and 1744,
but these figures are slippery. Flaxseed ships were commonly
reported as entering the Port of Philadelphia from New Castle on
the Delaware, where they presumably discharged both passengers
and cargo. Others sailing from Belfast or Derry called at some
intermediate port.[45]

A Ship Calculated for Passengers

One of the first results of the burgeoning flaxseed trade was a flur-
ry of orders from Londonderry and Belfast merchants for ships to
be built for them in New England or along the Delaware. William
and Robert Hogg of Londonderry had two ships built for them at
New England yards in 1735 and the following year their partner
James Mackey supervised the building of a snow for them at
Chichester, below Philadelphia. A group of Belfast merchants
ordered a brig from the same shipyard at the same time. William
Harper and his Londonderry associates had a ship built at
Philadelphia in 1737. All of these vessels were of modest size, displacing 60, 70, and 80 tons, and could normally accommodate
only 50 or 60 passengers.[46] This was probably close to the number
actually carried on these and other flaxseed ships. Two vessels
arrived together at Philadelphia in September 1738 from
Carrickfergus on Belfast Lough "with 130 Passengers and Servants
from Ireland." This number was in marked contrast with ships
bringing Germans. In September 1738 one ship arrived with 360
Palatines, three more brought a total of 1,003, and two others
brought 440 Palatines. It was little wonder that "Most of the Ships
which bring Dutch Passengers this Year have been visited with a
Sickness that has carried off great Numbers."[47] The expanding
flaxseed trade generally eliminated such dangerous overcrowding
on vessels from Ulster ports. The fact that nine ships were waiting
to sail from Belfast with passengers in April 1736 is an indication

that would-be emigrants had a choice of vessels for the Atlantic crossing and, as the flaxseed fleet increased in number and tonnage, ship-owners competed for their business.

Several larger ships were built for merchants in Belfast and Derry in the 1740s, under the supervision of Philadelphia flaxseed merchants. The *Wilmington*, registered at 140 tons, was launched at a Wilmington, Delaware shipyard for James Ross and other Belfast merchants and their American partner David Bush in 1741. William Hamilton of Londonderry joined Redmond Conyngham of Philadelphia in building the *Hamilton Galley* and the *Prince William*, both of 100 tons, at Philadelphia. Theophilus Gardner of Philadelphia had the ship *Bendall* built at Philadelphia for Davis Bendall and William Whitehead of Londonderry. Three other Derry merchants, Ninian Boggs, Richard Bateson, and John McConnel, had the snow *Success* of 100 tons built at Wilmington.[48] A merchant like William Hogg of Derry wanted ships suitable for carrying large numbers of passengers across the Atlantic and instructed his correspondents to keep a weather eye out. Hugh Davey and Samuel Carsan wrote him that

> We have been Looking out for a vessel for you, but none hath fallen in our way, three of our Privateers are return'd without Doing any thing, three more are out, if they shou'd Bring in any vessel Such as we think will Suit the Passenger tread, we Shall Endeavour to purchase her, and be Concerned with you therein.

The firm had already purchased a ship for Londonderry merchant John Fairly in 1745, "a Cheape ship and one that will out Last any vessel belonging to your Port and better Calculated for Passengers than any we know." This was evidently *La Pomone*, taken as a prize by a privateer.[49]

Supervising construction of ships suitable for the passenger and flaxseed trade was one of the services American merchants performed at a commission for their business associates in Ulster. British merchants had relied on ship's captains, like Robert Hogg, to oversee shipbuilding projects, and often sent over skilled craftsmen with him, but they came to see that American artisans were more than equal to the task, so "a Merchant who understands how to deal with these folk is by much the properest person" to direct the project and could "build a vessel 10 to 15 pCt Cheaper than any Stranger possibly can." Davey and Carsan declined William Hogg's offer of a share in a new vessel he intended building at Philadelphia, but urged him to wait until summer, since "none of our master Carpenters Incline to build in the winter, as the days are short the Journeymen can neither Doe so good work nor so much as in the Summer & their wages are pretty much the same." They apologized to Vance and Caldwell of Londonderry that "the vessel ye have ordered to be built is not as forward as we expected in the beginning," but assured them "we shall use our endeavours to forward her."

The snow *City of Derry* was launched in the spring and registered in June 1748 as the property of Andrew Gregg, Arthur Vance, and William Caldwell of Londonderry. Davey and Carsan arranged for Gregg to "take a freight for Lisbon and back here with Salt and by that time he might fill with flaxseed for Derry." The new owners were sufficiently pleased with the *City of Derry* to order another ship built for them; but Davey and Carsan were able to buy "a Vessell already on the stocks much cheaper than Coates or any other Person here would engage for." The brig *Diamond* was launched in time to take a flaxseed cargo.[50] The next year Davey and Carsan bought the ship *Liberty* for Vance and Caldwell and sent her to Derry with flaxseed, flour, barrel staves, and pig iron.[51]

Pioneers in the Flaxseed Business

Hugh Davey and Samuel Carsan were typical of the Ulster-born merchants who pioneered in the flaxseed trade from Philadelphia in the range of their business activities. Merchants who specialized in the flaxseed trade with Ulster had perforce to be engaged in many other branches of commerce. In addition to buying and shipping flaxseed, flour, and other articles for correspondents in Londonderry, Belfast, and Newry, they supervised the building of ships for Ulster merchants in the flaxseed and passenger trade and sold linen and the time of servants and redemptioners on their account. They also imported English woollens and other cloth. With few exceptions, the Scotch-Irish merchants of Philadelphia freighted ships for the West Indies and for Lisbon and Madeira with flour, ship's bread, barrel staves and beeswax, importing rum, Jamaica spirits, and molasses from the sugar islands and wine and dry goods from Portugal. A few ventured into the provisions trade with Cork and the coastal trade of the Colonies.

All of the Philadelphia merchants who specialized in flaxseed also sent flour, bread, and other provisions to Barbados, Jamaica, Antigua, and St. Kitts. Davey and Carsan, for example, had correspondents in each of these islands and relied on them for shipments of rum, spirits, and sugar. They re-exported much of their West Indian imports to Ulster and at least some Irish gammons and beef in barrels to Barbados. Hugh Davey's brother-in-law Joseph Sims was one of a firm of brothers in the West Indies trade. As a possible result of the family connection, Davey and Carsan had business dealings with Joseph and Buckridge Sims. Their major correspondent in Antigua was Colonel John Murray, an old friend of Carsan's from Strabane. Davey and Carsan also shipped flour and wheat to William Shee in Lisbon, ordering wine and cloth from him.

Their primary business, however, was to ship flaxseed ordered by merchants in Derry and Strabane, as is evidenced by their surviving letter book in the Library of Congress. Their correspondents were primarily in Londonderry and included such prominent merchants as Alderman William Hogg, Ninian Boggs, Arthur Vance and his several partners. Vance and Caldwell were long the major firm in the passenger trade from Londonderry; Samuel Carsan's association with Vance began before 1738, when he sold cloth for Vance in Delaware, and continued for many years afterwards. Others were in Carsan's home town of Strabane.[52] Davey and Carsan imported linens, hats, and dry goods from Dublin merchants William Alexander, Hosea Coats, and Joseph Fade. Correspondence with Fade and with Robert Travers in Cork related primarily to earlier sales of servants.[53] But flaxseed shipments to Londonderry held primacy of place with Davey and Carsan, judging by the sheer volume and the seasonal nature of the correspondence in their one surviving letter book. They went into the flaxseed business early and stayed with it as demand and competition increased.

Linen Bounty Acts in 1743 and 1745 broadened colonial markets for low-priced linens and stimulated demand for flaxseed. A report to the Linen Board in 1750 noted that Ireland exported nearly 3.9 million yards of linen in 1723 and over 9.5 million yards in 1749.[54] The Irish linen industry experienced another burst of rapid growth in the 1740s, exporting 4 million more yards of linen in 1750 than in 1745, and, as a result, Ulster farmers needed to plant more flax. In 1744 Irish imports of American flaxseed amounted to 11,252 hogsheads and the following year reached 11,828 hogsheads. There was considerable fluctuation in the next few years, due to poor crops in America and the wartime interruption of trade in Baltic and Holland flaxseed. The general trend, however, was upward, reaching a peak in 1753 when the American Colonies shipped 22,146 hogsheads of flaxseed to ports in Ireland. Import figures rarely fell below that number until the American Revolution and averaged closer to 40,000 hogsheads a year in 1767–75.[55]

Philadelphia merchants did not normally wait for flaxseed and flour to come to market. As demand for flour, wheat, and flaxseed increased, merchants in Philadelphia reached into neighbouring Delaware and Maryland and the Pennsylvania backcountry. Like many of their competitors who created networks in the country to supply them with commodities for export, Davey and Carsan operated a "flaxseed store" in New Castle, Delaware, and shipped hogsheads of seed by shallop from Christiana. They also "bought a Lot of Ground where a town is Intended at the head of N: East, where we have some thoughts of building a smal house" in Charlestown, Cecil County, Maryland, "and there we Can at any time, purchase wheat, flour, & flaxseed at Least 3d pr Bus[hel] Cheaper than here." Charlestown, founded in 1742, drew a number of flaxseed merchants. There were other advantages. In Maryland, "Convicts & Servants in a General way sell better" and, should flaxseed or flour be in short supply, "we can allways be serv'd with Lumber or a tobacco freight." The partners intended that "one of us during the Season will remain there", as Charlestown was but a day's ride from Philadelphia.[56] Maryland's Eastern Shore became a major source of flour and flaxseed for Philadelphia merchants in later years and, on the opposite shore of Chesapeake Bay, the new town of Baltimore would draw established merchants like Samuel Carsan to establish a branch of his firm in the 1770s.[57]

Davey and Carsan were also typical of Philadelphia merchants in the flaxseed and passenger trade because of their connections in Ireland. Samuel Carsan owned property in Strabane, County Tyrone, where his brother Andrew Carsan and brother-in-law Robert Barclay were merchants.[58] The Carsans had been merchants in the town at least since 1675, when Robert Carsan "of the Town of Strabane, Merchant" obtained land in the town and in the neighbouring townland of Dromalagh.[59] The Barclays were merchants and linen drapers with bleach greens near Strabane. His other brother-in-law, the Rev. John Maxwell, Presbyterian minister at Armagh, had business connections in Newry.[60] Samuel Carsan's partner was from Londonderry. Hugh Davey, Jr. also belonged to a mercantile family. He had survived a harrowing voyage in an emigrant ship bound to America. His father had commanded the *Katharine*, which sailed from Londonderry in August 1728, and after more than five months at sea and 109 deaths, his father among them, Hugh Davey, Jr ran her aground on the coast of Mayo. He reported the disaster to his uncles, Samuel Davey, merchant in Londonderry, and William Delap, merchant in Dublin.[61] A few years later Davey joined Carsan in Philadelphia.

The partners brought enough capital to have the *Catherine*, a ship of 60 tons, built for them at Philadelphia.[62] In 1738, in one of his first ventures in the American trade, Samuel Carsan took the *Catherine* to Dublin to take on servants and found none were to be had. He and John McKnight, the ship's captain, were obliged to load a cargo of salt at Liverpool, making it a less profitable voyage.[63] The firm advertised for freights for Dublin on her return voyage. They also noted that "A Choice Parcel of Irish Linnen are to be sold by said Davey and Carsan."[64] They advertised for freights for Derry for Archibald Cunningham's ship *Rundell* and for the *Prince of Orange*.[65] While they advised their correspondents of the state of the market for servants and occasionally handled the sale of servants sent by a correspondent in Derry as a remittance for flaxseed shipped him, they were no longer concerned in the servant trade on their own account.[66]

Ulster merchants who sent orders, but no ship to carry them home, left it to their American correspondent to find a ship willing to take flaxseed on freight. This was not always easy, as the Belfast or Londonderry ship-owner might have ordered enough flour, wheat, or other commodities to fill his own vessel to capacity. Once the flaxseed ships left, it was nearly impossible to find a ship sailing for an Irish port. Without available shipping, flaxseed orders could remain in a warehouse in Philadelphia or New York and finally arrive in Ireland too late to be sold that season.[67] The merchant to whom a ship was consigned could begin loading her at once with the seed and other shipments ordered by her owner. But his orders could be insufficient to fill her hold and the American correspondent might lose precious days or weeks waiting for a full cargo or be obliged to load her with less valuable lumber or pig iron. The many advertisements in Philadelphia newspapers seeking freight for flaxseed ships returning to Belfast and Derry are an indication that this was a common plight.[68]

American merchants had other problems in the brief marketing season. Farmers and backcountry merchants frequently held back seed hoping for a rise in price, sometimes resulting in artificially high prices or a glut in December that lowered prices and rewarded seed buyers able to fill orders then. Worse these late purchases made it difficult to clean and pack the seed before the river iced over. Philadelphia merchants attempted to bring order to the flaxseed market in 1749, a year when seed was scarce:

> Whereas, for some years past, it has been the constant custom of the farmers of this province, to keep back their FLAXSEED from this market till the months of October and November, on a mistaken notion of having a better price for it, whereby the shippers have not time to clean the seed as it should be, which has occasioned general complaints from Ireland of what is sent there from this place, and it is to be feared we shall lose that branch [of trade] entirely, as the seed they have from the other provinces is cleaner, and better liked, merely from their having it sooner from the country; This, therefore, is to desire those concerned in flaxseed, to bring it to town some time next month at farthest, and that they may depend on having at least as good a price for it, as when they kept it so late in the year, that the merchants were obliged to send it off any how, for fear of being shut up by the winter.[69]

In contrast with the factors employed by Whitehaven and

Glasgow merchants to manage their stores in Maryland and Virginia, American correspondents of Ulster firms were free agents. They could accept orders for flax and other commodities from many different merchants and consign ships to one or another. Merchants in Ireland were no less free to drop one correspondent and send their ships and orders to a rival firm. In spite of personal services rendered and care taken in filling orders, Davey and Carsan found their Ulster clients a fickle lot. They lost some of their most important accounts to Conyngham and Gardner and complained of their treatment. Although they bought *La Pomone* for John Fairly and freighted her to Londonderry, Fairly consigned his new ship to Conyngham and Gardner on her return voyage. Carsan asked Fairly, "what Cou'd Posses you to Change an old Experienced friend for a new one" and argued that "had yr Ship Pomone Come to us as indeed we had a good dale of Right to Expect, she had been with you as Soon if not before as any vessel that belongs to Londonderry." Their experience with Archibald Cunningham was much the same and similarly resented.[70] Prize ships, like John Fairly's *La Pomone*, became part of the flaxseed fleet. John Mease and partners purchased the snow *Hannah* "Taken from the French" in 1746 and Daniel Mussenden and William Blair owned shares in the snow *Peggy*, "A Prize from the Spanish."[71]

Wartime Problems

Wartime brought additional hazards to the Atlantic crossing. Belfast merchant James Burgess advertised for passengers, redemptioners, and servants to sail for Philadelphia on the letter of marque ship *William and Mary*, commanded by Captain William Blair. They might feel more secure knowing they had booked passage on a privateer, armed and equipped to capture enemy shipping on the high seas.[72] Great Britain and Spain went to war in 1739, the so-called War of Jenkins' Ear which lasted until 1742. All the major European powers were engaged in the War of Austrian Succession from 1741 to 1748. After a short breathing space, they resumed the conflict in the Seven Years' War from 1756 to 1763, which began in America in 1754 as a struggle between the French and British for control of the Ohio Valley.

With every declaration of war came an invitation to merchants and ship-owners to fit out privateers, authorized by a letter of marque and reprisal to prey on any vessel flying the enemy's flag. Merchants in Philadelphia, New York and other colonial ports were quick to arm their ships and dispatch some of them in search of French or Spanish prizes. At the same time their own ships sailing to or from British and Irish ports and especially to the West Indies were exposed to capture by privateers sent out by France and Spain. Flaxseed ships were also armed. Davey and Carsan advertised in 1741 for freight or passage to Londonderry on the ship *Rundell*, "Burthen 200 Tons, 10 Guns, Men answerable." Other ships sailing to Belfast, Dublin, and Newry that season advertised their armaments as well.[73] The ship *Francis and Elizabeth*, bound for Londonderry, in 1742, and taking "Flax-seed on Freight, at Ten Shillings per Hogshead," was "Mounted with Eight Guns, Men Answerable." The *Robert and Alice*, sailing for Newry, was fitted with "Six Guns."[74] There was good reason to want an armed ship. The brig *Debby*, Captain Zachariah Whitpain, "bound here from Dublin with 140 Servants and Passengers," was off the Delaware Capes in September 1744, when a Spanish privateer took her and carried her to Havana. Captain Whitpain came to Boston under a flag of truce. The fate of the servants and passengers was not reported.[75]

The *Arundel Galley* from Londonderry was taken by a Spanish privateer on the high seas in 1746. Matthew Rowan, her captain, agreed to ransom his ship and two passengers, Robert Macleheaney and William Colhoun, were delivered to the privateer "to secure the payment of the ransom." After the *Arundel* arrived at New Castle, Delaware, an admiralty court determined the proportion of the ransom money due from the owners of the ship, those who had shipped cargo on her, and the individual passengers. After this was settled, she sailed for Derry with flaxseed.[76] The master was traditionally allowed to ransom his ship by paying or pledging a substantial sum of money. Thus a French privateer returned the snow *George*, sailing from Dublin with servants, to Captain Nathaniel Ambler on payment of £500 Sterling. He brought her safely to Philadelphia.[77] Captain Ambler threw all of his papers overboard when his ship was taken, so the invoice for linens shipped on the

George to Davey and Carsan was lost, although the boxes of linens were delivered to them.[78]

Ships bound to and from the West Indies were especially vulnerable. Davey and Carsan acquired the sloop *Warren's Prize* of 30 tons, taken from the French by the privateer *Warren* early in 1745. They dispatched her to Antigua in December, intending to send her to Ireland with flour in the Spring. She sailed from Antigua in February and disappeared, leading them to believe she was taken by a privateer.[79] They were already in correspondence with a London insurer about the sloop *Charming Molly*, "taken by a Spanish privateer, retaken by one of ours & carried into Jamaica."[80]

Philadelphia Merchants

The expatriate business community continued to grow as other aspiring merchants came to Philadelphia from Ulster in the 1740s. Many, if not all, passed into the ranks of dry goods merchants.[81] Some, like John Knox, who shipped flaxseed to Londonderry and sold Irish linens and cambrics at his store, left little more at their deaths than flaxseed, store goods, and wearing apparel sold at public venue, but others established commercial dynasties.[82] By 1750 there were a good many Ulster-born merchants in Philadelphia, each vying for a share of the commerce in flaxseed, linens and servants. The rising star of Conyngham and Gardner eclipsed many of its rivals, which was especially galling to Carsan since Theophilus Gardner "was our clerk but now since sett up for himself."[83]

The new firm of Conyngham and Gardner came into being in 1746. Gardner's partner was Redmond Conyngham, who came to Philadelphia in 1741 from Letterkenny, County Donegal. The Letterkenny Conynghams were a family of minor landowners, claiming descent from a seventeenth-century bishop of Raphoe. Conyngham had important business connections in Derry, notably with Archibald Cunningham and William Hamilton. He had responsibility for Cunningham's ship *Rundell Galley* in 1742.[84] He was living at that time with the family of William Harper, who had been a partner of William Kirkpatrick of Londonderry and Hugh White and Robert Finlay of Dublin.[85] Harper died in 1741 and his widow Alice carried on the business as best she could.[86] Redmond

Conyngham, not long in Philadelphia from Londonderry, advertised his dry goods for sale at the Widow Harper's shop.[87]

Whatever their business rivalries might be, they formed a fairly
close-knit community, possibly because they all came from similar
backgrounds in Ulster. Samuel Carsan attempted to help Alice
Harper collect money owed her late husband, engaging John
McEvers in New York to look out for her interests while she was in
that city. He also worked with her husband's creditors in
Londonderry and Dublin, pointing out that she was left with "a
numerous family of Small Children" and would need time to make
payments.[88] Rose Harper, the eldest of that large family, married
Randle Mitchell, another Ulster-born merchant, in 1751.[89]

Merchant and Shipmaster

Command of a ship in the flaxseed and passenger trade was often
entrusted to a member of a mercantile family, usually himself a
part-owner of the ship. Francis Boggs, for instance, was master of
ships owned by his brother Londonderry merchant Ninian Boggs
and Walter Marshall commanded flaxseed ships belonging to his
brother Thomas Marshall, also a merchant in Londonderry.[90] Not
a few men made the shift from the quarterdeck to the counting
house as merchants themselves and there were some who straddled
both professions. Such a man was William Blair, who arrived in
Philadelphia before 1729 when he married Mary Steel at First
Presbyterian Church. He sailed from Belfast in 1733 as master of
the brig *Prosperity* in time to take a flaxseed cargo to Ireland. Blair
made annual voyages thereafter in his ship *William and Mary* carrying passengers from Carrickfergus on Belfast Lough. Captain
William Blair and William Woodlock were the registered owners of
the ship *William and James* in 1736. Three years later James Agnew
of Larne, as her owner, advertised for apprentices and redemptioners to sail for New Castle and Philadelphia on the *William and
James*, but failing to find as many willing to indenture themselves
as he wanted, took on convicts from Downpatrick jail to transport
to America.[91] Blair, Woodlock, and Agnew would be associated
with the American trade for many years to come.

By 1741 Blair had formed a partnership with William and David

McIlvaine as dry goods merchants in Philadelphia. They dissolved their firm in 1745, although Blair and the McIlvaine brothers continued in the flaxseed business. Blair had Belfast connections, advertising for freight for the *Paisley*, "lately arrived from North Britain and Ireland." She had already loaded half her flaxseed cargo and "will be clear to sail in two Weeks time for Belfast."[92] Blair himself sailed "for Great Britain and Ireland" in March 1742, leaving his wife Mary to conduct his Philadelphia business.[93] He was a business associate of James Burgess, just one of Belfast's merchants with an interest in the flaxseed and emigrant trade. James Blair, Captain Blair's son, married Isabel Burgess. Her tombstone in the graveyard of First Presbyterian Church, Philadelphia, reminded passers-by that she was "Daughter of Mr. James Burgess, late of Belfast, Merchant."

From 1745 Blair owned shares in a half dozen ships together with other Philadelphia businessmen. He was part owner of two other ships, one with John and James Ritchie of Glasgow and one with Daniel Mussenden of Belfast.[94] Blair took his own ship *William and Mary*, fitted out as a privateer, to Belfast and returned to Philadelphia with passengers in September 1746.[95] Advertisements in the *Pennsylvania Gazette* suggest he was at least based in Philadelphia during the next few years, finding freights for ships in the flaxseed trade. He commanded the *William and Mary* on a voyage to Dublin in 1751, leaving his son James to manage affairs in Philadelphia.[96] Both father and son were in Belfast the following year, when they joined James Burgess in advertising for passengers, redemptioners, and servants for Blair's *Earl of Holderness*, William Simpson, master.[97] William Blair came as a passenger on this ship, advertising for freights for her return voyage to Newry, and promptly sailed for Belfast, again as a passenger, on the *William and Mary*.[98]

Young James Blair must have stayed in Belfast, as father and son joined James Burgess in advertising the *William and Mary's* return passage to Philadelphia.[99] She arrived at New Castle in August: "The Ship William and Mary, Captain Peele, is in the River from Belfast, with a great Number of People on Board, chiefly Passengers."[100] The younger generation had taken over by then. William Burgess advertised for passengers for Philadelphia on ships

sometimes commanded by James Blair, who assumed responsibility for the firm's American interests when his father was at sea.[101]
James Burgess died in 1759, but his son continued to be active in
the flaxseed and passenger trade until the American Revolution.[102]
This type of transatlantic partnership had become more common
by the 1750s as both the flaxseed and passenger trades expanded to
meet new needs.

Notes

1   Nathaniel Magee, Samuel Payton, Joseph Westray, Henry McLaughlin, George
    Beard, James Stewart, John Martindale, and Henry Laird, Petition, April 19,
    1736 (Mussenden Papers, D/354/508, PRONI).

2   *Pennsylvania Gazette*, September 9, 1736, September 30, 1736, October 26,
    1736, December 16, 1736.

3   James Stewart to Thomas Penn, April 1736 (Penn Papers, HSP). Henry Jones
    Ford, *The Scotch-Irish in America* (Princeton, NJ, 1915), 196–8. Dickson,
    Ulster Emigration, 189–91.

4   This was not the Isle of May on the east coast of Scotland, but Ilha de Maio in
    the Cape Verde Islands for a cargo of salt. Naval Officer's Returns, Port of
    New York (CO/5/114/111–12, LC).

5   Naval Officer's Returns, Port of New York *Pennsylvania Gazette*, September 14,
    1733.

6   His brothers Charles McEvers and Nicodemus McEvers of London had
    dealings with Mussenden as well. John McEvers to Daniel Mussenden,
    August 1, 1734. John Roosevelt and John McEvers to Isaac and George
    Macartney, December 9, 1734 (Mussenden Papers, D/354/684, /685,
    PRONI).

7   John Fowler, master of the *Bruerton*, Belfast, May 29, 1729 (Mussenden Papers,
    D/354/477, PRONI).

8   *Belfast News Letter*, April 20, August 8, December 18, 1750.

9   Charter Party, July 22, 1726, September 1, 1726, Invoice, April 1, 1734
    (Mussenden Papers, D/354/389, /391, /491, PRONI).

10 Malcomson, "Introduction to the Mussenden Papers" (D/354, PRONI).

11 *Belfast News Letter*, May 19, 1758, September 5, 1758.

12 *Belfast News Letter*, March 25, 1763.

13 He spelled his surname Gregg. His sons spelled the name Greg. *Belfast News
    Letter*, April 19, 1765, January 1, 1771. Thomas M. Truxes, ed., *Letterbook
    of Greg and Cunningham, 1756–57 Merchants of New York and Belfast*
    (Oxford, 2001), 36. *Burke's Landed Gentry* (London, 1972), III, 400.

14 Michael J. O'Brien, *In Old New York: The Irish Dead in Trinity and St. Paul's
    Churchyards* (New York, 1928) 25–6. Howard I. Durie, *The Kakiat Patent
    in Bergen County, New Jersey, with Genealogical Accounts of Its Early
    Settlers* (Pearl River, NY, 1970), 4–7. Francis M. Marvin, *The Van Horn
    Family History* (East Stroudsburg, PA, 1929), 106. On the Van Horne
    merchants, see Cathy Matson, *Merchants and Empire: Trading in Colonial
    New York* (Baltimore, 1998), 135–6, 143.

15 Daniel Mussenden and John Gregg to James Van Horne, April 8, 1735
    (Mussenden Papers, D/354/692, PRONI).

16 Account of Sales, May 3, 1735, June 9, 1735 (Mussenden Papers, D/354/503,
    /504, PRONI).

17 Daniel Mussenden and John Gregg to James Van Horne, June 11, 1735.
    Mussenden and Gregg to Abraham Van Horne, July 11, 1735 (Mussenden
    Papers, D/354/695, /697, PRONI).

18 *American Weekly Mercury*, August 3, 1732. Hood, "Flax Seed," 153.

19   Daniel Mussenden and John Gregg to Abraham Van Horne, Jr., April 8, 1735
     (Mussenden Papers, D/354/691, PRONI).

20   *Pennsylvania Gazette*, May 2, 1738.

21   John McEvers to Daniel Mussenden and John Gregg, December 21, 1734.
     Daniel Mussenden and John Gregg to John McEvers, April 8, 1735.
     Invoice, April 8, 1735 (Mussenden Papers, D/354/494, /690, /501,
     PRONI).

22   Naval Officers Returns Port of New York (CO/5/114/111–12, LC).

23   John Moore, Robert Watts, David and Matthew Clarkson, Paul Richards,
     Anthony Rutgers, Joseph Reade and Robert Livingston owned the
     Amsterdam; Moses Levy, Robert Livingston, David and Matthew Clarkson,
     and Paul Richards owned the *Prince Frederick*.

24   Davey and Carsan to John McEvers, May 8, 1746, August 17, 1746,
     November 16, 1746 (Davey and Carsan Letterbook, LC).

25   Gerard G. Beekman to William Snell, November 16, 1749, in *Beekman
     Mercantile Papers*, I, 92.

26   Gerard G. Beekman to Robert Shaw and William Snell, November 25, 1747,
     in *Beekman Mercantile Papers*, I, 31–2.

27   Naval Officers Returns Port of New York (CO/5/114/111–12, LC).

28   One or more ships each year were recorded only as sailing "to Ireland."
     Abstracted from *The New York Gazette and Weekly Post Boy*. Michael J.
     O'Brien, "Some Interesting Shipping Statistics of the Eighteenth Century,"
     Journal of the American Irish Historical Society, 13(1914), 191–201.

29   Francis G. James, "Irish Colonial Trade in the Eighteenth Century," *William
     and Mary Quarterly*, 3rd series, 20(1963), 582–3.

30   *American Weekly Mercury*, August 3, 1732. Adrienne D. Hood, *The Weaver's
     Craft: Cloth, Commerce and Industry in Early Pennsylvania* (Philadelphia,
     2003), 43.

31   Arthur L. Jensen, *The Maritime Commerce of Colonial Philadelphia* (Madison,
     WI, 1963), 85–6.

32   Wokeck, *Trade in Strangers*, 197.

33   In 1729 two vessels arrived at Philadelphia from Belfast, the snow *John and
     David* of Glasgow, and the *Hopewell*, on her way to South Carolina, and
     one from Carrickfergus, William Blair's *Prosperity*, all three bringing
     emigrants and returning to Glasgow, rather than Belfast (*Pennsylvania
     Gazette*, July 24, 1729, July 31, 1729, August 7, 1729). The *John and
     David* and the snow *Brunswick* came in 1730 (*Pennsylvania Gazette*, June
     11, 1730, July 23, 1730). The *Brunswick* returned in 1731, 1732, and
     1733, clearing for Glasgow, and the *Prosperity* in 1732, clearing for Dublin
     (*Pennsylvania Gazette*, August 12, 1731, September 30, 1731, August 14,
     1732, November 16, 1732, December 14, 1732, March 15, 1733, August
     9, 1733).

34   *Pennsylvania Gazette*, October 11, 1733.

35   *Pennsylvania Gazette*, September 5, 1734, September 12, 1734, October 3,
     1734, October 17, 1734, November 21, 1734, December 4, 1734.

36   Bezanson *et al.*, *Prices in Colonial Pennsylvania*, 67.

37   *Pennsylvania Gazette*, April 8, 1736.

38 *Charming Molly* was an American ship owned and commanded by James
    Chalmers of New Castle, later of Wilmington, Delaware. *Pennsylvania
    Gazette*, August 7, 1735, September 30, 1736, February 14, 1738.
39 *Pennsylvania Gazette*, September 11, 1735, September 25, 1735, October 16,
    1735, October 30, 1735.
40 "Ship Registers for the Port of Philadelphia," *PMHB*, 23(1899), 381–2, 384
41 *Pennsylvania Gazette*, November 20, 1735, December 11, 1735, January 22,
    1736, January 29, 1736.
42 *Pennsylvania Gazette*, August 7, 1736, September 2, 1736, September 9, 1736,
    September 23, 1736, September 30, 1736, October 7, 1736, October 21,
    1736, October 28, 1736, November 4, 1736, November 18, 1736,
    November 25, 1736, December 2, 1736.
43 *Pennsylvania Gazette*, September–December 1739. Bezanson *et al.*, *Prices in
    Colonial Pennsylvania*, 68.
44 The number of ships sailing to and from Irish ports in 1740–41 from New
    York and Philadelphia was greater than usual because of crop failures and
    famine in southern Ireland resulting in large shipments of grain and other
    provisions. Three quarters of these ships went to southern Irish ports. I have
    limited my figures to the flaxseed shipping season. On the Irish famine, see
    John D. Post, *Food Shortage, Climactic Variability, and Epidemic Disease
    in Preindustrial Europe: The Mortality Peak in the Early 1740s* (Ithaca, NY,
    1985), 174–8.
45 Wokeck, *Trade in Strangers*, 180.
46 "Ship Registers for the Port of Philadelphia," *PMHB*, 23(1899), 381–5, 501.
47 *Pennsylvania Gazette*, September 7, 1738, September 14, 1738, September 21,
    1738, October 26, 1738.
48 "Ship Registers for the Port of Philadelphia," *PMHB*, 24(1900), 112, 359, 502,
    511.
49 Davey and Carsan to William Hogg, November 25, 1745, to John Fairly,
    November 25, 1745 (Davey and Carsan Letterbook, LC).
50 Davey and Carsan to Nathaniel Alexander, February 15, 1746/7, to William
    Hogg, November 26, 1746, December 8, 1746, to Vance and Caldwell,
    November 26, 1747, March 28, 1748, to Vance, Gregg and Caldwell, June
    29, 1749, October 3, 1749, to Arthur Vance, July 21, 1748 (Davey and
    Carsan Letterbook. LC). "Ship Registers," *PMHB*, 24(1900), 504.
51 Davey and Carsan to William Alexander, November 22, 1750, to Vance and
    Caldwell, November 23, 1750 (Davey and Carsan Letterbook, LC). "Ship
    Registers," *PMHB*, 25(1901), 125.
52 They shipped flaxseed and flour to Londonderry on the accounts of Nathaniel
    Alexander, Ninian Boggs, John Campbell, Archibald Cunningham, Samuel
    Ewing, John Fairly, Henry and Mossom Gamble, William Hogg, James
    Ramage, William Scott, Jr., Arthur Vance and his associates. Their Strabane
    correspondents were Samuel Carsan's brother Andrew Carsan and brother-
    in-law Robert Barclay, Alexander Auchinleck, Hugh and William Brown,
    James Hamilton, Robert and Thomas Parkinson, and John and Robert
    Porter. They also shipped seed and wheat to William Drummond of
    Ramelton, County Donegal, and to the Newry merchants Matthew
    Henderson and Robert Hutchinson.

53   Davey and Carsan to Joseph Fade, May 20, 1746, to Robert Travers, July 17, 1746 (Davey and Carsan Letterbook, LC).

54   W. H. Crawford, *The Impact of the Domestic Linen Industry in Ulster* (Belfast, 2005), 185.

55   Gill, *Rise of the Irish Linen Industry*, 10. Hood, *Weaver's Craft*, 43. Truxes, *Irish-American Trade*, 33, 284.

56   Davey and Carsan to Robert Travers, June 5, 1746, to Alexander Auchinleck, December 12, 1746 (Davey and Carsan Letterbook, LC).

57   *Maryland Gazette*, November 10, 1774. Thomas M. Doerflinger, *A Vigorous Spirit of Enterprise: Merchants and Economic Development in Revolutionary Philadelphia* (Chapel Hill, NC, 1986), 113.

58   Carsan's right to a freehold in Strabane, part of the Abercorn Estate, was disputed in 1744, but he retained it at his death in 1778. John H. Gebbie, ed., *An Introduction to the Abercorn Letters* (Omagh, County Tyrone, 1972), 7–8.

59   It is interesting that he signed his name Robert Carsan. Fee farm grant, 1675 (T/808/1438, PRONI).

60   Registry of Deeds, Dublin, vol. 100, p. 354, #70771, vol. 307, p. 396, #204220, vol. 380, p. 112, #252964. Samuel Carsan to Rev. John Maxwell, November 29, 1750 (Davey and Carsan Letterbook, LC). *Belfast News Letter*, December 27, 1763.

61   *New York Gazette*, May 26, 1729.

62   *Pennsylvania Gazette*, December 20, 1739. "Ship Registers for the Port of Philadelphia," *PMHB*, XXIV (1900), 515.

63   Davey and Carsan to the Rev. William McKnight, January 1, 1745/6 (Davey and Carsan Letterbook, LC).

64   *Pennsylvania Gazette*, December 20, 1739.

65   The *Prince of Orange* arrived with passengers in September 1742. *Pennsylvania Gazette*, October 29, 1741, September 30, 1742, January 18, 1743, February 17, 1743.

66   Davey and Carsan to William Hogg, December 31, 1745, June 24, 1746, to Samuel Ewing, March 28, 1748 (Davey and Carsan Letterbook, LC).

67   Gerard G. Beekman to William Hogg, November 29, 1758, in *Beekman Mercantile Papers*, I, 334.

68   Davey and Carsan Letterbook (LC). James Fullton Papers (Historical Society of York County, York, PA).

69   *Pennsylvania Gazette*, August 17, 1749.

70   Davey and Carsan to Archibald Cunningham, June 22, 1746, to John Fairly, September 22, 1746, December 10, 1746, to William Hogg, February 15, 1747 (Davey and Carsan Letterbook, LC). *Pennsylvania Gazette*, October 23, 1746.

71   "Ship Registers," *PMHB*, XXIV (1900), 358, 511.

72   *Belfast News Letter*, June 10, 1746. According to R. J. Dickson, this was the only ship to advertise for emigrants between 1740 and 1746, but few issues of the paper survive for those years (Dickson, *Ulster Emigration*, 52).

73   She was also advertised as the *Rundell Galley*. *Pennsylvania Gazette*, October 29, 1741.

74 *Pennsylvania Gazette*, October 28, 1742.

75 *Pennsylvania Gazette*, November 8, 1744.

76 It is interesting that all the passengers landed at New Castle. *Pennsylvania Gazette*, October 9, 1746, November 27, 1746, February 17, 1747.

77 *Pennsylvania Gazette*, September 26, 1745.

78 Davey and Carsan to William Alexander, November 22, 1745 (Davey and Carsan Letterbook, LC).

79 Davey and Carsan to John Jourdan, December 13, 1745, to Edward Bayly, April 23, 1746 (Davey and Carsan Letterbook, LC). "Ship Registers," *PMHB*, XXIV (1900), 350.

80 Davey and Carsan to Patrick and Robert Mackey, January 6, 1745/46 (Davey and Carsan Letterbook, LC).

81 In addition to Davey and Carsan, flaxseed merchants Conyngham and Gardner, James Wallace, John Erwin, Randle Mitchell, William and David McIlvaine, John Martin, and Walter Shee were among Philadelphia's dry goods importers who advertised newly-arrived spring and fall goods at their stores in the 1740s. *Pennsylvania Gazette*, July 2, 1747, August 13, 1747, June 22, 1749, June 29, 1749, July 20, 1749, August 3, 1749, October 19, 1749, November 2, 1749.

82 *Pennsylvania Gazette*, January 7, 1752.

83 Samuel Carsan to the Rev. William McKnight, January 1, 1746 (Davey and Carsan Letterbook, LC).

84 *Pennsylvania Gazette*, March 3, 1742, October 23, 1746. Horace Edwin Hayden, ed., "The Reminiscences of David Hayfield Conyngham 1750–1834 of the Revolutionary House of Conyngham and Nesbitt, Philadelphia, Pa.," *Wyoming Historical and Genealogical Society Proceedings*, 8(1903), 187.

85 He regularly advertised servants and linens for sale. *Pennsylvania Gazette*, July 27, 1738, June 28, 1739, January 1, 1741. "Ship Registers" *PMHB*, XXIII (1899), 501.

86 *Pennsylvania Gazette*, August 20, 1741.

87 *Pennsylvania Gazette*, March 3, 1742.

88 Davey and Carsan to William Alexander, December 31, 1745, to James Evory, December 31, 1745, to John McEvers, July 1, 1746, to Joseph Fade, July 4, 1746 (Davey and Carsan Letterbook, LC).

89 "Marriage Licenses," *PMHB*, XXXII (1908), 345.

90 Gerard G. Beekman to Conyngham and Gardner, December 26, 1752, Beekman to Thomas Marshall, December 14, 1754, in *Beekman Mercantile Papers*, I, 130, 240.

91 *Belfast News Letter*, April 13, 1739, June 29, 1739, July 3, 1739. "Ship Registers," *PMHB*, 23(1899), 385.

92 *Pennsylvania Gazette*, October 30, 1740, November 19, 1741, July 11, 1745. "Ship Registers," *PMHB*, XXIV (1900), 111.

93 *Pennsylvania Gazette*, February 24, 1742, March 10, 1742.

94 "Ship Registers," *PMHB*, XXIV (1900), 221, 353, 360, 363, 365, 366

95 *Belfast News Letter*, June 10, 1746. *Pennsylvania Gazette*, June 5, 1746, September 18, 1746.

96   *Pennsylvania Gazette*, April 25, 1751, May 23, 1751, October 3, 1751, October 31, 1751.

97   *Belfast News Letter*, June 19, 1752.

98   *Pennsylvania Gazette*, November 2, 1752, November 16, 1752.

99   *Belfast News Letter*, February 6, 1753.

100   *Pennsylvania Gazette*, August 30, 1753.

101   *Pennsylvania Gazette*, October 3, 1751, October 31, 1751, November 21, 1751, October 25, 1752.

102   *Belfast News Letter*, September 4, 1759.

4

Transatlantic Partners
Patterns of Trade

THE FLAXSEED TRADE HAD SETTLED INTO its long-term patterns by 1750 with merchants on both sides of the ocean dispatching ships at the appropriate seasons. The passenger trade, too, was now an important part of the commercial life of Belfast and Londonderry, Newry and Coleraine. This meant that there were now regular predictable sailings from all of the Ulster ports and a wide choice of shipping available to prospective emigrants. As on the American side, merchants and ship-owners in Ulster made every effort to dispatch their ships on time with a full complement of passengers, redemptioners or servants and to see that they made a second profitable voyage in the months between arriving with flaxseed and flour and departing with emigrants. Both sides of this trade favoured the northern ports. Gerard Beekman found "It is difficult getting a vessel among us to go to Dublin. They chuse any other port in Ireland before it."[1]

Flaxseed, which was shipped only to Ireland, was now Pennsylvania's third most important export after flour and bread, the staples of Philadelphia's European and West Indian trade.[2] Apart from the short crop in the 1749 growing season, the amount of American flaxseed imported into Ireland rose steadily over the next decade, doubling the average export of the previous ten years. Philadelphia merchants shipped 21,336 bushels of flaxseed in 1749, when seed was scarce and expensive, 44,527 bushels in 1750, and 69,295 bushels in 1751. In most years New York sent more flaxseed to Ireland than Philadelphia did, "making it one of the few items of trade in which New York could claim leadership."[3] Since a hogshead contained seven bushels of seed, Philadelphia shipped roughly 3,000 hogsheads in 1749, 6,000 in 1750, and 10,000 in 1751.[4] During the winter of 1752–3 flaxseed ships sailed from Philadelphia and New York carrying 22,146 hogsheads of seed and the total amount imported from America each year thereafter remained close to this figure. New York merchants usually shipped a shade over half of each year's export and Philadelphia a little less than half.[5] While seed from Holland and the Baltic was still held in high esteem, seed from the American Colonies almost totally supplanted it on the Irish market. Except for the flax planting season of 1750, when American seed was in short supply and Belfast merchants advertised Riga flaxseed for sale, nearly all the flaxseed sold in Ireland came from North America.[6]

The steadily growing import of American flaxseed into Ireland financed the importation of Irish linen into the Colonies which was increasing just as rapidly and the greater demand for flaxseed to meet the needs of the Ulster linen weavers required a greater shipping capacity to bring it home in time for spring planting. Advertisements began appearing in nearly every issue of the *Belfast News Letter*, the only newspaper in the North, for ships sailing for New Castle, Philadelphia, or New York, commonly extolling the ship's advantages for passengers, redemptioners, and servants. The more ships in the trade the more choices for passengers and the more opportunities for merchants in Ulster ports and in the Colonies.

New firms came into the flaxseed and passenger trade on both sides of the Atlantic in these years. In Belfast Thomas Greg and Waddell Cunningham were among the more prominent new arrivals on the commercial scene; Cunningham represented the interests of the firm in New York while Greg directed operations in Belfast. And there were other firms new to the flaxseed business beside the Lagan, among them Mussenden, Bateson and Co., James Ross, and Thomas Sinclaire.[7] Many of the Londonderry merchants trading with America in the 1730s and 1740s were still active, but there were new faces there, too, men such as Adam Schoales, Alexander and Francis Knox, Henry Gamble and Mark Bellew. Transatlantic partnerships were characteristic of the trade in flaxseed and emigrants in these years.

Although merchants in the port cities tended to dominate the trade, there was room for a host of dealers in rural market towns such as Strabane and Ramelton to directly import flaxseed, export linens, butter, beef and other products, and arrange passage to America for emigrants. Alexander Ogilby, a linen draper of Limavady, County Londonderry, for instance, did all of these things.[8]

Another interesting development in the 1750s was the growing importance of the Ulster out ports, reflecting the greater volume of the passenger trade. In the first ten or twelve years of emigration from Ulster, Coleraine, Portrush, and Larne had been ports of embarkation for settlers from their immediate neighbourhood. Once flaxseed ships began regular sailings from Derry, Belfast, and Newry, the passenger business concentrated there. More numerous sailings from the out ports represented efforts to accommodate would-be emigrants. The rise of Larne on the north Antrim coast as an emigrant port brought new firms there into the transatlantic shipping business. James Agnew, Robert and John Wilson, and Hugh Montgomery were all active in the passenger trade in the 1750s and later. The Galt and Laurence families of Coleraine and George Dunlope of Ballycastle also owned ships that carried emigrants to America.[9]

In New York, where the flaxseed commerce was largely in the hands of men born in America, merchants from Ulster, notably Waddell Cunningham, George Folliot, and William Neilson, became prominent in the 1750s and gradually took the lion's share of the business, while in Philadelphia, where Scotch-Irish merchants dominated the trade in flaxseed and emigrants, young men from the North of Ireland came out every year to join long-established firms or begin new ones. A growing number of firms in both port cities had business partners in Belfast, Londonderry, or Newry, rather than simply representing a number of correspondents in the Ulster ports.

The Atlantic World of Goods

Increased exports of Irish linen to American and English markets and resulting demand for American flaxseed in Ireland were part of a larger pattern of consumption. The years after 1740, on both sides of the Atlantic, saw a remarkable expansion in the importation of consumer goods and by mid-century what has been termed the consumer revolution had become a way of life.[10] By 1750 the British market absorbed each year nearly 2 pounds of tobacco, 16.9 pounds of sugar, and slightly more than a pound of tea for every man, woman and child in England and Wales and falling prices brought what had once been luxury goods within the reach of most of them. Textiles had also come within a price range that made it possible for ordinary people to pay less to own more.[11] The American Colonies shared in this rising standard of living as anyone who has sampled the inventories and records of estate sales in the probate courts can testify, with tea pots and coffee pots, delft dishes, and imported fabrics now commonplace everywhere. Consumption of British goods rose steadily, but took off dramatically after 1740. In fact, by mid-century the per capita consumption of British manufactures in the American Colonies outpaced the population growth – which doubled every 25 years.[12]

All kinds of British manufactures shared in this dynamic American market. British woollens, a staple of overseas trade, had no real market in the Colonies until mid-century. As late as 1750 continental Europe absorbed from 80% to 90% of the different varieties of woollen goods exported from England.[13] The small export of wool textiles to Pennsylvania, New York and New England was limited to luxury grades for wealthy customers. This began to change dramatically in the 1750s both in quantity and quality. With such a great supply and variety of textiles on the market, consumers had a wide choice of goods and even in the backcountry demanded "fashionable" colours and weaves. Dry goods merchants in New York and Philadelphia had hitherto relied on their British correspondents to select the goods they shipped. Orders now included patterns and specified colours goods were to be dyed, "a service which they expected for cheap and mid-priced Yorkshire cloth as well as fine West Country broadcloth."[14]

Irish linens shared in this rapidly expanding market. In 1750 Great Britain exported 11,200,460 yards of linen, an increase of more than 4 million yards over 1745. This was the biggest leap in linen exports in the century.[15] To be sure, not all of this linen was woven in Ulster, but Ulster's market share had risen steadily from less than 2.5 million in the second decade of the century to almost 8 million in the 1740s and 17 million in the 1760s.[16]

Consumer demands were reflected in the advertisements placed by dry goods merchants in colonial newspapers. While some importers were content to offer no more than "an assortment of European and East India goods," others provided a column-long list of specific sizes, grades and varieties of cloth to attract the custom of the shopkeepers they supplied. This plethora of goods, bewildering to a twenty-first century reader, but full of meaning for eighteenth-century shoppers, is also reflected in the inventories of shops in the Pennsylvania backcountry.[17]

City merchants had to keep up with the current London styles if they wanted to sell the textiles they received by "the latest ships from Britain and Ireland." They had to be equally cognisant of backcountry tastes.[18] In Pennsylvania goods were sometimes advertised as "specially selected for the Germans."[19] American merchants regularly informed their Ulster correspondents that the linens they sent were a drug on a market already oversupplied and increasingly warned them that linens shipped to the American Colonies had to be of better quality, more uniform size, or otherwise suitable to the demands of colonial buyers.[20]

Supplying the Ulster Market

In 1743 Philadelphia merchant Samuel Powel wrote a London correspondent that "the call for flaxseed to Ireland continues & increases" and that "It puts our people to sowing a great deal" of flax.[21] How much flax were Pennsylvanians growing in response to the export market? In Chester County farmers cultivated anywhere from a quarter acre to an acre and a half of flax for household use and for sale to flaxseed buyers.[22] There are hints of growing flax on a commercial scale. A farmer in Lancaster County wrote in 1755 of a 150-acre farm he bought the previous year: "We have eight or nine acres of wheat, as well as six acres of oats, three acres of field corn and one of flax. We have seeded sixteen acres of flax for the next harvest."[23] Shopkeepers in the backcountry accepted flaxseed in payment for store goods and then sold it to Philadelphia merchants or their agents. One merchant's flaxseed accounts indicate purchases of seed in large quantities from 14 shopkeepers in York and Cumberland counties, the smallest 60 bushels, substantial amounts from seven other Philadelphia flaxseed merchants, and "Cash at sundry prices" paid for 913 hogsheads and 696 bushels from unidentified suppliers. Since this merchant employed agents to buy flaxseed for him, some may have come directly from growers.[24] New York's flaxseed supply came by water from Connecticut and eastern Long Island on small craft carrying from 1,000 to 3,000 bushels at a time.[25] The flaxseed trade was an important part of the Connecticut economy, second only to the West Indies trade. An estimated 3,000 farmers sent at least some flaxseed to New York through a similar network of rural shopkeepers and merchants in the seaport towns on Long Island Sound.[26] Seed normally arrived in New York in very large quantities, 1,200 bushels from Long Island in a single vessel.[27] It also came later in the season than at Philadelphia, since New York harbour was ice free, never reaching the market before December, "Neither does the body of it Come Until Near Christmas."[28]

The diary kept by a farmer's son in southern New Jersey gives a glimpse of flaxseed production from the grower's viewpoint. His father did mixed farming near Greenwich in Cumberland County. He evidently grew flax for household use and for seed to send to market, treating each differently. Early in October, having threshed both wheat and rye, they cleaned the floor for flaxseed. The cleanliness of flaxseed was a major issue for both exporters and importers, and consequently for the producers. While many, perhaps most, merchants shipping flaxseed cleaned their own seed, the price of flaxseed depended in part on its being well-cleaned and free of dirt, stones, stalks, etc. They began to beat their flax. This was the process sometimes called rippling, whereby the flax was pulled through iron teeth on a wooden block. This would be to separate the seed and to begin the initial separation of the flax fibers from the stalk. In mid-October the flax stalks were spread out on the ground to rot, called dew-rotting. (In some places the stalks were left to soak in pools of water, water-rotting, which caused a terrible stench, but did the job in less time.) They began cleaning their flaxseed November 4, a process which continued for three days when they had ten bushels of seed ready for market. A week later they "carted down" their flaxseed, presumably to a storekeeper in Greenwich, who would sell it and ship it by shallop to a merchant in Philadelphia. In the meantime, they were busy "spreading the flax" on the ground and turning it, shifting the plants decaying on the ground. After a snowfall in early December, they turned the flax for the last time and took up the flax the next day. The long fibers could now be separated from the stalks by breaking on a flax break, a simple hand-operated machine with grooved rollers that broke up the outer skin and the woody core of the plant, and by scutching, using an apparatus with flat wooden blades that removed the skin and core, leaving only the fibers. The final stage involved combing the fibers with a hackle, untangling the fibers and preparing the dressed flax, ready for spinning. They seem to have been at this through the winter, with entries from January through March, making in all 164 pounds of dressed flax. In April they "finished plowing, sowing & harrowing two acres of flax" and the process began anew.[29]

As with any agricultural product, flaxseed buyers, like farmers, were dependent on the vagaries of weather. The right combination of rain and warm dry days could yield a bumper crop and low prices when it came to market. Unseasonable weather, too little or too much rain, would make seed scarce and expensive in the buying season.

The 1749 crop was remarkably short as the result of prolonged drought, so prices soared. Flaxseed hovered around 3/– a bushel in 1745, 1746, and 1747, according to the current prices included by Carsan and Davey in their letters to customers in Ulster. In December 1748 flaxseed was quoted at 8 shillings a bushel; a year later at 11/6. Samuel Carsan, just back in Philadelphia from Derry, wrote one brother-in-law that "in North America has not been rais'd the one sixth part of what we generally used to have."[30] That spring Gerard Beekman in New York anticipated flaxseed "will Run high this year" since "the new Crops is almost destroyed with frost and drought."[31] He was right. Merchants like Davey and Carsan had great difficulty filling orders from Ulster. They explained in nearly identical words to a host of correspondents that

> The scarcity & Extravagant price of flaxseed prevented us from shipping you the Seed you wrote for. We presume none will be shipped off for Less than 11/– per Bush[el] & are Confident a great Deall will be shipped at 12/–.[32]

For some customers, who may have set no limits on the price they would pay, the firm did better, sending Vance, Gregg and Caldwell 600 hogsheads by their *City of Derry* and 200 more by their brig *Diamond*. Sam Carsan's brother-in-law Robert Barclay had another 100 hogsheads on the *City of Derry*. Hugh Davey wrote him that

> Since we have known this Country, there never was such a scarcity of Seed; that article has got up to 12/– pr Bus[hel] & the fourth part of the orders for said article cannot be effected if the buyers would give 20/– pr bus[hel]. There will not be ship'd from this Port this Season 2,500 hhds of Seed & we are inform'd by Letter from our Correspondent Mr. Paul Richard of New York that there will not be Ship'd from thence above one thousand hhds.[33]

They also shipped 50 hogsheads each to Samuel Ewing and to William Scott, Jr.[34]

In New York the situation was much the same. Gerard Beekman was unable to fill an order for 100 hogsheads from William Snell, an Ulsterman from Ballymoney, County Antrim, who was now a London merchant and Beekman's banker, but he was able to ship fifty to Newry on Snell's account. Beekman was "to give the Market price when delivered Let it be what it will." He would not have sent any seed, "if I was not afraid to Disoblidge you for I am of opinion all Shippers from hence will Lose by it this season." John McEvers, Joseph Hayne and Clarkson had orders for 3,000 hogsheads, Beekman wrote, "and will not Ship 300 between all." Cornelius Van Horne and Paul Richards also had orders for 3,000 hogsheads "and don't think they will get 1000 between them for its not in the Cuntry."[35] Despite Beekman's claim that flaxseed merchants would all suffer losses, he clearly believed their future prospects were good, for he planned

> this Spring to build me a Large Store on Purpose to follow the flaxseed business and Convert the better Part of my Stock in[to] that Commodity wether I have orders for it or not.[36]

The next season brought a better supply of flaxseed, but not enough to keep prices from running higher than in a normal year.

"Our Crops of flaxseed promise to turn out in greater plenty this year than Last, though we have had Exceeden dry Season," Beekman reported in June 1750, but "will not be so plenty as we had it some years past." New York prices started at 5/– a bushel and got to 7/2 by the first of October.[37] All of Davey and Carsan's old customers sent orders for seed and the firm had no difficulty filling them.[38] The rest of the flaxseed merchants were in the same situation. Prices at Philadelphia peaked in early November and dropped through the season as there was enough seed to satisfy all the shippers. Flaxseed was selling at 9/6 a bushel the first of November, 8/6 a week later, and only 7/– by early December.[39] With high prices on the Philadelphia market, Beekman sent New York flaxseed there in anticipation of it bringing 11/– a bushel, although he expected the New York would soon be 9/6 or 10/– a bushel.[40] Flaxseed merchants in the two cities kept a close watch on price trends in the other, asking a correspondent to buy seed where prices were lower. Taking advantage of the price differential, Redmond Conyngham had Beekman fill his flaxseed orders for John Gordon of Belfast and William Lecky and Adam Schoales of Londonderry.[41] As Beekman explained to potential customers in 1752:

> The Philadelphians have this season the advantage of us in shipping seed much cheaper than can be done from this place for which reason I judge the next season most orders will go there and then we shall have the advantage in our turn when shall be proud to execute any order you or your friends send me.[42]

Philadelphia shipped about 45,000 bushels of flaxseed in 1750 and over 70,000 bushels the next year. As supplies increased, prices naturally fell. Moderate prices prevailed for the next five years. The highest price paid for the 1751 crop was 5/7; although the *Pennsylvania Gazette* quoted 5/9 in early November, the newspaper reported 5/6 as the going price every other week. Flaxseed reached 6/11 at one point in 1752 and 6/4 in 1753. After this the price of flaxseed dropped still lower, averaging 4/6 through 1756.[43]

By that time flaxseed shippers faced new problems, in addition to weather-based shortages and price swings, as Britain and France were again at war. Shipments of flaxseed to Ireland continued at the same volume through the war years, rarely dipping below 20,000 hogsheads.[44] Fifteen ships sailed from New York with flaxseed in the 1756–7 season, seven for Belfast and Larne, three for Londonderry, two for Dublin, one each for Newry and Drogheda, and one for Killybegs and Sligo.[45] Philadelphia sailings, as reported in the *Pennsylvania Gazette* in the same period, included six to Belfast, six to Londonderry, and seven to Newry, nineteen in all.

Emigrants from Ulster

The larger number of ships in the flaxseed fleet facilitated an increase in the number of emigrants taking passage to America. With around thirty ships from Irish ports arriving at Philadelphia each year, a figure of 1,500 emigrants a year in the 1750s might be a conservative estimate.[46] New York's flaxseed ships were as numerous as those sailing for New Castle and Philadelphia, although New York was less attractive as a destination for emigrants. Shipowners got around this difficulty by advertising that their vessel would call at New Castle on the Delaware before proceeding to New York. As a result, we can safely assume that the greatest number of the Ulster emigrants in the 1750s landed at New Castle or Philadelphia. There is no way of knowing how many they were, only how many could have been more or less comfortably accommodated on the ships that actually made the crossing in those years. The number of newspaper advertisements is an indication the passenger trade was competitive with enough people buying passage to America to make it worthwhile. The location of agents authorised to book passages and of the ship's place of departure is an indication of where the emigrants who took these ships lived in Ulster.

There are significant gaps in the files of the *Belfast News Letter* for this decade; for instance, no single issue from 1751 is known to survive. R. J. Dickson's compilation of advertisements in extant issues from 1750 through 1759 demonstrated the overall pattern of emigration in these years. Of advertisements that specified a destination, 59 were bound for the Delaware Valley, only eight for New York, and five for North Carolina. The advertised tonnage of these ships averaged 200 tons, so they had the capacity to take a larger number of emigrants than most vessels in the earlier peak years of emigration, whether that potential was utilized or not. Dickson found twenty advertisements for passengers to sail from Belfast and two more for sailings from Belfast and Larne and from Belfast and Portrush. Only four were for passengers to New York. Five advertisements invited passengers to Wilmington and Cape Fear in North Carolina. The others were to New Castle and Philadelphia or New York and Pennsylvania. Ten advertisements were for ships sailing from Londonderry, all of them to Philadelphia, and there were just three for ships from Newry, two for Philadelphia, one for New York. There were fourteen ships from Larne offering passage, nine to Philadelphia and three to New York, two to "America". Portrush accounted for ten passenger advertisements, all for Philadelphia.[47]

Direct sailings for North Carolina ports represented an exceptional situation that proved the more general pattern. While most emigrants intended to land at New Castle or Philadelphia, with a smaller number choosing New York, Governor Arthur Dobbs of North Carolina made an effort to divert the stream of Irish Protestant migrants to his own lands in that colony. Dobbs, whose home was at Castle Dobbs near Carrickfergus, enlisted the veteran flaxseed merchant John Gordon to find passengers for a Liverpool ship bound for Cape Fear in North Carolina in 1753.[48] Gordon's own snows, the *Lord Russell*, the *Henry*, and the *Entwistle* regularly sailed with passengers for Philadelphia and New York.[49]

That Larne and Portrush should between them account for 45% of the passenger trade advertisements may well reflect the efforts by ship-owners in Larne, Coleraine, and Ballycastle, already involved in the flaxseed trade, to fill their ships with paying passengers, redemptioners, or servants on the outward voyage to America, but it may equally be the result of would-be emigrants from north Antrim securing passage on these ships from a more convenient point of embarkation.

James Agnew, a merchant in Larne, engaged in trade with the American Colonies over many years. As early as 1739 he advertised his ship *William and James*, "built for the passenger trade," to sail between Belfast and Philadelphia. John Boyd, an importer of American flour and flaxseed, was his Belfast agent.[50] Agnew and John Armstrong, merchants of Larne, advertised for passengers, redemptioners and servants to sail on his snow *Antrim* for New York in 1750. The *Antrim* was already a regular sailer in the New York flaxseed trade. Gerard Beekman wrote of her as "a fine Dubble Deckt Snow" and Captain William Woodlock as "a particular acquaintance of mine." To accommodate passengers, her owners promised in subsequent advertisements that she would call at either New Castle or Philadelphia.[51] James Agnew and Robert Wilson of Larne owned the snow in 1753 and 1754, when she sailed from Larne with passengers for Philadelphia and New York.[52] The outward voyage in summer was usually uneventful, but sailing from Philadelphia or New York in midwinter was always hazardous. The *Antrim* was rounding the Antrim coast on the last leg of her homeward voyage in February 1756 when she was blown off course and lost with all hands in Machrihanish Bay in Scotland.[53]

The *Elinor* of Coleraine and the *William and George* of Ballycastle sailed from Portrush on the north Antrim coast in 1754 with passengers for America. In 1755 George Dunlope of Ballycastle and Hugh Montgomery of Larne advertised for passengers for the *William and George*, to sail from Larne bound for New Castle and Philadelphia. She continued to make this circuit for several years.[54] Dunlope and Montgomery had ties to the Philadelphia firm of Scott and McMichael who held a share in the *William and George*.[55] George Dunlope, a merchant in the small north Antrim town of Ballycastle, would later be associated with George Fullerton of Philadelphia and still later with his own son George Dunlope in the Philadelphia firm of Orr, Dunlope and Glenholme.[56] His partner Hugh Montgomery was a son of John Montgomery, senior, a merchant in Larne and Hugh's brothers John and William were also Larne merchants. The Montgomerys, including Hugh's son Samuel, owned ships in the flaxseed and emigrant trade and advertised each year through 1775 for passengers to Philadelphia or New York.[57]

William Galt of Coleraine, John Caldwell of Ballymoney, and William Humphreys of Philadelphia were joint owners of the ship *Lord Dunluce* of 150 tons in 1754.[58] Galt and Caldwell advised passengers that their ship *Lord Dunluce* would sail from Portrush in June 1755 for New Castle and Philadelphia. She sailed the following summer from Larne for New York and made six more voyages

with passengers to New York, New Castle or Philadelphia, returning with flaxseed.[59] The Galts, a mercantile family in Coleraine,
had a share in nearly all the ships sailing from Portrush for America.
The Caldwells of Ballymoney, a small inland town between
Ballycastle and Coleraine, were already a transatlantic family.
Merchant John Caldwell, Jr. was a nephew of William Caldwell,
one of those from the townland of Ballywattick in Ballymoney
parish who emigrated to Londonderry, New Hampshire, in 1718.
John's brother, another William Caldwell, was a Londonderry merchant in the firm of Vance and Caldwell, which became Caldwell,
Vance and Caldwell, when younger brother Richard completed his
apprenticeship and joined the firm. James Caldwell, the youngest
brother, went out to Philadelphia to go into partnership with his
cousin as Andrew and James Caldwell, merchants in the flaxseed
trade like his brothers.[60]

Londonderry drew on a large hinterland in Donegal, Tyrone, and
Fermanagh as well as neighbouring County Londonderry for passengers for the American colonies. Based largely on its transatlantic
commerce in flaxseed and emigrants, Derry's overseas fleet grew in
number and tonnage. In 1763 there were "upwards of 40 vessels
belonging to the City, many of which were from 200 to 300 tons
burthen."[61] Vance, Gregg and Caldwell, the partnership of Arthur
Vance, Andrew Gregg and William Caldwell, owned quite a few of
them, regularly advertising for passengers to New Castle and
Philadelphia.[62] Their firm, like many other Derry flaxseed merchants, consigned their ships to Davey and Carsan in Philadelphia,
as did Alderman William Hogg and James Stirling.

Sam Carsan's Londonderry business connections can be seen
from his partnerships with Derry ship-owners. Carsan owned the
ship *King George* in partnership with Andrew Gregg and his new
partner in Derry, James Thompson.[63] Carsan also owned the ship
Willy in partnership with William Hogg and the brig *Ann and
James* in partnership with Thomas Parkinson of Strabane, and
Thomas James, Thomas Moore, and William Hope, all
Londonderry merchants.[64] He shared ownership of the *Admiral
Hawke* and the brig *Success* with William Caldwell and of the ship
Phoenix with William Caldwell and James Stirling.[65] Carsan owned
a share in the brig *Betty*, together with Derry merchants William

Caldwell, William Kennedy, James Stirling, James Mitchell and his own brother-in-law Robert Barclay of Strabane.[66] Carsan was also part-owner of four large ships famous in the flaxseed and passenger trade, all built at Philadelphia under his direction. The ship *Recovery* belonged to Arthur Vance and William Caldwell of Londonderry and Samuel Carsan of Philadelphia. Carsan and William Hogg owned the ship *Lecky*. The ship *Walworth* belonged to "Messrs. Caldwell," James Stirling and James Mitchell and Samuel Carsan. The ship *James and Robert* was the property of James Major, Robert McCausland and James Huey of Derry and Samuel Carsan of Philadelphia.[67] William Caldwell, Arthur Vance, and John Hamilton, all of Londonderry, shared ownership of the brig *Independent Whig* in 1758. Carsan dispatched all these ships in the flaxseed fleets.[68]

By no means were they the only Derry merchants active in the flaxseed and passenger trade in the 1750s. Gerard Beekman, for instance, shipped seed to brothers Thomas and Walter Marshall, Archibald Cunningham and Adam Schoales, who sent their own ships to New York for cargoes of flaxseed, wheat and flour. They also dealt with Conyngham and Gardner and with Walter Shee in Philadelphia.[69] The Marshalls as well as James and Thomas Harvey consigned ships to Shee. Alexander Knox, who was chosen as Derry's Lord Mayor in 1750, was a close associate of Conyngham and Gardner. Redmond Conyngham and Alexander Knox as owners of the ship *Alexander* registered her in December 1752.[70]

Belfast merchants also strengthened their ties with Philadelphia and New York in the 1750s. Benjamin Legg, John Hyde and Thomas Greg advertised for passengers, redemptioners and servants to take passage for Philadelphia and New York on the snow *Ross*, which they owned with James Ross of Belfast.[71] The *Ross*, from Liverpool and Belfast, arrived safely at Philadelphia, where George Duncan, the ship's captain, offered Irish linens for sale "on board the snow Ross," before proceeding to New York.[72] She sailed from New York for Belfast with a flaxseed cargo.[73] This voyage marked the entry of Thomas Greg into the flaxseed trade, although his father, John Gregg, had been one of the first Belfast merchants to import American seed.

Thomas Greg had a hand in many enterprises. In 1750 he joined

Benjamin Legg, Alexander Legg, John Stewart, John Hyde, and James Templeton in the firm of Leggs, Hyde and Co. to operate a sugar refinery at the Sugarhouse in Rosemary Lane, Belfast.[74] From sometime before 1754, Greg had an interest in manufacturing delftware in Belfast, an enterprise that continued into the 1770s.[75] His main activity was as a general merchant, selling rum, brandy, Lisbon wine, cider, and hardware, occasionally in partnership with James Templeton.[76] Greg's American trade was developing during these years. He first advertised American flaxseed in 1753 and offered New York flaxseed for the first time in 1755. He had American wheat flour for sale in 1757.[77]

In 1756 Greg formed a partnership with Waddell Cunningham, from Killead, County Antrim, who was already in New York. Each partner was to invest £2,000 New York currency in the firm. With this start-up capital they would import woollens and linens and other British manufactures and ship flaxseed and flour from New York to Belfast.[78] On this foundation both Greg and Cunningham rose to become pre-eminent in Belfast's commercial life.

Philadelphia Merchants, Shopkeepers, and Ship's Captains

The eighteenth-century use of the term "merchant," like the use of "esquire" or "gentleman" was supposedly hedged about by rules understood by everyone. Any person engaged in commerce had once been called a merchant, but by 1750 the word primarily connoted a wholesale trader, especially one involved in importing or exporting goods.[79] It was commonly accepted that "shopkeepers" were retail traders, however extensive their business might be. In actual practice, the terms seem more slippery. Merchants who imported their own goods in bulk did not necessarily sell at wholesale and nearly all of them kept a retail shop.[80] Nor did tax assessments and other legal documents always make a clear distinction between the one and the other. The same man might appear in different years as either merchant or shopkeeper or without any occupation assigned him. Allowing for a margin of error, local tax assessments provide at least a rough estimate of the composition of the mercantile community in any colonial port or backcountry town, but the relative amount of taxable wealth credited to each is only a

rough gauge of their actual wealth. Since merchants generally rented their warehouses and shops and usually lived above the store,
owning no real property, and much of their wealth, like credit, was
intangible or untaxable, a tax assessment may seem a dodgy way of
evaluating merchants, but it works as a way of ranking them within their own group.

Merchants in colonial cities were generally twice as wealthy as
shopkeepers. Robert Oaks found that on the eve of the American
Revolution, for instance, Philadelphians designated "merchant" on
the 1774 tax assessment were assessed a mean average £77 and
those who were called "shopkeepers" were assessed a mean average
£40.[81] In a general way, this would be true of merchants and shopkeepers over the previous twenty years.

The men who drew up the 1756 tax assessment of the City of
Philadelphia designated 170 individuals as "merchants." They
recorded only 88 "shopkeepers."[82] There was considerable range in
taxable wealth in both categories. One merchant was assessed over
£500, one over £400, seven over £200, and nineteen over £100,
making 28 merchants in all assessed £100 or more. They were
among the most important men in transatlantic and coastal trade,
many of them Quakers, with names recognisable today. Among the
merchants were a few assessed no more than £12 or £16, hardly
men who moved in the same business circles. As many as 35 of the
88 shopkeepers were women. Two shopkeepers were assessed at
over £100, more than five-sixths of the merchants. One shopkeeper's assessment was a mere £8. The greatest number of shopkeepers
fell into a range between £10 and £25.[83]

Flaxseed merchants, as we have seen, had a hand in many aspects
of commercial life, but they were not among the twenty-odd leaders of the business community. All of them were assessed below
£100. John Mease led the list at £90. Scott and McMichael, and
Conyngham and Nisbett were close behind at £80. Tench Francis
was assessed at £70. George Bryan's assessment was £50 as was that
of his late partner James Wallace. Samuel Carsan, John Erwin, and
Abraham Usher were each assessed £40. Hugh Donaldson,
Benjamin Fuller, Theophilus Gardner, and Randle Mitchell, were
each in the £36 category. (Since Donaldson and Fuller were partners, their firm would rank fourth among flaxseed exporters.)

Captain William Blair, Alexander Lunan, Thomas Wallace, and Walter Shee were assessed at £30. James Eddy, James Mackey and James Blair had the lowest assessment, just £20. There are some anomalies. Thomas Campbell, listed as a shopkeeper, was rated at £80. He was a dry goods merchant and linen bleacher. James Wallace, George Bryan's partner, was assessed as a shopkeeper at £50. John Bleakley, who owned ships trading with Ireland, was also listed as a shopkeeper, assessed at £34. A scattering of flaxseed merchants lived in other wards of the city, but they concentrated in the Dock Ward with the shallopmen, flatmen, and ship's captains who brought flaxseed, flour and timber to their warehouses and carried it across the ocean.

There are other ways to measure the standing of Philadelphia flaxseed merchants, such as membership in elite social clubs. The first Philadelphia Assemblies were held in the winter of 1748–9 with dances at Andrew Hamilton's House and Stores, then tenanted by merchant John Inglis. The 59 initial subscribers included a good many of the more opulent merchants and their wives, men like Charles and Alexander Stedman, Buckridge Sims, David Franks, Samson Levy, and Joseph Shippen. Redmond Conyngham, William and David McIlvaine, Samuel McCall, and William Humphreys were the only ones with an interest in the Irish trade. Very few flaxseed merchants participated in the fishing clubs that brought together many of Philadelphia's most prominent men. Only Redmond Conyngham, John M. Nesbitt, and John Shee belonged to the prestigious Mount Regale Fishing Company in 1762. The more staid Presbyterians and Quakers would decline an invitation to such frivolous entertainments, of course, but Conyngham and Nesbitt were at the top of their profession by this measure, too.[84]

North Antrim Neighbours

To become a merchant anywhere in the Colonies required, at the least, excellent credit and good connections with the British firms who supplied the stock of dry goods and hardware that merchants sold to retailers.[85] Even with British manufactures on long credit, a retail linen draper would need a minimum of £1,000 and "to engage in foreign trade to any great advantage" a beginning merchant required from £3,000 to £4,000, according to a manual published in 1747.[86] To set up business in Belfast and New York in 1756, Greg and Cunningham calculated they would need £3,000 in the first six months.[87] Merchants dealing in flaxseed needed, in addition, the support of merchants and linen drapers in Belfast or Derry and in Dublin. Randle Mitchell, Hugh Donaldson, and a third young man, Benjamin Fuller, who was employed as Mitchell's clerk, had all of these advantages. Fuller's connections were with Dublin and Cork where family members were in business. His father Abraham Fuller, a merchant in Cork, was kin to the Dublin Quaker linen merchant Joseph Fade, who left bequests to Benjamin, his brother and sisters.[88] Mitchell and Donaldson, neighbours in Glenarm, County Antrim, both came from families who held considerable acreage in north Antrim on long-term leases from the Earl of Antrim and Donaldson's brother was agent for the Earl's massive estates in north Antrim. In this regard, they were typical of the young men who went out to America to go into the flaxseed trade.

Randle Mitchell, one of the flaxseed merchants from Glenarm, offered "Very good Irish linnens" at his store in Water Street, Philadelphia, in 1749.[89] Within a year another man from Glenarm had come to Philadelphia and set up as a merchant. Hugh Donaldson was in business in Philadelphia as a dry goods merchant in 1751, when he and his partner John Troy also had Irish linens for sale at their store in Front Street, as well as some men and women servants who came from Dublin on John Troy's snow *Three Friends*. Randle Mitchell advertised for freight for the snow on her return voyage to Dublin with Captain Troy.[90]

The small town of Glenarm is a few miles up the coast from the busy port of Larne. The remains of the old castle of the McDonnells, Earls of Antrim, stood in the centre of the town. The Donaldson family held the "Old Castle" and the "Old Abbey" property in Glenarm for many years.[91] In the seventeenth century, the Catholic Earls of Antrim encouraged the settlement of Lowland Scots on their lands and north Antrim became a stronghold of the Presbyterian Church and the Scots language. The Mitchells and Donaldsons were among the Scottish settlers in north Antrim.

Both families were early established at Glenarm. Being kinsmen of the McDonnells of Antrim, the Donaldsons were treated liberally with grants of land, beginning in 1626 with leases to John Donaldson of Glenarm, who became Sheriff of County Antrim in 1633. His son, also John Donaldson, lived in the old castle in Glenarm. A staunch Presbyterian, he helped organise an association in defence of Protestant interests in 1688 and defended Derry against his old friend, the Earl of Antrim, a Catholic and a Jacobite. Being on different sides did not damage the good relations between the two families.[92]

Hugh Donaldson, the future Philadelphia merchant, held an estate known as Drumnasole, between Glenarm and Carnlough. In 1707 Randal McDonnell, 4th Earl of Antrim, leased for 41 years nearly 2,000 acres near Carnlough, including the quarterland of Drumnasole, the Old Castle and Old Abbey property in Glenarm, and land near Larne, to "John Donaldson, Gentleman of Drumnasole". An endorsement on the deed recorded that in 1740 John's son Alexander Donaldson of Drumnasole sold this lease to his brother, Hugh Donaldson.[93] The 5th Earl confirmed a lease of the same lands "as formerly held and enjoyed by his father Mr. John Donaldson" to "Hugh Donaldson, Gentleman, of Drumnasole," in 1744.[94] Hugh Donaldson of Drumnasole mortgaged all of this property in 1750 to William Hamilton, Doctor of Physick, and prepared to sail for Philadelphia.[95] He arrived there with capital raised from the mortgage, but retained his Ulster property. Ulster bleachers and linen drapers usually raised money by mortgaging a lease of property. He made an unsuccessful attempt to sell his lands in 1764.[96]

Randle Mitchell's family also settled at Glenarm in the seventeenth century. Alexander McDonnell, Esq. of Glenarm, soon to succeed his brother as 3rd Earl of Antrim, leased property to John Mitchell of Glenarm and to his brother James Mitchell of Glenarm.[97] The Mitchells were a mercantile family. James Mitchell borrowed money from his brother John to purchase a share in the ship *Rose* of Belfast in 1698.[98] Alexander Mitchell of Glenarm was a merchant in Dublin by this time and his brother Hugh Mitchell was already established at Cork.[99] Alexander Mitchell died at Dublin in 1712.[100] The next generation continued the tradition.

In 1755 Randle and Alexander Mitchell, Merchants of Philadelphia, acknowledged payment of a legacy from "our late Honour'd Father William Mitchell late of Dickstown in the County of Antrim" paid by "our Brother Hugh Mitchell of Dublin Merchant, one of the Executors," by the hand of "Mr. Tench Francis junr. of the said City of Philadelphia," in a document witnessed by John Troy and John Shee.[101] We know very little about their father. William Mitchell was "one of the Owners and Supercargo" on a Belfast ship the *Brothers* when she ran aground in a storm near Dublin in March 1732 on a voyage from Holland with flaxseed. With a good deal of local help, Mitchell saved both ship and cargo and brought them safely to Belfast. James Arbuckle of Belfast, the other owner, carried a letter signed by the sovereign, burgesses and principal merchants of Belfast to the Earl of Meath, thanking him for his kindness to "Mr. William Mitchell of Belfast and the Ship and Cargo under his Care."[102] Apart from this glimpse, we know nothing of his business career, but he did have land near Glenarm. In 1737 Alexander McDonnell, Earl of Antrim, leased "forever" substantial acreage near Glenarm to "William Mitchell, Gentleman, of Dickeystown."[103]

Four of William Mitchell's sons went to Philadelphia. Hugh Mitchell joined his brother Randle and the firm became Hugh and Randle Mitchell in 1750. Their brother Alexander was one of their clerks, replacing Benjamin Fuller, who had become Hugh Donaldson's business partner. The two firms were on the best of terms. For example, Benjamin Fuller, Randle Mitchell, and Hugh Donaldson jointly owned the sloop *Charming Sally*, probably used for coastal voyages, in 1754.[104]

Hugh Mitchell was already established as a merchant in Dublin and did not remain long in America. Randle Mitchell of Philadelphia and Hugh Mitchell of Dublin owned the ship *Lennox* of 100 tons, which they registered in November 1751, and the ship *Betty and Sally* registered in June 1752 at the same tonnage, both built at Philadelphia. They also owned the ship *Jenny and Betty* and the brig *Rose*, built at Marcus Hook, and evidently named for Randle Mitchell's bride Rose Harper Mitchell.[105] Hugh Mitchell was dead by 1757. Hugh Mitchell of the City of Dublin, merchant, wrote his last will in 1754, leaving all his property in Great Britain or Ireland or in any other part of Europe or in America and the West Indies in trust to his widow and children with William Lennox, Esq. of Dublin as sole trustee.[106]

Randle Mitchell and Company believed in the power of advertising, publishing detailed lists of the goods they had for sale and reminding newspaper readers that "Said Randle Mitchell gives ready money for good clean FLAX SEED." Randle went home with the flaxseed ships in the 1752–3 season, leaving Alexander Mitchell to conduct the business while he was abroad. On his return the firm became Randle and Alexander Mitchell.[107] Later on he was in business with Abraham Usher as Usher and Mitchell.[108]

John Mitchell, the youngest brother, was at home in Glenarm at school in the 1750s. Later, as Lieutenant John Mitchell he marched with Glenarm volunteers when the French landed at Carrickfergus in 1760.[109] He served an apprenticeship with Belfast merchants James and William Burgess before beginning on his own in Dominica, West Indies in 1762.[110] A few years later, he joined his brother Randle in Philadelphia. John's wife Sally was Benjamin Fuller's niece.[111]

The Mitchells, Donaldson and Fuller were important men in Philadelphia trading circles for several decades. Hugh Donaldson was also a prominent Freemason, which created other links, but, like other flaxseed merchants in the 1750s, they were all expatriates – and ties forged in Glenarm trumped the rest.[112] In 1774 William Harris of the firm of Harris and Donaldson in Baltimore wrote a letter of introduction to John Mitchell on behalf of "a Sober, honest, industrious Young man" who needed Mitchell's help to set up as a tanner in Philadelphia. It was enough for Harris to write that the young man was from Glenarm in County Antrim to be certain that Mitchell would do everything he could for him.[113]

Transatlantic Partners

About the same time that Mitchell and Donaldson arrived in Philadelphia, other young men went to New York to represent Londonderry and Belfast merchants. George Folliot, the twenty-three year old son of Derry merchant William Folliot, was a partner in Archibald Cunningham's firm when he started as a flaxseed merchant in New York in 1753. James Thompson, whose brother Andrew Thompson was an established merchant in Newry, arrived a year earlier. He later returned to Ulster to form a partnership with William Caldwell of Londonderry.[114] Another newcomer in 1753, Hugh Wallace offered "a large Assortment of Irish Linnens" at his store. In a later advertisement Wallace had a wide variety of goods for sale, but he specialised in Irish linen.[115] Wallace acted for a number of merchants in Ireland and as a vendue master, selling goods at auction, from the 1750s. By his marriage in 1760 to a daughter of New York merchant Cornelius Low, he consolidated his position and rose from middling stature to prominence.[116] John Torrans from Londonderry owned the snow *Prince of Wales*, built at New York in 1753, with George Folliot, John Neilson, and Waddell Cunningham and dispatched her to Newry in 1754 with flaxseed, barrel staves and lumber.[117]

In 1754 John and Jonathan Holmes of Belfast sold their snow *Prince of Wales* to John Torrans, George Folliot, and Waddell Cunningham of New York, and John Neilson, captain of the snow.[118] The *Prince of Wales* carried flaxseed from New York to Belfast.[119] Torrans sent flaxseed cargoes to Londonderry as well. He moved to Charleston, South Carolina in 1758. William Neilson from Maddybenny, near Coleraine, represented Newry merchants Although they never formed such a cohesive group as their Philadelphia counterparts in the flaxseed trade, Gerard Beekman observed in 1757 that "the Irish Gentlemen" seemed to act in concert in such matters as finding freight for a ship loading for Londonderry.[120]

In New York, as in Philadelphia, connections with mercantile firms at home were of paramount importance. Waddell Cunningham, for instance, counted eighteen Belfast merchants as his correspondents in addition to his partner Thomas Greg. He included five Dublin firms and five in Newry, but only one correspondent in Londonderry.[121]

Family connections meant a great deal in forming partnerships and taking on associates. Alexander Lang, for instance, came from the heart of the linen-making district around Banbridge, County Down. His family had a freehold estate in the townlands of Greenan and Bovennett, in the parish of Aghaderg, amounting altogether to 323 acres, and houses in the village of Loughbrickland. His brothers James and Hugh were both linen merchants in Dublin and had some interest in collieries in County Tyrone.[122] Their sister married Jonathan Nesbitt of Loughbrickland. In 1747 the Nesbitts sent their seventeen-year-old son to his uncle in Philadelphia to learn the mercantile business; Alexander Lang apprenticed his nephew John Maxwell Nesbitt to his friends Conyngham and Gardner. Alexander Lang died in November 1748, unmarried, leaving his estate to his brothers and his nephew, with Redmond Conyngham and Theophilus Gardner as executors. Young Nesbitt continued with Conyngham and became a partner in 1754 when the firm became Conyngham and Nesbitt, after Gardner left the firm, ultimately for Jamaica, where he became a merchant and sugar planter.[123]

Mercantile families sent their young sons as apprentices to established merchants on both sides of the Atlantic to learn the business, "to meet the people they would later have to deal with, and to pick up what they could of the most modern techniques of commerce."[124] Several other rising stars came to Philadelphia and New York in this way. George Bryan's father sent him to James Wallace in Philadelphia in 1752 and launched him on a business and political career. Wallace was in business as a dry goods merchant selling Irish linens and other goods imported from London and Liverpool and had frequent dealings with Samuel Bryan, one of Dublin's Presbyterian linen drapers, offering "a choice parcel of Irish linens, imported from Dublin."[125] James Wallace of Philadelphia and Samuel and James Bryan of Dublin registered their ship *Friendship* built at Marcus Hook in 1751. Wallace advertised for freights for the *Friendship* on her return voyage as well as his own European and East India goods. The following year the brig *Jenny* and the snow *Lucas* were registered as owned by James Wallace and George Bryan.[126]

Samuel Bryan sent his twenty year old son to Philadelphia on the *Jenny* to become Wallace's resident partner. He was not as conscientious at first as he might have been. The elder Bryan scolded George for writing home about "pleasure boating on the river" with his friend John Bleakley, Jr. and not reporting "how the present crops have proved in corn and flaxseed," matters "very proper to be taken notice of at the time of your writing."[127] The merchant at home needed eyes and ears in the Colonies, too. Wallace went home with the flaxseed fleet, leaving young Bryan to sell linens and "a parcel of likely men and women servants".[128] Wallace and Bryan extended their West Indian trade, sending their snow *Lucas* with Wallace's brother Thomas to Barbados and the Leeward Islands.[129] Their partnership did not last long and was finally dissolved in 1755. George Bryan struck out on his own, while James Wallace and his brother did business at the old stand.[130] The brothers continued together through 1764. Wallace later formed a partnership with James Fullton.[131] Bryan took no other business partners, but worked closely with Conyngham and Nesbitt and with George Folliot in New York.[132] His trade was largely with Dublin, importing both linen and servants, but he also shipped flaxseed and flour to Newry and Londonderry.[133] With William Gilliland of New York, Bryan also traded to Quebec, sending his sloop *Greyhound* there in 1762.[134]

There was no shortage of new faces among flaxseed merchants in Philadelphia and in New York. Ten of the twenty flaxseed merchants on the 1756 Philadelphia tax assessment had, in fact, arrived in the city after 1750.[135] John Mease, Conyngham and Nesbitt, and the new firm of Scott and McMichael headed the list. John Mease, like Samuel Carsan, came from Strabane, where his family of merchants and ministers were later prominent in founding Strabane Academy. Mease established himself as a flaxseed merchant in Philadelphia by 1736, and married Mary Steel at First Presbyterian Church the following year. He first advertised in the *Pennsylvania Gazette*, however, in 1746 for freight to Belfast for the brigantine *Elizabeth*.[136] Like Carsan, Mease was a Presbyterian. He was ordained an elder at First Presbyterian Church in Philadelphia before 1749 and was one of the original trustees of The Corporation for Relief of Poor and Distressed Presbyterian Ministers in 1759.[137] John Mease died in 1768, leaving a reputation as "a compassionate and liberal Helper of the Poor and Distressed of every Denomination." In his will he devised his estate to Presbyterian charities and to his numerous relatives, among them his cousin William Alison and his children and Alison's stepchildren, David Caldwell's son and daughter. He also left a

legacy to John McMichael's widow.[138] Mease took his brother
Robert's sons into his business and James, John, and Matthew
Mease continued in the flaxseed trade.[139]

John Scott and John McMichael were from Belfast, although
Scott's home was in Armagh. Scott and McMichael owned the ship
Fanny, built at Philadelphia in 1753, and, in partnership with
George Dunlope and Hugh Montgomery of Larne, the ship
William and George, advertising for freights and passengers to
Belfast for both ships.[140] Both the Ulster and Philadelphia firms
had business ties with Waddell Cunningham, sending the *William
and George* round to New York consigned to him.[141] Scott and
McMichael rapidly expanded their operations, purchasing ships in
the flaxseed and West Indies trade and dispatching flaxseed cargoes
to Belfast, Londonderry, and Newry.[142] Over the next few years
they acquired shares in fifteen vessels and were sole owners of seven
more.[143] Along with many other American merchants, notably
Greg and Cunningham, Scott and McMichael dabbled in "the
Dutch trade," landing smuggled tea and textiles from the
Netherlands. Thomas Wallace had a hand in this, too.[144] They may
have overreached, for by 1763 they were bankrupt. They owed
more than £50,000 and their failure affected other merchants who
had accepted their bills and given them credit.[145] John McMichael
died in 1764. Scott returned to Belfast, where he was afterwards
associated with James Henderson in the American and Baltic
trade.[146]

George Bryan, James Wallace, Samuel Carsan, Abraham Usher,
Hugh Donaldson, Benjamin Fuller, Theophilus Gardner and
Randle Mitchell were in the next rank. Abraham and Matthew
Usher came from a family of linen drapers in Lurgan, originally
from Magheralin.[147] Two of their brothers were linen merchants
and bleachers in Lisburn. Others of the family were in the linen
business in Dublin and London.[148] They offered linens imported
from Belfast in the *Lord Russell* and "in the Dursley Galley from
Belfast" at their store in Front Street, where they sold "dry goods,
ironmongery, tea, loaf and muscavado sugar, pepper, allspice, coffee, chocolate, long and short pipes, salt, &c. at the lowest rates."
The Ushers also supplied peddlers and chapmen.[149] The *Dursley
Galley*[150] brought a flaxseed cargo to Belfast merchant Gilbert Orr

and John Pollock, a merchant in Newry, who sent her back from Belfast to Philadelphia with passengers.[151] Matthew Usher, store keeper, died in 1753. Walter Shee and James Harvey witnessed his last will.[152] A third brother, Robert Usher became Abraham's partner until in 1759 he joined Randle Mitchell.[153] That partnership dissolved in 1763 when Abraham Usher added sugar refining to the firm's operations and Mitchell chose to concentrate on dry goods.[154]

Walter Shee and James Eddy were among the other more prominent flaxseed merchants in Philadelphia. Walter Shee came from a landed family in County Westmeath, but his business associations were with Londonderry. Shee settled in Philadelphia by 1745 and was soon established as a dry goods merchant with his sons.[155] His partners in Derry were James Harvey, Thomas Harvey, and William Caldwell. They were also partners in the ship *Lydia* built at Philadelphia in 1752, although Caldwell alone advertised for passengers.[156] Shee's partnership with the Harveys expired in 1755.[157] His other Derry correspondents included Walter Marshall, his brother Thomas Marshall, and Robert Houston, who owned the brig *Boscawen* with Shee in 1759.[158] His sons John and Bartles were his partners until 1765 when Walter Shee and Sons was dissolved, John Shee going into trade on his own, and Walter and Bartles Shee forming a new partnership.[159] Walter Shee was one of the first to open an office for marine insurance, a sideline he continued for many years.[160] He was also prominent in Masonic affairs.[161]

James Eddy was also a merchant in the flaxseed trade.[162] Eddy and his partner Thomas Walker owned the ship *Earl of Holderness* in 1754. Eddy evidently bought Captain William Blair's interest in his old ship. Captain James McCullough then bought out Walker. McCullough and Eddy owned the *Earl of Holderness* in 1757.[163] She brought passengers from Belfast and Larne, returning with flaxseed to Dublin.[164] Like William Blair, James McCullough was shipmaster as well as merchant. He owned the brig *Princess Louisa*, registered in 1751, with Blair and William and Andrew Hodge and the *Charming Polly*, registered in 1752, with the Hodges.[165] McCullough and Eddy informed the public in 1759 that the *William and George* would be "ready in a few Days to take in Flax Seed" for Belfast and Larne. They also had for sale "A Parcel of good

Irish Butter and Beef, some Crates of English Earthen and Glass Ware, Irish Linens, and fine Tiles for Chimneys."[166] McCullough's death in 1759 brought the partnership to an end. Besides providing for his wife and children, he left money to the Pennsylvania Hospital and "the poor children of the Presbyterian meeting house on Arch street."[167] James Eddy continued in business, dispatching flaxseed ships for Belfast or Newry, sometimes with Samuel Purviance, Sr., and selling Irish linens, English stone and delftware and china and occasionally servants at his store.[168] He died in 1769, leaving a large family. Abraham Usher was executor and Randle Mitchell a witness to his will.[169]

There were other new faces among Philadelphia's flaxseed merchants by the last of the 1750s. William Humphreys shipped flaxseed to Belfast as early as 1750. He had close business ties with the Galts of Coleraine and John Caldwell of Ballymoney. They were co-owners of the ship *Lord Dunluce* in the passenger and flaxseed trade. Humphreys left legacies to his friends William Galt of Coleraine and William White of Dublin as well as his Humphreys and McIlvaine relations in the will he dictated in 1776.[170]

William West landed in Philadelphia in 1751. He married William Hodge's daughter at First Presbyterian Church in 1757. With his brother Francis West he went into business as a dry goods merchant, taking a special interest in the Indian trade. Francis West moved to Carlisle on the western frontier, while William West remained in Philadelphia. As early as 1754 William West, merchant of Philadelphia, purchased Lot 108 in Carlisle which he sold for a nominal sum to Francis West, merchant of Carlisle. In 1756 Cumberland County voters chose William West as their representative in the Pennsylvania Assembly, where he served for one term as a very active member.[171]

Samuel Purviance was nearly forty when he came to Philadelphia from County Donegal in 1754 with his wife and sons. He evidently had accumulated capital as he set up immediately as a dry goods merchant and ship-owner.[172] He also had good connections in Philadelphia. In 1755 Purviance owned a share in the snow *Dunbar* together with James McCullough, the snow's captain, and William Correy of Philadelphia and with Correy, William Wishart, and Widow Mina Edwards in the snow *Industry*. Purviance shipped flaxseed to Belfast in the *Dunbar*.[173] He owned a number of other vessels, too.[174] By 1757 he had taken his older son into the firm, doing business as Samuel and Samuel Purviance, offering European and East India goods "imported in the last ships from London, Bristol and Ireland."[175] The following year, Samuel Purviance, Sr. was again on his own as Samuel Purviance, Jr. formed a new partnership with David Caldwell who came from Londonderry.[176] Caldwell died in 1762.[177] A year or two later the younger Purviance and his brother Robert set up as general merchants in Baltimore and built a rum distillery there, although Samuel Jr. remained in Philadelphia until 1768.[178] The Purviances, like George Bryan, had a strong commitment to the Presbyterian Church and a gift for politics in both church and state. Samuel Purviance, Jr. was one of the board members of the Corporation for the Relief of Poor and Distressed Presbyterian Ministers and emerged in the 1760s as a spokesman for Presbyterian interests.[179]

David Caldwell, the other partner in Purviance and Caldwell, married Grace Allison, the daughter of Patrick Allison, an early settler on Conewago Creek in Donegal Township, Lancaster County.[180] Allison moved from the Susquehanna to Somerset County on Maryland's Eastern Shore, where he was a tavernkeeper and storekeeper in the town of Princess Anne, leaving his only child an estate of £1,451 with instructions that she be educated in Philadelphia. He made his brother Robert Allison executor and named John Mease one of the trustees.[181] After David Caldwell's death, his widow married her cousin Captain William Allison, who was also John Mease's cousin.[182]

James Fullton, who freighted flaxseed ships to Londonderry, was in partnership with Valentine Standley by 1755, offering "Madeira and Lisbon Wines, West India and Philadelphia Rum, Muscavado and White Sugars, Cocoa, Coffee, Tea, Chocolate, Pepper, Allspice, best French Indigo, Rice, Mackerell, Oil, &c." at their store on Market Street. Their partnership was dissolved in 1760.[183] His brother John Fullton was a merchant in Ramelton, County Donegal, and his "kinsman" James Fullton a merchant in Londonderry. They were all in business with Derry merchant and ship-owner Ninian Boggs for the next thirty years.[184]

Newcomers and old hands alike shared in interconnecting webs of business alliances and personal friendships, illustrated most poignantly by the merchants who gathered at a colleague's bedside to record his last will and bid him farewell. These networks reached across the Atlantic swells, linking merchants in Belfast and Derry with the men who found flaxseed freights for their ships, sold their linens and other goods, and made the necessary arrangements for passengers, redemptioners, and indentured servants who came ashore at New Castle, Philadelphia, or New York after a long Atlantic crossing. For these men this was an Atlantic world.

Notes

1   Gerard G. Beekman to William Snell, November 13, 1750, in *Beekman
        Mercantile Papers*, I, 130.

2   Marc Egnal, "The Pennsylvania Economy, 1748–1762: An Analysis of Short-
        Run Fluctuations in the Context of Long-Run Changes in the Atlantic
        Trading Community," Ph.D. dissertation, University of Wisconsin (1974),
        63. Cf. Hood, "Flax Seed," 154.

3   Jensen, *Philadelphia Commerce*, 86.

4   White, *The Beekmans of New York*, 248.

5   Truxes, *Irish-American Trade*, 206, 284.

6   Advertisements for Riga flaxseed in *Belfast News Letter*, February 23, 1749/50,
        April 6, 1750, April 27, 1750.

7   Daniel Mussenden, James Bigger, Thomas Bateson and Valentine Jones were
        partners in Mussenden, Bigger and Co. in 1746. Mussenden, Bateson and
        James Adair, merchants and bankers, formed Belfast's first bank in 1752.
        Mussenden retired in 1758 and died in 1763. Mussenden, Bateson and Co.
        continued to 1766, when it reorganised as Thomas Bateson and Co.

8   Gerard G. Beekman to Alexander Ogilby, December 25, 1752, in *Beekman
        Mercantile Papers*, I, 162.

9   Dickson, *Ulster Emigration*, 112–15.

10   Neil McKendrick, John Brewer and J. H. Plumb, *The Birth of a Consumer
        Society: The Commercialization of Eighteenth-Century England* (London,
        1982), 30–33.

11   Carole Shammas, "Changes in English and Anglo-American consumption from
        1550 to 1800," in John Brewer and Roy Porter, eds., *Consumption and the
        World of Goods* (London, 1993), 180–82, 192–3.

12   T. H. Breen, "The meaning of things: interpreting the consumer economy in
        the eighteenth century," in Brewer and Porter, *Consumption and the
        World of Goods*, 252. Cary Carson, "The Consumer Revolution in British
        North America," in Cary Carson, Ronald Hoffman and Peter J. Albert,
        eds., *Of Consuming Interest: The Style of Life in the Eighteenth Century*
        (Charlottesville, VA, 1994), 490–91. T. H. Breen, "An Empire of Goods:
        The Anglicization of Colonial America, 1690–1776," in Stanley Katz, John
        Murrin and Denis Greenberg, eds., *Colonial America: Essays in Politics and
        Social Development* (New York, 1993), 385–6.

13   G. D. Ramsay, *The English Woollen Industry, 1500–1750* (London, 1982), 36.

14   John Smail, *Merchants, Market, and Manufacture: The English Wool Textile
        Industry in the Eighteenth Century* (London, 1999), 76–8.

15   Adrienne D. Hood, "Flaxseed, Fibre and Cloth: Pennsylvania's Domestic Linen
        Manufacture and Its Irish Connection, 1700–1830," in Brenda Collins and
        Philip Ollerenshaw, eds., *The European Linen Industry in Historical
        Perspective* (Oxford, 2003), 148.

16   W. H. Crawford, *The Impact of the Domestic Linen Industry in Ulster* (Belfast,
        2005), 134, 185.

17   See, for instance, complete listings of the stock in John Mitchell's stores at
        Reading and Caernarvon in Berks County (John Mitchell Papers, MG–92,
        PSA).

18 Thomas M. Doerflinger, *A Vigorous Spirit of Enterprise: Merchants and Economic Development in Revolutionary Philadelphia* (Chapel Hill, NC, 1986), 84–7. Thomas M. Doerflinger, "Farmers and Dry Goods in the Philadelphia Market Area, 1750–1800," in Ronald Hoffman *et al.*, eds., *The Economy of Early America: The Revolutionary Period, 1763–1790* (Charlottesville, VA, 1988), 166–95.

19 *Pennsylvanische Berichte*, March 25, 1760.

20 Davey and Carsan to Richard Bateson, March 3, 1749/50, to William Hogg, November 30, 1750 (Davey and Carsan Letterbook, LC). Gerard G. Beekman to John and David Ross, January 4, 1757, to Adam Schoales, January 8, 1756, January 16, 1758, February 16, 1758, in *Beekman Mercantile Papers*, I, 270, 288, 320–22.

21 Anne Bezanson, Robert D. Gray and Miriam Hussey, *Prices in Colonial Pennsylvania* (Philadelphia, 1935), 267.

22 Hood, *Weaver's Craft*, 46.

23 John E. Engle and Eugene K. Engle, "A Letter from Immigrant Ulrich Engel to Switzerland in 1755," *Pennsylvania Mennonite Heritage*, 16(July 1993), 11–18.

24 "Flaxseed Account," April 1, 1765 (James Fullton, Day Book, 1763–6, Historical Society of York County, York, PA). See Chapter 5 for more on commercial networks in the backcountry.

25 White, *The Beekmans of New York*, 240–41.

26 Thomas M. Truxes, "Connecticut in the Irish-American Flaxseed Trade, 1750–1775," *Eire-Ireland*, 12(1977), 34–62.

27 Gerard G. Beekman to Conyngham and Gardner, December 3, 1750, in *Beekman Mercantile Papers*, I, 131.

28 Gerard G. Beekman to William Hogg, November 29, 1758, in *Beekman Mercantile Papers*, I, 334.

29 F. Alan Palmer, ed., *The Beloved Cohansie of Philip Vickers Fithian* (Greenwich, NJ, 1999), 47–53, 91.

30 Samuel Carsan to the Rev. John Maxwell, November 21, 1749 (Davey and Carsan Letterbook, LC).

31 Gerard G. Beekman to William Snell, June 3, 1749, in *Beekman Mercantile Papers*, I, 83.

32 Davey and Carsan to Uriah McDowell and Matthew Gibson, to Hugh and William Brown, to Robert Brown, to Richard Bateson, to John McConnell, to William Hogg, to Andrew Ferguson, to John and James Porter, all November 21, 1749 (Davey and Carsan Letterbook, LC).

33 Davey and Carsan to Vance, Gregg and Caldwell, November 21, 1749, to Robert Barclay, November 21, 1749 (Davey and Carsan Letterbook, LC).

34 Davey and Carsan to Samuel Ewing, to William Scott, Jr., November 21, 1749 (Davey and Carsan Letterbook, LC).

35 Gerard G. Beekman to William Snell, November 16, 1749, in *Beekman Mercantile Papers*, I, 92.

36 Gerard G. Beekman to William Snell, December 22, 1749, in *Beekman Mercantile Papers*, I, 97.

37 Gerard G. Beekman to William Hogg, n.d. [June 1750], to William Snell, October 4, 1750, in *Beekman Mercantile Papers*, I, 108, 125.

38   Davey and Carsan to William Hogg, November 23, 1750, to Vance and
      Caldwell, November 23, 1750, to Samuel Ewing, November 29, 1750, to
      Thomas Barclay, November 30, 1750 (Davey and Carsan Letterbook, LC).

39   *Pennsylvania Gazette*, November 1, 1750, November 8, 1750, December 11,
      1750.

40   Gerard G. Beekman to Thomas Gilbert, October 29, 1750, in *Beekman
      Mercantile Papers*, I, 127.

41   Gerard G. Beekman to Redmond Conyngham, November 13, 1750, to
      Conyngham and Gardner, November 18, 1750, November 26, 1750,
      December 3, 1750, in *Beekman Mercantile Papers*, I, 130–34.

42   Gerard G. Beekman to Samuel Stewart and Samuel Montgomery, January 21,
      1752, in *Beekman Mercantile Papers*, I, 136.

43   *Pennsylvania Gazette*, October 14, 1751, November 7, 1751, November 28,
      1751. Bezanson *et al.*, *Prices in Colonial Pennsylvania*, 69.

44   Truxes, *Irish-American Trade*, 284.

45   *Belfast News Letter*, February 25, 1757.

46   This is admittedly a circular argument, since any estimate of the number of
      emigrants can only be based on the known number of ships from northern
      and southern Irish ports. Wokeck, *Trade in Strangers*, 172, 180.

47   For obvious reasons, Londonderry and Newry merchants were less likely and
      Belfast merchants more likely to advertise in a Belfast newspaper. The
      volume of Londonderry's passenger trade would thus be underestimated by
      any count of advertisements. Dickson, *Ulster Emigration*, 229, 282–7.

48   *Belfast News Letter*, May 29, 1753. For a full account of Dobbs' emigration
      scheme, see Dickson, *Ulster Emigration*, 128–34.

49   *Belfast News Letter*, January 16, 1749/50, June 19, 1752, February 8, 1754,
      August 23, 1757.

50   *Belfast News Letter*, February 29, 1739, April 13, 1739.

51   Gerard G. Beekman to Cunningham and Gardner, November 18, 1750, in
      Beekman Mercantile Papers, I, 133. *Belfast News Letter*, August 12, 1750,
      June 19, 1752, July 31, 1752.

52   *Belfast News Letter*, July 27, 1753, August 3, 1753, August 10, 1753, August
      17, 1753, May 17, 1754, July 19, 1754.

53   *Belfast News Letter*, February 20, 1756, April 23, 1756.

54   *Belfast News Letter*, April 30, 1754, August 27, 1754, December 10, 1754,
      January 24, 1755, May 23, 1755, April 29, 1757, June 10, 1757.

55   "Ship Registers," *PMHB*, 25(1901), 407.

56   *Belfast News Letter*, May 14, 1765, May 28, 1765, April 11, 1769.

57   Hugh Montgomery, merchant of Larne, County Antrim, died in 1778. His will
      provided for his daughters Martha and Margaret and his widow Martha
      Brown Montgomery and left his "freeholds and leasehold interests in Larne
      and all my personal fortune" to his son Samuel Montgomery, merchant of
      Larne. His father and Robert McKedy of Ballymena were named overseers
      (will of Hugh Montgomery, dated June 24, 1772, D/282/27, PRONI).
      Dickson, *Ulster Emigration*, 113n.

58   "Ship Registers," *PMHB*, 25(1901), 415.

59   *Belfast News Letter*, May 15, 1755, August 6, 1756, May 27, 1757, May 30,
      1758, August 22, 1758, July 3, 1759, September 4, 1759, June 20, 1760,

February 3, 1761, June 5, 1761, August 7, 1761, July 2, 1762, August 23, 1763.

60   John Caldwell, "Particulars of History of a North County Irish Family" (typescript, T/3541/5/3, PRONI). The original ms. of Caldwell's memoir, completed in 1841, is in the New York Historical and Genealogical Society Library, New York, NY.

61   Robert Simpson, *The Annals of Derry* (Londonderry, 1847), 216.

62   *Belfast News Letter*, February 13, 1749/50, April 10, 1753, July 2, 1754.

63   "Ship Registers," *PMHB*, 25(1901), 574

64   "Ship Registers," *PMHB*, 26(1902), 133, 142.

65   James Stirling was usually styled "of Wallworth." "Ship Registers," *PMHB*, 27(1903), 101, 106.

66   "Ship Registers," *PMHB*, 27(1903), 350.

67   "Ship Registers," *PMHB*, 27(1903), 358, 364.

68   "Ship Registers," *PMHB*, 26(1902), 133.

69   Gerard G. Beekman to Walter Marshall, July 9, 1753, to Cunningham and Schoales, January 17, 1755, in *Beekman Mercantile Papers*, I, 179, 243.

70   Londonderry merchants were influential beyond the world of commerce. Adam Schoales was Lord Mayor of Derry in the 1750s and Sheriff of County Londonderry in 1763. William Hogg became Lord Mayor in 1760. Simpson, *Annals*, 204. *Belfast News Letter*, November 13, 1750. "Ship Registers," *PMHB*, 25(1901), 401.

71   *Belfast News Letter*, March 13, 1749/50, May 8, 1750, May 29, 1750.

72   *Pennsylvania Gazette*, August 16, 1750, August 30, 1750.

73   *New York Gazette*, January 22, 1750/51.

74   *Belfast News Letter*, August 3, 1750.

75   Peter Francis, *A Pottery by the Lagan* (Belfast, 2001), 5–6.

76   *Belfast News Letter*, May 22, 1753, February 22, 1754, May 24, 1754.

77   *Belfast News Letter*, April 20, 1753, March 28, 1755, February 22, 1757.

78   Thomas M. Truxes, ed., *Letterbook of Greg and Cunningham, 1756–57, Merchants of New York and Belfast* (Oxford, 2001), 32–4.

79   David Hancock, *Citizens of the World: London merchants and the integration of the British Atlantic community, 1735–1785* (Cambridge, 1995), 9–10.

80   Virginia D. Harrington, *The New York Merchant on the Eve of the Revolution* (New York, 1935), 58.

81   Jackson Turner Main, *The Social Structure of Revolutionary America* (Princeton, NJ, 1965), 86–7. Robert F. Oaks, "Philadelphia Merchants and the American Revolution 1765–1776," Ph.D. dissertation, University of Southern California (1970), 11.

82   Since not every individual was assigned an occupation, Thomas Doerflinger estimated the total number of merchants in 1756 would be close to 230. Doerflinger, *A Vigorous Spirit*, 17.

83   A transcript of this assessment is in Hannah Benner Roach, *Colonial Philadelphians* (Philadelphia, 1999), 109–44.

84   "The Mount Regale Fishing Company," *PMHB*, 27(1903), 88–90.

85   Doerflinger, *A Vigorous Spirit*, 56. The entire section "How to Become a Merchant" is instructive.

86   Hancock, *Citizens of the World*, 241–2.

87   Truxes, *Letterbook of Greg and Cunningham*, 33.

88   P. Beryl Eustace and Olive C. Goodbody, *Quaker Records Dublin Abstracts of Wills* (Dublin, 1953), 67.

89   *Pennsylvania Gazette*, July 20, 1749.

90   *Pennsylvania Gazette*, January 15, 1750/51, February 12, 1750/51.

91   Randal McDonnell, 2nd Earl of Antrim, built a new Glenarm Castle near the town in 1636, but it was burned in 1642 by the Scottish army and only the walls remained in the eighteenth century. The McDonnells moved to Ballymagarry House, near their ancient stronghold of Dunluce Castle, but another fire in 1750 left this a ruin. The 5th Earl decided to rebuild Glenarm Castle and his project was completed in 1756. Felix McKillop, *Glenarm: A Local History* (Glenarm, 1987), 5–6.

92   Jimmy Irvine, "Drumnasole," *The Glynns*, 11(1983), 1–6.

93   Randal, Earl of Antrim to John Donaldson, December 11, 1707 (D/2977/3A/4/1/38, PRONI).

94   Alexander, Earl of Antrim to Hugh Donaldson, November 17, 1744 (D/2977/3A/4/1/69, PRONI).

95   Hugh Donaldson to William Hamilton, August 18, 1750 (D/282/11, PRONI).

96   Crawford, *Domestic Linen Industry*, 16. *Belfast News Letter*, April 3, 1764.

97   Alexander McDonnell to John Mitchell, March 23, 1674, March 26, 1674, to James Mitchell, February 3, 1682 (D/2977/3A/4/65/7, /8, /26, PRONI). He also granted a lease for property in Glenarm to the Mitchells' neighbour, John Donaldson, Gentleman, who was mentioned in the Mitchell lease of 1674 as occupying the adjacent house. Alexander McDonnell to John Donaldson, April 28, 1679 (D/2977/3A/4/65/24, PRONI).

98   Receipt, James Mitchell to John Mitchell, September 16, 1698 (D/2977/5/1/3/16/1, PRONI).

99   Agnew, *Belfast Merchant Families*, 182–5.

100   "Last night I was at the funeral of my long acquaintance and good friend Mr. Alex Mitchell, he was interr'd in St. Paul's Church." Daniel Forest to John Donaldson, May 10, 1712 (D/2977/5/1/4/14, PRONI).

101   John Shee was a son and partner of Walter Shee. Randle Mitchell and Alexander Mitchell, Acknowledgement, October 9, 1755 (D/282/15, PRONI).

102   *Faulkner's Dublin Journal*, April 29, 1732, June 10, 1732.

103   Alexander, Earl of Antrim to William Mitchell, December 14, 1737 (D/2977/3A/4/1/57A–C, PRONI).

104   *Pennsylvania Gazette*, December 6, 1750, November 28, 1751, January 14, 1752, May 28, 1752. "Ship Registers," *PMHB*, 25(1901), 563.

105   "Ship Registers," *PMHB*, 25(1901), 269, 275, 279.

106   Will of Hugh Mitchell, no date, [proven] March 1757 (T/502, PRONI).

107   Mitchell regularly advertised dry goods imported from London and less frequently servants from Dublin and Bristol. *Pennsylvania Gazette*, October 19, 1752, January 2, 1753, September 20, 1753.

108   *Pennsylvania Gazette*, October 4, 1759.

109   *Belfast News Letter*, March 28, 1760.

110 William Burgess to John Mitchell, January 14, 1763 (John Mitchell Papers, MG–92, Box 1, PSA).

111 Benjamin Fuller to Sally Mitchell, April 8, 1774 (Benjamin Fuller Letter Book, I, 34, HSP).

112 *Pennsylvania Gazette*, June 22, 1755. Campbell, *Friendly Sons*, 31.

113 William Harris to John Mitchell, July 20, 1774 (John Mitchell Papers, MG–92, PSA).

114 Truxes, *Letterbook of Greg and Cunningham*, 11.

115 *New York Mercury*, October 23, 1753. "Hugh Wallace sells on very reasonable Terms Madeira, Mountain, Sherry and benecasto Wines, Rum, Molasses, White and Muscavado Sugar, Oranges and Lemmons, Sallad Oil, Olives, Capers and Anchovies, Gold and Silver Lace, Men's Shoes and Pumps, Boots and Spatterdashes, Silk Handkerchiefs, Scots Carpets, Men's and Women's Gloves, Irish Linnens and sundry European Goods." *New York Mercury*, March 29, 1762.

116 *New York Mercury*, May 12, 1760. Cathy Matson, *Merchants and Empire: Trading in Colonial New York* (Baltimore, 1998), 276.

117 New York Naval Officer's Returns (CO 5/1227/242 and CO 5/1228/25, PRO, Microfilm, LC).

118 Norman E. Gamble, "The Business Community and Trade of Belfast 1767–1800," Ph.D. dissertation, University of Dublin (1978), 20. Truxes, *Letterbook of Greg and Cunningham*, 32–4, 115n.

119 *Beekman Mercantile Papers*, I, 298.

120 Gerard G. Beekman to to Thomas Marshall, January 31, 1757, to Archibald Cunningham and Adam Schoales, February 2, 1757, in *Beekman Mercantile Papers*, I, 292–3.

121 John Greg, Sr., John Hyde, Samuel Hyde, James Ross, Leggs, Hyde & Co., John Henderson, James Henderson, James McQuatters [McWaters], John Potts, Hugh Donaldson, James Park, John Brown, Samuel McTier, John Gordon, John Calwell, Robert Calwell, Robert Gordon, Blair & Cunningham, and John Campbell were his Belfast correspondents. Waddell Cunningham to Thomas Greg, May 10, 1756, in Truxes, *Letterbook of Greg and Cunningham*, 110.

122 They traded extensively with Philadelphia. James and Hugh Lang to John Mitchell, July 31, 1773 (John Mitchell Papers, Pennsylvania State Library). *Belfast News Letter*, March 24, 1761, October 12, 1762, November 27, 1764, August 12, 1766. James Lang was evidently a merchant of importance as he subscribed to the Marine Society with the Archbishop of Dublin, the Earl of Kildare, and other prominent people. Other Dublin merchants in the Marine Society were James Evory, Joseph Fade, and William Alexander, all correspondents of Davey and Carsan. *Belfast News Letter*, March 30, 1759.

123 Philadelphia County Wills, J–1. Hayden, "Reminiscences," 188–9.

124 Bernard Bailyn, *Atlantic History: Concept and Contours* (Cambridge, MA, 2005), 47–8.

125 *Pennsylvania Gazette*, June 22, 1749, May 10, 1750, May 24, 1750, July 18, 1751.

126 *Pennsylvania Gazette*, October 24, 1751. "Ship Registers," *PMHB*, 25(1901), 269, 275, 277.

127 Burton A. Konkle, *George Bryan and the Constitution of Pennsylvania* (Philadelphia, 1922), 19–20.

128 *Pennsylvania Gazette*, July 30, 1752, August 27, 1752, November 9, 1752.

129 *Pennsylvania Gazette*, June 6, 1754.

130 *Pennsylvania Gazette*, October 10, 1754, January 21, 1755, February 4, 1755, March 4, 1755, March 11, 1755, February 29, 1756

131 *Pennsylvania Gazette*, May 19, 1763, February 2, 1764, July 9, 1767. *Pennsylvania Journal*, May 19, 1763, March 29, 1764.

132 Bryan, Conyngham and Nesbitt registered the ship *Hayfield* of 100 tons as their property in 1756. George Bryan owned a share in the brig *Hannah* with Conyngham and Nesbitt. He registered the snow *Patty*, a prize taken from the French, as his property in 1759. The same year Bryan and George Folliot of New York registered the brig *John and William* and the *Charming Sally*, both taken from the French as prize ships. "Ship Registers," *PMHB*, 25(1901), 573, 26(1902), 391, 398.

133 *Pennsylvania Journal*, October 20, 1763, November 10, 1763, December 15, 1763.

134 Joseph S. Foster, *In Pursuit of Equal Liberty: George Bryan and the Revolution in Pennsylvania* (University Park, PA, 1994), 7.

135 Even Homer's catalogue of ships and men has caused generations of schoolboys to nod, and a lengthy list of flaxseed merchants and the ships consigned to them may have a soporific effect on the reader, but how else to understand the complex web of transatlantic partnerships?

136 *Belfast News Letter*, March 5, 1771, August 5, 1785. *Pennsylvania Gazette*, October 30, 1746.

137 He was still an active elder in 1763. *Pennsylvania Journal*, November 24, 1763. Alexander Mackie, *Facile Princeps: The Story of the Beginning of Life Insurance in America* (Lancaster PA, 1956), 75.

138 *Pennsylvania Gazette*, January 7, 1752, January 21, 1768. Philadelphia Wills, O–190.

139 John H. Campbell, *History of the Friendly Sons of St. Patrick* (Philadelphia, 1892), 120.

140 *Pennsylvania Gazette*, November 8, 1753, October 17, 1754. "Ship Registers," *PMHB*, 25(1901), 404, 407.

141 Waddell Cunningham to George Dunlope, May 10, 1756, Truxes, ed., *Greg and Cunningham*, 97.

142 *Pennsylvania Gazette*, January 13, 1757, Otober 27, 1757, November 8, 1759.

143 They registered the ship *King George* of 150 tons and the ship *Philadelphia* of 110 tons in 1757. Scott and McMichael were the sole owners of the ship *Prince George* in 1758. They owned the brig *Wolfe* with William White and Robert McGee of Dublin. They had the brig *Mary* built for William Benson of Dublin and owned her in partnership with him. They also owned the snow *Triton*, a prize taken from the French, with John Taylor of Philadelphia. In 1759 Scott and McMichael registered the snow *Prince Edward*. They were part owners of the ship *Hamilton* and the snow *Gordon*

in 1760 and sole owners of the ship *King George*, registered at 200 tons, and the Bermuda-built sloop *Recovery* in 1761. They also registered the brig *Spy* and the schooner *Fox* that year, both prizes taken from the French.

144 Waddell Cunningham to John Scott and John McMichael, August 9, 1756, August 12, 1756, in Truxes, *Letterbook of Greg and Cunningham*, 188–92. On smuggling, see Jensen, *Maritime Commerce*, 130–52.

145 James and Drinker to Neale and Pigou, December 20, 1763 (James and Drinker Letterbook, HSP).

146 *Pennsylvania Gazette*, December 29, 1763. *Pennsylvania Journal*, January 4, 1764. Benjamin Fuller to John Scott, August 26, 1768 (Benjamin Fuller Letterbook, I, 8, HSP).

147 *Belfast News Letter*, February 22, 1754, April 5, 1754, May 10, 1754, May 24, 1754.

148 Philadelphia County Wills, M–193. *Belfast News Letter*, January 18, 1757, April 15, 1768.

149 *Pennsylvania Gazette*, June 28, 1750, August 6, 1752, March 6, 1753.

150 The *Dursley Galley* belonged to John Rowan, a merchant and brewer, on Society Hill in Philadelphia. She made a number of crossings to and from Belfast and Newry. In addition to importing Irish linens, Rowan brought over race horses, such as Young Tifter, "bred by Charles O'Neill, Esq. of Shanes Castle," County Antrim. Rowan died in 1759, making John Mease executor of his last will with his widow. *Pennsylvania Gazette*, September 28, 1751, November 14, 1751, December 17, 1751, August 13, 1752, September 14, 1752, June 28, 1753, April 25, 1754. "Ship Registers," *PMHB*, 25(1901), 126. Philadelphia County Wills, l–357.

151 Gilbert Orr and his son Andrew were later concerned in Orr, Dunlope and Glenholme of Philadelphia. *Belfast News Letter*, February 9, 1753.

152 Philadelphia County Wills, K–99. *Pennsylvania Gazette*, September 27, 1753, January 15, 1754.

153 William West and John Shee were appointed executors of Robert Usher's will, witnessed by Randle Mitchell. Philadelphia County Wills, M–193. *Pennsylvania Gazette*, November 29, 1759.

154 *Pennsylvania Journal*, May 5, 1763.

155 *Pennsylvania Gazette*, November 2, 1749. Campbell, *Friendly Sons*, 132.

156 "Ship Registers," *PMHB*, 25(1901), 276. *Belfast News Letter*, May 3, 1757.

157 *Pennsylvania Gazette*, July 3, 1755.

158 "Ship Registers," *PMHB*, 26(1902), 288.

159 *Pennsylvania Gazette*, March 28, 1765.

160 *Pennsylvania Gazette*, September 23, 1756.

161 *Pennsylvania Gazette*, June 22, 1755.

162 *Pennsylvania Gazette*, August 8, 1753, July 25, 1754, August 8, 1754.

163 "Ship Registers," *PMHB*, 25(1901), 414, 26(1902), 126.

164 Oddly there is only one advertisement in the Belfast paper. *Pennsylvania Gazette*, December 14, 1752.

165 The Hodges also owned the *Prince of Orange* and the *King of Prussia*, both flaxseed ships. "Ship Registers," *PMHB*, 25(1901), 127, 277, 403.

166 *Pennsylvania Gazette*, November 29, 1759.

167   He belonged to Second Presbyterian Church. Philadelphia County Wills, L–516. *Pennsylvania Gazette*, September 18, 1760.

168   *Pennsylvania Gazette*, October 23, 1760, November 13, 1760, October 29, 1761, August 26, 1762.

169   Philadelphia County Wills, 0–410.

170   *Pennsylvania Gazette*, September 20, 1750. "Ship Registers," *PMHB*, 25(1901), 415. Philadelphia County Wills, S–1.

171   Cumberland County Deeds, 2A–81, CCCH. *Pennsylvania Gazette*, December 16, 1756, July 7, 1757. Craig W. Horle, "William West," *Lawmaking and Legislators in Pennsylvania: A Biographical Dictionary* (Philadelphia, 1997), 2 (1710–56), 1055–64.

172   *Pennsylvania Gazette*, May 4, 1754.

173   *Pennsylvania Gazette*, November 13, 1755, October 28, 1756. "Ship Registers," *PMHB*, 25(1901), 566, 569.

174   Correy, Wishart, and Edwards were co-owners with Purviance of the ship *Louisburg*. He owned the brig *Mary and Hannah* in partnership with John Mifflin, Jr. and the brig *Recovery*, a prize taken from the French, in partnership with Thomas Lightfoot and George Houston. Purviance was the sole owner of the snow *Joannah*. "Ship Registers," *PMHB*, 26(1902), 136, 141, 280, 396.

175   *Pennsylvania Gazette*, August 4, 1757.

176   *Pennsylvania Gazette*, May 25, 1758, October 12, 1758, July 12, 1759.

177   Samuel Purviance, Jr. witnessed his last will, which named John Mease as executor with Caldwell's widow and his brother Samuel. Philadelphia County Wills, M–365.

178   *Maryland Gazette*, January 31, 1765. Robert Purviance, *A Narrative of Events Which Occurred in Baltimore Town During the Revolutionary War* (Baltimore, 1849), 32.

179   Corporation for the Relief of Poor and Distressed Presbyterian Ministers, Minutes, I, 16 (PHS).

180   On his death in 1748, Grace Caldwell inherited 175 acres patented by him in 1737, which David Caldwell, merchant of Philadelphia, and his wife Grace sold in 1761. Lancaster County Deeds, CC–123.

181   I am indebted to John F. Polk of Havre de Grace, Maryland for this information, taken from the estate papers in the Maryland Hall of Records, Annapolis, MD.

182   Daniel McHenry, a merchant in Ballymena, sent his son James to his friend William Allison in 1771 and followed with the rest of the family a year later, going into the flaxseed business first in Philadelphia, then in Baltimore. Bernard C. Steiner, *Life and Correspondence of James McHenry* (Cleveland OH, 1907), 75.

183   *Pennsylvania Gazette*, March 11, 1755, June 14, 1759, October 9, 1760, April 2, 1761.

184   James Fullton Letter Book (typescript), LCHS. The original has been lost.

5

Into the Backcountry

Opportunities in Wartime

"The Season is very favourable both for A Crop of grain and Flaxseed," Waddell Cunningham wrote Newry merchant David Gaussan in June 1756. But, he warned, "The Province of Pennsylvania will fall short of Both, as a great Part of the Province is now deserted."[1] Fear of Indian raids depopulated the frontier counties from which much of the wheat, flour, and flaxseed shipped from Philadelphia came. The amount of flaxseed imported into Ireland from the American Colonies fell below pre-war levels in 1756 and did not recover until the planting season of 1759 when the threat to the Pennsylvania backcountry had largely evaporated.[2] As early as July 1755, before the first attacks struck, the *Pennsylvania Gazette* reported the "Back Settlers are in general fled, and are likely to be ruined for the Loss of their Crops and Summer's Labour."[3] In 1756 the countryside west of the Susquehanna river was nearly deserted and it was said that from Carlisle to Virginia, "there is not an Inhabitant to be seen, a few in Shippensburg excepted." From Carlisle, Adam Hoops reported to the Governor of Pennsylvania that there were 3,000 men fit to bear arms in Cumberland County in 1755 and a year later, exclusive of the provincial forces, "they did not amount to an hundred." Hoops wrote that detachments of volunteers protected farmers harvesting their crops, but, he added, on a general alarm that Indians were coming, "The Farmers abandoned their Plantations, and left what Corn was not then stacked or carried into Barnes, to perish on the Ground."[4]

As settlement moved westward in Pennsylvania, Shawnee and Delaware and other native peoples abandoned their villages east of the Susquehanna river and gradually withdrew beyond the Allegheny mountains to the Ohio country. Traders followed them into a region that the French in Canada claimed as their own. The French began constructing barrier forts across western Pennsylvania and the Ohio Company of Virginia sought to checkmate them with a fort at the Forks of the Ohio, site of Pittsburgh. France won the match in 1754 building Fort Duquesne at the Forks and compelling the surrender and withdrawal of a military force sent from Virginia under command of Col. George Washington. The stage was set for an imperial reaction. The British government sent General Sir Edward Braddock with two regiments of regulars to America to dislodge the French. By the time he was ready to march towards Fort Duquesne, Braddock had 2,500 men at his command, regulars and colonial troops, as his army inched its way through the wilderness. On July 9, 1755, Braddock's column blundered into a French and Indian ambush and, after two hours of slaughter, the remnants of his army withdrew from the field. Col. Thomas Dunbar, who took command after Braddock's death, still had a considerable military force and greatly outnumbered the French and their Indian allies.[5] But he ordered a general retreat, abandoning artillery and supply wagons, and marched his men through Shippensburg, Carlisle, and Lancaster to the safety of Philadelphia. With the Delaware and Shawnee already gone over to the French, the Pennsylvania frontier was suddenly in danger.[6]

Adam Hoops and William Buchanan were typical of the frontier leaders who found scope for their abilities in the emergency and profited from wartime opportunities to each become "Merchant" and "Gentleman." They were not without connections. Buchanan, an innkeeper-storekeeper in the Marsh Creek settlement and then in the town of Carlisle, was the son of Robert Buchanan, Sheriff of Lancaster County. Hoops, whose origins are shrouded in mystery, was himself a justice of Cumberland County.[7]

"Only some Scotch-Irish kill'd"

By 1755 the Scotch-Irish were emphatically the people on the frontier, clearing land and raising crops in the backcountry of
Pennsylvania and in the Shenandoah Valley of Virginia, and pressing on to south-western Virginia and the North Carolina piedmont. Their image as restless frontiersmen, moving on as soon as
they could see smoke rise from a neighbour's chimney, is pervasive,
but they were driven by the same impulse that led them to negoti-
ate a lease for a new farm in Ulster on better terms than their present landlord offered. In contrast to the vision of church leaders,
who favoured compact communities capable of supporting a settled
minister, they had solid economic reasons for selling out and starting over in a new location. They saw land as a commodity to be
bought and sold to the best advantage. Rev. James Anderson, minister in the Donegal settlement in Lancaster County, complained in
1730 that members of his congregation "with a regard to their own
private Interest only are for disposing of their Improvement to the
best Bidders who are generally the Dutch."[8] A generation later the
problem was widespread. Edmund Burke ascribed the settlement of
the Southern backcountry to Irish migrants, "who not succeeding
so well in Pensylvania, as the more frugal and industrious Germans,
sell their lands in that province, and take up new ground in the
remote counties in Virginia, Maryland, and North Carolina. These
are chiefly presbyterians from the Northern part of Ireland, who in
America are generally called Scotch Irish."[9] Longer-settled parts of
Pennsylvania gradually became more German as the Scotch-Irish
moved to the backcountry. The Presbyterian Synod of Pennsylvania
declared in 1759 that:

> The Inhabitants are inconstant and unsettled, and are always
> shifting their Habitations, either from a Love of variety, or
> from the fair Prospect of more commodious Settlements on
> the Frontiers of this, or the Neighbouring Provinces; … When
> our People remove they are generally Succeeded by Strangers
> from Europe, who incline at their first arrival to purchase or
> hire cultivated Lands; [so that] one of our most promising
> Settlements of Presbyterians, may in a few Years, be entirely
> possessed by German Menonists, or Moravians, or any other
> Society of Christians.[10]

Germans also settled on the frontiers and many of them fell victims to Delaware and Shawnee war parties, but it was seared into Scotch-Irish consciousness that their people suffered disproportionately "from the fury of the heathen," while Quakers and others lived in security. This view was reinforced by a careless remark of Nathaniel Grubb, a Quaker who represented Chester County in the Pennsylvania Assembly, who "being informed that sundry of the Back Inhabitants were cut off, and destroyed by our savage Enemies, replied, 'That there were only some Scotch-Irish kill'd, who could well be spared."[11]

Across the Susquehanna

Not all Scotch-Irish abandoned Pennsylvania, of course. Emigrants from Ulster settled in Chester and Lancaster counties in south-eastern Pennsylvania in the 1720s, with Donegal and Paxton townships on the east bank of the Susquehanna as their advance guard. They crossed the river in the 1730s, while others pressed on to Virginia, and by 1745 these Scotch-Irish settlers had formed ten Presbyterian congregations within the bounds of what was to be Cumberland County.[12] Because of this, Pennsylvania west of the Susquehanna river early became the domain of the Scotch-Irish. Soon settlement had spread beyond the Susquehanna to such an extent that two new counties were created in 1749 and 1750. York County included an area along the southern boundary of the colony. Cumberland County formed a wide arc around York, from the Susquehanna to the Maryland line.

As settlement moved westward, commercial interests followed. Lancaster, established in 1729, was the first of the inland towns to become part of the trading network. The shopkeepers of the town depended on Philadelphia merchants for their supply of dry goods and the wide variety of hardware, wines, sugar, coffee, and tea that made up their stock. And a city merchant would often engage a Lancaster shopkeeper "to buy and ship to him certain agricultural and industrial products of the interior regions." Lancaster was initially a base for the Indian trade as well.[13]

The new counties of York and Cumberland demanded a place where local government could be conducted with a court house, jail, and other public buildings. The Proprietor of Pennsylvania Thomas Penn authorised two new "Proprietary towns," as they were called, to meet this need. York was the first to be laid out in 1741.[14] Penn took a personal interest in planning Carlisle, the county town for Cumberland County. With "near fifty Houses built, and building," in 1751, Carlisle promised to be a considerable place, "a great thorough fare to the back Countries, and the Depositary of the Indian Trade."[15]

Never simply an administrative centre, Carlisle was intended from the first as a channel for the trade of central Pennsylvania.[16] As a frontier outpost, Carlisle was the collection point for Indian traders as well as a distribution point for backcountry grain, flour and flaxseed and British manufactured goods. Established athwart the main road leading from Harris' Ferry on the Susquehanna into the backcountry, Carlisle was fourteen miles from the ferry and fifty miles by road from Lancaster. The new town was thirty two miles from the slightly older York.[17] Within a few short years of its founding, Carlisle became a frontier outpost of a different kind, the furthest bastion of imperial power, a refugee camp for settlers fleeing more exposed frontier settlements and the base for the British army's operations in western Pennsylvania. War temporarily disrupted the Cumberland County economy with farmers afraid to harvest their crops and the fur trade stagnant, but for a few Carlisle merchants and traders the war provided a larger commercial stage and a boost in capital formation. The necessities of moving troops and supplies in wartime caused roads to be built into the wilderness of western Pennsylvania and into Maryland that would at last make Carlisle the "great thorough fare to the back Countries."

"People who keep Shops and Public Houses"

Colonel William Eyre, chief military engineer of the British army in America, wrote of Carlisle in 1762 as "mostly compos'd of People who keep Shops and Public Houses."[18] William Buchanan did both. He came to Carlisle in 1752 from the Marsh Creek settlement, the later Gettysburg, where he was also an innkeeper.[19] In August 1752 a local carpenter mortgaged his house and lot in Carlisle to "William Buchanan of Carlisle, innholder."[20] During his years in Carlisle, Buchanan was more than an innkeeper. As early as 1753 he was associated with Robert Callender and Michael Taaffe in the Indian trade.[21]

When General Braddock asked for roads to be constructed to facilitate his army's march and the movement of materiel and supplies, George Croghan, John Armstrong, William Buchanan, James Burd, and Adam Hoops were appointed commissioners to oversee construction of two roads from Carlisle, one to Will's Creek, where Braddock planned to locate his base camp, the other to the Forks of the Ohio. The commissioners started from Carlisle at the end of March and followed an old traders' path from Shippensburg across the mountains and along Raystown Creek. Deserted by their Indian guides and threatened by scouting parties of French and Indians, they stopped short of the Youghiogheny River and retired to the safety of Fort Cumberland.[22] Armstrong and Buchanan advertised in April and May for "two Hundred Labourers … to work on Clearing the new Road … thro' Cumberland County towards the Ohio."[23]

Governor Morris was at Carlisle when news came of Braddock's defeat. In the immediate aftermath of the disaster, Morris "at the request of the People laid the Ground for a Wooden Fort in the Town of Carlisle and … formed four Companies of Militia to whom I distributed some Powder and Lead." Companies of volunteer associators formed to meet the emergency and elected their own officers. William Buchanan commanded the company raised in Carlisle.[24]

The frontier waited through the summer and early autumn for the Indians to strike. On Saturday afternoon, November 1, 1755, a hundred Delaware and Shawnee fell upon the Big Cove settlement (present McConnellsburg) and destroyed it. When news reached Carlisle the next day, John Armstrong, John Smith, and William Buchanan decided to send a company of volunteers to Shippensburg.[25] For the time being, Carlisle and Shippensburg served as refuges for settlers fleeing more exposed frontier settlements.

The French and Indian War interrupted trade with western tribes, but it gave fresh opportunity to Carlisle shopkeepers and Indian traders in supplying the needs of British and provincial troops. In May 1756 Col. John Armstrong was given the command of all forces west of the Susquehanna and William Buchanan and Adam Hoops shared responsibility for provisioning all the military posts west of the river. Armstrong was unhappy with their perform-ance, writing that "the Contract with Messrs. Hoops & Buchanan gives a general Umbrage" as "an Extravagant sum thrown into the hands of two private persons for a Service of not more than two months in ye whole year." Buchanan was also reimbursed for his "Expences fortifying Carlisle" and arms and ammunition sent him for its defense. His brother-in-law John Smith had similar accounts paid.[26]

John Smith and William Lyon were the only ones listed as "mer-chant" on the 1759 tax assessment, but seven others on the tax roll were identified on later returns as either merchant or shopkeeper.[27] Smith was the son of Samuel Smith from Ballymagorry, near Strabane, County Tyrone, an Indian trader and one of Cumberland County's original justices. William Lyon from County Fermanagh was John Armstrong's nephew and as an assistant surveyor helped him in laying out the town of Carlisle in 1751.[28]

Carlisle's merchants were the recognized leaders of the communi-ty. Voters chose William West as their representative in the Pennsylvania Assembly in 1756 and sent John Smith there in 1759. Francis West, William's brother, and John and William Smith, both brothers-in-law of William Buchanan, were named justices of the county court in 1757.

Command of the second expedition against Fort Duquesne in 1758 fell to General John Forbes, but getting the army there and supplying them on the way was the responsibility of Swiss-born Col. Henry Bouquet. He turned to Adam Hoops to organize much of this as an army contractor, strictly as Agent to the Contractors for Victualling His Majesty's Forces, since he represented Joshua Howell, who was in turn Philadelphia agent for Baker, Kilby, and Baker of London who held the contract. Hoops made his head-quarters at Carlisle and enlisted his son-in-law Daniel Clark and William Buchanan as his assistants.[29] Hoops had little previous experience except as a backwoods justice, but successfully organized a network of suppliers stretching from Philadelphia to the South Branch of the Potomac on the Virginia frontier. His letters to them and to army officers are written in his own version of grammar and spelling, but reflect a sagacity and drive that served him well in a complicated business.[30]

Bouquet was at Carlisle in May 1758 and at a dozen other places east of the Susquehanna arranging for wagons and teams and for flour, oats, beef and pork. He ordered the Berks County magistrates, for instance, to send sixty wagons and teams "to Barney Hughes' and also to Thomas Harris' Mill" on Conewago Creek in Lancaster County to load flour and oats and proceed with them to Carlisle.[31] Long trains of wagons passed up the road on their way to Carlisle. "I have sent off 40 Waggon load of artillery stores & ammunition yesterday." Contractors were busy filling orders. "I shall send with the Convoy 1,000 pairs of shoes, and shall order another 1,000 to be made, and have ordered Mr. [Joshua] Howell to send up some tuns of salt." General Forbes complained about the wagons, the pork, the bad flour and meal that Hoops supplied. He insisted "our men must not be poisoned." Supply wagons and droves of cattle continued to pass over the same route all summer. "There is plenty of Cattle moving up with a large escort of wagons loaded with flour and pork."[32]

The army had to cut a new road and improve existing roads through more than 200 miles of wilderness, slowing the advance. The British were poised to attack Fort Duquesne on November 24, 1758, when the French commander evacuated it and marched his men away in the night. The British occupied the partially-destroyed fort and General John Forbes wrote a report to his superiors, dated from "Fort Duquesne, now Pittsbourg."[33]

The war was far from over and the need to garrison and supply frontier outposts continued. Captain Robert Callender of Carlisle and Barnabas Hughes, a tavernkeeper of Donegal Township in Lancaster County, had a contract to supply the army with 1,000 packhorses in 1758–9. General Stanwix was well enough satisfied to give them another contract for additional packhorses in July 1759.[34] Hughes moved to Baltimore in 1761 as William Buchanan's business partner, acting for Colonel Bouquet as well. Victualling the army and supplying wagons and packhorses continued to be an important source of income for Scotch-Irish businessmen in Carlisle and their employers in Philadelphia and London through 1760. Early the next year creditors were warned to present their claims before March 25, when the books would close, to representatives in Philadelphia and Lancaster or, for those west of the Susquehanna, to Adam Hoops at Carlisle.[35]

Army contracts proved invaluable in the upward trajectory from counting-house or shop counter to city merchant and landed gentleman.[36] They clearly played a similar role in the careers of Adam Hoops and his colleagues in Carlisle. Hoops leased his house on the square in Carlisle in 1761 and moved his family to Philadelphia. He continued to take an interest in the Presbyterian Church in Carlisle, but his business interests were now directed to importing dry goods and exporting flaxseed and flour to Ulster ports with his son-in-law Daniel Clark.[37] Hoops took his family home to Belfast on his own ship *New Hope* in 1763 and returned the following year by way of Liverpool.[38] His other daughter was the wife of Sam Carsan's nephew and partner, Thomas Barclay. In later years he devoted time to his investments in Pennsylvania and Nova Scotia land and retired to his country home in Bucks County, where he died in 1771.[39]

William Buchanan left Carlisle for Baltimore in 1761, where he went into partnership with Barnabas Hughes from Donegal Township in Lancaster County as general merchants. Buchanan maintained his Carlisle connections, however, and was involved in several trading ventures cut short by Pontiac's War in 1763. Buchanan and his partner Barnabas Hughes joined Thomas Smallman, a Carlisle Indian trader, in sending goods to the Ohio and Illinois country. George Croghan was a silent partner, backing his cousin Smallman financially. When the Indian trade reopened at Fort Pitt, they were among the first to ship trade goods to Smallman's store there. Croghan took an active role in the business. "According to Smallman's clerk, James Harris, 'Any thing we do here is promoted by the influence of Mr. Croghan, without which it would not be worth while to keep a store open at this place.'"[40] The partners lost heavily in ventures beyond Fort Pitt in 1763. Their severest loss was a shipment of goods valued at £3,000 sent "under the care of Hugh Crawford to Waweachteny [on the Wabash] and Miamy [upper Miami in Indiana]." Other losses were incurred on trade goods sent to the Lower Shawnee Town [near the

juncture of Scioto Creek and the Ohio River] with Thomas
Smallman, to Muskingum [in Ohio] under the care of John Bard,
and to Illinois under Smallman's charge as well as "two Houses
Destroyed at Fort Pitt by the Indian War in June 1763" and "two
Cows Drove from Fort Pitt in June or July 1763."[41] The fur trade
was the anchor for Philadelphia interests in Carlisle, since much of
the western trade passed that way.[42]

Buchanan was just one of the enterprising Ulstermen thrust forward by wartime needs. His brother-in-law John Smith, a merchant
in Carlisle from 1751, also migrated to Baltimore and became
Buchanan's partner after Hughes died in 1765. Both partnerships
sent cargoes of flaxseed and flour to Belfast. Buchanan's other
brother-in-law William Smith moved his family to Baltimore, too.
Sligo-born Daniel Clark was introduced to London Quaker merchants Daniel Mildred and William Neale by his father-in-law
Adam Hoops, ordering dry goods from both firms on their joint
account with the request that "As I am but a Beginner and not Bred
to the Business Some Improprieties in my Order may happen
which please to amend."[43]

Ulster-born John Montgomery remained in Carlisle. John
Montgomery described himself as merchant and shopkeeper in
deeds, although he is better-remembered for his service in the
Pennsylvania Assembly, the Pennsylvania Committee of Safety and
the Continental Congress and as co-founder of Dickinson College.
He married Sidney Smith, John Smith's younger sister, in 1755.[44]
The operations of a backcountry merchant were meticulously
recorded in Montgomery's one surviving store ledger. He evidently
relied on William West, James Fullton, Samuel Purviance Sr. and
his own brother-in-law John Smith for his stock in trade and
offered a bewildering variety of textiles and every other article from
six-plate iron stoves to Philadelphia beaver hats. Customers of every
social class appear to have demanded cloth of many different kinds,
weaves, colours and quality. They paid him in as many different
ways: cash, credit for work performed, bills of exchange, cash paid
to his creditors, turnips, cider, wheat, corn, whiskey, furs and deerskins. Flaxseed was not a major item in his store credits, but he
charged Robert Miller for "Carriage of Flaxseed to Phila. and goods
back." Montgomery oversaw the Cumberland County interests of

Philadelphia merchants Adam Hoops and James Fullton and of John Smith, Merchant in Baltimore Town, paying taxes, collecting rents, keeping their Carlisle property in repair and marketing their share of the tenant's crops on their plantations. Carlisle was still a frontier crossroads. John Boyd who bought a "sett of Philadelphia china cups & saucers" and a "China pint bowl" settled his account with 397 pounds of fall Deerskins. Joseph Spear, the Indian trader, sent furs to Philadelphia through Montgomery. It was also a centre for education. John Creigh, schoolmaster, was paid for schooling Montgomery's young daughters and charged for a copy of John Dickinson's *Letters of a Pennsylvania Farmer*. He also paid the Rev. John Steel for schooling his son Sammy and his nephew John Smith, Jr. By 1773 the minister's school had become the Carlisle Grammar School, with John Montgomery as one of its original board of trustees.[45]

While French influence over the Ohio Indians was gone, the tribes remained restive. They agreed nevertheless to come to Lancaster for a definitive peace treaty in August 1762. As spokesman for the Scotch-Irish of the frontiers, the Corporation for the Relief of Poor and Distressed Presbyterian Ministers pressed Governor James Hamilton to give first priority to the return of captives taken by the Indians and sent five flaxseed merchants, William Humphreys, John Mease, John McMichael, Adam Hoops and George Bryan, and five ministers to the treaty making as observers. The Indians took umbrage at the Governor's peremptory demand for surrendering all captives and departed angrily for the Ohio, many of them ready to resume warfare.[46] Carlisle was again the staging point for a British expedition and its supply base in 1763 when the Ottawa chief Pontiac united the western tribes and struck at frontier forts. Col. Bouquet assembled another force of provincials and British regulars, won a decisive battle at Bushy Run, and relieved the siege of Fort Pitt in August.[47] During that summer hundreds of settlers were killed and many more took refuge in Carlisle. Indian traders, scattered throughout the west, were especially vulnerable.[48]

The backcountry remained nervous for months after Bushy Run. A letter from Carlisle published in the *Belfast News Letter* in May 1764 reported that:

> The distresses of the back inhabitants are greater than can be
> conceived. Two hundred miles of an extended frontier are so
> exposed to the incursions of Indians, that no man can go to
> sleep within 10 or 15 miles of the borders, without being in
> danger of having his house burnt, and himself and family
> scalped, or led into captivity, before the next morning.[49]

In spite of this uncertainty, a mood of optimism swept across the
backcountry from 1761, manifesting itself in new towns as nodules
of expanding commercial networks that linked the back counties
with Philadelphia and Baltimore.

Town-Building Fever and Mercantile Networks

James Fullton was one of those flaxseed merchants who depended
on a large number of backcountry customers for the seed and flour
he shipped to Londonderry. Fullton regularly advanced money to
Joseph Larimore, a storekeeper at Chestnut Level in southern
Lancaster County, and to John Morrison and James Hunter in
western York County "to buy flaxseed" on his account.
Backcountry merchants, such as George Erwin in York, Seth
Duncan "near Wright's Ferry" in Hellam Township, York County,
Elijah Sinclair "over Susquehanna River near Nelson's Ferry" in
Chanceford Township, York County, and Samuel Gettys at Marsh
Creek (Gettysburg) in York (now Adams) County, often figured in
his "Flaxseed Account." Fullton's network of customers and com-
modity buyers included other storekeepers in Lancaster, and in
Martic, Drumore, Donegal, and Paxton Townships in Lancaster
County, at Swatara (Middletown) and Harris' Ferry (Harrisburg) as
well as in Carlisle, Shippensburg, Rocky Spring (Chambersburg),
"Conigogigg" (Mercersburg) and York.[50]

In his first years in business Fullton attempted to supply a broad
range of dry goods, hardware, wine and rum to his customers. By
the 1760s he concentrated on wine, rum, sugar, lemons and other
West Indian products, supplemented by Irish linens shipped by his
Londonderry correspondents. At the same time he was buying
flaxseed, iron, staves, and flour to ship to Ireland and flour and
other articles for the West Indies. This meant that his backcountry
customers necessarily dealt with other merchants for some store

goods and sold them hemp, iron and other produce.[51] William
McCord, one of Fullton's Lancaster customers, for instance,
stocked his shop with dry goods from partners Isaac Whitelock and
Benjamin Davis, and Isaac Wikoff. McCord, in turn, supplied
other backcountry shopkeepers, such as Hannah Haines in
Maytown, James Knox and James Dysart in Paxton Township,
James Dowdall and George Erwin "Stoarkeeper," in York, extend-
ing the network in both directions.[52]

Every backcountry storekeeper accepted flaxseed and other produce in payment for consumer goods. John Cameron of Lancaster
sold all the flaxseed he took in to Carsan, Barclay and Mitchell of
Philadelphia, but had no other dealings with this firm. He sold the
hemp he acquired from Samuel Bethel at Susquehanna to Henry
Keppele.[53] Cameron's extensive dealings with other Philadelphia
merchants in the flaxseed trade involved the shipment of bar iron
to such firms as Mease and Miller, John and David Rhea, Robert
Montgomery, and White and Caldwell.[54] Cameron obtained the
iron from Curtis and Peter Grubb at Hopewell Forge and from
Thomas Smith and Co. at Martic Forge. Peter Grubb dealt directly with White and Caldwell, but also relied on Cameron for dry
goods and cash in payment for bar iron.[55] Cameron had his own
network, too, supplying a number of shopkeepers, among them
Usher and Donaldson and George Stevenson in York, John Lowden
"at Susquehanna," Caleb Johnston, Joseph Solomon, and William
McCord in Lancaster, James Patterson, John Allison and James
Fullton in Donegal Township and Joseph Spear, Indian trader at
Carlisle, who made his remittance in deer skins and beaver skins.[56]
Cameron's own stock in trade came from Philadelphia merchant
Daniel Wister, amounting to no less than £59,997.10.3, for a total
indebtedness of £65,077.9.5 by 1769.[57] Wister understandably felt
free to draw on Cameron for cash and bills, for example to pay
Carsan, Barclay and Mitchell for Irish linens, draining away what-
ever specie his store accumulated. When Cameron died early in
1770, he was resented by other Lancaster traders because "he
received three or four times as much money as all the rest of the
Shopkeepers put together" but nearly all of it "was always sent to
Philadelphia, so that there would be but very little Cash circulating
among us."[58]

While one Philadelphia merchant's ledgers will reveal his customers in the backcountry, these more complicated networks can
also be traced in court proceedings. James Fullton, John Shee, and
the heirs of Robert Usher each proceeded against Alexander Brown,
a shopkeeper in Mountjoy Township, probably in Elizabethtown,
for unpaid goods. The judgment for Fullton was levied on Brown's
house and three acres of ground.[59] Some country storekeepers
obtained stock from many different wholesalers. Flaxseed merchants John Shee, William West, Thomas Charlton, Abraham
Usher and Randle Mitchell, William McCausland, William
Crichton, and Henry Keppele obtained judgments against Roger
Anderson, a shopkeeper in Leacock Township, for store goods each
one advanced him on credit.[60] Bankruptcy also brought commercial networks to light. In 1766 Lancaster shopkeeper Robert Fulton
deeded his property to William West, Joseph Swift, and Samuel
Purviance, Jr. He was also indebted to William Moore, Isaac
Wikoff, Richard Parker, George Fullerton and James Fullton.[61]

Backcountry customers, like any business associates, needed to be
nurtured by personal contacts. Every three months Fullton made a
tour through Lancaster, Cumberland and York counties and into
Maryland to settle accounts. Each time he recorded "My Expences
in the Country" along with "Sundry accounts received at their
homes." His travels took him to nearly all the principal Scotch-Irish
settlements in the lower Susquehanna valley and interestingly his
contacts outside of the Philadelphia mercantile community were
exclusively with Scotch-Irish businessmen. Whatever he did with
this knowledge, he was in a position to know a great deal about
backcountry Pennsylvania. A few of his extant letters refer to taking passengers on board ship at Londonderry for the voyage to
America, but none mention information shared with them when
they reached Philadelphia, even in the case of his own relatives.
Despite the lack of documentation, one might think that Fullton
used his backcountry network to inform emigrant families about
land prices and prospects in one settlement or another.[62]

Like other merchants, Fullton acted as a banker for his backcountry customers, co-signing a note for Lancaster shopkeeper Robert
Fulton in 1764, for instance, and asking another Lancaster shopkeeper to advance money to a third party on Fullton's account.[63] As

James T. Lemon observed, "Rural Pennsylvanians were connected by a chain of credit through Philadelphia and Baltimore and through merchants, millers, and shopkeepers in smaller places with London merchants."[64] British wholesalers sent textiles and other manufactures on long credit and the city merchants shipped goods to backcountry shopkeepers on credit for a shorter time, usually six months.

Daniel Clark, Adam Hoops' son-in-law and partner, needed a network of shopkeepers in Shippensburg, York and elsewhere in the backcountry to distribute the dry goods he imported from England and Ireland. Clark also shipped goods for the Indian trade. For example, Clark offered to supply a stock of goods at six months credit, "the usual time," to Captain John Clark, who kept a tavern and store at Bird-in-Hand, six miles east of Lancaster on the Philadelphia road.[65]

The Mitchell brothers from Glenarm, County Antrim, developed a different sort of network. John and Randle Mitchell each supplied dry goods to many backcountry merchants who sent them flaxseed and other produce. George Erwin of York and Charles Hamilton of Lancaster, who was married to a Mitchell niece, were typical in that they had extensive dealings with John Mitchell year after year.[66] While most of their business was conducted through their principal and autonomous Philadelphia firms, the Mitchells inclined to form separate partnerships with country storekeepers, such as Randle Mitchell's partner Francis Murray at Newtown in Bucks County.[67] John Mitchell had similar business relationships, for example, with John Reynolds at Allentown. This led the Mitchells to acquire town lots in many of the new towns created in the 1760s. Nor were they alone in choosing new towns as business centres.

Town-making Fever

Merchants like Fullton and the Mitchells depended on at least passable roads to send goods by wagon to customers as far away as Fort Ligonier and bring flaxseed, flour, hemp, even bar iron by the same wagons to Philadelphia. "The traveler who headed west from Philadelphia would find the road rutted and muddy, thanks to heavy use by hundreds of Conestoga wagons loaded with produce."

Wagons and teams crossed the broad Susquehanna with some difficulty by ferryboat.[68] Crossroads taverns and stores provided collection points for country produce and the advantages of laying out
a town at such points were readily understood.

Initially stores, often in connection with taverns, were widely dis-
persed in the back counties. Both were situated at the distance of a
day's journey on main highways and at ferries. With the creation of
proprietary towns as centres of local government, some traders settled there, while others continued to do business at rural crossroads
that would in many cases be the site for new towns in the 1760s.[69]

James T. Lemon wrote of a "town-making fever" that led to the
founding of more than twenty-nine new towns in the Pennsylvania
backcountry between 1756 and 1765, more than in all of
Pennsylvania in the previous 75 years.[70] This fever reached its peak
in 1761–2, with the end of Indian raids on the frontier and a pos-
itive economic outlook based on wartime profits on backcountry
produce. It also reflected the commercial development of the county towns in the backcountry, notably Lancaster, York, and Carlisle,
as secondary centres for the distribution of manufactured goods
and the shipment of wheat, flour, flaxseed, beef and pork to
Philadelphia and a market overseas. Lemon suggested that some of
the new towns, such as McAllisterstown (Hanover) in York County
and Chambersburg and Shippensburg in Cumberland County,
developed in the 1760s as satellites of the county towns, important
transport centres at major crossroads. He also recognized a different network for which the established county towns and the new
towns were nodal points, the commercial network linking
Philadelphia merchants and backcountry shopkeepers.[71]

New towns sprang up along the main roads. Stretching across the
Pennsylvania backcountry from Northampton Town (Allentown)
in the "Irish Settlement" on the Lehigh River to Taneytown in
western Maryland at least a dozen new towns were laid out and lots
sold in 1761–2 alone. Edward Shippen of Lancaster, one of the
principal merchants in the Indian trade, began selling lots in
Shippensburg in Cumberland County in February 1763. The 173
lots went mainly to Scotch-Irish buyers. The deeds described the
lots as "within a certain new town called Shippensburg," but there
had been a small settlement there before 1750.[72] Benjamin

Chambers from County Antrim settled at the site of the Falling Spring by 1734, but he laid out the town of Chambersburg only in 1764.[73] Richard McAllister laid out his town, later called Hanover, in 1763 or 1764 to the great amusement of his German neighbours. He was the son of Archibald McAllister, an Ulster emigrant, who settled near the Big Spring in Cumberland County in 1732.[74]

Although a few established merchants, like John Cox, Jr., Edward Shippen and Barnabas Hughes, laid out backcountry towns and others played ancillary roles in their development, much of the impetus for town-making came from local interests, from the tavernkeepers, shopkeepers, and land speculators of the back counties, who were often enough one and the same person.[75] They seized on the real or imagined advantages of a place on the main roads or the river as a link in the chain that bound them to the transatlantic commerce of Philadelphia and Baltimore. These rural entrepreneurs were not simply retailers of imported dry goods making remittances in country produce. They frequently acted as purchasing agents for city merchants, assembling large orders of flaxseed or flour, and handled other business for their principals in the seaport. While staking out town lots in a rocky pasture alongside a crossroads tavern or store would add to their annual income, the founders of backcountry towns primarily aimed at consolidating the trade of their rural neighbourhoods.

Overlapping Hinterlands

Richard McAllister operated a tavern and a store where the high road from Carlisle to Baltimore crossed the road leading to York and Philadelphia. When he announced his intention to make a town there, his neighbours thought it a good joke. McAllister persisted and in 1763 or 1764 offered lots subject to an annual rent. At the suggestion of an influential neighbour, McAllisterstown became Hanover.[76] "Richard M'Callister's store at Hanover-town in York county" was broken into on an October night in 1767 and a great variety of calico, linens, handkerchiefs and other dry goods taken away, together with about six pounds in cash.[77] Records of both store and town are extant.[78] McAllister's accounts are mainly of small purchases by customers who lived in his immediate neighbourhood and at McSherrystown, Abbotstown, Littlestown, Spring Forge, and Mary Ann Furnace. A few of these customers paid in flaxseed. His accounts with his suppliers are more revealing. He ordered "Sundries" of considerable value from David M'Lure, John and Alexander M'Lure, James Sterrett & Son, all of Baltimore, beginning in 1774, and from Baltimore merchants Joseph McGoffin and William Neill, beginning in 1775. He also had dealings with John Montgomery, a merchant in Carlisle. His account with "John Smith, Merchant", presumably the well-known Baltimore merchant of that name, differs from the others in that the amount of McAllister's cash payments greatly exceeded the value of "Sundries" supplied.[79]

Carlisle still looked eastward over Harris' Ferry to commercial links with Philadelphia. Between 1763 and 1775 twelve Cumberland County residents, including five Carlisle shopkeepers, mortgaged property to Philadelphia merchants to secure debts and only three, all local merchants, mortgaged property to Baltimore merchants.[80] An equal and opposite force drew the trade of Carlisle and the western shore to the new commercial centre of Baltimore. Its rise was due in part to the migration of several rising merchants from Carlisle to Baltimore beginning in 1760.[81] Baltimore claimed a lion's share of the trade in grain, flour, and flaxseed within the Cumberland Valley. This was especially true of the region west of the Susquehanna, where by 1770 no fewer than eight major roads led south to Baltimore.[82]

Shippensburg and Chambersburg were in many ways satellites of Carlisle. Both new towns would seem to have an even closer relation to Baltimore firms, since the distance there by road was so much less than to Philadelphia. Samuel Jack and Robert Boyd of Chambersburg, shopkeepers, mortgaged real estate to Alexander M'Clure and William Goodwin, merchants of Baltimore, to secure payment of a bonded debt in 1773, but Samuel Jack mortgaged other property the same year to Caleb and Amos Foulke of Philadelphia.[83]

With Philadelphia merchants like Samuel Carsan and Samuel Purviance opening branches of their firms in Baltimore in the 1760s, others found correspondents in the new town, supplying one another's needs, so that the relationship between the two cities

was more symbiotic than a simple trade rivalry.[84] In 1771, a
Philadelphian could nevertheless write that:

> Baltimore town in Maryland has within a few years past car-
> ried off from this city almost the whole trade of Frederick,
> York, Bedford, and Cumberland Counties, its situation on the
> West side of the river Susquehannah and its vicinity to these
> counties will always be a prevailing inducement with the
> inhabitants of those parts to resort to Baltimore for trade,
> rather than to be at the expense of crossing the river
> Susquehannah and afterwards to drag their wagons along a
> road rendered almost impassable by the multitude of carriages
> which use it, and the insufficiency of our road Acts to keep it
> in repair.[85]

Another Philadelphian observed that "immense quantities" of
wheat and flour "are now carried to Baltimore in Maryland" and
"that, not only all the Inhabitants to the westward of Susquehanna,
but also a large tract of the country adjacent, on the east side of said
river, transport their commodities to that growing town."[86]

East of the Susquehanna

With the threat of Indian raids gone, settlers moved up the
Susquehanna and the Juniata, both navigable by flatboats or rafts at
certain seasons of the year. New towns sprang up along the river to
capture their trade for Philadelphia. John and Thomas Simpson
sold lots in their new town "on the eastern side of Susquehana,
about two miles above Mr. Harris's ferry, in the township of
Paxton" on a bitter cold day in February 1765, but advertised a second lottery when the weather was less severe. They claimed their
town was "the most convenient for trade of any yet formed in the
back parts of this province, where the new settlers in Sherman's
Valley, on Juniata, and up Susquehana, may easily repair by
water."[87] John Cox, Jr., a Philadelphia merchant and partner of
Samuel Purviance, Jr. in western land speculation, offered lots in
Estherton, his new town, also in Paxton Township.[88]

Towns in this part of Pennsylvania sprang up along the main
roads leading to Philadelphia. George Fisher, son of a Philadelphia

merchant, sold the first lots "in a certain new Town, called Middletown, in Paxtang" in 1761.[89] According to one Middletown boomer, merchants there traded up the Susquehanna and produce was brought down the river to Middletown "with many thousand bushels of wheat, rye, and Indian corn annually unloaded here."[90] Barnabas Hughes, by this time a Baltimore merchant, made the first deeds for lots in Elizabethtown, the town he laid out around a central diamond and named for his wife, in 1763. Both towns lay on the main road from Harris' Ferry to Lancaster.[91]

Another road from Harris' Ferry swung southeast through Lancaster County to meet the main Philadelphia road. In 1762 Frederick Hummel bought land in Derry Township from John Campbell and laid out Hummelstown athwart this road.[92] A few miles further east John Campbell divided another piece of his "property into lots, for the purpose of erecting a town or village," called Campbellstown.[93] This road continued past Ephrata Cloister to the Blue Ball tavern in Earl Township, where Robert Wallace opened a store in 1762, and on to the distant metropolis.[94] Another road forked off from this road near Hummelstown going northeast through the new town of Lebanon to Reading. George Stites deeded 365 acres "including land platted into Town of Lebanon" to his grandson George Reynolds in 1761 "for the purpose of building a town."[95]

Several town founders had stores or taverns or both as the nucleus for their new town. George Reynolds and his partner John Nicholas Henicke were storekeepers in Lebanon. Philadelphia merchants Henry Keppele, Philip Benezet, Isaac Myer, Owen Jones and Daniel Wister, Moses Heyman, and Marcus Kuhl supplied them with goods and obtained judgments against them when they failed to pay. The debts were levied on "a brick messauge" and other houses and lots in Lebanon Town.[96] Frederick Stump conveyed a lot on Market Street in Fredericksburgh in Bethel Township in May 1761. The buyer agreed to build a sixteen-foot-square house with a good chimney within eighteen months.[97] Matthias Bush and Henry Keppele of Philadelphia each sued him to be paid for store goods.[98] George Newman, another storekeeper and town founder, owed both Jones and Wister and Whitelock and Davies for goods.[99]

The new towns east of the Susquehanna were generally inhabited by Germans, who had recently arrived in Pennsylvania. This was true even in areas with substantial Scotch-Irish rural populations. Travelling from Lancaster to Maytown, Elizabethtown, Middletown and Hummelstown to visit Lutheran congregations in 1769, the Rev. Henry Melchior Muhlenberg commented on each community in almost the same words: "The inhabitants of this town are young newcomers and for the most part poor."[100] The men who laid out these towns were sometimes Germans, but most often of British ancestry. Shopkeepers in these towns and villages were more likely born in Scotland or Ireland.

Shopkeepers and Debtors

The 1760s were not particularly good years for retail traders. Many backcountry shopkeepers were overextended and found themselves unable to meet their obligations. William McCord, a shopkeeper in Lancaster, was bankrupt in 1767. Joseph Swift, Cadwallader Morris, George Fullerton and Isaac Wikoff were his principal creditors.[101] George M'Dowell of Middletown, Lancaster County, shopkeeper, signed over all his effects and debts to John Boyle and John Murray in 1767.[102] The same year William McCullough, storekeeper in Hanover Township, mortgaged his property to Joseph Swift and Caleb Foulke, trustees for themselves and his other creditors, Owen Jones and Daniel Wister, Charles Willing, Alexander Todd, Benjamin Davis, Benjamin Fuller, Samuel Hudson, Robert Lloyd, and Daniel Wister.[103] McCullough evidently recovered since he later advertised land in Lancaster County, including lots in Miller's town [Millersville] in Manor Township, Frederick's Town [Hummelstown] and Jones' town for sale in 1769.[104] James Wilson granted 201 acres in Paxton Township to Matthew Smith, who then conveyed the property in trust to Samuel Purviance Jr and Caleb Foulke, merchants of Philadelphia, who were to sell it for the best price and pay debts owed by Wilson to John and Joseph Swift of Philadelphia, then themselves, Abel James, and the assignees of Wilson's other creditors, Mordecai Yarnel, Jeremiah Warder, Richard Parker and Matthias Bush.[105]

Many backcountry shopkeepers were young men hoping to rise to the status of merchant. One such was Hugh Swan, who came to

Pennsylvania with a stock of linen from north Antrim markets. Like William Pollard who "embarked for Philadelphia with the intent of setting up as an importer of woollen goods from his native West Yorkshire," Swan discovered that connections at home were not enough to offset the advantages London held for established dry goods merchants.[106] Swan's story is told in terms of actions for debt. Isaac Whitelock and Benjamin Davis, merchants of Philadelphia sued Hugh Swan, shopkeeper of Paxton Township, in August 1763 for a debt of £493.17.10 which Swan then paid. At the next session of the court James Simm brought an action against Hugh Swan of Lancaster County, "otherwise called Hugh Swan of Killead Parish, County of Antrim, linen draper," for a small sum. He also settled this debt. In February 1764 the court ordered the sheriff to seize 200 acres in Paxton and 250 acres in neighbouring Hanover Township to settle claims by William Hay for £2000 and by Andrew Elliott for a small sum. Hugh Swan, merchant, was taken into custody in August 1764 at the suit of Philadelphia merchant Jeremiah Warder. He evidently paid all of these creditors. In May 1765 Robert Thompson, John Singleton and Allen Gillespie, John Lindsay, and John Hughes were granted executions levied on Swan's land. He again paid his debts and held onto his real estate.[107] In 1771 Hugh Swan, storekeeper in Hanover Township, and his wife mortgaged his property to William Sitgreaves, a Philadelphia merchant.[108] They returned home at a time when other Ulster families were sailing to Pennsylvania. Hugh Swan joined his relatives in County Antrim, where he had a long career as a respected linen merchant and owner of bleach greens.[109]

Merchants of substance were not immune to the shifting tides of the Atlantic economy. Adam Hoops, now retired to his country estate, deeded much of his property in Cumberland County to his son-in-law Daniel Clark, who promptly transferred title to his creditors, Jeremiah Warder, Abel James, and William West. Clark and his wife evidently needed her father's help to stave off bankruptcy.[110]

A Chain of Retail Shops

Many flaxseed merchants owned lots in the new towns springing up at every crossroads. James Fullton, for instance, invested in houses and lots in Middletown and Shippensburg. The Mitchell brothers were unusual in acquiring property in the new towns as a marketing strategy. Like more modest ventures into the backcountry trade, it also led ultimately to business failure.

One of several regional centres in eastern Pennsylvania, Reading was a market town and the county seat of Berks County. As in the county, German settlers predominated in Reading. Thomas Penn chose the site where a main road crossed the Schuykill River, laid out the town and the sale of lots began in 1749. By the end of 1763 Reading counted 210 families or 1,300 inhabitants. Ten shopkeepers and four wagoners employed hauling goods to and from Philadelphia lived in Reading in 1767. The Mitchells chose the town as the site for one of their first retail outlets in the backcountry. Randle Mitchell, Benjamin Lightfoot, Thomas Dundas and Adam Witman had their shops on Penn Square in the centre of town.[111] Robert Patton was employed to manage the Reading store and given considerable freedom to act on his own. When the store was short of cash, a perennial problem in the back counties, Patton obtained a loan from Carsan, Barclay and Mitchell which he had some difficulty repaying. His surviving correspondence with John Mitchell reflects the high level of consumer preferences that drove retail business as Patton ordered cloth in specific colours, patterns and quality that he believed suitable for Quakers or for Germans.[112] Patton moved on to manage the Baltimore store. His successors bought flaxseed for the Mitchells.[113]

Allentown, originally Northampton Town, was another of the new towns platted in 1762. Only thirteen persons paid taxes in the town the first year and there were just thirty eight names on the 1766 tax list, but they included two shopkeepers. John Reynolds kept the Allentown store for the Mitchells, sending down pork, corn, beeswax and cheese taken in payment for store goods and buying barrel staves.[114] Reynolds was also busy buying flaxseed in season.[115]

Charles Hamilton, whose wife was a sister of Randle and John Mitchell, and his partner William Moore were sons of merchants in

Londonderry. They established a mercantile business in Lancaster in 1771. Hamilton and Moore sent flaxseed to John Mitchell, ordering goods from him.[116] Their store occupied "the premises where John Cameron had his store." They promised "the highest price for Bees Wax, Hemp, Flax Seed, in its season, and country made Linen, and most sorts of Country Produce."[117] Hamilton & Moore dissolved their partnership in 1774 and William Moore moved to Reading.[118] Hamilton asked Mitchell,

> to Ship in the first Vessell that Sails to LondonDerry 2Hhds. Flaxseed for Charles Hamilton in Broadpath Consigned to William Moore Merchant Londonderry which Charge to William Moore of Reading who will Remit you the Cash Immediately, he Sends my Father the Two Hhds Seed in Consequence of a present of £33 Interest I made him in our Settlement when we dissolved our Partnership."[119]

Hamilton was assiduous in finding new customers for Mitchell, not always with the best results. Hamilton recommended Michael Montgomery, "a person that lives & keeps Store in Maytown & tavern which is about 14 Miles from this place," and wanted Mitchell to send him goods on credit for which he would remit in flour.[120] Montgomery wrote to Mitchell and sent his own brother with his wagon to Philadelphia for a selection of goods suitable for a store, since "Your Brother Mr. Hamilton Mercht. In Lanchaster promised that I should Get as good treatment as he gets."[121] Unfortunately, with the assortment of store goods in hand, Montgomery took off for Shamokin on the upper Susquehanna and Mitchell and Hamilton had great difficulty reclaiming their property.[122]

Their partner in Middletown caused them no less grief. Randle and John Mitchell drew up an agreement with John Williams, "to furnish a Store to be kept by said Williams at Middletown aforesaid with all kinds of Goods and Merchandises that might Be necessary for the same." Williams would have "for his Trouble and Attendance on said Store One third part of the Issues and profits arising from the sale of all such goods as he should dispose of on account of said Partnership." After several years Williams was in debt to the Mitchells for a considerable sum and conveyed his house and lot in Middletown and all claims on the business to them.[123] With little incentive left to be loyal to his employers, Williams removed the store goods and prepared to leave for the frontier settlement on the Holston River in Virginia. Charles Hamilton reported:

> Williams is this Morning Lodged safe in Our Gaol, the sheriff took him Friday last in Middletown and he pretended he had no objection to come with the Sheriff but in the night made his escape leaving his Pocket Book and every Stick of his Cloaths that he had taken off when he went to bed & got himself dressed in others. the Sheriff then Advertised a Reward and Raised a party & after a long pursuit Retook him in Cumberland County. he had sent his Chest three days before he was taken toward Holstens River Virginia by one of his Associates and had got his Horse Ruff Shod & every thing packed up to follow the next day after he was first taken.[124]

Such were the perils of doing business in the backcountry. Randle Mitchell had returned to Belfast in 1770 with the flaxseed ships, leaving his friend Hugh Donaldson to conduct his business.[125] He came back to Philadelphia, determined to retire from trade. Mitchell offered to sell the Reading store to his competitor Thomas Dundas.[126] He offered his stock in goods at prime cost to merchants and shopkeepers and sold off the Middletown, Caernarvon and Reading stores.[127] But John Mitchell was apparently still convinced that opening new retail stores to absorb more and more British goods was the way to wealth. Benjamin Fuller recorded the denouement.

> I make no doubt that you will have heard that our friend Jack Mitchell has been obliged to stop, it was an act of his own before his affairs should become desperate, and deserves its merit. He very imprudently greatly over imported himself, in proportion to his original capital; however from the present appearance of his affairs, there will be a sufficiency to pay all his debts, but it will take time to bring them into a narrow compass.[128]

Notes

1   Waddell Cunningham to David Gaussan, June 17, 1756, Truxes, *Letterbook of Greg and Cunningham*, 155.

2   Imports reflected the previous year's harvest. Truxes, *Irish-American Trade*, 284.

3   *Pennsylvania Gazette*, July 31, 1755. On the impact of these frontier raids on backcountry society, see Matthew C. Ward, *Breaking the Backcountry: The Seven Years' War in Virginia and Pennsylvania, 1754–1765* (Pittsburgh, PA, 2003), 64–8, 71–3.

4   *Pennsylvania Gazette*, August 19, 1756. Adam Hoops to Robert Hunter Morris, September 6, 1756, in *Colonial Records*, VII, 242.

5   William Buchanan wrote from Carlisle with news of Braddock's defeat. "It is now reduced to a certainty that our Army are defeated, the General & Sir John are dangerously wounded, about the number of one thousand men lost with the train of Artillery & baggage. The remain[in]g part of the Army have destroy'd all their baggage except two Six pounders which was in Dunbar's Regiment and Provisions necessary for their retreat to Wills' Creek where I expect they are by this time." William Buchanan to William Franklin, July 21, 1755 (HSP).

6   John Richard Alden, *General Gage in America* (Baton Rouge, LA, 1948), 24–6. Governor Morris was outraged at the idea that "all that extensive and Rich Country which lies West of the Sasquehannah be abandoned and laid waste." Robert L. D. Davidson, *War Comes to Quaker Pennsylvania 1682–1756* (New York, 1957), 150–51. Francis Jennings, *Empire of Fortune: Crowns, colonies, and tribes in the Seven Years War in America* (New York, 1988), 159.

7   Priscilla H. Roberts and James N. Tull, *Adam Hoops, Thomas Barclay, and the House in Morrisville Known as Summerseat, 1764–1791, Transactions of the American Philosophical Society Held at Philadelphia for Promoting Useful Knowledge, Volume 90, Pt. 5* (Philadelphia, 2000), 11.

8   James Logan to James Anderson and Andrew Galbraith, March 2, 1730 (Logan Letterbooks, III, 170, HSP).

9   Edmund Burke, *An Account of the European Settlements in America* (London, 1760), II, 216.

10   Minutes of the Corporation for the Relief of Poor and Distressed Presbyterian Ministers, 1759, in Maurice W. Armstrong, Lefferts A. Loetscher, and Charles A. Anderson, eds., *The Presbyterian Enterprise: Sources of American Presbyterian History* (Philadelphia, 1956), 71.

11   Grubb denied that he said anything of the sort. *Pennsylvania Gazette*, June 10, 1756.

12   William M. Swaim, "The Evolution of Ten Pre-1745 Presbyterian Societies in the Cumberland Valley," *Cumberland County History*, 2(1985), 3–30.

13   Jerome Wood, Jr., *Conestoga Crossroads: Lancaster, Pennsylvania 1730–1790* (Harrisburg, PA, 1979), 93, 103–08.

14   Paul Erb Doutrich, "The Evolution of an Early American Town: Yorktown, Pennsylvania 1740–1790," Ph.D. dissertation, University of Kentucky (1985), 17–18.

15   Judith Anne Ridner, "A Handsomely Improved Place: Economic, Social, and

Gender Role Development in a Backcountry Town, Carlisle, Pennsylvania, 1750–1815," Ph.D. dissertation, College of William and Mary (1994), 26–7.

16   Indian trade was seen as the lifeblood of the new town. Governor James Hamilton wrote in 1752 that the trading partnership of George Croghan and William Trent "drew a great deal of trade to that part of the country, and made money circulate briskly," but their unexpected bankruptcy "will, I fear, retard the progress of the town." Hamilton to Thomas Penn, June 19, 1752 (Penn MSS, Official Correspondence, V, 183, HSP, as quoted in Nicholas B. Wainwright, *George Croghan Wilderness Diplomat* (Chapel Hill, NC, 1959), 45).

17   James T. Lemon, *The Best Poor Man's Country: A Geographical Study of Early Southeastern Pennsylvania* (Baltimore, 1971), 104.

18   Ridner, "A Handsomely Improved Place," 92.

19   *Pennsylvania Gazette*, February 11, 1752.

20   Cumberland Deeds, A–30 (CCCH). Buchanan's tavern was located on Lot 109. In January 1760, William Buchanan of Carlisle, gentleman, and his wife Esther conveyed this property to James Pollock of Carlisle, tavernkeeper, for the substantial sum of £1200 Pennsylvania currency, since the Buchanans were about to move to Baltimore. Merri Lou Scribner Schaumann, *A History and Genealogy of Carlisle, Cumberland County, Pennsylvania, 1751–1835* (Carlisle, PA, 1995), 55.

21   Robert Callender and Michael Taaffe to William Buchanan, September 2, 1753, in *Colonial Records*, V, 684.

22   Albert T. Volwiler, *George Croghan and the Westward Movement 1741–1782* (Cleveland, OH, 1926), 92–4.

23   Ridner, "A Handsomely Improved Place ," 91.

24   William A. Hunter, *Forts on the Pennsylvania Frontier 1753–1758* (Harrisburg, PA, 1960), 171.

25   Hunter, *Forts on the Pennsylvania Frontier*, 177. See also, Jane T. Merritt, *At the Crossroads: Indians and Empires on a Mid-Atlantic Frontier 1700–1763* (Chapel Hill, NC, 2003), 176–81. Armstrong was from County Fermanagh.

26   Hunter, *Forts on the Pennsylvania Frontier*, 200–02, 441, 447. Adam Hoops, first resided in present Franklin County, PA., later moving to Carlisle.

27   Stephen Duncan, Thomas Donnellan, William Spear, and Francis West, merchants, and Andrew Grier, John Montgomery, and Elizabeth Ross, shopkeepers. Tax List in Schaumann, *History*, 173–4.

28   Lyon's business records from 1759 are in the Cumberland County Historical Society, Carlisle, PA.

29   Roberts and Tull, *Adam Hoops*, 11–15.

30   Numerous letters from and to Hoops are in the Henry Bouquet Papers. His birthplace is unknown, but his Ulster associations suggest he was born in Ireland. Roberts and Tull, *Adam Hoops*, 3–4.

31   Barnabas (Barney) Hughes, who was also an army contractor, kept "The Sign of the Bear in Donegal" at Elizabethtown, a town he laid out in 1763. Sylvester K. Stevens, ed., *The Papers of Henry Bouquet* (Harrisburg, PA, 1951), II, 31–2.

32   Alfred P. James, ed., *Writings of General John Forbes Relating to his Service in North America* (Menasha, WI, 1938), 97–111, 178.

33   James, *Writings of General John Forbes*, 262.

34   Donald H. Kent, ed., *The Papers of Henry Bouquet* (Harrisburg, PA, 1976), III, 112–13, 289–91, 293–5, 429.

35   *Pennsylvania Gazette*, February 19, 1761.

36   This is one of the themes developed in David Hancock, *Citizens of the World: London Merchants and the Integration of the British Atlantic Community 1735–1785* (Cambridge and New York, 1995), 224–7.

37   Roberts and Tull, *Adam Hoops*, 17–22. Daniel Clark Letterbook, 1759–61 (HSP).

38   *Pennsylvania Gazette*, October 22, 1761. *Pennsylvania Journal*, November 15, 1763, June 14, 1764. Hoops also owned the snow *Elizabeth* in partnership with William Hodge of Philadelphia and Thomas Montgomery of Delaware. "Ship Registers," *PMHB*, 27(1903), 98, 353.

39   Roberts and Tull, *Adam Hoops*, 28.

40   Harris to Buchanan and Hughes, June 21, 1762, as quoted in Wainwright, *Croghan*, 190–91.

41   "An Account of Losses sustained by William Buchanan, Barnabas Hughes & Thomas Smallman in Sundry Adventures of Trade to the Indian Countries by Indian Hostilities in the Year 1763" (AM–2229, HSP).

42   On Carlisle's role in the fur trade in the 1760s, see also Judith Ridner, "Relying on the 'Saucy' Men of the Backcountry: Middlemen and the Fur Trade in Pennsylvania," *PMHB*, 129(2005), 133–62.

43   Daniel Clark to William Neale, December 20, 1759, August 27, 1760, to Daniel Mildred, November 15, 1760, November 29, 1760 (Daniel Clark Letterbook, 1–9, 12, 27, 30, HSP).

44   Cumberland County Deeds, B–45, C–304 (CCCH). "Smith Family Genealogy" (1729/179, Special Collections, Alderman Library, University of Virginia, Charlottesville).

45   [John Montgomery], "Leger 3 1765–71" (Joseph Kent Collection, MS 092–31, Virginia Polytechnic Institute and University, Blacksburg). On the Grammar School, Merri Lou Scribner Schaumann, *History and Genealogy of Carlisle, Cumberland County, Pennsylvania* (Dover, PA, 1987), 213.

46   "Minutes of the Corporation for the Relief of Poor and Distressed Presbyterian Ministers," 37–41, PHS. *Colonial Records*, VIII, 723ff. Guy S. Klett, ed., *Journals of Charles Beatty 1762–1769* (University Park, PA, 1962), 32–3. Ward, *Breaking the Backcountry*, 214–6.

47   Howard H. Peckham, *Pontiac and the Indian Uprising* (Princeton, NJ, 1947), 37ff. Niles Anderson, *The Battle of Bushy Run* (Harrisburg, PA, 1966), 5–6.

48   George Croghan estimated 2,000 killed or captured by Indians and thousands "drove to beggary." Wainwright, *Croghan*, 199. Volwiler, *George Croghan*, 265–6.

49   *Belfast News Letter*, May 25, 1764.

50   Ledger A (1761–65), November 26, 1761, November 19, 1763. Day Book (1763–66), November 11, 1763, April 1, 1765 and *passim* (James Fullton Papers, HSYC).

51 Fullton's business career is sketched in Richard K. MacMaster, "James Fullton, A Philadelphia Merchant and His Customers," *Familia* 17(2001), 23–34.

52 Invoices, William McCord to Whitelock and Davies, November 27, 1763, William McCord to Isaac Wikoff, November 28, 1763. Account, Mr. Jas. Dowdall to Wm McCord Dr. Dec. 17, 1764–Sep. 4, 1766. Invoice Book, 9. Ledger, 6, 32 (William McCord Papers, MG–2, Pennsylvania State Archives).

53 Samuel Carsan, his nephew Thomas Barclay, and William Mitchell comprised this firm. Samuel Bethel was a storekeeper at present Columbia, PA. John Cameron Ledger 1767–70, 108–09, 198 (Wistar Papers, HSP).

54 Cameron Ledger, 47, 110, 202, 208 (Wistar Papers, HSP).

55 White and Caldwell to Peter Grubb, July 22, 1767, October 7, 1767, June 2, 1768; John Cameron to Peter Grubb, July 29, 1767, July 22, 1768 (Grubb Papers, HSP).

56 Cameron Ledger, 111 (Wistar Papers, HSP).

57 Cameron Ledger, 138 (Wistar Papers, HSP).

58 *Pennsylvania Chronicle*, January 29, 1770. Edward Shippen to James Hamilton, August 21, 1770, Shippen Letterbook, American Philosophical Society, as quoted in Wood, *Conestoga Crossroads*, 100.

59 Lancaster County Fieri Facias, May 1763, November 1763, February 1764 (LCHS).

60 Lancaster County Fieri Facias, August 1763, August 1764 (LCHS).

61 Lancaster Deeds, M–142, M–144 (LCCH).

62 Ledger A (1761–65), January 3, 1765, February 27, 1765. (James Fullton Papers. HSYC). James Fullton to John Fullton and Ephraim Campbell, December 19, 1766, June 30, 1767 (James Fullton Letterbook (typescript), LCHS).

63 Bond, James Fullton and Robert Fulton to John Ross, November 27, 1764. James Fullton to William McCord, February 12, 1765 (Stauffer Collection, 27/2152, 21/1616, HSP).

64 Lemon, *Best Poor Man's Country*, 27.

65 Daniel Clark to John Clark, March 15, 1761 (Clark Letterbook, 54, HSP).

66 Numerous letters in John Mitchell's correspondence from Charles Hamilton, Hamilton & Moore, and George Erwin. On the family connection, Charles Hamilton to John Mitchell, June 1, 1774 (Mitchell Papers, MG92, PSA).

67 *Pennsylvania Gazette*, April 27, 1769, August 16, 1770.

68 Doerflinger, *A Vigorous Spirit*, 76.

69 A. G. Seyfert, "The Wallace Family and the Wallace Store of East Earl," *Journal of the Lancaster County Historical Society*, 28(1924), 20–29.

70 Lemon, *Best Poor Man's Country*, 29, 143.

71 Lemon, *Best Poor Man's Country*, 133–4.

72 *History of Cumberland County, Pennsylvania* (Chicago, 1886), 257–61. James Fullton to Robert Magaw, September 10, 1766 (James Fullton Letterbook (typescript), LCHS).

73 *Pennsylvania Gazette*, July 19, 1764. I. H. McCauley, *Historical Sketch of Franklin County* (Chambersburg, 1878), 9, 22.

74 John Gibson, ed., *History of York County, Pennsylvania* (Chicago, 1886), 574–5, 592.

75   On storekeeper-tavern keepers, see Diane Wenger, "Delivering the Goods: The
      Country Storekeeper and Inland Commerce in the Mid-Atlantic,"
      Pennsylvania Magazine of History and Biography, 129 (2005), 60. Daniel
      Thorp found tavern keeping and storekeeping was the practice in rural
      North Carolina, but less common in urban areas where the larger
      population allowed people to specialize. Daniel B. Thorp, "Doing Business
      in the Backcountry: Retail Trade in Colonial Rowan County, North
      Carolina," *William and Mary Quarterly*, 3rd ser., 48(1991), 391.

76   John Gibson, ed., *History of York County, Pennsylvania* (Chicago, 1886), 574.

77   *Pennsylvania Journal*, October 15, 1767.

78   McAllister kept his store accounts from 1773 to 1781 in a ledger that already
      was stamped "Paul Zantzinger, Lancaster." The first 69 pages are missing. It
      was understandably accessioned as Paul Zantzinger Ledger, MG–2,
      PSA. McAllister's Store Book, 1781–5, and Rent Roll, 1782, are in
      McAllister Papers, MG–81, PSA.

79   "Paul Zantzinger" Ledger, 248, 375, 400, 408, 446, 464, 493 (MG–2, PSA).

80   Cumberland County Deeds, B–72, B–146, B–208, B–211, B–245, C–113,
      C–302, C–327, C–333, C–363, C–437, C–450, D–402 (Cumberland
      County Court House, Carlisle, PA).

81   Richard K. MacMaster, "Scotch-Irish Merchants and the Rise of Baltimore:
      Identity and Community, 1755–1775," *Journal of Scotch-Irish Studies*
      1(Summer 2001), 19–32.

82   James Weston Livingood, *The Philadelphia-Baltimore Trade Rivalry 1780–1860*
      (Harrisburg, PA, 1947), 4–6.

83   Cumberland County Deeds, C–399, C–436 (CCCH).

84   The idea of a symbiotic relationship was proposed by Jo Hays for the
      nineteenth century, but it seems valid for the eighteenth as well. Cf. Jo N.
      Hays, "Overlapping Hinterlands: York, Philadelphia, and Baltimore
      1800–1850," *Pennsylvania Magazine of History and Biography*, 116 (1992),
      295–321.

85   A Friend of Trade, "An Address to the Merchants and Inhabitants of
      Pennsylvania," Library of Congress, Pennsylvania Broadsides, fol. 143, as
      quoted in Livingood, *Philadelphia-Baltimore Trade Rivalry*, 6.

86   "Philo-Pennsylvaniensis," *Pennsylvania Chronicle*, February 17, 1772.

87   *Pennsylvania Journal*, February 14, 1765, March 7, 1765, July 25, 1765.

88   *Pennsylvania Journal*, March 21, 1765, June 6, 1765.

89   Lancaster County Deeds, N–1–59, O–1–445 (LCCH).

90   *Pennsylvania Gazette*, March 8, 1775.

91   Lancaster County Deeds, O–1–368, O–1–370 (LCCH).

92   Lancaster County Deeds, X–1–42 (LCCH).

93   Lancaster County Deeds, R–1–568, S–1–519, Q–1–462 (LCCH).

94   Records of the Wallace store from 1762 are Accession 1004, Hagley Museum
      and Library, Wilmington, Delaware. A. G. Seyfert, "The Wallace Family and
      the Wallace Store of East Earl," *Journal of the Lancaster County Historical
      Society*, 28(1924), 20–29.

95   Lancaster County Deeds, G–1–95 (LCCH).

96   Lancaster County Fieri Facias, May 1762, August 1762, February 1763, May
      1763, November 1763 (LCHS).

97   Lancaster Deeds, H–295, R–495 (LCCH).

98   Lancaster County Fieri Facias, May 1762, November 1762 (LCHS).

99   Lancaster County Fieri Facias, May 1762, August 1762 (LCHS).

100   Theodore G. Tappert and John W. Doberstein, eds., *The Journals of Henry Melchior Muhlenberg* (Philadelphia, 1944), II, 389–90.

101   *Pennsylvania Journal*, April 23, 1767, June 11, 1767.

102   *Pennsylvania Journal*, September 3, 1767.

103   Lancaster Deeds, M–194, M–216 (LCCH).

104   *Pennsylvania Gazette*, July 27, 1769.

105   Lancaster Deeds, P–11 (LCCH).

106   Smail, *Merchants, Markets and Manufacture*, 1–2.

107   Merchant John Hughes was the Stamp Act collector. Lancaster County Fieri Facias, August 1763, November 1763, February 1764, August 1764, May 1765 (LCHS).

108   Lancaster Deeds, O–545 (LCCH).

109   *Belfast News Letter*, May 24, 1774, April 11, 1775.

110   Cumberland Deeds, 1–K–28, 1–K–30 (CCCH).

111   Laura L. Becker, "The American Revolution as a Community Experience: A Case Study of Reading, Pennsylvania," Ph.D. dissertation, University of Pennsylvania (1978), 18–26, 185.

112   Robert Patton to John Mitchell, January 8, 1772, June 1, 1772 (John Mitchell Papers. MG 92, PSA).

113   Murray and Conolly to John Mitchell, November 21, 1772, November 22, 1772 (Mitchell Papers).

114   John Reynolds to John Mitchell, January 17, 1772, June 19, 1772, November 6, 1772 (Mitchell Papers). Charles Rhoads Roberts, *History of Lehigh County, Pennsylvania* (Allentown, PA, 1914), I, 388–92.

115   John Reynolds to John Mitchell, October 23, 1772, November 13, 1772, November 18, 1772, November 20, 1772, December 4, 1772, December 15, 1772 (Mitchell Papers).

116   Hamilton & Moore to John Mitchell, December 30, 1771 (Mitchell Papers).

117   *Pennsylvania Journal*, December 22, 1773.

118   *Pennsylvania Gazette*, February 2, 1774.

119   Charles Hamilton to John Mitchell, December 9, 1774 (Mitchell Papers).

120   Charles Hamilton to John Mitchell, November 20, 1774 (Mitchell Papers).

121   Michael Montgomery to John Mitchell, November 10, 1774 (Mitchell Papers).

122   Charles Hamilton to John Mitchell, May 29, 1774 (Mitchell Papers).

123   Lancaster Deeds, N–1–644 (LCCH).

124   Charles Hamilton to John Mitchell, January 8, 1775 (Mitchell Papers).

125   *Pennsylvania Gazette*, August 16, 1770, October 18, 1770, December 27, 1770, April 18, 1771.

126   Thomas Dundas to John Mitchell, August 23, 1772 (Mitchell Papers).

127   *Pennsylvania Gazette*, September 22, 1773, October 6, 1773, November 10, 1773, January 5, 1774.

128   Benjamin Fuller to Anthony Stocker, November 15, 1773 (Benjamin Fuller Letterbook, I, 32–33, HSP).

6

From Ulster to the Carolinas

THE SOUTHERN COLONIES WERE OUTSIDE the region where flaxseed was a cash crop, so Irish merchants were rare birds south of Baltimore.[1] But three enterprising Ulstermen found a way to carry passengers to Charleston and Savannah and then pick up a cargo of flaxseed in Philadelphia or New York and to do so at a profit. John Torrans, John Poaug, and John Greg lobbied energetically for a bounty that would encourage Protestant settlers to come to South Carolina, petitioned successfully for land grants to accommodate them, and, with business associates in Ulster, arranged shipping to bring them to Charleston. They were largely responsible for beginning emigration from Ulster to South Carolina and for directing the flow to specific settlements in the Carolina backcountry.

In 1761 the South Carolina Assembly offered to pay four pounds sterling for the passage of each poor Protestant brought to the colony.[2] The bill, passed without opposition, was far from altruistic. Low country planters, already nervous about slave insurrection in a colony where enslaved Africans were in the majority, wanted a barrier between themselves and the Creeks and Cherokee and accepted sweeping changes in South Carolina's settlement policy without demur. "Thus the Commons abandoned its traditional opposition to immigrants unable to pay their passage, and sought to guard against the dumping of undesirables by demanding certificates of good character." The law ran for three years and proved so successful, that, after a brief lapse, it was renewed for another three years in January 1765.[3] Charleston merchants John Torrans and John Poaug used their influence to get this measure adopted and were eager to take advantage of the bounty. Immediately after the act passed, Poaug applied for a certificate of the bounty that he might transmit to Ireland.[4] Their third partner, John Greg, returned to Ireland to set the plan in motion. He arranged to bring out settlers from Belfast, where they had a network of business associates, while the three partners petitioned for land, not for themselves, but for the settlers they would bring to South Carolina. In their petitions to the governor of South Carolina, Torrans, Greg, and Poaug were joined by the Rev. John Baxter, John and David Rea and James Maghlin. Baxter came to the colony from Ulster in 1737 and served Presbyterian congregations in Charleston and later in Williamsburg.[5] John Rea of Rea's Hall, near Savannah, was an important man in the Indian trade, a partner of George Galphin and Lachlan McGillivary. He was later active in bringing emigrants from Ulster to Georgia.[6]

In June 1762 the *South Carolina Gazette* reported: "We hear that application has been made to his Excellency our Governor, by petition, for two townships, of 20,000 acres each, to be surveyed and reserved for a number of poor Protestants the petitioners engaged to bring over."[7] The petitioners were even allowed to select the sites for the land grants. In December 1762 two townships were laid out: Boonesborough of 20,500 acres at the head of Long Canes Creek and Londonborough of 22,000 acres on Hard Labor Creek. Their settlers were already on the high seas by that time.

In February 1763 about 70 persons arrived from Belfast and settled in Boonesborough.[8] They came on the brigantine *Success*, Thomas Morrison commander. The *Success*, a brigantine of 85 tons, built at Philadelphia in 1760, was registered there in 1761 by her owners, William Caldwell of Londonderry and Samuel Carsan of Philadelphia.[9] John Greg had returned to Belfast in 1762 and advertised for both passengers and servants to sail for Charleston on the *Success*. She was delayed by adverse winds on her anticipated sailing date, but the captain hoped to put to sea early in November.[10] The ship's troubles were not over. She arrived safely at Charleston in February 1763, after having been captured by a French privateer "and ransomed for 500 pounds Sterling".[11]

Within less than a week of their arrival, "in order that no time might be lost in settling those persons in either of the two new Townships lately laid out for Foreign Protestants," the Governor

and Council heard and granted the petitions for land and the bounty by 41 adult passengers on the *Success*. They received between 100
and 300 acres each, located at Long Cane in Boonesborough
Township.[12] The settlers from the *Success* moved out to their own
lands, with farm implements and seed provided by South Carolina,
and Torrans and Poaug collected the bounty. The newcomers were
apparently well satisfied, until the following winter when they
realised they were on an exposed frontier amid rumours of an
Indian war.

Settlements on Long Cane were devastated during the Cherokee
War in 1760 with many killed.[13] Nearly four years later, a party of
Creek Indians fell on the Long Cane settlement on December 24,
1763 killing fourteen settlers. Two days later a number of these settlers with four wagons arrived at Hard Labour, "where they resolved
to remain till they heard what was to be done concerning the murders committed by the Creek Indians."[14] The *South Carolina
Gazette* reported that:

> The Irish settlers, who arrived here last year, and are seated
> between Ninety-Six and Long-Canes, having complained,
> that they were in a most distressful situation, deserted by most
> of the neighbouring older settlers, and equally destitute of
> arms and ammunition to defend themselves in case they
> should be attacked, as of conveniences to remove their fami-
> lies to places of greater security, a supply of arms and ammu-
> nition has been sent them.[15]

Scotch-Irish Settlers in the Carolinas

The rapid settlement of the Carolina frontier caused friction with
the native inhabitants. In little more than ten years Pennsylvanians
and Virginians, mainly Scotch-Irish, had occupied the North
Carolina piedmont and upper South Carolina. In 1763 alone it was
reported "A great number of settlers from the northward, have
come by land into the western parts of this province [South
Carolina] during several months past."[16] The same year Benjamin
Franklin estimated that 40,000 persons had moved from
Pennsylvania to the Carolinas in the past few years.[17] Scotch-Irish
settlers had pushed the frontier along the eastern slope of the

Allegheny Mountains, moving up the Shenandoah Valley and the South Branch of the Potomac as far as the upper reaches of the Holston and New rivers in southwestern Virginia and southeast into the North Carolina piedmont. In 1759 a petition from Protestant Dissenters in Rowan County, "an Infant Settlement on ye Back frontiers of the Province of North Carolina," to Earl Granville was signed by 820 heads of families, "Mostly originally from the North of Ireland trained brought up under Presbyterian Church Government & we & our forefathers have mostly resided sometime in ye Northern Province of Pennsylvania Jersey & New York."[18]

The North Carolina settlements spilled over into South Carolina. In the 1750s settlers from the northward took up lands along the Catawba and upper reaches of the Wateree rivers in upper South Carolina, in the Waxhaws and Cane Creek.[19] Germans pushed on to the forks of the Broad and Saluda rivers, while families from Ulster chose lands further west around Fort Ninety Six.[20] This movement from older settlements in the Middle Colonies to North and South Carolina continued and gradually peopled the back-country. Despite the efforts of North Carolina Governor Arthur Dobbs in 1753–5 to arrange shipping from Belfast and Larne for prospective settlers, few of these emigrants from Ulster came direct from Ireland before Torrans, Greg and Poaug began promoting emigration to South Carolina.[21]

Torrans, Greg and Poaug

According to his tombstone in the graveyard of the Circular Congregational Church in Charleston, John Torrans Esq. "was born in the County of Derry in the north of Ireland" in 1702. He called his farm in St. Andrew's Parish "Derry," but nothing more is known of his birthplace or family background or, indeed, of his life before he came to America.[22] Torrans came to New York as a flax buyer for Londonderry firms and was soon established as a promi-nent merchant there. He was closely associated with another New York firm in the flaxseed trade, the partnership of Waddell Cunningham and Thomas Greg of Belfast. One of that new firm's first letters to a London correspondent was a ringing endorsement of "our Friend Torrans who we hope you'l continue your favours to and dare say you'l find him more and more deserving of them." His friendship with Greg and Cunningham survived Torrans' move to Charleston and proved important for both.[23] Torrans owned the snow *Prince of Wales* with his fellow Derryman George Folliot and Waddell Cunningham from 1754.[24] He and Waddell Cunningham of New York were registered as owners of a privateer, the schooner *Elisabeth* of Charleston in 1759.[25] Torrans had an interest in privateers outfitted in New York to capture enemy shipping during the French and Indian War. He left New York for South Carolina in March 1758. Henry and John Cruger, Beverly Robinson, Henry Holland, and William Kelly, "owners with John Torrans of the privateer Brigg Hawke," gave a power of attorney to "John Torrans one of the owners of said Brigg who is now Bound to Charlestown in South Carolina" to handle the ship's affairs for them, including the potentially lucrative sale of prize ships and their cargoes.[26] Mr. John Torrans, Merchant in Charles-Town, was also owner/agent for "the Private Ship of War Oliver Cromwell, Commanded by John Nicoll," a Charleston privateer.[27]

In March 1761 Torrans announced the formation of Torrans, Greg and Poaug.[28] His new partners were John Greg, Jr., and John Poaug. John Greg was the older brother of Thomas Greg of Greg and Cunningham. He was born in 1716, son of a Scottish merchant who settled in Belfast only the year before. John Greg did not stay long in South Carolina, returning home to manage their European business. He left the firm at the end of 1764, when he moved to the West Indian island of Dominica, with a government appointment as Commissioner for the Sale of Land and became a sugar planter.[29] John Poaug was also from Belfast, but possibly of Scottish birth. His brother Charles Poaug married a Belfast merchant's daughter and commanded ships in the flaxseed and emigrant trade. On New Year's Day 1763 John Poaug married Charlotte Wragg, one of the daughters of a prominent South Carolina planter and officeholder. His wife was related to the Duboses and Manigaults and other prominent Charleston mercantile families.[30]

The new partnership imported flour from Philadelphia and kept a wide range of store goods in stock. They advertised "Choice old

Teneriffe Wine, bottled Claret, Jamaica, Barbados, and Northward Rum, ship Bread, double Beer, London Porter, a small quantity of Iron, pimento, flour, and muscavado Sugar, to be sold reasonably by Torrans, Greg and Poaug." They also sold hyson and bohea tea and "India Muslins, strip'd, sprig'd, and plain".[31] The firm freighted ships "For Liverpool, Bristol, or Cowes and a Market," for Philadelphia, for Havana, and for Jamaica.[32] Like other Charleston merchants, Torrans, Greg and Poaug were also briefly involved in the slave trade. John Greg in London handled both the European and African side of the business. They brought a shipload of Fantee slaves from the Gold Coast in August 1764 and advertised "about Seventy very healthy New Negroes, picked out of sundry Cargoes at the Havana," in October.[33] In other words, Torrans, Greg and Poaug carried on the same business ventures as their competitors, shipping rice, indigo, and deerskins, operating a general store, importing the goods they sold, and finding cargoes to fill their correspondents' ships. But they were not an ordinary firm.

Importing Foreign Protestants 1763–64

Their first venture obviously profitable, Torrans, Greg and Poaug moved on to new efforts. John Greg left Belfast for London, where he arranged for the transit of French Protestant refugees from the region of Bordeaux to South Carolina.[34] His brother Thomas Greg of Greg and Cunningham managed the Ulster end of their business. In the summer of 1763 Thomas Greg advertised for passengers and servants for South Carolina on the ship *Falls* of Belfast, normally a flaxseed ship, scheduled to sail in October. Passengers may have been slow to sign on because late in October Greg added agents in Downpatrick, Dromore, Lisburn, and Antrim authorised to book passages on the *Falls*.[35] The ship *Prince of Wales*, owned by Mussenden, Bateson and Company of Belfast, was also advertised for Charleston that summer and consigned to Torrans, Greg and Poaug. The only agent was William Beatty of Belfast, making his debut in the emigration business.[36]

John Rea of Rea's Hall was one of the petitioners for South Carolina lands for poor Protestants. In 1765 Rea launched his own scheme to bring Ulster settlers to the Georgia backcountry, a plan closely modelled on that of Torrans, Greg and Poaug, but in 1763 he was looking for ways to profit from the South Carolina scheme. His brother Matthew Rea of Drumbo advertised for servants to go out to his brother on either the *Falls* or the *Prince of Wales*.[37] It may not be immediately clear why anyone would agree to go as a servant, when his passage to South Carolina would be free in any case. Emigrants without resources believed they could amass enough capital working for a few years under an indenture to be able to take advantage of the promise of free land in South Carolina. This had been the experience of some indentured servants in Pennsylvania. When the *Falls* arrived at Charleston on January 8, 1764 several passengers looked for this kind of employment, which would also be advantageous for planters:

> Sunday last arrived here the ship Falls, Captain Henry, in eight weeks from Belfast, with about 90 passengers, natives of the north of Ireland, who are for the present lodged in the new barracks. Several of them are able young men, and ready to enter into the service of any gentlemen who are obliged by law to have one white person to every ten slaves on their plantations; the due observation of which law, we are told, is intended to be enforced, very soon, by upwards of fifty informations.[38]

The previous day the South Carolina Council received petitions from 86 persons who had come on the *Falls* and granted their requests for the bounty and land rights. Of the *Falls* passengers 60 presented evidence they had paid their passage and personally collected the bounty; 53 of the passengers shared seven surnames, suggesting they were members of extended families. The final group of 26 petitioners had not paid their passage and the bounty went to Torrans, Greg and Poaug. Nineteen of them shared the same surnames as the majority of paying passengers. Having a son or daughter in service was not uncommon at home and in America. The Council agreed that the acting commissary "should endeavour to get Masters for as many of those people as should want them and do everything in his power to prevent their being cheated or imposed upon." The others received land as promised.[39]

The *Prince of Wales* also arrived safely in January 1764 with 170 passengers.[40] One hundred and five passengers on the *Prince of Wales* paid their own passages and received both land warrants and bounty money. Another 47 passengers received land warrants, but their bounty was paid to James Egger, master of the *Prince of Wales*, presumably for the owners, Mussenden, Bateson and Company.[41] Both the *Prince of Wales* and the *Falls* sailed in March for Cowes laden with rice for the Dutch market by Torrans, Greg and Poaug.[42]

That Spring Torrans and Poaug were busy with the French Protestants sent by John Greg. "On Thursday last arrived here from Plymouth, in the ship Friendship, 131 French Protestants, from the country about Bourdeaux and Montpelior." Torrans and Poaug collected the bounty from the South Carolina treasury, paid freight, and furnished provisions and accommodations until the newcomers were established in their new home. John Greg presented his account with Torrans and Poaug to the Commissioners of Trade and Plantations in London in July 1764.[43] Henry Laurens reported in October that "The French Refugees are highly pleased with their New settlement & the Irish are satisfied & I am in hopes of seeing in a few Years a fine Colony rising upon the Spots where they are fixed."[44]

The bounty system appeared to be working well for both South Carolina and the transatlantic partnerships involved in transporting foreign Protestants as settlers. Torrans Greg and Poaug had arranged for 410 newcomers from Ulster to take up land in the South Carolina backcountry and, after a propitious start, continued their scheme to bring Ulster emigrants to South Carolina.

Bound for Charles Town

Emigrants from Ulster to South Carolina had to formally petition the Governor's Council and present documentation that they were Protestants and of good reputation at home in order to qualify for the cash bounty and a grant of land. It is moving to stand in the small chamber where the Council met and imagine these newly-arrived settlers, hat in hand, waiting for the clerk to record their names, but in most cases Torrans and Poaug would have drawn up the essential documents and presented them, leaving nothing to chance since they would collect the bounty themselves. The certificates, signed by the the Presbyterian minister and his elders or the Church of Ireland rector and the church wardens, were returned to the newcomers to be kept in the family Bible or a notebook and eventually lost. This process resulted nevertheless in official records with more information than we possess about other eighteenth-century Ulster emigrants. Except for those who came ashore at Philadelphia in 1768–72, there are no passenger lists, no record even of the number on board ship. For the South Carolina bounty emigrants, we have enough data to generalise about this particular migration.

Although the South Carolina government paid their passage to America as "poor Protestants," the emigrants, by and large, did not lack resources. The demography of the bounty emigration resembled that of Ulster emigrants who paid their own passage to Philadelphia and of emigrants to seventeenth-century New England. They were more likely to be 35 to 45 year old parents with several children. They travelled in family groups, sometimes extended families, and many of them were farmers and weavers at home.[45] This was in contrast to the emigrants from German-speaking lands in the 1760s, who were more commonly unmarried men and women in their upper teens or twenties with few resources beyond their ability to work.[46]

This was emphatically a family migration. Two thirds at least came with their families, although young single men and occasionally single women accounted for up to a third of those who qualified for the South Carolina bounty. This seems to have been the pattern throughout with the preponderance of families becoming greater as time went on. In some cases the family groups were multigenerational or two brothers, their wives and children travelled together. Thus of 41 passengers who arrived on the *Success* in 1763, 28 belonged to eight families and a dozen single men and one single woman evidently came on their own.[47] Passengers on the *Countess of Donegall* in 1765 included 48 persons in nine family groups. Fathers ranged from 32 to 49 years and mothers from 28 to 40 years. There were 14 single men on board from 16 to 24 years old and three single women aged 18 to 20. The average age for emigrant heads of households was 37 and for single emigrants twenty.[48]

The *Earl of Hillsborough* arrived at Charleston with 230 passengers in 1767. There were 43 families on this ship, 196 men, women and children, and just 30 single persons. No ages of men, married or single, survive, but the average age of mothers was 37.5 in a range from 30 to 60 years and there were 36 children aged 15 years or more, which would suggest the average age of male heads of households was probably over forty.[49] The *Britannia*, which sailed from Newry brought 34 families, 176 persons in all, and 24 single persons to Charleston in 1767. The average age of mothers on this ship was 38.9 years and there were 42 children in these families who were more than 15 years old, so again these were not young families or recently married couples.[50] There were 91 passengers on the *Admiral Hawke* in 1768. Since they sailed from Londonderry, they were most likely from the north-western counties of the province of Ulster, Donegal, Fermanagh, west Tyrone and Londonderry. There were 15 families on board, 69 men, women, and children. These families were somewhat younger than on other ships. With the exception of Dougal and Elinor McDougal, 56 and 54, with children in their twenties, there were no children older than fourteen. The average age of male heads of households was 35 and that of married women just 29. The proportion of single persons on the *Admiral Hawke*, 22 in all, was higher than on other ships. While most of these passengers were 19 to 21, a few were considerably older.[51]

To the general picture of emigrants from Ulster to South Carolina as middle-aged parents of large families, we can add that they came in the main from County Down where there was a concentration of farmer-weavers. Until the last years of the bounty brought other ports into play, Belfast and Newry provided all the shipping for Charleston. In recruiting passengers for South Carolina, Belfast ship-owners sent agents to the linen weaving district in County Down and nowhere else. It would be reasonable to assume that most emigrants came from the linen triangle.[52] This pattern changed after 1770 when more emigrants came from north Antrim and the northwest counties.

What was the advantage to Torrans and Poaug and to the merchants and ship-owners with whom they worked? The Rev. Alexander Hewatt, Presbyterian pastor at Charleston at this time, observed that once merchants realised they would receive £4 sterling for every passenger they brought to Charleston, "from avaricious motives," they "crammed such numbers of them into their ships that they were in danger of being stifled on the passage." This was certainly true of the infamous *Nancy*, but is there evidence that merchants and ship-owners routinely overloaded their ships bound to Carolina? The minister was convinced that more than one shipping merchant ill served passengers and Hewatt was clearly in a position to know that emigrants "sometimes were landed in such a starved and sickly condition, that numbers of them died before they left Charleston."[53] There was often a discrepancy between the tonnage claimed in an advertisement for freight and passengers and that recorded in the customs house. As R. J. Dickson pointed out, there were good reasons for maximising the one and minimising the other. In some cases the difference was trifling, in others considerable. William Caldwell of Londonderry and Samuel Carsan of Philadelphia registered their ship *Admiral Hawke* at 100 tons in 1760, but claimed 250 tons in newspaper advertisements. Whatever the more accurate figure might be, *Admiral Hawke* carried only 91 passengers from Londonderry so there was no question of overcrowding. Similarly their brig *Success*, registered at 85 tons in 1761, brought just 70 passengers to Charleston. Other ships are more problematic, especially those sailing in 1767. The Newry ship *Britannia* was advertised at 300 tons, but the Naval Officer at Charleston listed her at 70 tons; since *Britannia* brought 180 passengers on one voyage and 200 on another one hopes the latter figure was a clerk's error. The Newry owners of the *Lord Dungannon* advertised her tonnage as 200 tons in 1767, but the same owners registered her at Philadelphia at just 100 tons. Since 141 passengers crossed on *Lord Dungannon*, this ship should have been at least 150 tons to accommodate them.[54]

The bounty certainly took the risk out of carrying servants and redemptioners across the ocean and securing buyers for their indentures, but in the first years of the bounty emigration, with fewer passengers, profits must have been small. John Poaug's argument before the Council that passengers had signed over all their bounty rights and consequently Torrans and Poaug were entitled to the twenty shillings appropriated for tools and seed for each settler is an indication that the profit margin was too narrow to permit them to be generous.[55] Their real profits however lay in freighting ships that their owners would otherwise not have sent to Charleston.

Bounty Emigration at Full Tide 1765–66

The *Belfast News Letter* advertised only one sailing for Charleston in 1764, a return voyage by the *Prince of Wales*.[56] But 1765 was different. Besides their close ties with Greg and Cunningham, Torrans and Poaug had by this time found new associates in the emigrant trade from Belfast. The firm of Daniel Mussenden and Thomas Bateson, long associated with the flaxseed trade, entered wholeheartedly into the bounty emigration scheme. And William Beatty, who had been their only agent for the *Prince of Wales* on her first voyage to South Carolina, began promoting emigration to Charleston on ships owned by both firms. William Beatty was agent for all Greg and Cunningham's ships advertised for Charleston.[57]

Greg and Cunningham sent their ship the *Countess of Donegall* to South Carolina with passengers in September 1765 and she arrived safely at Charleston in November. A letter signed by William Crossley in behalf of all on board testified to the captain's kindness to his passengers.[58] William Crossley headed the list of poor Protestants from "Belfast in Ireland" granted warrants for land "In Boonesborough or Belfast Township" at the meeting of the Council in December, so the 73 men, women and children who qualified for the bounty were evidently passengers on the *Countess of Donegall*. Six men and one woman had not paid their passages and Torrans and Poaug received their certificates for the owners of the ship.[59]

Mussenden, Bateson and Company began advertising for passengers, redemptioners, and servants for the *Prince of Wales'* next voyage to Charleston in August 1765, but with repeated postponements of her sailing date, she did not actually put to sea until January 1766.[60] Beatty advertised for servants to go out on this voyage. He intended for Charleston himself, he said, and promised to "clothe them in a genteel manner, pay their passage, and take care to have them happily settled in that country, where industry is amply rewarded and poverty a stranger."[61] In January "Being now ready to depart for South Carolina on board the ship Prince of Wales," he left his son in charge of his Belfast business.[62] The *Prince of Wales* brought 51 settlers who were granted land in Belfast Township by the South Carolina Council and at least 21 others who went into service with a hope of future land grants.[63] As soon as the ship docked at Charleston in March, Beatty made his way to Torrans and Poaug, where he made his headquarters.

> Just arrived in the Ship Prince of Wales, James Egger, Master, William Beatty, Merchant and Linen-Draper, from Belfast, who has to dispose of the Times of 21 Servants, among whom are 9 Women, Sempstresses, Knitters, and two Cooks, some Young Men, among whom are Mechanicks, who can write good Hands, and can be recommended to the Purchaser.
>
> He has likewise to sell, a Parcel of Linen, well manufactured, and bleached in the best and safest Manner. Enquire for said Beatty, at Messrs. Torrans, Poaug, & Co. Store, or at his Lodgings at Captain Foskey's, in Church Street.[64]

Torrans and Poaug freighted the *Prince of Wales* with rice for the Rotterdam and Hamburg market and she sailed for Cowes on April 19.[65]

Londonderry merchants William Caldwell, Arthur Vance and Richard Caldwell again sent their ship the *Falls* to Charleston with passengers. The *Falls* arrived from Derry on March 7, 1766 and cleared for Philadelphia the last day of April.[66] She also brought "a few Servants from the North of Ireland, who have Certificates of their good Behaviour from their Infancy," all consigned to Torrans and Poaug.[67]

The next ship to convey emigrants from the north of Ireland to South Carolina brought a new player on stage. William Beatty had earlier been associated with Robert Wills, a hardware and general merchant in Belfast, in promoting emigration from Ulster to Philadelphia, travelling to different market towns to sign up passengers.[68] Wills himself went to Philadelphia in 1764 and was established in a business partnership with Samuel Jackson from Dundonald, County Down, as importers of linen and hardware.[69] Wills and his partner owned a flaxseed ship of 100 tons built at

Philadelphia in 1765 called the *Belfast Packet*.[70] Wills sailed home on her maiden voyage to Belfast. Wills advertised in February 1766 that:

> The Owners of the Belfast Pacquet, finding that the Passengers, who came over in her from Philadelphia, could not get their Families ready against the appointed Time to proceed with said Ship to that Port, have ordered her to Sea.[71]

The ship sailed for New Castle, Delaware, and Philadelphia. Wills and Jackson advertised as "just imported in the ship *Belfast Packet*, from Belfast" Irish beef, Irish linens, and servants, "all likely lads, from 12 to 20 years of age." The Belfast Packet returned immediately to Belfast.[72] Wills advertised her to sail again in July for New Castle and Philadelphia, but ten days later he invited passengers, redemptioners and servants to sail for Charleston on the *Belfast Packet*. Matthew Rea of Drumbo was now one of the agents, traveling to Lisburn, Ballynahinch, and Dromore to explain the South Carolina bounty.[73] Rea had a successful tour through the parts of County Down where he and his family were known and the *Belfast Packet* sailed in August with 78 passengers.[74] Captain Thomas Ash brought her safely from Belfast "with between eighty and ninety Irish settlers."[75] They made the voyage in seven weeks and all were in good health.[76] She sailed for Philadelphia in November in time to load a flaxseed freight.[77]

William Beatty missed recruiting passengers for the *Packet*, as he was still in Charleston. As soon as he returned to Belfast, he set about organising another shipload of passengers and servants for South Carolina. He announced that "William Beatty of Belfast, just returned from the Province of South Carolina (now the most flourishing Province in America)" would have a vessel ready to sail there and offered a free passage from Belfast to Charleston.[78] Beatty promised to visit Ballynahinch, Lurgan, and Dromore in County Down each week "to treat and settle with such as intend to go to South Carolina in his ship."[79] He arranged with Gregs and Cunningham to dispatch their ship the *Earl of Hillsborough* to Charleston. She sailed on Christmas Eve 1766.[80] The *Earl of Hillsborough* reached Charleston on February 19, 1767, "with two hundred and thirty protestant settlers, encouraged by the large bounty given by this province, and the success their countrymen have met with in their several settlements here." She sailed for Cowes early in March with a cargo of rice.[81]

Bounty emigration had not proven an unqualified success. As far as can be gleaned from newspaper reports and the Council Journal, only some 400 men, women and children from the north of Ireland sailed directly to South Carolina in 1765 and 1766. While there are no comparable figures for the movement of other settlers into upper South Carolina from other colonies, the general impression is that migration from Pennsylvania, Virginia, and North Carolina was a more important factor in the settlement of the backcountry. The majority of the bounty emigrants came in family groups and were all directed to Boonesborough or Belfast Township. But a growing number were indentured servants. If the original vision was for an orderly settlement by groups of foreign Protestants, it had been only partially achieved.

Debacle 1767

The winter of 1766 was a time of distress in Ireland due to the failure of that year's harvest. Wheat and oats were in short supply and prices high throughout the kingdom. The partial failure of the next year's potato crop added to the problem and the shortage of food was most acute in 1767. A letter written from Cork in July gave a grim picture:

> We have a greater scarcity of provisions of all sorts this year in Ireland, than has been felt for thirty years past, inasmuch that unless we are supplied from America our poor will be in great danger of suffering dreadfully. Our last crop grately failed, whereas we find you had a very plentiful one; we have got a few cargoes of wheat and flour, but expect more.[82]

A series of unfavourable seasons and spoiled harvests everywhere in the British Isles led to soaring grain prices, despite an Order in Council in September 1766 forbidding the export of grain. The rise in prices attracted heavy imports of grain in 1767–8 in England and Ireland.[83] It also gave a boost to emigration.

Two ships were scheduled to sail for Charleston early in 1767.

William Beatty and Matthew Rea of Drumbo were both advertised as agents for the *Prince of Wales*. She returned to Charleston May 14, when "about 250 Irish protestants arrived here from Belfast, in order to settle in this province, encouraged by the large bounty granted by the legislature." They were all in good health.[84]

The other ship, the *Nancy*, was to be at the centre of a scandal because of gross overcrowding. Robert Wills of Belfast and William Ray of Ballyreany in the parish of Dundonald, County Down, who owned the *Nancy* with Samuel Jackson of Philadelphia, promised a free passage on their ship.[85] The *Nancy's* owners told of two crops in one year in South Carolina and that the authorities there would give 100 acres free to the head of the family, and 50 more for each child or servant, free of rent or taxes for ten years. Passengers were to bring a certificate from "the Church Minister and Wardens or the Dissenting Minister and Elders."[86] William Ray and Captain Samuel Hannah of the *Nancy* visited Ballymena, Coleraine, Garvagh, Cookstown, Armagh, Portadown, and Lurgan in February and March to secure passengers.[87] They were too successful. The owners claimed their vessel was 300 tons, but the *Nancy* was actually only 80 tons. *Nancy* was a new ship, built at Philadelphia and registered there in 1766 by Jackson and Wills as 80 tons.[88] By the rule of thumb used at that time, *Nancy* should have carried 80 "full" (i.e. adult) passengers. They signed on nearly 300 for the voyage. Comparison with another government-assisted emigration scheme in 1764 is instructive. The committee stipulated "two ships of not less than 200 tons each, to carry the Poor Palatines to South Carolina, and to carry no more than 200 persons in each ship."[89]

How many passengers were crowded into the ship? The *Nancy* arrived June 5, with "about 240 protestants from the north of Ireland, intending to settle in this province, on the large bounty granted by the legislature."[90] When the South Carolina Council met June 22 to allocate land and pay the bounty for the *Nancy's* passengers, they were presented with a list of 237 names, with their ages, apparently arranged in family groups. This list can be broken down to 128 passengers 21 years old or older, 38 from 13 to 20 years, and 71 children aged 12 or younger. Torrans and Poaug claimed bounty on 291 passengers.[91] The Council ordered the bounty paid to the owners of the *Nancy* through Torrans and Poaug. The governor however stopped payment until a full investigation could be made by the legislature. Their final report gave the figure as 193 adult passengers and 50 children 12 or younger.[92] Since Wills and Ray admitted that "about thirty died" before the ship reached South Carolina, *Nancy's* passengers must have numbered close to 300 when they sailed from Belfast Lough.[93]

Wills and Ray entered into a written agreement with the passengers for their diet on the voyage. Full passengers were each promised seven pounds of beef, seven pounds of bread, one pound of butter and fourteen quarts of water weekly, while "half passengers," those aged between two and twelve years, were to receive half these amounts. This was a Spartan diet compared to what the Germans on the *Dragon* had to eat on their voyage to South Carolina in 1764. In addition to a daily pound of bread, they each received beef, flour, fruit, pease, fish, butter, cheese, potatoes, pork, rice and grits every week. Still beef, bread and water were standard shipboard fare. The problem on the *Nancy* would not be adequate food, but adequate space.[94]

Her passengers were in sad condition, suffering from ship fever (typhus). The editor of the *South Carolina Gazette* visited them in their temporary quarters in the Barracks where he found "Many dying, some deprived of their senses, young children lying entirely naked whose parents had expired a few weeks ago."[95] Charleston responded with generosity. Nathaniel Russell, a visitor in Charleston, reported that, in addition to money, "Blankets, Linen, Cloaths, & every necessary that the sick and naked stood in need of" was collected in two days.[96] The editor of the *South Carolina Gazette and Country Journal* wrote:

> The distressed Situation of the poor Irish Protestant Settlers lately arrived here, having excited the Compassion of several worthy Gentlemen, a Subscription, for their immediate Relief, was set on Foot, and in a very short Time, to the Honour of the Inhabitants of this Province, upwards of Two Hundred Pounds Sterling was raised, which will afford great Assistance to these unhappy People, who are much in Want of the Necessaries of Life. Subscriptions continue to be received by the Church Wardens of both Parishes.[97]

Public opinion rallied to the *Nancy* emigrants when they petitioned in July that Captain Hannah "not only nipped them of the provisions allowed them but heaped them one upon the other, to such a degree in their births that it must be absolutely impossible they could survive as appears by the mortality which rages amongst them to this day." They had been treated with inhumanity, pinched in provisions and water, and so crowded together that it was probably the cause of their sickness. When Torrans and Poaug applied to the treasurer for payment of the bounty as usual, they learned it was withheld by order of the governor. Since sixty of the passengers had already died, Governor Montagu with consent of the council stopped payment to Torrans and Poaug as agents for the owners. By grossly overcrowding their ship, the *Nancy's* owners "endeavoured at the expense of Justice and humanity to convert to a private emolument, those Sums, which were given with the most liberal and laudable views to promote the Public good." In January 1768 Governor Montagu asked the assembly to concur with his decision. A committee of investigation reported in March that the emigrants' complaints were well founded. The ship-owners were "covetous and avaricious" and lacking in "Humanity and Principle of Justice," and the bounty money was permanently withheld.[98] When news of the death toll on the *Nancy* reached Ulster, it did little to stem the tide of emigration. But the plight of her passengers undoubtedly turned the South Carolina Assembly against renewing the bounty once it expired.

Last Call for the South Carolina Bounty

John Bynan and David Gaussan, merchants in Newry, advertised their ship the *Britannia* for Charleston, offering a free passage to South Carolina.[99] Passengers asked for a delay in sailing to give them "time to dispose of their effects," but the owners insisted all be on board by May 4, "so the Ship, by the blessing of God, will then proceed on her intended Voyage for the Land of Promise."[100] The *Britannia* came from Newry on August 23, "with about 180 Protestant settlers, all in good health."[101] When Gregs and Cunningham announced their brig *Chichester* would sail for Charleston in late summer, they reminded readers of the *Belfast*

News Letter that the South Carolina bounty would soon expire, information presumably sent them by Torrans and Poaug.

> Gregs and Cunningham received Advice Yesterday from Charles Town in South-Carolina, that the Bounty to Passengers ceases the first of January 1768. Those that have agreed to proceed in their Brig Chichester, William Reed, Master, are desired to be ready to go on board the 25th of September next, for she will sail the first Wind after ... [and] after this Bounty ceases they will not have an Opportunity of a free Passage.[102]

With the bounty payments about to expire, ship-owners in the north of Ireland hastened to get their share before it was too late. Caldwell, Vance and Caldwell of Londonderry dispatched their ship *Admiral Hawke* to Charleston. They advertised that "Joseph Burnet, who long resided in South Carolina, and is now in this Neighbourhood [i.e. Londonderry], will return in said Vessel, and can give a full and satisfactory Account of that Country to all who please to apply to him."[103] James McVickar of Larne had been advertising the snow *James and Mary* "for New-York in America," but announced that she would sail for Charleston in September.[104] In August 1767 Belfast merchants John Campbell and Hugh Donnaldson, John Ewing, whose trading interests were primarily with Baltimore, and John Gregg announced the sailing of the ship *Earl of Donegall* for Charleston. She was then on a voyage to Norway, but arrived in Belfast Lough in time to sail in September.[105] Late in the season Gregs and Cunningham advertised "A Free Passage to Charles-Town in South-Carolina by the Snow *Betty Greg*." Another group of Belfast merchants, Campbell and Donnaldson, James Henderson, and John Greg dispatched the brig *Lord Dungannon* to Charleston at the same time.[106] The two ships, normally part of the flaxseed fleet, sailed together for Charleston early in October.[107]

These ships brought a sudden influx of Ulster emigrants. The *Earl of Donegall* arrived at Charleston on December 10 with "about 250 passengers" from Belfast.[108] Torrans and Poaug were paid the bounty due on 266 passengers. The brigantine *Chichester* from

Belfast and the ship *Admiral Hawke* from Londonderry both landed passengers in the last days of December.[109] Torrans and Poaug
collected the bounty payments for 146 passengers on the *Chichester*
and 71 who came on the *Admiral Hawke*.[110] The snow *James and
Mary* from Larne arrived early in January 1768. The *James and
Mary* brought "about 150 more passengers from the North of
Ireland to settle in this province."[111] Torrans and Poaug received
bounty money for 186 passengers on this ship. *Lord Dungannon*
and *Betty Greg* reached Charleston in February.[112] The *Lord
Dungannon* brought 141 passengers and the *Betty Greg* 145 passengers. Torrans and Poaug claimed the bounty for both ships. The
editor of one of the three Charleston papers observed:

> About 300 settlers arrived here last from Ireland, encouraged
> by the large bounty given by this province. These it is thought,
> will be the last that receive any benefit from the present act,
> which expires with the next session of assembly.[113]

Without the bounty to guarantee a profitable voyage, Ulster
shipowners had little reason to dispatch ships to their friends in
Charleston, Torrans and Poaug. And, like all good things, the
bounty came to an end. "By the Prorogation, this Day, of the
General Assembly, the large Bounty, granted by the Province to
Protestants coming to settle here, ceases and determines."[114]

What had the South Carolina bounty accomplished? Settlers had
come to the province who would otherwise have gone elsewhere
and taken up lands on the frontiers, where they provided a buffer
between the Low Country planters and the Indians. Was this a
good thing? It depended on one's point of view. The Rev. Charles
Woodmason, who saw everything in the Colonies as a plot against
the Church of England, complained in his diary

> That above £30,000 Sterling have been expended to bring
> over 5 or 6000 Ignorant, mean, worthless beggarly Irish
> Presbyterians, the Scum of the Earth, and Refuse of Mankind,
> and this, solely to balance the Emigration of People from
> Virginia, who are all of the Established Church.[115]

Emigration After the Bounty

Emigration from Ulster to South Carolina did not end, although the stream was temporarily diverted to Georgia, where George Galphin, John Rea, and other promoters had secured similar advantages for newcomers. Matthew Rea and William Beatty acted as their agents in Ulster.[116] The sloop *Two Arthurs* brought 60 passengers from Wexford in September and Captain Conolly McCausland brought the ship *Walworth* from Londonderry to Charleston in October.[117] Caldwell, Vance and Caldwell dispatched their ship with passengers for South Carolina. Since there was no bounty to be paid, the number of passengers is not recorded. Passengers on the *Walworth* petitioned for aid as "several dyed since their arrival here, and others continue sick and suffering." Their petition was referred to a committee of the Assembly including John Poaug who was now a member of the Commons House. Other momentous events took precedence. The South Carolina Assembly considered an invitation from the Massachusetts and Virginia Legislatures to join them in opposition to the Townshend Revenue Acts. Poaug was appointed to another committee instructed to formulate a response. They endorsed the two letters and instructed the colony's London agent to lobby for repeal of the acts. On learning this, Governor Montagu dissolved the Assembly, but not before they voted £200 to provide the poor Protestants lately arrived "with Wagons and necessaries to transport them to their Settlements in the back part of this province."[118] The *Walworth* sailed from Charleston at the end of November "for Cowes and a Market," freighted with rice by Torrans and Poaug.[119] It was more than a year before other Ulster people landed in Charleston and they came by way of Savannah.

> Yesterday 35 Passengers from the North of Ireland, arrived here from Georgia, to settle in this Province. They came out with that Intent in the ship Hopewell, Captain Ashe, arrived at Savannah.[120]

But this was only a temporary decline. After 1770 the emigrant trade moved again into high gear. The *Hopewell* again sailed that year for Charleston and Savannah, bringing "155 Irish Passengers from Belfast" to settle in South Carolina, after landing 45 more at Savannah.[121] John Montgomery of Larne dispatched his brig *Jupiter* to Charleston with "above 200 passengers."[122] William Beatty now busied himself in promoting emigration to both South Carolina and Georgia, while Matthew Rea concentrated on finding settlers for his brother's lands in Georgia. The *Britannia* sailed for Savannah and the *Hopewell* for Charleston on the same day with the settlers they recruited. The *Britannia* sailed with 200 for Georgia and the *Hopewell* brought "250 Irish Settlers" to Charleston.[123]

This was only a foretaste of the numbers who left Ulster in 1772, when a half dozen ships carried more than 1,200 emigrants to South Carolina. The Rev. William Martin of Kellswater, County Antrim, a Covenanter, is often credited with the whole of that year's emigration, but this seems to be a myth.[124] Martin placed an advertisement in the *Belfast News Letter* noting "the want of Gospel Ordinances in South Carolina" and his intention to supply that need, embarking with his family from Belfast or Larne in September. Some of his "present hearers and their families," he said, intended to embrace this opportunity to have "the comforts of life in abundance" and free exercise of their "religious sentiments" and would accompany the Martins to Charleston.[125] Since he neglected to consult with the Reformed Presbytery before making this decision, they censured Martin, but his congregation rallied to him and pledged to emigrate with him.[126] In May, having "already agreed for a considerable Number of Passengers," Martin made arrangements with John Montgomery for a ship from Larne and then offered his lease on a farm by Kellswater in Connor parish, his furniture, his crops, and cattle at auction in July.[127] John Montgomery had announced in April that his ship *Betty* would sail from Larne to Charleston that summer, but in August he advertised the *Lord Dunluce* of 400 tons for Charleston. Passengers were required to pay part of the passage money by September 5 as an earnest of their intention to sail on her, "a much greater Number offering than the Vessel can carry." In mid-September, after several families had withdrawn their names, the *Lord Dunluce* had room for 200 more passengers and Montgomery advertised for additional passengers. This would suggest that Martin could not recruit enough to fill one large ship, much less five. The *Lord Dunluce* sailed from Larne in October and reached Charleston in December in company with three other emigrant ships.[128]

In 1772 the Ulster economy was too weak and the passenger trade to Charleston too well established to require any special promotion. John Montgomery's brig *Jupiter* sailed from Larne in May and disembarked 300 passengers at Charleston in July.[129] James McVickar dispatched his snow *James and Mary* from the same port in August and she reached Charleston in October taking seven weeks for the crossing.[130] William Beatty, still active in finding settlers for South Carolina sent the *Hopewell* back to Charleston from Belfast.[131] John Ewing and Samuel Brown of Belfast first offered the *Pennsylvania Farmer* for Philadelphia, then for Charleston. Rev. John Logue, Presbyterian minister at Broughshane, County Antrim, who was going to South Carolina with his family, was their agent.[132] David Gaussan and his partners in Newry sent their *Free Mason* to Charleston as well.[133] The *Pennsylvania Farmer, Lord Dunluce, Hopewell,* and *Free Mason* arrived at Charleston on four successive days in late December, "all with Irish Passengers, above 1,000 Souls."[134] Another of David Gaussan's ships, *Britannia*, "full of Settlers for this Province," came early in January.[135] Although all of them paid their own passage and there is no indication of servants or redemptioners among them, many of these emigrants were quite poor. Of the *Britannia's* passengers, for instance, only seven were able to pay the fee for their land warrants and the others were described as "poor people who have severally sworn they are not worth five pounds sterling."[136] Once again Charleston was overwhelmed by an influx of needy people and once again responded generously. The Rev. William Tennent preached a charity sermon at the Independent Church and the Rev. Robert Cooper at St. Michael's raising more than £1,275 "for the Relief of the poor Irish Settlers lately arrived here."[137]

There were more emigrant ships in 1773. Londonderry merchants advertised for passengers for Charleston on the *Walworth*, the brig *Louisa*, and the *Helen*. James Stirling of Walworth and Abraham McCausland owned the *Walworth*, commanded by Conolly McCausland, and the *Helen* belonged to Abraham McCausland and Dickson Coningham. *Louisa* was Robert

Alexander's vessel. Samuel Curry advertised his brig *George* for Charleston, too.[138] Robert Alexander offered both the *Ann*, "the ship being mostly engaged to a number of creditable families," and the *Elizabeth* for Charleston.[139] William Beatty promised to have "a good ship from Belfast," his own *Liberty and Property* scheduled to sail in September.[140] John Montgomery proposed again sending his ships *Lord Dunluce*, *Jupiter* and *Betty* from Larne to Charleston.[141] James McVickar sent his snow *James and Mary* on a return voyage and Thomas Waring of Newry dispatched his brigantine *Elliott* to Charleston with passengers.[142] James Patterson, James Templeton, and John Henderson, Belfast merchants, advertised their brig *Lord Chatham* for South Carolina, too.[143]

The *Elliott* was the first to arrive "with about 200 Passengers." A week later there were "about 300 Irish Passengers, in the *Walworth*, Captain McCausland, from Londonderry."[144] In September the *South Carolina Gazette* reported that:

> Yesterday arrived here the Brigt. Helena, James Ramage, Master, with upwards of 120 Passengers, from Londonderry. Several other Vessels were to follow; and the Spirit of Emigration from Ireland to America, instead of being checked, seemed to have encreased: But the poor People had not been acquainted, that they could not obtain Lands here as formerly.[145]

The *Jupiter* with "about 200 Souls on board" and the *Ann* bringing "260 Persons, who Intend to settle in this Province" came in October.[146]

South Carolina was the destination of many who left Ulster before and after the American Revolution. That this was so resulted in no small part from the vision of John Torrans and John Poaug, who saw a way to make a trade in emigrants profitable for Ulster ship-owners and used their own networks in South Carolina, New York, Belfast, Londonderry, and London to make it happen. Their experience is a clear example of the determining role that merchants on both sides of the Atlantic played in directing the flow of emigration. Far from being passive ticket brokers, who accepted a freight in emigrants when it offered, they shaped the process of emigration from beginning to end. To understand Ulster emigration we need to understand these transatlantic mercantile networks.

The firm of Torrans and Poaug was reorganised in 1771 to meet a cash flow problem, doubtless the result of non-importation agreements.[147] They continued to be active in the shipping business, with emigrant ships again consigned to them. In 1773 the *Belfast News Letter* published a testimonial by John Poaug, merchant of Charleston, to Conolly McCausland of the *Walworth* and James Ramage of the *Hellena* who landed passengers in good health and spirits.[148] Both John Torrans and John Poaug died in Charleston in 1780.

Notes

1   Flax was widely grown for domestic use. In the 1760s tobacco planters were
    urged to diversify by planting flax. John Wily, *A Treatise on the Propagation
    of Sheep, the Manufacture of Wool, and the Cultivation and Manufacture
    of Flax, with Directions for making several Utensils for the Business*
    (Williamsburg, VA, 1765), 30.

2   *South Carolina Gazette*, August 1, 1761.

3   Robert L. Meriwether, *The Expansion of South Carolina, 1729–1765*
    (Kingsport, TN, 1940), 241–3.

4   Leila Sellers, *Charleston Business on the Eve of the American Revolution*
    (Chapel Hill, NC, 1934), 250.

5   George Howe, *History of the Presbyterian Church in South Carolina*
    (Columbia, SC, 1870), I, 204, 255. The South Carolina Council allowed
    him 500 acres and another 600 acres "between Broad and Savannah Rivers"
    when the first bounty settlers received their land in 1763. Janie Revill, *A
    Compilation of the Original Lists of Protestant Immigrants to South
    Carolina, 1763–1773* (Columbia, SC, 1939, reprinted Baltimore, 1968), 6.

6   E. R. R. Green, "Queensborough Township: Scotch-Irish Emigration and the
    Expansion of Georgia, 1763–1776," *William and Mary Quarterly*, 3rd
    series, 17(April 1960), 183–99. Michael P. Morris, "Profits and
    Philanthropy: The Ulster Immigration Schemes of George Galphin and
    John Rea," *Journal of Scotch-Irish Studies*, 1(2002), 1–11.

7   *South Carolina Gazette*, June 19, 1762.

8   Boonesborough, also known as Belfast Township, was named for Governor
    Thomas Boone. Both townships are in Abbeville and Greenwood counties,
    SC. Meriwether, *Expansion of South Carolina*, 250–52. Revill, *Original Lists
    of Protestant Immigrants*, 6.

9   "Ship Registers of the Port of Philadelphia," *PMHB*, 27(1903), 106.

10 *Belfast News Letter*, August 17, 1762, October 26, 1762.

11 *South Carolina Gazette*, February 19, 1763.

12 This is near Abbeville, SC. Revill, *Original Lists of Protestant Immigrants*, 5–6.

13 William L. McDowell, ed., *Documents Relating to Indian Affairs 1754–1765*
    (Columbia, SC, 1970), 495.

14 *South Carolina Gazette*, January 14, 1764. *Pennsylvania Journal*, February 2,
    1764. *Belfast News Letter*, March 20, 1764.

15 *South Carolina Gazette*, January 21, 1764.

16 *Pennsylvania Journal*, February 2, 1764.

17 Harry Roy Merrens, *Colonial North Carolina in the Eighteenth Century*
    (Chapel Hill, NC, 1964), 54.

18 Petition, n.d. [1758] (Papers of the Marquess of Bath, Longleat, England,
    microfilm in North Carolina Department of Archives, Raleigh).

19 Peter N. Moore, *World of Toil and Strife: Community Transformation in
    Backcountry South Carolina, 1750–1805* (Columbia, SC, 2007), 19,
    21–3.

20 Meriwether, *Expansion of South Carolina*, 136–9. George Lloyd Johnson, Jr.,
    The Frontier in the Colonial South: South Carolina Backcountry, 1736–1800
    (Westport, CN, 1997), 50.

21   As few as eighteen families came on Dobbs' ships. Dickson, *Ulster Emigration*, 128–34.

22   Charleston County Wills, 19:27. While in New York, Torrans married into a family of New York lawyers, Presbyterian in religion and Whig in politics, allied with the powerful Livingston clan. His much-younger wife, Elizabeth Blanche Smith, was the daughter of Judge William Smith, Sr., Attorney General and member of the Governor's Council, and the sister of Chief Justice William Smith, Jr.

23   Truxes, *Letterbook of Greg and Cunningham*, 125.

24   *Beekman Mercantile Papers*, I, 292–4, 298. Truxes, *Letterbook of Greg and Cunningham*, 32–4, 115n.

25   R. Nicholas Olsberg, "Ship Registers in the South Carolina Archives 1734–1780," *South Carolina Historical Magazine*, 74(October 1973), 219.

26   Charleston County, Miscellaneous Records, Book 86–8, 53–4.

27   *South Carolina Gazette*, December 15, 1758.

28   *Beekman Mercantile Papers*, I, 371, 379.

29   *Burke's Landed Gentry*, 1972, III, 400. Gamble, "Business Community and Trade of Belfast," 185, 273.

30   *South Carolina Gazette*, January 8, 1763. Henry A. M. Smith, "Wragg of South Carolina," *South Carolina Historical Magazine*, 19(1918), 122–3. Leola Wilson Konopa, "The Isaac Dubose Family of South Carolina," *Transactions of the Huguenot Society of South Carolina*, 78(1973), 112–14.

31   *South Carolina Gazette*, April 18, 1761, April 25, 1761, January 15, 1763, December 3, 1764.

32   *South Carolina Gazette*, December 5, 1761, October 2, 1762, November 20, 1762, March 5, 1763, September 10, 1763.

33   *South Carolina Gazette*, August 25, 1764, October 29, 1764. Sellers, *Charleston Business*, 138–9.

34   *Belfast News Letter*, June 29, 1764. Sellers, *Charleston Business*, 114.

35   The Londonderry firm of Caldwell, Vance and Caldwell owned the ship. *Belfast News Letter*, August 12, 1763, September 2, 1763, October 7, 1763, October 21, 1763.

36   *Belfast News Letter*, August 12, 1763.

37   *Belfast News Letter*, October 7, 1763. On Matthew Rea, Dickson, *Ulster Emigration*, 164–73.

38   *South Carolina Gazette*, January 14, 1764.

39   Revill, *Original Lists of Protestant Immigrants*, 7–9.

40   *Belfast News Letter*, March 27, 1764.

41   The *Prince of Wales* is called the *Prince Henry* in the Council minutes. Revill, *Original Lists of Protestant Immigrants*, 9–13.

42   *South Carolina Gazette*, March 10, 1764, March 17, 1764.

43   *South Carolina Gazette*, April 18, 1764. *Belfast News Letter*, June 29, 1764. Sellers, *Charleston Business*, 114–17.

44   Philip M. Hamer, ed., *The Papers of Henry Laurens* (Columbia, SC, 1968–80), IV, 464.

45   David Cressy, *Coming Over: Migration and Communication between England and New England in the Seventeenth Century* (Cambridge, 1987), 66–7.

46 Wokeck, *Trade in Strangers*, 47–9, 187.

47 The remaining 29 passengers were children. Revill, *Original Lists of Protestant Immigrants*, 5–6

48 Revill, *Original Lists of Protestant Immigrants*, 46–8.

49 Revill, *Original Lists of Protestant Immigrants*, 67–70.

50 Revill, *Original Lists of Protestant Immigrants*, 81–4.

51 Revill, *Original Lists of Protestant Immigrants*, 97–9.

52 *Belfast News Letter*, October 21, 1763, June 27, 1766, July 8, 1766, October 14, 1766.

53 Alexander Hewatt, *An Historical Account of the Rise and Progress of the Colonies of South Carolina and Georgia* (London, 1779), in Batholomew Rivers Carroll, *Historical Collections of South Carolina* (New York, 1836, reprinted 1973), I, 488.

54 "Ship Registers," *PMHB*, 27(1903), 101, 106, 491. Dickson, *Ulster Emigration*, 231–3.

55 Revill, *Original Lists of Protestant Immigrants*, 49–50.

56 *Belfast News Letter*, March 27, 1764. *South Carolina Gazette*, January 7, 1765.

57 Interest in South Carolina was not as great as Greg and Cunningham expected. They advertised the *Pitt*, scheduled to sail from Larne in August, and the *Prosperity*, sailing from Belfast in August, for Charleston. The *Pitt* normally sailed with passengers for New York or Philadelphia and carried flaxseed from New York. At the last minute, the owners changed her destination to New York. *Prosperity* continued to be advertised for South Carolina through September, when her sailing was postponed and the *Countess of Donegall* replaced her. *Belfast News Letter*, June 11, 1765, July 12, 1765, July 23, 1765, August 2, 1765, August 20, 1765, September 10, 1765, September 13, 1765.

58 *Belfast News Letter*, September 27, 1765, February 18, 1766.

59 These passengers arrived at a time when the *South Carolina Gazette* suspended publication rather than conform with the Stamp Act, so there is no newspaper report. Revill, *Original Lists of Protestant Immigrants*, 46–8.

60 *Belfast News Letter*, August 30, 1765, October 29, 1765, November 26, 1765, December 10, 1765, January 3, 1766, January 21, 1766.

61 *Belfast News Letter*, October 29, 1765.

62 *Belfast News Letter*, January 17, 1766.

63 This number may include passengers on the *Falls*. Dickson, *Ulster Emigration*, 118. Revill, *Original Lists of Protestant Immigrants*, 58–9.

64 *South Carolina Gazette and Country Journal*, April 1, 1766.

65 *South Carolina Gazette and Country Journal*, April 22, 1766.

66 *South Carolina Gazeteer and Country Journal*, March 18, 1766. *South Carolina Gazette*, June 2, 1766.

67 *South Carolina Gazette* and Country Journal, May 6, 1766.

68 *Belfast News Letter*, February 19, 1765, March 5, 1765, March 15, 1765.

69 They were associated with John Pringle and his brothers, merchants in Newry. *Pennsylvania Journal*, September 27, 1764, November 1, 1764.

70 "Ship Registers," *PMHB*, 27(1903), 366, 492.

71 *Belfast News Letter*, February 25, 1766.

72 *Pennsylvania Journal*, March 20, 1766, April 24, 1766, May 1, 1766.

73   *Belfast News Letter,* June 17, 1766, June 27, 1766, July 8, 1766.
74   Dickson, *Ulster Emigration,* 168.
75   *South Carolina Gazette,* October 20, 1766, *South Carolina Gazette and General Advertiser,* October 24, 1766. There is a puzzling statement in the Council Journal about assigning the bounty to "the owners of the ship Belfast Packet which they came over in" as they had not paid their own passages, since it refers to a list of German emigrants. Revill, *Original Lists of Protestant Immigrants,* 64.
76   *Belfast News Letter,* February 9, 1767.
77   *South Carolina Gazette,* November 3, 1766, *South Carolina Gazette and General Advertiser,* November 7, 1766.
78   *Belfast News Letter,* October 7, 1766.
79   *Belfast News Letter,* October 14, 1766.
80   *Belfast News Letter,* November 7, 1766, November 25, 1766, December 30, 1766.
81   *South Carolina and American General Gazette,* February 20, 1767. *South Carolina Gazette and Country Journal,* March 17, 1767.
82   *Pennsylvania Journal,* October 29, 1767.
83   J. D. Chambers and J. E. Mingay, *The Agricultural Revolution 1750–1880* (London, 1966), 111.
84   *South Carolina and American General Gazette,* May 15, 1767.
85   *Belfast News Letter,* December 30, 1766, January 3, 1767. Jackson was also from Dundonald.
86   *Belfast News Letter,* February 6, 1767.
87   *Belfast News Letter,* February 20, 1767.
88   "Ship Registers," *PMHB,* 27(1903), 491.
89   Robert A. Selig, "Emigration, Fraud, Humanitarianism, and the Founding of Londonderry, South Carolina, 1763–1765," *Eighteenth-Century Studies,* 23(1989), 17.
90   *South Carolina and American General Gazette,* June 5, 1767.
91   This number would suggest *Nancy* sailed with as many as 320 passengers. Revill, *Original Lists of Protestant Immigrants,* 74–80.
92   SC Assembly Journal, March 2, 1768, 545.
93   PRO CO5/114/111–112d.
94   PRO CO5/114/111–112d. Dickson, *Ulster Emigration,* 207. Selig, "Emigration, Fraud, Humanitarianism," 18–19
95   *South Carolina Gazette,* June 29, 1767.
96   Warren B. Smith, *White Servitude in Colonial South Carolina* (Columbia, SC, 1961), 42.
97   *South Carolina Gazette and Country Journal,* June 30, 1767
98   South Carolina Assembly Journal, January 21, 1768, January 27, 1768, March 2, 1768, pp. 508, 517 and 543. Hamer, *Laurens Papers,* V, 505. Sellers, *Charleston Business,* 118–19. For a more extended account of this incident and its aftermath, see Richard K. MacMaster, "The Voyage of the Nancy 1767," *Familia,* 19(2003), 64–73.
99   *Belfast News Letter,* February 24, 1767, March 3, 1767.
100   *Belfast News Letter,* April 14, 1767.
101   *South Carolina and American General Gazette,* August 28, 1767.

102 *Belfast News Letter*, July 28, 1767, August 7, 1767.

103 *Belfast News Letter*, August 18, 1767.

104 *Belfast News Letter*, July 28, 1767, August 14, 1767, September 4, 1767.

105 *Belfast News Letter*, August 14, 1767, September 4, 1767.

106 *Belfast News Letter*, September 8, 1767.

107 *Belfast News Letter*, October 6, 1767.

108 *South Carolina and American General Gazette*, December 11, 1767.

109 *South Carolina Gazette and Country Journal*, December 29, 1767. *South Carolina and American General Gazette*, January 1, 1768.

110 There are 91 names on the list of passengers on the *Admiral Hawke* who qualified for land as foreign Protestants. Revill, *Original Lists of Protestant Immigrants*, 93–9.

111 *South Carolina Gazette and Country Journal*, January 4, 1768, January 5, 1768, January 12, 1768.

112 *South Carolina Gazette*, February 16, 1768.

113 *South Carolina and American General Gazette*, February 12, 1768. The emigrant ships carried some goods from Belfast and Londonderry for sale in America, but no cargo paid as well as emigrants. From the *Betty Greg's* cargo, for instance, Torrans, Poaug and Co. advertised "excellent Irish Potatoes, at 20 sh. per Bushel, and new Butter at 3/6 per Pound." *South Carolina Gazette*, March 1, 1768.

114 *South Carolina and American General Gazette*, July 8, 1768.

115 Journal, September 3, 1768, in Richard J. Hooker, ed., *The Carolina Backcountry on the Eve of the Revolution: The Journal and Other Writings of Charles Woodmason, Anglican Itinerant* (Chapel Hill, NC, 1953), 60.

116 Dickson, *Ulster Emigration*, 57. Green, "Queensborough Township," 189–93.

117 Since there was now no bounty money, merchant Newman Swallow advertised "A few Irish Families, Passengers on the *Two Arthurs*, to be indented for their passage money." *South Carolina and American General Gazette*, September 23, 1768, November 4, 1768. *South Carolina Gazette and Country Journal*, October 11, 1768, November 1, 1768.

118 South Carolina Assembly Journal, November 18, 1768, pp. 16 and 19–22. *Belfast News Letter*, May 27, 1768. *South Carolina and American General Gazette*, November 25, 1768.

119 *Charleston Gazette*, December 1, 1768.

120 *South Carolina Gazette and Country Journal*, December 28, 1769.

121 *South Carolina Gazette*, January 10, 1771. *Belfast News Letter*, March 19, 1771.

122 *Belfast News Letter*, April 23, 1771, July 26, 1771. *South Carolina Gazette*, October 17, 1771.

123 *Belfast News Letter*, July 30, 1771, September 6, 1771, September 10, 1771, November 1, 1771. *South Carolina Gazette*, January 21, 1772.

124 Jean Stephenson, *Scotch-Irish Migration to South Carolina, 1772: Rev. William Martin and his Five Shiploads of Settlers* (Washington, DC, 1971).

125 *Belfast News Letter*, December 31, 1771.

126 Emily Moberg Robinson, "The Covenanter Diaspora: Presbyterian Rebellion in the Atlantic World," unpublished paper presented at the Irish Atlantic conference, College of Charleston, Charleston, SC, March 1, 2007.

127 *Belfast News Letter*, December 31, 1771, May 26, 1772, July 17, 1772.

128 *Belfast News Letter*, April 28, 1772, August 28, 1772, September 15, 1772, October 9, 1772. *South Carolina Gazette*, December 24, 1772.

129 *Belfast News Letter*, March 10, 1772, September 15, 1772. *South Carolina Gazette*, July 9, 1772.

130 Robert Chesney, who farmed near Ballymena, his wife and eight children were among the passengers. His farm "being too small for his family," he moved from one to another within the parish of Kirkinriola, County Antrim and then to South Carolina. Small pox broke out on the passage, taking the lives of five children, and forcing the survivors to remain in quarantine seven weeks after they reached Charleston. *Belfast News Letter*, July 28, 1772. *South Carolina Gazette*, October 18, 1772. Bobby Gilmer Moss, ed., *Journal of Capt. Alexander Chesney, Adjutant to Major Patrick Ferguson* (Blacksburg, SC, 2002), 4–6. The passengers on the *James and Mary* were more than satisfied with their treatment aboard ship and 37 of them signed a letter of thanks to McVickar penned by the Rev. Robert McClintock, one of the passengers. *Belfast News Letter*, December 22, 1772. McClintock was not a Covenanter but a licentiate of Ballymena Presbytery. George Howe, *History of the Presbyterian Church in South Carolina* (Columbia, SC, 1870), 414.

131 *Belfast News Letter*, June 16, 1772, August 21, 1772.

132 *Belfast News Letter*, July 24, 1772, August 28, 1772.

133 *Belfast News Letter*, July 28, 1772.

134 *South Carolina Gazette*, December 24, 1772. These ships, consigned to Inglis and Lloyd and to Powell, Hopton and Co., all loaded rice for Cowes and the German market. *South Carolina Gazette*, January 7, 1773, February 15, 1773.

135 *South Carolina Gazette*, January 14, 1773.

136 Revill, *Original Lists of Protestant Immigrants*, 128.

137 Tennent, who was incidentally John Torrans' pastor, was the son of the Rev. William Tennent, Jr. and nephew of the Rev. Gilbert Tennent, Presbyterian leaders in the "Great Awakening." *South Carolina Gazette*, January 21, 1773, January 28, 1773.

138 Abraham and Conolly McCausland were grandsons of Col. Robert McCausland of Fruit Hill and James Stirling was their uncle. *Londonderry Journal*, April 1, 1773, April 23, 1773, May 25, 1773, May 25, 1773.

139 *Londonderry Journal*, June 11, 1773, June 15, 1773, June 25, 1773.

140 *Belfast News Letter*, May 7, 1773, August 6, 1773.

141 Advertised sailings were repeatedly delayed, and only *Jupiter* reached Charleston in 1773. *Belfast News Letter*, March 2, 1773, May 18, 1773, June 22, 1773, August 31, 1773, September 10, 1773.

142 *Belfast News Letter*, April 16, 1773, April 23, 1773.

143 *Belfast News Letter*, August 10, 1773.

144 *South Carolina Gazette*, August 25, 1773, August 30, 1773.

145 *South Carolina Gazette*, September 15, 1773.

146 *South Carolina Gazette*, October 11, 1773, November 1, 1773. *South Carolina and Country Gazette*, November 2, 1773.

147 *South Carolina Gazette*, October 24, 1771.

148 *Belfast News Letter*, November 26, 1773.

7
Merchants in Politics

Changing Times

The Treaty of Paris in 1763 brought the Seven Years' War to a close and stripped France of its North American empire, apart from two tiny islands in the Gulf of St. Lawrence. Spain acquired all of Louisiana west of the Mississippi and, in exchange for British evacuation of Havana, transferred East and West Florida to the British Crown. Faced with the need to protect an empire that stretched from Labrador to the Gulf of Mexico, a task undertaken by ten thousand men of the British army, and with a crushing national debt from the last war, government looked to new sources of revenue. There was never any question of making the Colonies pay for their own protection or even make a significant contribution to the costs of empire. The Sugar Act of 1764 promised a modest revenue enhancement by raising the duty on foreign sugar and molasses and a range of other imports and tightening enforcement of customs rules. It incidentally encouraged production of Ulster linen by making German and Dutch linens more expensive. Unfortunately passage of this legislation came at a moment when the American Colonies were sliding into an economic downturn.[1]

It was not a propitious time to go into business. Daniel Clark complained that "Goods are so monstrous high in England, so plenty here," it was hard to make a go of it. "We owe heavy sums in England," but with "sales dull, goods high and scarce at home, here plenty," merchants had trouble paying their creditors or collecting debts owed them, with "Money prodigious scarce and not easily collected from the inhabitants."[2] The failure of several small traders in 1763 was followed by the collapse of the Philadelphia flaxseed merchants Scott and McMichael, "which is likely to prove the most considerable break ever known here." They owed more than £50,000 and their failure affected other merchants who had accepted their bills and given them credit.[3]

Supplying the British army proved to be a lucrative business and gave a boost to the economy of many of the Colonies, notably Pennsylvania. Record prices for wheat, flour and bread in 1762–3 were owing in part to the demands of the British military on the mainland and in the West Indies.[4] A writer in the *Pennsylvania Journal* noted the difference after the province was no longer on a wartime footing. "The price of country produce is low, and likely to get lower." The West Indies, "our only market for flour," could not absorb the quantities Pennsylvania produced. "The army, which has hitherto kept up the price of meats for several years, is now removed, consequently the profits of grazing must be less than in times past." The anonymous writer pointed to the one break in this cloudy prospect. The demand for flaxseed in Ireland was growing every year to meet the needs of Ulster weavers and prices were on the rise. He urged his fellow Pennsylvanians to concentrate on exporting flaxseed.[5]

The price of flaxseed on the Philadelphia market increased each year from 1756 through 1762 and remained high thereafter. Prices for flour, bread, beef and pork followed much the same trajectory in the war years. There was a major upswing in these Pennsylvania staples, "which lasted until the close of the French and Indian War and in the case of pork carried it to even higher levels in 1763 and 1764 after peace was restored." But these prices began falling and by 1765 had dropped by half. Flaxseed prices continued high, however, despite substantially increased exports each year except in years of natural scarcity from drought or crop failure. Philadelphia shipped 95,000 bushels of seed in 1760, compared to 73,000 bushels the previous year. A bushel of seed sold for six shillings in 1760, eight shillings in 1761, and nine shillings in 1762 and remained in that range through the decade.[6] Flaxseed brought eleven shillings a bushel in 1764, when prices for wheat, flour and other commodities reached their nadir, and was quoted at from eight to ten shillings in 1765.[7] Exports continued to swell. During the 1765–6 shipping season Philadelphia sent 12,994 hogsheads of flaxseed to Ireland and New York shipped a further 11,037 hogsheads.[8] The following year New York shipped 18,851 hogsheads. More than two thirds of the New York flaxseed went to Londonderry, Newry, and "Belfast and Learn," more than half the total to the first two ports.[9]

The 1760s were a golden age for the flaxseed merchants and new firms entered the business in Philadelphia, New York and Baltimore. The Philadelphia merchants in the trade "numbered no fewer than sixty men at its peak in the late 1760s."[10] It was also a period of expansion for the passenger trade with more sailings from Ulster ports for the Middle Colonies as well as for Charleston and Savannah. Londonderry merchants and ship-owners testified to the importance of their American trade not only to Ulster and its linen manufacture, but to all British commercial interests, when an oversight by a parliamentary draftsman would, unless remedied, put a stop to their imports at the beginning of "the time for loading flaxseed at New York, a very principal mart for that commodity."[11]

Transatlantic trade became a weapon in the increasingly bitter arguments over the right of the Parliament at Westminster to levy direct or indirect taxes on the American Colonies and merchants on both sides of the ocean found themselves in the front lines of the dispute. Since the men who shipped flaxseed and flour to Belfast and Londonderry imported dry goods and hardware from London and Liverpool, non-importation agreements needed their cooperation. The economic depression that formed the backdrop for colonial resistance was also felt in England and riots erupted there over a tax on cider and textiles imported from France while New England merchants protested an increased levy on foreign molasses.[12]

In these years Ulster-born merchants in the principal North American towns were faced with other choices, too. Were they Irish, British, American or "Scotch-Irish"?

Affinity, Ethnicity and Identity

Elizabeth Graydon McIlvaine, the widow of flaxseed merchant David McIlvaine, died in 1763. In her last will she left bequests to family members and to her friends, Mary, wife of William West, Mary Donaldson, wife of Hugh Donaldson, and Polly West, and named Hannah, wife of William Humphreys, and Philadelphia merchant William Humphreys as executors of her estate.[13] In the absence of diaries and private letters, wills and estate settlements offer a window into the connections that flaxseed merchants and their families made in Philadelphia. While business associations might be enough to connect men in the same commercial circles, friendships among their wives must have another explanation. Elizabeth Graydon, daughter of an Irish lawyer who became a judge in Pennsylvania, married David McIlvaine, who came with his brother William from Ayrshire, Scotland about 1745. The McIlvaines were dry goods merchants who shipped flaxseed to Belfast. Mary Hodge, daughter of William Hodge, a Philadelphia merchant in the flaxseed trade, married William West in 1753. Her husband came from Sligo in 1750. Hugh Donaldson and his wife arrived from Glenarm that year. William Humphreys and his wife came from Coleraine about the same time.

Among other things all of these people had in common, all of them were Presbyterians, active in First Presbyterian Church, Philadelphia, where William McIlvaine was an elder. That merchants and their families would socialize with other mercantile families who attended the same church is hardly surprising. Should we make more of the fact that merchants Benjamin Fuller, George Fullerton, Blair McClenachan, James Mease, Randle Mitchell and William West, attorney George Campbell, and apothecary Sharp Delany were early members of the Hibernia Fire Company? Or that Fuller, Mease, John Maxwell Nesbitt and West formed a dining club they called the Irish Club in 1765? Or that William McIlvaine was a founding member of the parallel St. Andrew's Society? Were they making a statement of ethnic identity or were they merely clubable? These and other Philadelphia merchants organized the Friendly Sons of St. Patrick in 1771 and made provision for honorary members who had no claim on Ireland's patron saint, but they did not include Irish-born artisans or others outside their own circles.[14] Were they asserting a common Irish identity, parallel to that of the United Irishmen of the 1790s, or something broader? When the Sons of St. Patrick celebrated with "an elegant dinner" at

John Byrne's tavern in 1769, the 36 formal toasts included the King, the Queen, and the Corsican patriot Paoli, but all the others had reference to American liberties and political issues in Pennsylvania.[15] Were these Irishmen at the same time British and Americans?

Identity and especially ethnic identity was a new concept in the eighteenth century and far more fluid than it would be a century or two later. Ned Landsman observed that nice distinctions among emigrants from Scotland, the north of Ireland, Ireland, or elsewhere in the British Isles were rarely made by contemporaries and that Scots, Englishmen, Welshmen, and Irishmen who found themselves in predominantly Scotch-Irish Presbyterian settlements in the Pennsylvania or Virginia backcountry readily assimilated to the majority. He concluded that "Ethnic identifications in the eighteenth century, among British immigrants at least, were not fixed in quite the way that is sometimes supposed," reflecting "both a circumstantial and a volitional quality to ethnic identifications in the eighteenth-century British and Anglo-American worlds."[16]

Like Scots and Englishmen at home, Pennsylvanians and North Carolinians were trying on a new British identity. Development of a consciousness of being British stressed "its antitheses: France and Popery" and reached its zenith during the Jacobite rising of 1745–6. "The victory at Culloden was the culmination not only of an anti-Jacobite, but of a pro-British campaign," W. A. Speck noted. It was no happenstance that English volunteers marching against Bonnie Prince Charlie inscribed on their banners: "For Liberty and the Protestant Religion." These were the touchstones of a British identity. While being British was encouraged by government as a new national awareness at home and in the Colonies, a different "colonial American identity was a subconscious evolution from a cultural awareness towards a national character." The experience of the French and Indian War on the one hand strengthened a British identity in the Colonies and simultaneously raised a consciousness of being American. "These two developments met in the emergence of multiple identities." As Linda Colley pointed out, "Identities are not like hats; human beings can and do put on several at a time." It was possible to be many things at once, an American, a Pennsylvanian, and a loyal British subject – and for men and women who came to the Colonies from Ulster a recognition that all three were compatible with their own Protestant heritage.[17]

The Philadelphia merchants in the trade were mostly Ulstermen, many of them Ulster Presbyterians. They not only facilitated emigration, but assisted their countrymen in America. As historian Thomas Truxes noted, "The Philadelphia group was the most cohesive of any in the Colonies, with leading members active in promoting the political interests of the colony's Irish immigrants, particularly Scotch-Irish Presbyterians." Truxes is certainly correct in concluding that "deep sectarian divisions" were not evident among the flaxseed merchants of Philadelphia, despite the dominance of Presbyterians in the trade.[18]

According to a list of contributions by members of First Presbyterian Church to the Corporation for the Relief of Distressed Presbyterian Ministers, as minuted in 1760 by William Humphreys, the treasurer, at least 25 flaxseed merchants were members of that one Philadelphia congregation. The list included John Mease, William Humphreys, Adam Hoops, George Bryan, John McMichael, John Bleakley, Sr. and Jr., Peter Chevalier, William Hodge, John & Peter Chevalier, David Caldwell, Samuel Purviance, Jr., Alexander Huston, William McIlvaine, William West, James Cannon, Hugh Donnaldson, James Harvey, John Fullerton, Robert Corry, John Corry, Mark Kuyl, James Fulton, John Wallace, and William Murray.[19] Similar lists from the other Presbyterian churches in the city would add nearly all the other men in the flaxseed trade.

This is hardly surprising. The trade in flaxseed and emigrants was primarily with Ulster and Presbyterians accounted for a very high percentage of the merchants in Belfast, Londonderry, Newry, and the other northern ports. Presbyterians were no less prominent in Dublin mercantile circles, especially in the linen trade, and well represented in other Irish ports, such as Waterford, Cork, and Sligo. When these firms sought correspondents in America, they naturally turned to men already known to them, often enough a relative or a former apprentice.

Business associations did not require subscription to the Westminster Confession, of course, and Presbyterian merchants in

Ireland and America readily entered into formal and informal partnerships like that of Anglican Hugh Davey and Presbyterian
Samuel Carsan. Personal friendships also regularly ignored labels
like Churchman and Dissenter, as in the guest list for the dinner
hosted by Oliver McCausland for Samuel Carsan on one of his visits to his native Strabane.[20] What did come into play on both sides
of the Atlantic was the similar social background of virtually all the
mercantile class. It was less significant that Redmond Conyngham
went to the parish church and Hugh Donaldson to the dissenting
meeting house than that each owned Ulster acreage in his own
right, not on the scale of the nobility or the great Anglo-Irish proprietors to be sure, but sufficient to qualify as gentlemen.

American scholars are notoriously chary of social class as an
explanation for anything and, in the case of eighteenth-century
Ulster emigrants, are more comfortable with the categories of contemporary Irish nationalism and Ulster unionism in crafting an
identity for "the people with no name" whom we recognize as
Scotch-Irish. Flaxseed merchants in Philadelphia and New York
had no more need to identify with the needs and aspirations of fellow emigrants from Ulster on the frontiers than opulent Boston
merchants and land speculators had to forge close ties with the poor
Yankees of western Massachusetts. When both groups made common cause it would be a deliberate choice and one with political
consequences.

Aftermath of a Massacre

Events conspired to thrust an identity on men and women who
might or might not have chosen it for themselves as Philadelphia's
flaxseed merchants were drawn together into closer community
with emigrants from Ulster in the Pennsylvania backcountry in the
aftermath of a massacre of friendly Indians in Lancaster County.
Early on the morning of December 14, 1763, in the midst of a
heavy snowstorm, a party of men from Donegal and Paxton townships, Scotch-Irish settlements along the Susquehanna river, rode
into the village of the Conestoga Indians some miles downstream,
killed all six people they found there and burned their huts. After
the massacre, the local magistrates instituted a search for the other

Conestogas, who were scattered about the countryside, and put fourteen of them in the Lancaster jail for their own safety. They would then be moved to a more secure refuge in Philadelphia. Before that could happen, on December 27, fifty or sixty Paxton Boys rode into Lancaster, broke into the jail, and set about killing the men, women and children there. Ten minutes later they were gone, mangled corpses mute testimony to the fury of their killing spree.[21]

Other friendly Indians, 140 Christian converts from the Moravian missions, had already been moved to the comparative safety of Philadelphia. On January 3, 1764, Governor John Penn and his Council read an anonymous letter warning them

> that Many of the Inhabitants of the Townships of Lebanon, Paxton & Hanover, are Voluntarily forming themselves in a Company to March to Philadelphia, with a Design to Kill the Indians that Harbour there.[22]

About the same time, Robert Fulton, a respectable Lancaster shopkeeper, told one of his Philadelphia suppliers that they could muster as many as 5,000 men and, while they were not looking for a fight, any "who should oppose them they should kill."[23]

It was another month before the Paxton Boys and their supporters took the road to Philadelphia. With armed men, rumoured to be 1,500 strong, on their way to the city, Governor Penn called on the citizens to form volunteer companies of infantry, cavalry, and artillery and instructed the commanding officer at the barracks, where the Indians were housed, to fire on any frontiersmen who refused to disperse. Philadelphians had several days of panic and comic relief, while the Paxton Boys halted at Germantown. Anglican and Presbyterian ministers went there to talk with the leaders and finally a delegation from the Pennsylvania Assembly persuaded them to go back to their homes in return for a serious consideration of their grievances.[24] Later in February spokesmen for the marchers delivered to the Governor and Assembly and had printed as a pamphlet *A Declaration and Remonstrance Of the distressed and bleeding Frontier Inhabitants*, complaining of the under-representation of the back counties in the Assembly and the failure to provide adequate defence of the frontier and relief for captives and refugees.[25]

Between the back inhabitants and the city merchants lay the deep chasm of social class. A letter from Philadelphia published in the *Belfast News Letter* dismissed the Paxton Boys as "consisting chiefly of convicts and others of ill character."[26] Reflecting on the back-country protest in his diary, merchant George Bryan was no less certain that the Paxton Boys were drawn from the "mean and lower sort of people." Bryan believed in the "necessity of supporting order" and the "danger of mobs," but he understood nonetheless that they were desperate and "for any government to drive people into such proceedings is neither polite nor safe."[27] One of the first pamphleteers to comment on these events addressed himself to men like Bryan, "the more sensible Part" of the community, asking them to "openly avow your Disapprobation of these Measures," since "the Lower Sort of People are very imitative of their Superiors" and the protest marchers "will disperse" at a sign from their betters.[28]

Criticism of the backcountry protesters had an unexpected result. By tarring all Presbyterians and all Ulstermen with the Lancaster murders, critics drew them together. Even before the first marchers reached Germantown, the Rev. John Elder, pastor of the Paxton congregation, wrote to a friend:

> The Presbyterians, who are the most numerous I imagine of any denomination in the province, are enraged at their being charged in bulk with these facts, under the name of Scotch-Irish, and other ill-natured titles, & that the killing of the Conestogoe Indians is compared to the Irish Massacres & reckoned the most barbarous of either.

The slaughter of Protestants in 1641 was part of Ulster's folk memory. They resented its being invoked to identify themselves with the wild Irishmen who killed helpless settlers. Blame for the Paxton outrage crossed class lines, no longer limited to "the lower sort of people." As the commanding officer of the Paxton Volunteers who made an unsuccessful foray against the Indians in 1763, Elder was himself under suspicion. He complained in the same letter that "some particular persons I'm informed are grossly misrepresented in Phila[delphia]," as somehow involved and "even my neighbour Mr. Harris, it's said is looked on there as the chief promoter of these riots." John Harris, Jr., son of the Yorkshire-born Indian trader who gave his name to the ferry across the Susquehanna and the town later built there, was a magistrate, a merchant, and a Presbyterian. Through marriage and business associations, the Harris family had become "foster children of the Ulster Scots" who settled beside them. This was enough to tar him as "Scotch-Irish." It is little wonder that, as Elder observed, the men marching on Philadelphia had "the good wishes of the Country in general." [29]

While the Rev. John Elder bristled at being called Scotch-Irish, the term was already in general use by Americans to designate settlers from Ulster. In the 1757 first edition of his *Account of the European Settlements in America* (and in subsequent editions over the next twenty years), Edmund Burke wrote of the Southern backcountry that

> They are growing every day more numerous by the migration
> of the Irish, who, not succeeding so well in Pennsylvania as the
> more frugal and industrious Germans, sell their lands in that
> province to the latter, and take up new ground in the remote
> counties in Virginia, Maryland, and North Carolina. These
> are chiefly Presbyterians from the northern part of Ireland,
> who in America are generally called Scotch-Irish.[30]

"Ill-natured title" it may have been, but Presbyterians and others from Ulster accepted the "Scotch-Irish" identity pressed on them by their neighbors. Indian traders selling guns, ammunition, and knives to the tribal people in the Ohio and Illinois country always alarmed the backcountry. Two different agents of the Philadelphia firm of Wharton, Baynton and Morgan reported from Carlisle that townspeople there were "continually prying into every Waggon and package that comes ... and often ask whether, there is any powder or Lead going back to kill the Scotch Irishmen." One of his colleagues told the same story of being asked as he loaded pack horses for Indian country "whether I had Got Powder and Lead in those Bundles to Kill the Scotch Irish." The shopkeepers and publicans of Carlisle clearly made common cause with settlers on the frontiers.[31]

Philadelphia's merchants trading with Ireland also found themselves in close alliance and had a common identity thrust upon them. The city erupted in a pamphlet war in 1764 with fully 63 separate publications arguing for or against the Paxton Boys and their petitions for redress of backcountry grievances.[32] As Elder had observed, some writers quickly turned to railing against all Presbyterians as the supposed allies of the Conestoga killers. Presbyterians were equated with the "Christian white savages of Peckstang and Donegall." Some writers tried their hand at a supposed Ulster dialect in dialogues about "fechting the Lord's battles, and killing the Indians at Lancaster and Connestogoe." The murderers did it all "in the Name of the Lord," for "we were aw Presbyterians."[33] One writer went so far as to aver that "the Presbyterians have been the Authors, and Abettors, of all the Mischief, that's happened to us."[34] Another asked, "What King has ever reign'd in Great-Britain, whose government has not been disturbed by Presbyterian Rebellions, since ever they were a people?" He denied them any role in the Glorious Revolution of 1688 and asserted that Presbyterians have held "the same rebellious Principles since the Revolution" as they did before it.[35] Indeed, as another writer asserted: "To be govern'd is absolutely repugnant to the avowed principles of Pr---ns."[36]

Presbyterians and Ulster emigrants were one and the same to these writers. The author of *A Looking-Glass for Presbyterians* sneered at their Ulster origins: the first "adventurers from Ireland" promptly sent "for their poor Relations to populate this Province; whose delightful Plains far surpass the barren Mountains of Carrentaugher, Slemish, or Slevgallion." He blamed "the Scotch Presbyterians," who earlier had "swarm'd like Locusts" into Ireland from their own barren hills, for the 1641 massacres, since the Irish Catholics were defending their country "against the Inroads and Depradations of those foreign Interlopers" and reminded his readers that the Scots had massacred Catholics at Islandmagee that same year.[37]

Pamphleteers who took up their pens on behalf of the backcountry folk turned this criticism on its head and appealed to the hallmarks of the new British identity, especially to their role in "the happy and glorious REVOLUTION, by which our civil and religious Rights, as ENGLISHMEN and PROTESTANTS, were secured on the present Footing."[38]

These backcountry settlers were "Descendants of the Noble Enniskillers, who were the great Means of setting their great and never to be forgotten Prince King William on the Throne."[39] They had ever since upheld British liberty and taken up arms against its foes.

> These, these are they, who always chose
> T'engage their King and Country's Foes
> Whose Grandsires too were bravely willing
> To fight or die at Ineskilling.[40]

Their understanding of British liberty mandated "inclusion in governing institutions and a just allocation of representation." They "yoked British rights with the Protestantism that buttressed it."[41] The Rev. Thomas Barton, Ulster-born Anglican minister at Lancaster, summed up the grievances of the Paxton Boys and their supporters in the back counties:

> That tho' born to Liberty, and all the glorious Rights and Privileges of BRITISH SUBJECTS, they were denied Protection, at a Time when the Cries of Murder and Distress might have made the very Stones relent; ... That they have suffered and bled in the Cause of their Country, and have done more to protect it from the Violence of a rapacious Enemy than any others in the Province ... That they have been treated as Aliens of the Common-wealth, and denied a just and proportionable Share in Legislation.[42]

Dr. Hugh Williamson, a member of the Presbyterian Committee, took up the charge of fair representation in the Assembly, "an intolerable grievance, as it deprives us of liberty," and "is contrary to an express stipulation in [William Penn's] Charter, for which we left our native country, and came to this howling wilderness."[43]

The Rev. William McClenachan entered the fray with *A Letter from a Clergyman in Town*. He was the older brother of flaxseed merchant Blair McClenachan and, as the title of his pamphlet suggests, an Anglican minister and rector of St. Paul's Church in Philadelphia. He argued, as others did, that protection and allegiance are reciprocal and carried the case for British identity a step further, separating the Ulster Scots from the native Irish:

> The Macs you know are a noble dignified Race in the Irish Annals, famed for their intire Renunciation of Popery; while the O's are rank Roman-Catholicks, and Native Irish that trot in our Bogs ... and always attended Mass in Ireland, whatever they may do in Pennsylvania.[44]

It was not just in Philadelphia that the rhetoric of newspapers and pamphlets fed a growing sense of solidarity. The controversy also strengthened group identity in the backcountry and encouraged them to assert their rights. As the dispute heated up, the rhetoric of the "the rights discourse employed by the Paxton Boys and their defenders served as a touchstone for group unity."[45] A new identity emerged from the controversy. Their adversaries had lumped together Ulster emigrants and folk from other backgrounds, Presbyterians and Anglicans, and men and women of every social class "under the name of Scotch-Irish, and other ill-natured titles." With or without that label, they accepted the identification. They were at the same time British and American. This multiple identity, based on British liberty and the Protestant religion, served them well as they moved into new phases of the old struggle. In 1764, fresh from the arguments over the Paxton Boys and backcountry representation, they challenged the petition introduced by the Quaker party in the Pennsylvania Assembly for an end to the proprietary government of the Penn family and direct rule from Whitehall. This battle would be fought in large part by the "Scotch-Irish" flaxseed merchants of Philadelphia, led by George Bryan and Samuel Purviance, Jr.

Merchants in Politics

In March 1764 "a few Gentlemen in the city of Philadelphia," nearly all of them merchants, met "with the Ministers of the Presbyterian denomination there" to draw up a plan for a political action committee. As the furore over the march of the Paxton Boys demonstrated, notwithstanding Presbyterians "are so numerous in the province of Pennsylvania, we are considered as *Nobody*, or a body of very little weight and consequence." Political leaders and anonymous pamphleteers did not hesitate to "misrepresent and asperse the whole body of Presbyterians, on account of the indiscreet conduct of individuals belonging to us." In response, they constituted a committee of 27 prominent Philadelphia Presbyterians to "correspond with their friends in different parts" and to consult with them on "what things may have a tendency to promote our union and welfare." They called for similar committees in every district to work with them and for a general meeting at Philadelphia or Lancaster in August.[46]

The 27 gentlemen who comprised the Philadelphia committee included at least eighteen merchants, among them William Allison, George Bryan, William Humphreys, John Mease, Samuel Purviance, Sr. and Samuel Purviance, Jr., and three physicians, Robert Harris, John Redman, and Hugh Williamson. Fifteen of them were members of First Presbyterian Church, where John Ewing was the pastor, and eight of Second Presbyterian Church.[47]

Although nowhere mentioned, lurking in the background was a petition from the Pennsylvania Assembly, on Benjamin Franklin's initiative, for royal government. They were frustrated by Governor John Penn's insistence that none of his family's vast landholdings be taxed "higher than the lowest Rate at which any located uncultivated Lands belonging to the Inhabitants ... shall be assessed." On the same day that the Presbyterian committee drew up their circular letter, the Assembly agreed to consult their constituents whether to ask the King to take Pennsylvania under his direct rule and abolish the proprietary government.[48] The underlying issue of a fair assessment policy for frontier land might have appealed to both backcountry settlers and city merchants who themselves owned large tracts of "located uncultivated land," but the move by the Quaker or Anti-Proprietary bloc led by Franklin appeared in a more sinister light. Another circular letter from Presbyterian ministers Gilbert Tennent, Francis Alison, and John Ewing warned:

> This Affair is in all Probability, a Trap laid to ensnare the unwary, and then to cast an Odium on the Presbyterians for ruining or attempting to ruin the province. The Frontier Counties are now suing for a Redress of Grievances, and we have the greatest Reason to believe that it is no more than an artful Scheme to divide or divert the Attention of the injur'd Frontier Inhabitants from prosecuting their Petitions, which very much alarm them.[49]

They strongly recommended against signing the petitions circulated by the Quaker Party. George Bryan wrote in April that "in the country the petitions for a change in government are less liked, especially as you approach the frontier," where, of course, Presbyterians from Ulster were most numerous.[50] Another Philadelphia merchant observed that "There are Petitions handed about in every County," but the proponents of royal government "do not meet with that encouragement they expected."[51]

The 1764 election campaign was an apprenticeship in politics for flaxseed merchants. The first business of the newly-formed Presbyterian Committee was to organise for the upcoming Assembly election. They hoped to turn out Franklin and his cohort. Samuel Purviance, Jr., committee secretary, came into his own as a political operative, while George Bryan stood as a candidate in Franklin's Philadelphia constituency and won election to the Assembly. The committee met in Lancaster in August to adopt a "New Side" ticket, "but the Germans, who carry every thing in that country that goes by vote," remained aloof.[52] Worse, Purviance wrote of

> the Quakers & Menonists having made a powerful Party to thwart the Measures your Friends have so vigorously pursued of late for thrusting out of the Assembly those men who have lately endanger'd our happy Constitution by their precipitate Measures.

He proposed dropping two of the candidates endorsed at the

Lancaster meeting "and putting in two Germans to draw such a Party of them as will turn the Scale in our favor." At the same time, the "Irish" candidates had to be left on the ticket, as "it would be imprudent to offend them by rejecting one of their proposing." He was equally busy in Bucks, Chester, and Philadelphia counties.[53] In spite of Purviance's understanding of "political geography," the Old Side outfoxed him by choosing the same men as their candidates.[54] Indeed, Quaker Party leaders outside Philadelphia backed away from the royal government issue and presented themselves as champions of proprietary rule. Both Quakers and German Mennonites found the proposed change in government unsettling as it could threaten the religious liberty they enjoyed under Penn's Charter, so in the rural counties both Old and New Side candidates campaigned against it.[55] The 1764 election was at the end of the day less a referendum on royal government than a test of strength between the entrenched Quaker Party and the newly-politicised Presbyterians. Benjamin Franklin and Joseph Galloway, closely identified with the royal government agitation, lost their seats. The New Side elected George Bryan and Thomas Willing in the city and John Dickinson and five others in the county of Philadelphia. They were able to elect one member in each of the backcountry counties of Lancaster, Cumberland, and Northampton and two in York. The Quaker Party carried all the other contests.[56]

Passage of the Stamp Act in March 1765 overshadowed all other political issues for the next year. As the Pennsylvania Assembly election again drew near, Samuel Purviance, Jr. wrote, on behalf of the Presbyterian committee, that:

> You may possibly imagine from the general Silence with which our political Affairs have been conducted this year that perhaps we are relapsed again into the old passive humor of submitting the conduct of public Affairs to our former state Pilots & that if we at the Fountain head observe such a Conduct you at a distance shou'd follow the same non resisting plans in town. Be assured that nothing is less thought of by us than such a Scheme, tho matters go on very quietly, yet every thing is preparing for making a vigorous Stand at the ensuing election. ... The general committee of our Society meet this day & on Tuesday next & shall finally settle our Ticket.[57]

Purviance was buoyed by missteps his opponents had made. Franklin, in London as Pennsylvania's agent, failed to see the opposition this measure would meet in America and, like other agents, lobbied to get his associates appointed Stamp Act collectors.[58] On news of its passage, the Massachusetts House of Representatives invited the other colonies to send delegates to a meeting at New York in October to make a united appeal to King and Parliament for relief. The Pennsylvania Assembly was divided, but by a narrow 15:14 vote decided to send George Bryan, John Dickinson, and John Morton as their representatives to the Stamp Act Congress. John Hughes, the Stamp Act collector, and his Quaker Party allies formed the opposition. The same day the Assembly adopted a series of resolutions, asserting that only their elected representatives in the Assembly could levy taxes on the people of Pennsylvania and that the restraints on trade imposed by Parliament, "at a Time when the People labour under an Enormous Load of Debt," would have fatal consequences "not only to this Province, but to the Trade of our Mother Country."[59]

Purviance believed the opposition Hughes and his friends made to sending delegates to the Stamp Act Congress should prove fatal to their cause in the coming election. "This unpopular Action has greatly damp'd their Ticket … & even brought over some of their members in the house to our party by which means they carried the vote" to send Bryan, Dickinson and Morton to New York. He had been in Chester County and "there concerted some measures for dividing the Quaker Interest in that County that our friends may join one party of them." In Bucks County "we have appointed a considerable meeting of the Germans, Baptists & Presbyterians … in order to attempt a general confederacy of the three Societies in opposition to the ruling party." He had less hope of carrying the election in Lancaster County, but he suggested they could win if they could keep the Mennonites away from the polls. To do this they would need "to come well armed" and spread the rumour that at the least sign of partiality they were prepared to "thrash the Sheriff every Inspector Quaker & Menonist to Jelly." He wanted "all our friends warned to put on a wild face to be every man provided with a good Shilely, as if determined to put their threats into execution, tho' at the same time let them be solemly Charged to keep the greatest Order & peace."[60]

In spite of Purviance's efforts, the Presbyterian committee failed
to sway the voters. Even George Bryan and John Dickinson, delegates to the Stamp Act Congress, lost their seats. Israel Pemberton,
a prominent Quaker leader, reported:

> The Last Election in this province for representatives in assem-
> bly was the greatest ever known in this [Philadelphia] County,
> the Pre'[sbyteria]ns notwithstanding the utmost exertions of
> their labor & influence, came so farr Short of success that they
> have not Since recovered Sufficient Spirit to attempt what
> their aspiring & pernicious temper & principles would other-
> wise have prompted them to, after the Example of their
> Brethren in the Eastern Provinces.[61]

Had the effort been in vain? Far from it. The answer is to be
found in Israel Pemberton's identification of the opposition as "the
Presbyterians." The old Proprietary party based on loyalty to the
Penn family was gone and in its place a new organization based on
religious and ethnic identity had emerged. Purviance and the others on the Presbyterian committee had forged a political alliance
between the city merchants and the backcountry settlers who made
a common cause of otherwise regional issues. They succeeded in
broadening their base by reaching out to Germans, especially in the
Reformed churches, Baptists and Anglican evangelicals, notably the
congregation of St. Paul's in Philadelphia, where Rev. William
McClenachan was rector. This venture into identity politics would
last beyond the American Revolution.[62]

The petition for royal government was a dead letter by November
1765, although Franklin and Galloway tried to keep the issue alive
for a few more years.[63] Opposition to the Stamp Act took centre
stage. Philadelphia merchants presented a united front by pledging
to import no British goods until the act was repealed and cancelling
orders already sent, but there were no riots or destruction of property as in other colonies.[64] Pemberton and the Quakers took credit for the understated response in the city both to passage of the
Stamp Act and to its repeal in 1766, thus distancing themselves
from popular feeling.[65]

With the issues that caught the attention of Pennsylvanians no
longer current, Purviance and the Presbyterian committee found a

new cause to unite dissenters in the threatened appointment of a
Church of England bishop for the American Colonies. Purviance
travelled to Newport, Rhode Island, in August 1766, to enlist Rev.
Ezra Stiles and the New England Congregationalists as allies. He
brought a letter from Rev. Francis Alison proposing a "Union
among all the anti-Episcopal churches" so as to stand together
"against Episcopal Encroachments." Stiles found "Mr. Purviance
has been a Feast of Intelligence to me" and gave him letters of introduction to Rev. Charles Chauncy and other church leaders in
Boston.[66]

A few months later Samuel Purviance Jr. decided to join his
brother Robert in Baltimore. This did not mean a withdrawal from
politics. Both brothers were in the forefront of the defence of the
rights of the Colonies, so much so that a committee of Boston merchants anxious to secure the cooperation of Baltimore in a new
non-importation agreement in 1768 made their proposal to
Samuel and Robert Purviance alone.[67]

New York already had a Presbyterian party, led by lawyers and
centred on the Livingston family connections. Flaxseed merchants
William Neilson and Robert Boyd made common cause with them
in the Society of Dissenters formed in 1769 to defend "civil and
religious liberty." Neilson was also one of the committee of inspection appointed the same year to oversee the non-importation agreement.[68] By this time the identity as Presbyterian, Scotch-Irish and
British that united Pennsylvanians across class and region in a common struggle to preserve "all the glorious Rights and Privileges of
BRITISH SUBJECTS" would unite them with the other Colonies
in a new identity as Americans.

After Repeal

Merchants insisted "on business of all kinds going on as if no Stamp
Act pass'd," a Philadelphian observed in November 1765. They had
agreed with near unanimity to cancel all orders for Fall goods and
joined in a "Memorial to the Merchants and Manufacturers of
Great Britain" that same month asking their help to secure repeal.
James Mease, John Rhea, and J. M. Nesbitt were among those who
drafted it. With ships loading for Irish ports in the flaxseed season,

the Collector of the Port of Philadelphia decided to clear vessels without the technically unavailable stamps.[69] In agreeing to non-importation of goods from England, the Philadelphia merchants "determined to encourage the Irish trade by importing everything that can be lawfully brought from Ireland."[70] It was not only British merchants who supported the Americans in calling for repeal. A ship's captain, just arrived from Cork, told the *Pennsylvania Journal* that:

> The people of Ireland are highly pleased at the opposition the Stamp Act meets with in America; their general Toasts are: Destruction to the American Stamp Act; … In Ireland it was generally thought that the Stamp Act would be repealed or suspended at the meeting of the Parliament.[71]

Parliament voted repeal in February 1766 to general rejoicing on both sides of the Atlantic.[72] Henry Cruger, Jr., the Bristol merchant who corresponded with James Fullton and other flaxseed merchants, warned of "The unwillingness and backwardness of Merchants here trusting any more Goods to America where their Debts are already too enormous to venture much more."[73] American merchants were anxious to replenish their stock of textiles, hardware and other imports and ordered goods accordingly. Many found themselves in difficulty when backcountry shopkeepers fell behind in paying them and their British correspondents pressed for prompt payment. The experience of Benjamin Fuller, a Philadelphia flaxseed exporter and dry goods importer, was typical, if his solution was not.

> In the summer of 1766, I made a large order of Dry Goods, w[hi]ch added to a considerable Sum I already owed to Great Britain on the same account, made me greatly uneasy, as I found payment from the country very precarious, and the risque dayly increasing. I took a resolution to decline any further imports, until I could wind up my affairs, wch I foresaw would take up some time, therefore in the fall of the same year I erected a Vendue house, in the upper part of Second street, joining the limits of the City, wch has succeeded to my utmost wishes; it enables me to support my family genteelly.

Ordering too many British goods in a time of credit constriction brought others to ruin. "Misfortunes in trade has happened to many, since you have been here, and people in general have grown more familiar to accidents of that kind."[74]

Flaxseed merchants faced another crisis in 1766, but it was due to error and set right before any harm was done. A letter from Cork explained the situation:

> You will have seen, no doubt, before this reaches you, that the intercourse between America and Ireland, is totally cut off, from the 1st of January next, by the 35th section of the American act of last session, by the word Ireland being omitted, through mistake; a gentleman of this place, now in London, was the first that perceived it, and alarmed the people on this side the water; he has presented petitions to the Lord Lieutenant from all the principal trading towns in the kingdom, and his Excellency has given him the strongest assurance, that it will be repealed as soon as the parliament meets.[75]

The act in question forbade the exportation of colonial products to any port north of Cape Finesterre "unless bond be given that the same shall be landed in Great-Britain." All Irish ports were equally affected by the prohibition, but the northern ports depended on the flaxseed trade. Merchants in Londonderry protested that "the linen manufacture, the great and staple commodity of this country, must suffer unavoidable inconveniences, the American flax-seed being necessary to [its] very existence." They also pointed out that in the event of "a famine or scarcity of provisions in this country" American wheat and flour could not be imported to alleviate hunger. The Pennsylvania Assembly joined in the call for amending the act.[76]

Since the prohibition would not effect goods shipped before January 1, 1767, when Philadelphia's flaxseed season would be over, merchants there had less to fear than their counterparts in New York, where the season continued longer. Flaxseed prices hovered around six shillings through autumn and early winter. Because an early freeze prevented shallops from bringing seed to Philadelphia, James Fullton wrote in mid-December that "flaxseed is not to be got even at 6/6." There was clearly a rush to get the flaxseed ships to sea before the end of the year. Nine ships sailed for Belfast, six for Newry, eleven for Londonderry, two for Dublin and one for Waterford in December 1766.[77]

New York flaxseed merchants were also sanguine, urging their Connecticut and Rhode Island suppliers to ship early in the season.

> By late Advices from Ireland, they have not saved much Flaxseed of their own Growth, consequently they will want a Supply of American Seed. I believe the Price will be from 5/6 to 6/– Currency per Bushel, and would recommend to you to send what you buy as early as possible to Market.[78]

This problem was soon mended as the British Parliament corrected what was always an oversight. A copy of their new act reached Philadelphia and New York in January.[79] Nothing could be done about the weather and flaxseed promised to be in short supply for the 1767 shipping season. "Tis imagined we shall have a very bad crop of Flaxseed this season owing to the dryness of the weather," a Philadelphia firm warned in the summer. "We are sure there will not be the quantity raised that there was last year." By September they knew flaxseed would be "very scarce, as the crops in general are very indifferent." When the season was already advanced, flaxseed was in short supply, "as there is not above 300 hogsheads come to market yet, when formerly the most of the vessels used to be half loaded by this time." This firm had four flaxseed ships consigned to them to be loaded for Belfast and Newry. With so little flaxseed on the Philadelphia market, they turned to New York associates for enough to fill orders.[80] Despite the short crop, prices were only a shilling more than the year before, holding at seven shillings a bushel until December, rising to 7/6, dropping six pence for two weeks, and recovering at the New Year.[81] As the season drew to a close, William Glenholme estimated "the flaxseed export from here will not exceed 8,000 hogsheads" and there would be no more than 10,000 hogsheads shipped from New York.[82]

Short harvests in the British Isles caused the demand and the prices paid for wheat and flour to rise. William Lux, a Baltimore merchant, wrote in August 1767 that:

Our Crops of Wheat are shorter than formerly owing to a great draught early in the year, but the grain never was so good. Very little comes to Market yet, what does sells at 4/9. Flour 15/– but as this days Post brings advices of the Harvest failing in Europe and that large Orders are expected to be sent out to America, we expect the Price will be high here.[83]

Word reached Philadelphia in August "that there was little or no flour in Belfast." Like other flaxseed firms, Orr, Dunlope and Glenholme were already shipping flour to the West Indies and to Cork.[84] They sent a cargo of flour to Newry, but concentrated on their flaxseed business through the end of the season, while informing their correspondents that wheat and flour were both "extravagantly high."[85] James Fullton noted, "Flour so Extremely Dear here that there is Scarsly a Probability of its answering in any of the three Kingdoms."[86] Orr, Dunlope and Glenholme sent flour to Ballycastle and Belfast in March. There was no shortage of merchants in Philadelphia and in Baltimore ready to profit from the shortfall in provisions in the British Isles. Glenholme reported the "large number of vessels loading with wheat and flour for England."[87] Fullton offered to load a ship with 2,000 barrels of flour for Liverpool and informed his partners in Derry that "I find by Letters Rec'd from [Bristol] this Day that the ports of Great Britain is open for the Importing of Provisions, and that flour would pay a good freight."[88]

Passage of a new revenue act in 1767 brought on a fresh crisis for merchants in the Colonies. Bostonians were the first to agree to stop importing goods from Great Britain after a certain date to once again put pressure on the coalition of interests that won repeal of the Stamp Act. Rhode Island followed suit. In Providence a Town Meeting on December 2, 1767 condemned "Luxury and Extravagance in the Use of British and foreign Manufactures and Superfluities" and opened voluntary "subscription rolls for suppressing the unnecessary and destructive Importation of European goods."[89] New York merchants also adopted a non-importation agreement but cannily insisted it would only take effect if Philadelphia merchants agreed to the same terms. Most of them then agreed to a voluntary agreement to take effect October 1, 1768.[90] Philadelphia merchants were also wary of any precipitous action and adjourned their first meeting without any decision. A month's consideration of the issues did not increase their enthusiasm for what many saw as economic suicide. A second meeting in April left the matter to personal choice, much to William Glenholme's relief.

> In my last I advised you that the Merchants in Boston N. York & this place had come to a resolution not to import any dry goods from Britain the 1st of August next but the whole would not come into it therefore every person is at liberty to import what they please.[91]

The issue did not go away, however, and a lively debate continued in the ensuing months. New York merchants agreed to a more comprehensive ban in August 1768.[92] Early in 1769 the Committee of Merchants in Philadelphia secured more than 200 signatures to a pledge to send no orders to England and in March 1769 adopted a full-fledged non-importation agreement, the only exceptions being linens and provisions from Ireland.[93] There was a downside to this good news for the linen drapers of Ulster. Benjamin Fuller wrote to a friend in Armagh: "By our agreement Linens are not suffered to go to England for the bounty – they must be immediately from Ireland."[94]

These agreements were essentially voluntary ones with no mechanism to enforce compliance, so from the beginning there was pressure to break ranks. When Parliament relented and repealed the duties on everything but tea, many merchants were ready to reciprocate by dropping non-importation. Rhode Island and then New York abandoned this policy. In Baltimore, with John Smith in the chair, Samuel Purviance, Jr. moved not to purchase West Indian molasses brought in by Rhode Island vessels. New York's merchants were denounced by their Philadelphia counterparts as "traitors to their country, to themselves, and to ages yet unborn."[95] Philadelphia stood firm until September, when a majority of merchants voted to limit the ban to tea as New York had done. Flaxseed merchants were divided on the issue. William West, Hugh Donaldson, Randle Mitchell, Walter and Bartles Shee, and Tench Francis joined eight other merchants, all Quakers, in presenting the case for change in the newspapers. James Mease, John Maxwell

Nesbitt, Alexander Huston and nine others opposed this move and resigned from the committee in protest.[96] In Charleston, with "most of the dry goods stores now empty," none of the merchants proposed importing goods from Great Britain, "abhorring the example of New York." They soon discovered that Philadelphia had also dropped its ban on imports, except for the sole article of tea.[97]

Everywhere dry goods merchants responded with substantial orders to their British correspondents to restock empty shelves in anticipation of a buying spree by American consumers. This step would prove the undoing of some merchants and had grave consequences for the linen-based economy of Ulster.

Notes

1   Edmund S. and Helen M. Morgan, *The Stamp Act Crisis* (Chapel Hill, NC, 1953, New York, 1963), 36–9. Edmund S. Morgan, *Prologue to Revolution* (Chapel Hill, NC, 1959), 4–8.

2   Daniel Clark to Halliday, Dunbar & Co., November 14, 1761, to William Nicholson, March 16, 1762 (Clark Letter Book, HSP).

3   James and Drinker to Neale and Pigou, December 20, 1763 (James and Drinker Letterbook, HSP).

4   Geoffrey N. Gilbert, *Baltimore's Flour Trade to the Caribbean 1750–1815* (New York, 1986), 11.

5   *Pennsylvania Journal*, March 21, 1765.

6   Early in the 1761 shipping season Daniel Clark reported "its rising to 9/6 per Bushel delivered me." Daniel Clark to Edward Cochran, November 23, 1761 (Daniel Clark Letter Book, HSP). Bezanson *et al.*, *Prices in Colonial Pennsylvania*, 40, 69, 108.

7   *Pennsylvania Journal*, October 11, 1764, November 8, 1764, September 5, 1765, November 14, 1765.

8   *Pennsylvania Journal*, March 19, 1767.

9   *South Carolina Gazette*, April 27, 1767.

10 Truxes, *Irish-American Trade*, 106.

11 *Pennsylvania Journal*, October 30, 1766.

12 Lawrence H. Gipson, *The Coming of the Revolution 1763–1775* (New York, 1954), 84. Harrington, *New York Merchant*, 318–22. Jensen, *Maritime Commerce*, 154–6.

13 Philadelphia County Wills, M–533.

14 "Rules to be Observed by the Society of the Friendly Sons of St. Patrick," n.d. (Benjamin Fuller Letter Book, HSP). John H. Campbell, *History of the Friendly Sons of St. Patrick* (Philadelphia, 1892), 31–3.

15 *Pennsylvania Journal*, March 23, 1769.

16 Ned C. Landsman, "Ethnicity and National Origin Among British Settlers in the Philadelphia Region," *Proceedings of the American Philosophical Society*, (133, 1989) 170–77.

17 Linda Colley, *Britons: Forging the Nation 1707–1837* (London, 1992), 36. Mary K. Geiter and W. A. Speck, "Anticipating America: American mentality before the Revolution," in David Englander, ed., *Britain and America: Studies in Comparative History 1760–1970* (New Haven, CT, 1997), 34–5.

18 Truxes, *Irish-American Trade*, 106, 108–09.

19 Minutes, December 1760, as quoted in Alexander Mackie, *Facile Princeps: The Story of the Beginning of Life Insurance in America* (Lancaster, PA, 1956), 97–8.

20 Samuel Carsan to Col. John Murray, March 3, 1749/50 (Davey and Carsan Letterbook, LC).

21 *Pennsylvania Journal*, January 5, 1764, January 12, 1764. The best account of the massacre is still John R. Dunbar, ed., *The Paxton Papers* (The Hague, 1957), 23–33.

22 *Pennsylvania Archives*, IV, 156.

23   *Colonial Records*, IX, 126–7.

24   The Rev. William McClenachan of St. Paul's Church was one of their number.
     He, or someone pretending to be him, wrote that "when nobody could do
     it, I silenced the Paxton Boys, and brought them over to Peace." *A Letter
     from a clergyman in town; vindicating himself against the malevolent
     aspersions of a late pamphleteer letter-writer* (Philadelphia, 1764), 4.

25   Text in Dunbar, *Paxton Papers*, 40–46.

26   *Belfast News Letter*, March 2, 1764, March 30, 1764.

27   George Bryan, Diary, February 9, 1764, as quoted in Joseph S. Foster, *In
     Pursuit of Equal Liberty: George Bryan and the Revolution in Pennsylvania*
     (University Park, PA, 1994), 45.

28   *A Serious Address to Such of the Inhabitants of Pennsylvania, As have connived
     at, or do approve of the late Massacre of the Indians at Lancaster; or the
     Design of Killing those who are now in the Barracks at Philadelphia*
     (Philadelphia, 1764). Text in Dunbar, *Paxton Papers*, 91–7.

29   John Elder to Joseph Shippen, February 1, 1764 (Historical Society of
     Dauphin County, Harrisburg, PA). On Harris as Scotch-Irish, Hubertis
     Cummings, *Scots Breed and Susquehanna* (Pittsburgh, 1964), 53.

30   This book, which appeared anonymously, was apparently by Edmund and
     William Burke. *Account of the European Settlements in America* (London,
     1757), 209–10.

31   Judith Ridner, "Relying on the 'Saucy' Men of the Backcountry: Middlemen
     and the Fur Trade in Pennsysylvania," *PMHB*, 129(2005), 133 and 158.

32   Dunbar, *Paxton Papers*, 50.

33   *A Dialogue Between Andrew Trueman and Thomas Zealot* (Philadelphia,
     1764). Text in Dunbar, *Paxton Papers*, 89–90.

34   *An Answer to the Pamphlet Entitled the Conduct of the Paxton Men*
     (Philadelphia, 1764). Text in Dunbar, *Paxton Papers*, 324.

35   [Isaac Hunt?], *A Looking-Glass for Presbyterians* (Philadelphia, 1764). Text in
     Dunbar, *Paxton Papers*, 246. See also, [Isaac Hunt?], *A Looking-Glass, &c.
     Numb II* (Philadelphia, 1764). Text in Dunbar, *Paxton Papers*, 313.

36   *Remarks on the Quaker Unmask'd* (Philadelphia, 1764). Text in Dunbar,
     Paxton Papers, 227.

37   The writer was surprisingly well informed about Ulster geography and history.
     [Isaac Hunt?], *A Looking-Glass for Presbyterians* (Philadelphia, 1764). Text in
     Dunbar, *Paxton Papers*, 245, 248.

38   [David Dove?], *The Quaker Unmask'd* (Philadelphia, 1764). Text in Dunbar,
     Paxton Papers, 209.

39   *An Historical Account, of the late Disturbances, between the Inhabitants of the
     Back Settlements of Pennsylvania, and the Philadelphians* (Philadelphia,
     1764). Text in Dunbar, P*axton Papers*, 128.

40   *A Battle! A Battle!* (Philadelphia, 1764). Text in Dunbar, *Paxton Papers*, 178.

41   Griffin recognized British identity as a central issue. Griffin, *People With No
     Name*, 172.

42   Barton was from Carrickmacross, County Monaghan. [Thomas Barton?], *The
     Conduct of the Paxton Men* (Philadelphia, 1764). Text in Dunbar, *Paxton
     Papers*, 271. The author of *An Answer to the Pamphlet Entitled the
     Conduct of the Paxton Men* assumed it was written by a "Stark Naked

Presbyterian" who was "one of their esteemed Ministers, or one of his base Brethren." Dunbar, *Paxton Papers*, 324, 334. A strong case has been made by James Myers, "The Rev. Thomas Barton's Authorship of the Conduct of the Paxton Men," *PMHB*, 118(1994), 3–34. See also, Marvin F. Russell, "Thomas Barton and Pennsylvania's Colonial Frontier," *Pennsylvania History*, 46(1979), 313–34.

43   [Hugh Williamson?], *The Plain Dealer* (Philadelphia, 1764). Text in Dunbar, *Paxton Papers*, 341.

44   [William McClenachan?], *A Letter, from a clergyman in town; vindicating himself against the malevolent aspersions of a late pamphleteer letter-writer* (Philadelphia, 1764), 3–4. This pamphlet was a response to *True Copy of a Letter, from a Member of St. P---l's, to an intimate friend, shewing the Real Source from which the present Wranglings in that Congregation have Sprung* (Philadelphia, 1764). In its turn it was answered by *The Cheat Unmask'd: Being a Refutation of that Illegitimate Letter, said to be wrote by a Clergyman in Town* (Philadelphia, 1764). This last was certainly not by McClenachan, as the author "admits" to being an Irish Jacobite and the like, but it does suggest some doubt on the authorship of *A Letter, from a clergyman in town*. See also, Joseph McClenachan, "A Controversial Cleric: The Reverend William McClenachan," *Journal of Scotch-Irish Studies*, 1(2003), 80–103.

45   Griffin, *People With No Name*, 172.

46   The full text of the circular letter, dated March 24, 1764, and the "plan or articles" was published in *Pennsylvania Chronicle*, September 25, 1769.

47   The others could not be fully identified. Foster, *In Pursuit of Equal Liberty*, 56.

48   James H. Hutson, "The Campaign to Make Pennsylvania a Royal Province, 1764–1770," *PMHB*, 94(1970), 433–7.

49   Circular Letter, March 30, 1764, as quoted in *A Looking-Glass, Numb. II* (Philadelphia, 1764). Text in Dunbar, *Paxton Papers*, 311–2.

50   George Bryan to unknown correspondent, April 13, 1764, as quoted in Konkle, *George Bryan*, 48.

51   William Bingham to John Gibson, May 4, 1764 (Shippen Papers, HSP).

52   *Pennsylvania Chronicle*, September 25, 1769.

53   Samuel Purviance, Jr. to James Burd, September 10, 1764 (Shippen Papers, HSP).

54   James Burd to Samuel Purviance, Jr., September 17, 1764 (Shippen Papers, HSP).

55   James H. Hutson, *Pennsylvania Politics 1746–1770* (Princeton, NJ, 1972), 170. Hutson, "Campaign," 454–5. See also, Richard K. MacMaster, *Conscience in Crisis: Mennonites and Other Peace Churches in America 1739–1789* (Scottdale, PA, 1979), 171–4, 194–203.

56   Morgan, *Stamp Act*, 309.

57   Samuel Purviance, Jr. to James Bird, September 20, 1765 (Shippen Papers, HSP).

58   Gipson, *Coming of the Revolution*, 78–84.

59   *Pennsylvania Archives*, 8th series, VII, 5765, 5779–80. Morgan, *Prologue to Revolution*, 49–50.

60   Samuel Purviance, Jr. to James Burd, September 20, 1765 (Shippen Papers, HSP).

61   Israel Pemberton to Hinton Brown and Dr. John Fothergill, 12 mo. 17, 1765 (Pemberton Papers, HSP).

62   Hutson, *Pennsylvania Politics*, 4. Owen S. Ireland, "The Ethnic-Religious Dimension of Pennsylvania Politics, 1778–1779," *William and Mary Quarterly*, 3rd series, 30(1973), 423–48. Wayne L. Bockleman and Owen S. Ireland, "The Internal Revolution in Pennsylvania: An Ethnic-Religious Interpretation," *Pennsylvania History*, 41(1974), 125–60. See also, Owen S. Ireland, *Religion, Ethnicity and Politics: Ratifying the Constitution in Pennsylvania* (University Park, PA, 1995).

63   Hutson, "Campaign for a Royal Province," *PMHB*, 95(1971), 31–2.

64   Jensen, *Maritime Commerce*, 160.

65   *Pennsylvania Journal*, May 22, 1766. Theodore Thayer, *Israel Pemberton, King of the Quakers* (Philadelphia, 1943), 204.

66   Carl Bridenbaugh, *Mitre and Sceptre: Transatlantic Faiths, Ideas, Personalities and Politics 1689–1775* (Oxford and New York, 1962), 189, 272.

67   Purviance, *Narrative*, 107.

68   Herbert L. Osgood, ed., "The Society of Dissenters founded at New York in 1769," *American Historical Review*, 6(1901), 498–507. Carl L. Becker, *The History of Political Parties in the Province of New York, 1760–1776* (Madison, WI, 1960), 18–9, 75.

69   *Pennsylvania Gazette*, November 28, 1765. Letter from Philadelphia Merchants, November 25, 1765, in *Pennsylvania Journal*, May 10, 1770. Jensen, *Maritime Commerce*, 160–63.

70   Benjamin Marshall to Barnaby Egan, November 9, 1765, in *PMHB*, 20(1896), 209–10.

71   *Pennsylvania Journal*, February 6, 1766.

72   Morgan, *Stamp Act Crisis*, 350–52.

73   Henry Cruger, Jr. to Aaron Lopez, October 9, 1766, *Massachusetts Historical Society Collections*, 69(1914), 172.

74   Benjamin Fuller to John Scott, August 26, 1768 (Benjamin Fuller Letter Book, HSP).

75   *Pennsylvania Journal*, November 6, 1766.

76   *Pennsylvania Journal*, October 30, 1766. *Pennsylvania Archives*, 8th series, VII, 5946–7.

77   James Fullton to John Fullton and Ephraim Campbell, December 19, 1766 (James Fullton Letter Book (typescript), LCHS). *Pennsylvania Journal*, December 4, 1766, December 18, 1766, December 25, 1766.

78   Letter from a Gentleman in New York to his Correspondent in New Haven, October 27, 1766, in *Providence Gazette and Country Journal*, November 15, 1766.

79   *New York Journal*, January 29, 1767.

80   William Glenholme to Park, Henderson and Co., July 26, 1767, to Miller, Marshall and Co., September 3, 1767, to Walter Marshall and Co., November 7, 1767, to Bigger and Hulbert, November 7, 1767, to Greg and Cunningham, November 11, 1767 (Orr, Dunlope and Glenholme Letter Book, HSP).

81   *Pennsylvania Journal*, November 26, 1767, December 3, 1767, December 10, 1767, December 17, 1767.

82   William Glenholme to Walter Marshall, January 7, 1768, to Andrew Orr, January 7, 1768 (Orr, Dunlope and Glenholme Letter Book, HSP).

83   William Lux to Christopher Champlin, August 31, 1767, in *Massachusetts Historical Society Collections*, 69 (1914), 202.

84   William Glenholme to James Blair, July 23, 1767, to Andrew Orr, July 26, 1767, to Greg and Cunningham, August 15, 1767 (Orr, Dunlope and Glenholme Letter Book, HSP).

85   William Glenholme to William Beath and George Anderson, September 23, 1767, October 5, 1767, October 16, 1767, to James Lecky, December 2, 1767 (Orr, Dunlope and Glenholme Letter Book, HSP).

86   James Fullton to Messrs. Campbell and Fullton, December 4, 1767 (Fullton Letter Book (typescript). LCHS).

87   William Glenholme to Peter Robinson, February 17, 1768, to Andrew Orr, March 18, 1768, to Lane, Benson and Vaughan, March 19, 1768 (Orr, Dunlope and Glenholme Letter Book, HSP).

88   James Fullton to Holliday and Dunbar, January 4, 1768, to Ephraim Campbell and John Fullton, February 17, 1768 (Fullton Letter Book (typescript), LCHS).

89   *Providence Gazette and Country Journal*, December 5, 1767, December 12, 1767.

90   *New York Journal*, April 14, 1768.

91   William Glenholme to Andrew Orr, May 11, 1768 (Orr, Dunlope and Glenholme Letter Book, HSP). *New York Journal*, April 14, 1768. *Pennsylvania Journal*, April 28, 1768.

92   *New York Journal*, September 8, 1768. On the New York context, Becker, *Political Parties*, 63–71.

93   Jensen, *Maritime Commerce*, 179–80.

94   Benjamin Fuller to John Scott, September 5, 1770 (Benjamin Fuller Letter Book, HSP).

95   *New York Journal*, June 7, 1770, June 21, 1770, July 19, 1770.

96   *Pennsylvania Chronicle*, February 20, 1770, June 25, 1770, October 1, 1770. Jensen, *Maritime Commerce*, 186–95.

97   *South Carolina Gazette*, October 4, 1770, October 18, 1770, October 25, 1770.

8

A Scotch-Irish
Boom Town

Wheat, Flour and Flaxseed

In 1761 a group of businessmen in the small town of Baltimore in
the colony of Maryland announced a lottery to raise money to buy
a building site and erect a Presbyterian meeting house. There was
neither minister nor congregation as yet, but these merchants of
Baltimore and neighbouring Joppa formed a committee and enlisted the help of kinsmen and business associates in York and Carlisle
in Pennsylvania.[1] With one or two exceptions, they were newcomers to Maryland. The Rev. Patrick Allison, their first minister, writing in 1793, recalled that:

> The advantageous situation of the Town for Commerce
> induced a few Presbyterian Families from Pennsylvania to set-
> tle in it about the year 1761, who, with two or three of the
> same Persuasion, that had emigrated from Europe, soon
> formed themselves into a religious Society, and had occasion-
> al Supplies, when they assembled in private Houses.[2]

The network of Scotch-Irish merchants who assisted in organizing the first Presbyterian church in Baltimore also contributed to
the rise of Baltimore as a major port city, drawing the trade of York,
Carlisle, Lancaster, and the Susquehanna Valley to the Chesapeake
and giving Belfast, Londonderry and Newry firms ready access to
this market.

Baltimore's rise was inextricably bound up with the increased
demand for wheat and flour from America and Philadelphia's role
in the grain trade. From its early days as a commercial centre,

Philadelphia shipped flour, bread and lumber, mainly to the West Indies. But in the 1760s the Caribbean was gradually superseded as Philadelphia's most dynamic export market by Madeira, the Canaries, Spain, and Portugal. The West Indies and southern Europe together demanded more wheat than Pennsylvania alone could supply, so Philadelphia merchants regularly bought grain in Maryland and Virginia. As the Eastern Shore counties steadily shifted their emphasis from tobacco to wheat, the activity of Philadelphia firms in this part of Maryland increased.[3] The Scotch-Irish merchants of Baltimore had a direct link to the Philadelphia merchant community through their established business and personal contacts in Pennsylvania. They played a major role in bringing Philadelphia-based trade in wheat and flour to Baltimore. They also found a new market for Maryland grain through their contacts in Belfast, Newry and Londonderry.[4]

Town-building fever reached a climax in the Chesapeake region a bit earlier than in Pennsylvania. Both Maryland and Virginia adopted legislation in the 1740s requiring tobacco to be inspected and graded at official warehouses in each county. In an earlier downturn in tobacco prices, London houses largely surrendered the trade of Maryland and of the Potomac and Rappahannock rivers in Virginia to the factors sent out by merchants in Glasgow, Whitehaven and Liverpool. These men operated retail stores which they then clustered around the different inspection warehouses. The two colonial legislatures sanctioned a series of towns in the 1740s and 1750s laid out at the sites chosen earlier for inspection warehouses.

The Maryland General Assembly passed an act in 1729 authorising a town of sixty lots to be laid out and called Baltimore Town and the lots were duly surveyed the next year. In 1732 the legislature created another town at nearby Fell's Point. The two inchoate towns were combined as Baltimore Town by a new act passed in 1745, which also appointed seven men as a self-perpetuating board of commissioners to oversee the sale of lots, settle land disputes and otherwise guide the fortunes of their town.[5]

Baltimore remained a small place, insignificant even in the Maryland economy, until the 1760s. Tobacco was still the main export of the entire Chesapeake region and Baltimore lay on the fringe of the tobacco-growing area. Baltimore merchants, like James Houston and Jonathan Plowman, advertised in 1759 and 1760 that they would "purchase or take in payment, Turpentine, Cedar Plank, and Skins and Furs of all Kinds," and loaded ships with tobacco for their correspondents in England.[6] But the agricultural staple of the upper Chesapeake, including much of the Eastern Shore, changed from tobacco to wheat by the 1760s.[7] Cecil County, Maryland, at the head of Chesapeake Bay, had long supplied wheat and flour for Philadelphia's overseas trade and Philadelphia firms were prepared to expand into the Chesapeake wheat market. As early as 1746 Davey and Carsan – and several others – had established a base at Charlestown, Cecil County, Maryland where they could "purchase wheat, flour, & flaxseed" and, should flaxseed or flour be in short supply, "we can allways be serv'd with Lumber or a tobacco freight." In addition, they were aware that "Convicts & Servants in a General way sell better" in Maryland.[8] According to the records of the public warehouse there, Charlestown shipped a range of produce in 1755 including grain, salt, cider, flaxseed by the hogshead and by the barrel, iron and hemp, but no tobacco.[9] "During the 1760s Philadelphia traders pushed into the Eastern Shore of Maryland, purchasing huge quantities of wheat and corn, which were either exported directly from Maryland or brought back to Philadelphia."[10] Had the Susquehanna River been fully navigable to Chesapeake Bay, Charlestown might have become a major port. Since country produce, even bar iron, went to market by road, Charlestown was too far east to offer any advantage to shopkeepers in Carlisle or York. The traders and growers of central Pennsylvania would continue to look to Philadelphia, until a more promising alternative came along, while Philadelphia kept its hold on the trade of the Eastern Shore.

This shift to wheat was true on all the fringes of the tobacco region. Grain was the main crop raised on the upper Potomac, too, although the new towns of Alexandria, Virginia, and Georgetown, Maryland, were still mainly tobacco shipping points. The expansion of settlement in western Maryland and Virginia and a slump in tobacco prices greatly increased the amount of grain coming to market there and some Philadelphia and Whitehaven firms began regularly buying grain through merchants in Georgetown and Alexandria.[11] Georgetown was important enough as a market for grain to merit an essay on wheat prices there in the press.[12] Alexandria was also in transition from the tobacco trade. The lower Shenandoah Valley supplied substantial quantities of wheat to the Alexandria market by 1767, but none of the counties in the upper valley raised grain for market until after the American Revolution.[13] By 1775, however, Robert Carter of Nomini Hall could list a dozen "wheat purchasers" and two other firms that "purchase tobacco and wheat" among the twenty "merchants and factors" doing business in Alexandria.[14] Much of this trade would eventually go through Baltimore.

Demand for American wheat and flour in the British Isles in 1767–8 provided the necessary stimulus for Baltimore's grain trade with the town's Scotch-Irish merchants shipping wheat and flour to Londonderry, Belfast and Newry. They were not alone. Three brigantines from Whitehaven, for example, entered at Annapolis on the same day in 1767, but they "all came for Wheat, and sailed together from hence for Baltimore."[15] Even in these years, shipments to Lisbon and the Mediterranean were more important in determining prices for grain in Philadelphia.[16] The southern European market absorbed between 80 and 90 per cent of the wheat and wheat products shipped from Virginia, Pennsylvania and New York in 1768–72. Maryland demonstrated a different pattern with a quarter of the raw wheat and of the flour and bread shipped from Baltimore and Annapolis in 1768–72 going to Ireland. (Maryland grain exports nearly all came through Baltimore. Only one or two ships with cargoes of grain cleared from Annapolis in each of the years from 1765 through 1772.) Exports from Maryland ports, essentially from Baltimore, accounted for two thirds of the wheat and half the flour from the American Colonies imported into Ireland in 1768–72.[17]

John Stevenson, "a Native of Londonderry, in the Kingdom of Ireland, of a very respectable Family," led the way for others to follow. More than any other, this doctor from Derry was responsible for Baltimore's new status. He had lived in Baltimore for "upwards of Forty Years" before he died there in 1785, "formerly one of its most eminent Merchants." He was a regularly trained physician and had practiced medicine, although business ventures occupied him more and more in his Baltimore years. His obituary said:

> It may be remarked, that he was the first Exporter of Wheat and Flour from this Port, and consequently laid the Foundation of its present commercial Consequence; and it was the Delight of his Heart to promote and see the Increase and Prosperity of this Town in particular, and the State in general.[18]

Stevenson probably came to Baltimore, then no more than a village, about 1745; he was certainly established in Baltimore before 1753, when he was a town commissioner and one of the managers of a lottery to build a wharf.[19] As one of the town's leading merchants in the 1760s, he imported from London "well assorted Cargoes of Dry Goods," Barbados rum and muscavado sugar from the West Indies in his own sloop *Elizabeth and Betty*, to say nothing of "fine Irish pickled and dried Salmon."[20] The scope of his business ventures can be seen in an advertisement from 1767.

> Just Imported from Ireland, Madeira and Barbados and to be sold at my Store in Baltimore-Town, Fine Irish Linens, Table Cloths from 7/6 Sterling prime Cost to 36/0, Fine Diaper Napkinning, Choice Old Barbados Rum per the Hogshead or Barrel, Muscavado Sugars, Madeira Wine by the Pipe, Barrel or Quarter Cask, on very reasonable Terms, for Cash, by J. Stevenson.[21]

He was also one of the committee who organised the Presbyterian church in Baltimore.[22] Writing in 1769, William Eddis noted that Stevenson

> contracted for considerable quantities of wheat, he freighted vessels, and consigned them to a correspondent in his native country, the cargoes sold to great advantage, and returns were made equally beneficial. The commencement of a trade so lucrative to the first adventurers, soon became an object of universal attention. Persons of a commercial and enterprising spirit emigrated from all quarters to this new and promising scene of industry.[23]

In June 1767, Belfast merchant John Ewing advertised the arrival of the *Jane and Mary*, Brown, and the *Carlisle*, Taylor, with cargoes of "best Baltimore flour." He announced that Captain John Taylor would sail for Baltimore in the brigantine *Carlisle* in July and directed prospective passengers, redemptioners and servants to apply to John Ewing, Belfast, or the captain on board. The *Carlisle* was owned by William Buchanan and John Smith of Baltimore. The next summer the *Carlisle* brought another cargo of Baltimore flour to Belfast and sailed again for Baltimore with passengers, redemptioners and servants. She made a third voyage to Belfast in 1769 with flour, bar iron, and ship bread consigned to John Ewing and again returned with emigrants.[24] And there were more ships.[25]

John Ewing was also importing flaxseed from Baltimore. He advertised flaxseed, flour and shipbread landed by the *Jenifer* from Baltimore and the brig *Adventure* from Alexandria, Virginia, and for passengers to Maryland or Virginia for *Adventure's* return voyage.[26] Baltimore would never be as important to the flaxseed trade as Philadelphia and New York, although flaxseed was a significant part of Baltimore's overseas commerce. As one Baltimore merchant reported to his Belfast correspondents, in a normal year only about five per cent of the total flaxseed export came from Maryland:

> We find that you will have the Quantity ship'd this Season that you had last as we hear there will be 17,000 Hogsheads from New York 10,000 from Philadelphia and 1500 from this and no doubt some little from other Ports to the Northard.[27]

Baltimore's dependence on the grain trade with Ulster ports initiated by its Scotch-Irish merchants reached a highpoint in the 1770s. The columns of the *Belfast News Letter* carried many advertisements for ships sailing to Baltimore or the arrival of wheat and flour from Baltimore. On their outward voyage, ships from Belfast, Newry and Londonderry carried Ulster emigrants to Baltimore. Ulster merchants, like John Ewing, informed potential passengers of the advantages of Baltimore for access to the interior of Pennsylvania and Virginia. Baltimore merchants, like his brother Thomas Ewing, offered vast tracts of land for sale in western Virginia.[28]

The grain trade with Irish ports was uniquely a Baltimore venture.

Wheat exports to Irish ports from New York, Pennsylvania and Virginia, on the other hand, amounted to only 6% of their total. And trade with Ireland was a major element in Baltimore's commerce. Trade to Ireland, which was mostly wheat, flour and flaxseed, showed a marked increase. During 1757–62 an average of fewer than three ships a year sailed for Irish ports. No significant change in these shipments was recorded until 1769, when a rapid growth set in culminating in a high of 42 ships sailing for Irish ports in 1770 and an average of 25 ships a year from 1768 through 1773.[29]

Overseas shipments further stimulated grain production in the Chesapeake Colonies. "Maryland and Virginia shipped over half the corn, about three quarters of the raw wheat, and about one seventh of the bread and flour traded coastally among the mainland colonies in 1768–72." Much of this went to Philadelphia for shipment abroad. Exports of raw wheat from Maryland increased from 150,000 bushels in 1761 to 197,000 in 1768.[30] For its part Baltimore imported Irish linens and other textiles, small quantities of meat, potatoes, and a great many servants from Ireland. Baltimore emerged as a major port of entry for indentured servants, a trade in which all the Scotch-Irish merchants of the town participated.[31]

The grain trade would inevitably have drawn Philadelphia firms, if not to Baltimore, then to some other centrally located place on the Western Shore of Chesapeake Bay. What does not appear so inevitable is that the greater number of merchants who looked to Baltimore for new opportunities were men from Ulster or the sons of Ulster emigrants, many of them already established in the flaxseed trade. Glasgow, Whitehaven, Liverpool, and London were already represented in Baltimore's small community of tobacco buyers and dry goods merchants. It was the Scotch-Irish who made Baltimore not only a grain port, but part of their own transatlantic network exporting flaxseed, importing linen and bringing emigrants to the Chesapeake town.

This was true not only of its overseas trade, with its important relationship to Ulster, but also for Baltimore's ability to develop trade with a large hinterland in southern Pennsylvania through the Scotch-Irish merchants who migrated from Carlisle, York and

Lancaster and their business associates in the Pennsylvania towns. Baltimore's greatest advantage in drawing much of the trade of York and Cumberland counties in south-central Pennsylvania away from Philadelphia lay in the complex of good roads connecting the port-town to the backcountry. A correspondent of the *Pennsylvania Chronicle* complained in 1767 that

> the distance is so great, ferriages so high, and the roads so bad from Susquehanna to Philadelphia, that the countrymen to the westward of that river carry their produce to Baltimore in Maryland to the great detriment of Pennsylvania.

He added that the port of Baltimore was "daily increasing its trade" at Philadelphia's expense.[32] The presence of so many men who brought their own business connections with the backcountry to Baltimore was no less an advantage.

"Persons of a commercial and enterprising spirit"

The men who transformed Baltimore were part of a push into the backcountry by Philadelphia-based firms. While some gravitated to the inland towns, Lancaster, Carlisle, and York, others tapped the trade of the interior from the upper reaches of Chesapeake Bay. Beginning in 1760 many other Scotch-Irish merchants came to Baltimore, joining Dr John Stevenson. They came "from all quarters to this new and promising scene of industry," most from Carlisle and other towns in the backcountry and from Philadelphia. Seeing the way the wind was blowing, some flaxseed and grain buyers left Cecil County, a few tearing down their houses in Charlestown and shipping the materials across the Bay to build anew in Baltimore, among them Mark Alexander and the originally Irish Quaker Hollingsworths.[33]

The merchants who formed the nucleus of the Baltimore business community included a number of men from Carlisle with previous experience in the Indian trade. John Smith, merchant of Carlisle, was one of the first, coming to Baltimore in 1760.[34] John Smith's brother-in-law William Buchanan moved from Carlisle the same year. They would be among the most important merchants in the town, trading to Great Britain and Ireland, southern Europe and the West Indies. Both men came originally from the Donegal settlement in Lancaster County, as did Alexander, William and John McClure, William Smith, William Spear, and James Sterrett, who left there for Baltimore in 1761.[35] Samuel Carsan and Robert and Samuel Purviance, Jr., already established merchants in Philadelphia, set up new firms in Baltimore. All these newcomers retained their Philadelphia and backcountry Pennsylvania connections.[36] Thomas Ewing and Samuel Brown came direct from Belfast. Quite a few other Ulster emigrants came to this promising scene in the 1760s. Some, like George Patton, a merchant in the wine trade with Madeira, and James Calhoun gained almost immediate prominence as leaders of the radical Sons of Liberty.[37] It is little wonder that one scholar called Baltimore at this time a Scotch-Irish boom town.[38]

William Buchanan and his wife Esther sold a large stone house and lot in Carlisle to James Pollock, tavernkeeper, in January 1760 and went to Baltimore.[39] Buchanan and his business partner Barnabas Hughes shifted from Indian trade goods to supplies for the British army and provincial forces during the French and Indian War. Having profited as army contractors, they came to Maryland with money to invest in new ventures. Barnabas Hughes and his wife Elizabeth sold his property on Lime Street in Lancaster and leased his tavern "At the Sign Of the Bear" in Donegal Township in March 1760. He was in Maryland that month, arranging for a land purchase of 4,000 acres in western Maryland by his friend Col. Henry Bouquet and doubtless finalising his own move.[40] Bouquet was prepared to ask "my friend B. Hughs a Mercht. at Baltimore" to receive the widow of another Swiss officer into his own house and see to her interests when she moved to Maryland.[41]

As early as January 1762 Buchanan and Hughes accepted "merchantable Flour, Wheat, Hemp, &c." at their Baltimore store.[42] In 1763 Buchanan and Hughes announced the imminent dissolution of their partnership, advertising "a large Quantity of Dry Goods" for sale at their store. Like their competitors, they offered a variety of general merchandise. Hughes advertised a long list of goods for sale at his store in 1764, ranging from Irish linens to books, and from long-handled frying pans to madeira, sherry, and a few boxes of lemons.[43] He also maintained his interests in Pennsylvania, selling lots in Elizabeth Town, the town in Donegal Township, Lancaster County, he laid out and named for his wife, and obtaining judgements against the lessee of the Sign of the Bear.[44] Barnabas Hughes shifted his business interests more and more to iron manufacture at his Antietam Furnace and Forge in western Maryland, before he died in 1765. William Buchanan, Daniel Hughes and Samuel Hughes, as his surviving partners, advertised for payment of debts due to Hughes or to "the late Partnership of Buchanan and Hughes" or to "the Anti-eatam Company." William Smith and James Sterrett were his principal creditors. Since the ironworks absorbed all the cash Hughes could raise, it is obvious that his associates from Donegal Township were advancing him credit. Baltimore merchants Brian Philpot and William Aisquith made an appraisal of his estate, which came to £4,111 8s 7d in all, more than half of it "sundry European goods" in the shop amounting to £2,010 8s 5d and "Sundry other goods on hand" valued at £443 14s 1d "belong'g to the Antietam Comp'y."[45] Daniel and Samuel Hughes continued the ironworks with Samuel Beall, Jr.[46] William Buchanan and his brother-in-law John Smith owned commercial real estate in common from 1765 and eventually went into partnership as Smith and Buchanan, one of the most important Baltimore firms trading with Belfast.[47]

James Sterrett and William Smith arrived in Baltimore in May 1761 as business partners. They continued in partnership through 1770. By 1773 James and his son John Sterrett, merchants, were doing business in Baltimore.[48] They were involved in the wheat trade as was William Spear.[49]

Smith and Buchanan and Sterrett and Smith dealt with John Ewing of Belfast, who played an important role in developing trade between the two cities. By 1765 Ewing had a brother in Baltimore to further promote his interests. Thomas Ewing was one of three sons of Robert Ewing, a snuff manufacturer of Belfast. The eldest son, John Ewing, was the merchant in Belfast and the second son Robert Ewing Jr. represented his brother's interests in Barbados. Thomas Ewing completed the circle by handling their affairs in the Continental Colonies.[50] He was in Philadelphia early in 1765, selling Irish linens and Irish butter at James Harvey's store.[51] Samuel Brown sailed from Belfast in 1766 to join Thomas Ewing. They announced "the Partnership of Ewing and Brown" that year, offering Irish linens and "a neat Assortment of Fall Goods, suitable for the Country."[52] They lost no time in importing a stock of goods from Belfast and shipping cargoes of flaxseed and Baltimore flour. From 1767 on, John Ewing had regular shipments of both each Spring and Fall on ships consigned to him.[53] Ewing and Brown worked with Philadelphia merchants as well, notably with Orr, Dunlope and Glenholme and with George Fullerton.[54] In Baltimore David Stewart and John Smith were close associates.[55]

Neither Ewing had a monopoly on Maryland commerce. John Ewing joined with other Belfast merchants in the flaxseed and grain trade. John Ewing, John Gregg and John Campbell dispatched the ship *Earl of Donegall*, from Belfast for Baltimore in 1770. The *Lord Dungannon*, built at Philadelphia in 1766, first belonged to Andrew Orr and William Glenholme of Philadelphia and to the Belfast merchants John Campbell, Hugh Donaldson, John Gregg, James Henderson, and James Park. Normally one of the Philadelphia flaxseed ships, she returned to Belfast from Baltimore with flour and flaxseed in 1770 and 1771.[56] Addressed to one merchant, often the owner, a ship usually carried produce or goods ordered by a number of others. In the spring of 1771 William and John Brown and Jesse Taylor of Belfast imported American flour from Baltimore in the *Phoenix* and flour and flaxseed in the *Phillis*. The *Phillis* and *Fairfax*, *Chatham* and *Lord Dungannon* also brought flaxseed, flour and wheat from Baltimore for John Ewing.[57] That summer the *Dispatch* arrived with flour for John Ewing and Jesse Taylor and *Phillis* returned with wheat and flour for Ewing and Samuel Ashmore.[58]

In 1768 Samuel Brown returned to Belfast to marry Thomas Ewing's niece, Jane, daughter of James and Margery (Ewing) Simm of Belfast. Their son James Simm Brown was born in 1770 and baptised at the Presbyterian Church in Baltimore. During his stay in Baltimore, Samuel Brown joined Dr John Stevenson, John Smith, William Buchanan, William Smith, William Spear, James Sterrett, Robert and Samuel Purviance, David Stewart, Joseph Donaldson and others on the Presbyterian Church committee.[59]

In 1771 Samuel and Jane Brown of Baltimore sold his half of the business back to Thomas Ewing for £1,200 Maryland currency and sold him a house in Baltimore for an identical sum. Brown returned to Belfast where he was associated with John Ewing in business ventures that frequently included ships crossing between Baltimore and Belfast. The *Pennsylvania Farmer*, for example, arrived from Baltimore in 1772 with wheat and flour consigned to Ewing and Brown.[60] Samuel Brown returned to Baltimore and Philadelphia in the brig *Agnes* in 1773, but was back in Belfast within the year. In 1774 he advertised for passengers, redemptioners and servants for Baltimore in his own ship, the *Jenny Brown*.[61]

Thomas Ewing went into partnership with Walter Hall in 1771, after Brown left Maryland. Their partnership dissolved in 1774 and Ewing remained on his own until his death in 1776.[62] He continued in the grain trade. George Woolsey wrote that "T. Ewing has Ship'd two Cargoes of Wheat this Fall, one has gone to Belfast & the Vessel that carries this takes the other to Cork."[63] He advertised for flaxseed, offering to "give Market Price for any quantity."[64] Thomas Ewing was also one of those merchants who dealt in the time of redemptioners and servants. In his will he mentioned long association with George Fullerton, merchant of Philadelphia, and John Smith and David Stewart, merchants of Baltimore, and provided for two female servants, acknowledging their children as his own, and for his own brothers and sisters and their offspring.[65]

Robert Purviance was in business in Baltimore by 1763 with his brother Samuel who remained in Philadelphia. They operated a distillery, selling rum, molasses and sugar, as well as a general mercantile business. Samuel Purviance, Jr. "declined the dry goods business" in 1767 and moved to Baltimore after winding up his affairs. The Purviances had close ties with Londonderry firms and with William and Andrew Caldwell, later Andrew Caldwell and Joseph Wilson, as well as with Samuel and John Purviance in Philadelphia. They were also involved in land speculation in western Virginia with Philadelphia merchant John Cox, Jr., Samuel and Robert Purviance loaded the ship *Anne* at Fell's Point, Baltimore, for Londonderry and advertised "a few indented servants to be sold on board." *Anne* was owned by Robert Alexander and James Harvey of Londonderry. They also dispatched the *General Wolfe* for Cork.[66]

Another merchant with Londonderry connections, David Stewart offered Irish linens and India calicoes for sale at his Baltimore store and advertised for freight for the *Rose* to Londonderry, *General Wolfe* to Cork and the *Two Brothers* to Londonderry. Thomas Bateson and Co. of Belfast consigned their ship *Hawke* to him as well. Stewart was "a constant Purchaser of Wheat, Flour, Indian Corn, Bees Wax, Lumber, &c." He also dealt in servants from Ireland.[67]

Dr John Stevenson's connections were primarily with Londonderry, too. He found freights for the *Pitt* and the *General Wolfe* from Baltimore to Londonderry. He was also associated with David Gaussan of Newry and servants consigned to him arrived regularly from Newry on the brig *Venus*, one of Gaussan's ships.[68] Newry merchants established commercial ties with Baltimore early on. The owners of the *Britannia* advertised for passengers, redemptioners and servants for her voyage there from Newry in 1769. *Britannia* was consigned to Ewing and Brown.[69] In 1771 William and John Ogle, who operated the American Flour Warehouses on Canal Quay in Newry, sent the ships *Betsy*, *Peggy*, and *Jenny and Polly*, promising great encouragement to servants who chose to emigrate, and David Gaussan urged passengers to sail on the brig *Venus*.[70] The *Jenny and Polly* was chartered on arrival at Baltimore to load at Georgetown on the Potomac.[71]

Sons of Liberty

Political activity drew the Scotch-Irish from their shop counters and counting houses to work together in asserting the rights of the Colonies. "Together this clan of Scotch-Irish immigrants supplied revolutionary Baltimore with some of its most successful merchants and powerful politicians."[72] In 1763 a group of local merchants and tradesmen organised to provide some rudimentary policing and fire protection for the town. Mark Alexander proposed they call themselves the Mechanical Company, since so many of them were tradesmen or mechanics. Early in 1766 the Mechanical Company birthed the Baltimore Sons of Liberty. James Calhoun, George Patton, William Spear and James Sterrett were among the merchants who took a role in starting this radical political organization.

Samuel Purviance, Jr. had not yet settled in Baltimore when the Sons of Liberty formed, but became their leader once he did.[73]

When Boston merchants first proposed non-importation as a response to the Townshend Revenue Act in August 1768, they wrote Samuel and Robert Purviance with an invitation for Baltimore to follow suit.[74]

Baltimore merchants did not act on this until March 1769 and then under pressure from Philadelphia. Their initial agreement was sufficiently loose to permit merchants to import their fall goods as usual.[75] Dr John Stevenson chaired a meeting of a committee of merchants called to deal with "a premeditated Design to subvert the Association" by several merchants in Baltimore and Annapolis.[76] Dr Stevenson, John Smith, Jonathan Plowman, and Ebenezer Mackie, all four Presbyterians, lodged a protest against published reports of the committee action regarding the cargo of the *Good Intent* addressed to Dick and Stewart of Annapolis.[77]

The quasi-voluntary nature of the non-importation agreement, in response to Parliament's tax on certain enumerated articles, demanded virtual unanimity among importers from New England to Georgia to be effective. Since merchants in different cities were far from unanimous on the point, confidence in the measure eroded. News of the repeal of the Townshend act, leaving only a tax on tea, reached Maryland in May. Soon afterward Baltimore heard that Rhode Island had thereupon dropped its policy of non-importation. John Smith chaired a meeting of merchants who agreed to refuse any goods from Rhode Island. Samuel Purviance, Jr. spoke in favour of the boycott.[78] Rhode Island quickly returned to the fold, but by mid-summer New York had defected, to be followed by Philadelphia. A meeting of merchants of Baltimore "to judge of the expediency of continuing the Association" chose John Smith as chair and decided to permit imports from the British Isles of everything except tea. The meeting named John Smith, William Smith, William Buchanan, Samuel Purviance, Jr. and John McClure, with William Lux, to a continuing committee to represent their interests.[79] "An examination of the six men ... regarded as an informal executive board of the merchant community reveals the dramatic reshuffling in local leadership that had taken place" in only five years. Five Scotch-Irish Presbyterians, four from Pennsylvania, one from Ulster, had displaced the old leadership. Their rise to political dominance was thus essentially complete by 1770.[80]

Baltimore in the 1770s: New Firms as Trade Expands

The *Belfast News Letter* reported at least seven arrivals from Baltimore with cargoes of flaxseed and flour in 1773. John Ewing imported both on *Two Brothers* and *Charming Molly*. Andrew Thompson of Newry advertised Baltimore flour landed from the *Jupiter* of Londonderry, owned by his brother James Thompson and Andrew Gregg. The *Betty Greg* brought American flour to Waddell Cunningham and to Jesse Taylor.[81] The following year there were at least sixteen.

As Baltimore's overseas trade boomed and the town grew larger, more Scotch-Irish merchants migrated there. Old Sam Carsan established a branch of his firm in Baltimore with his brother Andrew's son from Strabane, trading as Samuel and Sam Carsan and Company at their store in Baltimore. His nephew, who was known as Samuel Carsan, Jr., was in charge. They imported Irish linens, Irish beef, and English woollens and found freights for Newry, Belfast and Larne for ships like the *Lord Dunluce* that brought redemptioners and servants as well as passengers to Baltimore. The elder Carsan remained active in Philadelphia under the same firm name.[82]

Daniel McHenry brought his family from Ballymena to Philadelphia in 1772 and moved to Baltimore the following year. He went into business with his son John importing dry goods, hardware, and wines.[83] Alexander Donaldson from Glenarm, trading as Alexander Donaldson and Co., sold dry goods and general merchandise at his store in Baltimore. By 1774 he had taken William Harris as his business partner. They relied on Randle and John Mitchell for much of their stock. In one letter, Donaldson assured John Mitchell "In general I have the best assorted Store in this Province but am in great want of several articles such as low priced Irish Linens Sheetings Osnabrigs &c."[84]

One new firm with transatlantic partners commenced business in 1774, although George Woolsey, the senior partner, was well-established in Baltimore long before then. George Salmon, his partner,

remained in Dublin. A full ten years of this firm's business correspondence has survived opening a window on Baltimore commerce
in the 1770s.

In 1767 George Bryan advertised for freight for the *Earl of
Chatham*, George Woolsey, commander, now lying at Baltimore
Town. She was one of the flaxseed ships and returned to
Philadelphia the following year from Dublin.[85] Captain George
Woolsey was from Portadown, County Armagh, heart of the linen
triangle. His father, John Woolsey, was a merchant there with an
interest in the American market. Migrating to Dublin, he was
employed as a ship's officer by John Armstrong and by Arthur
Bryan, the younger brother of George Bryan of Philadelphia. As
George Woolsey, mariner, he was married in 1769 to Catharine
Darley of Dublin. Her family were also from the north of Ireland.
Moses Darley, stonecutter, builder and later merchant, moved from
Newtownards, County Down, to Dublin, where he died in 1754
when Catharine was eighteen.[86]

By 1770 Woolsey commanded the *Hercules* of Dublin. She sailed
in July for Philadelphia with passengers and linen, consigned to
John Pringle.[87] Like many another sea captain, Woolsey wanted to
use his abilities and his connections to better advantage as a merchant. He seems to have been in business with a "Mr. C" in
Philadelphia that did not end well.[88] His connection with Pringle
gave him an opportunity to represent the firm of Fisher, Donaldson
and Pringle in Baltimore and reoriented him to Newry, where they
had their base.[89] The Darleys were also prominent in Newry, where
John Darley was Collector of Customs and Hill Willson, merchant
and ship-owner, was married to Mary Darley.[90]

The *Baltimore Packet*, a new vessel, brought merchandise from
London to Newry in December 1772. She sailed again for
Baltimore with passengers from Dublin in June 1773 and advertised a second voyage in August of that year from Liverpool and
Dublin. George Woolsey, merchant in Baltimore, was loading the
ship with flaxseed, wheat, and flour for a return voyage to Newry
in November 1773. The *Baltimore Packet* was addressed to David
Gaussan and she sailed for Newry in January 1774.[91] The ship's
owners, David Gaussan, John Woolsey of Portadown, and Thomas
McCabe of Belfast, announced her speedy return to Baltimore,
inviting passengers, redemptioners and servants to take passage.

John Woolsey was George Woolsey's father and Thomas McCabe, a Belfast watchmaker, was his brother-in-law.[92]

Baltimore's emergence as a grain port coincided with a steady rise in prices for American wheat and flour from 1767 to 1772. While prices fell slightly from the high of that year, they remained close to that high point through 1774. An extended period of high prices freed farmers and millers from the necessity of selling their produce at any price and let them insist on what they considered a fair price. With demand from Lisbon and Cadiz unabated, merchants in Ireland had to pay these prices or go without. David Gaussan, for instance, ordered eighty tons of wheat shipped to Newry, but stipulated that Woolsey purchase it at less than 5/– a bushel. With wheat at 5/10 and rising, Woolsey was "fearful we shall not be able to compleat your order of Wheat at your limits."[93]

If wheat prices were high, the price of flaxseed continued to climb from 1770 on. "The People here are Mad they have run Flaxseed up to Day to 9/– and Wheat to 5/10 Yet we are in hopes it will get lower," Woolsey wrote early in the season.[94] Prices continued to rise. With the last flaxseed ships at sea, Woolsey wrote in January that "Flaxseed has been very high this Season and that Very high Price has brought in Quantitys that would not have come if the Price had been low on Acct. of the distance from Market."[95] High prices compensated for the cost of transporting seed to market, bringing large and small quantities to Baltimore from distant places and allowing growers to hold back their seed until late in the year, creating a temporary scarcity to push prices still higher. Flaxseed prices in Philadelphia, as quoted in the *Pennsylvania Journal*, started at 12/– a bushel and rose to 13/6 before the end of November.[96] Woolsey wrote John Pringle in Philadelphia for advice:

> We wish you would advise us what lengths we might go for Flaxseed, as it is expected scarce here, & is now 10/– to 10/6 by the small parcel and 12/ to 12/6 by the Quantity and we may perhaps miss many parcels if we do not get good advise and soon from you. Indeed we have engaged some ourselves at these high Prices for fear of being disappointed.[97]

Woolsey also asked John Mitchell's "opinion about flaxseed with you and at New York as here it's scarce and high."[98] He assured

David Gaussan that the Irish market could bear the higher cost, since there would be less shipped than usual. "Altho the Flaxseed is very high yet we think it will be a good article with you as we think the Crop has failed in the Country."[99]

Short crops in Pennsylvania and Maryland contributed to the rising price of flaxseed in the 1774 shipping season. Woolsey observed in December that:

> Flaxseed this season is very Scarce, there will not be above 1000 hhds Ship'd from here or perhaps 1200. At Philadelphia it will be short also, but it's imagined New York will ship as much as last year nearly. It has been 13/– 14/– in Phila. No Prices yet at New York and it's now 12/6 here.[100]

By mid-December flaxseed reached 14/– to 14/6 in Philadelphia and 14/6 in New York, Woolsey reported, and "the Quantity that goes from this & Phila. is not equal to two thirds of what went last year."[101]

His obligation to John Pringle led him to favour Andrew Thompson of Newry over his own friend Gaussan. He gave John Pringle first refusal of 210 hogsheads of flaxseed, which he would otherwise send to David Gaussan and engaged the brig *Friendship* for Newry to take 400 hogsheads, 300 for Pringle addressed to Andrew Thompson and 100 for Gaussan.[102] When Thompson's ship *Lord Dunluce* arrived at Baltimore from Larne for flaxseed, it was consigned to Samuel and Sam Carsan.[103] Woolsey was unable to fill flaxseed orders for some of his correspondents.[104] He made an exception for his brother- in-law Thomas McCabe in Belfast and shipped flaxseed to him on the *Lord Dunluce*.[105] Woolsey wrote to Thompson when the ship was ready to sail early in the new year:

> The present goes by yr own Ship the Lord Dunluce and is merely to give you a state of our Markets … Since the 20th last month Flaxseed has been from 12/ to 15/ but mostly 13/– to 13/6 there is better than 1500 [bushels]will be shipped from this[106]

In the last weeks of December more flaxseed ships came to Baltimore. "There is a vessel loading for Newry, Mr. Thompson's

Ship which we believe will sail soon, and another loading for Belfast We cannot Say When She will Sail." The ship for Belfast was John Ewing's ship *John*, which arrived from Cork. Her captain was Charles Poaug, the brother of John Poaug of Charleston and Ewing's brother-in-law.[107] The snow *Patowmack* brought linens and other goods from Liverpool and Dublin, after the non- importation agreement took effect. "Capt. Graham is arrived Safe but what he has Brot is Stored," Woolsey wrote to Pringle, "What will be done with it by the Committee we can't Say." David Stewart was loading the snow with flaxseed "and I believe we will be able to make up your Quantity of seed."[108]

George Woolsey was himself concerned with the brig *Hope*, which arrived from Dublin at the turn of the year. Woolsey had "160 hhds Seed on board and 400 bbls flour" and was loading "1600 bushels Wheat or more if the room will hold it." The brig belonged to Robinson and Sandith of Dublin. Before the end of January Woolsey could report to his partner George Salmon "The Hope is full ... only 60 Hhds Flaxseed on board on freight 50 bbls Bread 50 do. Flour 50 Hhds Seed & 1500 bushels wheat for the owner the rest for our Selfs which will go to GD." He informed his brother-in-law George Darley, a merchant in Dublin, "I have Ship'd per the Brig Hope for Dublin and to your address say 100 bbls Bread, 192 do. Flour, 140 of Wheat meal, 52 Rye meal, 60 hhds Flaxseed on acct. of Woolsey & Salmon."[109]

With the sailing of the *Hope* Baltimore's meteoric rise as a port shipping wheat, flour and flaxseed to Ireland came to at least a temporary end. Unless matters were soon resolved, the Colonies were pledged to stop all exports to Great Britain in September. Woolsey advised his Ulster correspondents that flaxseed prices were high, "but as you Expect none from us next Season we think tho it cost high it must answer with you."[110]

Back in Belfast, Samuel Brown, as staunch a friend of American liberty as when he lived in Baltimore, had written to a business associate: "I hope if you come to Resolutions not to export goods, you will allow poor Ireland some Flaxseed, or they wont be able to pay their passages to go to you.'[111]

Convicts, Servants and Paying Passengers

As Baltimore's importance as a port grew, it gained another distinction: it became the primary marketplace for convict servants. Maryland and the Chesapeake generally had long been the best market for convicts, persons sentenced by the courts in Great Britain and Ireland to transportation overseas. What Charleston was to the slave trade and Philadelphia to the servant trade, as the principal port of entry and primary market, first Annapolis and then Baltimore were to the convict trade.[112] The appeal of convicts over ordinary indentured servants lay in their longer contracts. In Maryland in 1767–75 the average labour contract for a convict servant ran for nine years, while other servant indentures averaged just 3.9 years. The difference was reflected in the prices paid for each at the same time and place, convicts bringing an average £11 and other servants averaging £8 8s. There were thus distinct advantages to the importer who brought a cargo of convict servants. Any merchant would accept such a consignment, of course, but the trade was largely in the hands of a few specialist firms. John Stewart and Duncan Campbell had the London transportation contract from 1757 through 1773.[113] They had a number of agents in Baltimore and in tobacco-growing southern Maryland, trading as Stewart and Lux and Russell and Hodge.[114] James Cheston of Baltimore and his partners in Bristol were responsible for 93% of the convicts sent from Bristol to America. The Irish courts also sentenced criminals to transportation. No one firm seems to have had a monopoly on shipping them to the Chesapeake, although Stewart and Lux had a hand in this trade, too.[115]

Jonathan Plowman, James and Robert Christie, and Ashburner and Place were among the Baltimore firms who advertised British and German servants. John Ridgely imported 57 servants from Dublin on the brig *Achsah* which then brought flaxseed and flour from Baltimore to Belfast for John Ewing on her return voyage.[116] Certainly all the flaxseed and grain merchants had some involvement in the servant trade. John Stevenson offered "healthy Indented Servants, Men and Women," from Ireland in the brig *Venus*, which sailed from Newry, among them "Weavers, Shoemakers, Blacksmiths, Bakers, a Miller, House Carpenter, Sailmaker, Brazier, Hatter, Schoolmaster, and sundry Farmers." He advertised both "Indentured Servants and Redemptioners" by the same ship in other years.[117] Samuel and Sam Carsan had for sale "the times of a few redemptioners and servants" who came from Larne on the *Lord Dunluce* and David Stewart offered men and women servants "lately arrived on the brigantine Industry from Waterford."[118]

George Woolsey announced healthy men and women servants had "Just arrived in the Baltimore Packet" from Newry.[119] Captain Benjamin Fleming brought the *Isabella* from Dublin later that year. Thanks to his Dublin correspondent John Armstrong, "Capt Fleming through your recommendation has addressed his servants to me," Woolsey wrote "I have sold about forty of them and hope in a short time to get clear of the rest."[120] He advertised:

> A Number of healthy four, five, six, and seven years indented servants, among whom are several tradesmen, and men used to country work, whose indentures will be disposed of for cash, country produce, or short credit by Woolsey and Salmon.[121]

The long term indentures suggest some at least, if not all, were convict servants. They sold rapidly and well. "I have sold 60 of Flemings Servants amongs Whom are all the Women which have averaged £15.7.0"[122] This relatively high price proved the average. "Flemings sales are now finished he has £1450 for 101 Servants but I am obliged to allow him one third of the Commission."[123] The schooner *Industry*, commanded by his brother William Woolsey, arrived from Dublin in December. Its human cargo proved a disappointment.

> I think there is about 12 of the Schooners Servants dead with a Bad fever there is also 8 more Yet Sick with flux. ... I have sold half of What is Alive pretty well but have not raised L 200 Cash The rem'g half I believe will sell low & of course command no Cash.[124]

Convicts banished beyond the seas had no choice about the conditions on board ship. Men and women who feely chose to go to the Colonies as servants could bargain. Ships sailing for Baltimore routinely invited redemptioners and servants to seek passage. Agents recruited others. A certain Charles Hamilton advertised for tradesmen for Baltimore, promising that he "will be in Enniskillen, Omagh, Strabane and Londonderry" on specific days to make arrangements for them. He was possibly filling orders, as among others, he sought "a lad that understands waiting upon a single person, shaving & dressing hair."[125] If he met with success, they were probably among those who sailed from Londonderry on James Thompson's *Prince of Wales*.

"Freedom, Wealth, and Happiness"

A passage on the *Prince of Wales* was a passage to the Promised Land, if one could believe a newspaper advertisement:

> The town of Baltimore is commodiously situated for a ready Communication with all the back parts of Pennsylvania, Maryland, and Virginia, to which most new Settlers resort. It is a hundred miles nearer than Philadelphia to Fort Pitt on the River Ohio – a new Province of vast Extent, of the most fertile fine Lands in North America, and in the most agreeable moderate Climate, is now settling very fast along the Banks of that famous River, where Tracts of the richest Lands in the World and of greater Extent than most Kingdoms in Europe, are yet unsettled, and will for many Ages to come afford the most happy Asylum for all that choose to exchange a Land of Poverty, for Freedom, Wealth, and Happiness.[126]

When the *Prince of Wales* finally reached Baltimore and disembarked her passengers, the editor of the local newspaper rose to the same rhetorical heights.

> Yesterday arrived the Ship Prince of Wales, Capt. Morrison, from Londonderry, with about 200 Passengers, which makes no less than 3500 that has left that Port only within one Year, and come to seek in our back extensive and happy Territory, peaceable and comfortable Residences, which those loyal and industrious People could not enjoy in their native Land, from the ill-judged Oppression exercised over that sinking Country by Great Britain. Let the deplorable State of the once prosperous

Land fill Americans with wary Apprehensions, and rouse them with animated Warmth to resist every Attempt of Parliamentary Tyranny under what specious or plausible Pretext or Guise so ever it may be offered – for, the smallest Restriction of our Liberty admitted, all will be lost.[127]

Since Baltimore was far less familiar a destination to people in Ulster than New York or Philadelphia, ship-owners stressed the easy access to the backcountry as well as the advantages Maryland afforded newcomers. One of David Gaussan's advertisements said that

Baltimore is a new Town and improving every Day, and promises to be a great and flourishing City, being situated in the Heart of as fine a Corn Country as any in America. It is very convenient to the Province of Pensilvania , and has two Packet Boats plying between them twice a Week, so that at all Times those who desire to go to Pensilvania may have their Passage for 6/– Currency.[128]

One of Maryland's appeals for emigrants from Ireland was its tradition of religious freedom and the comparatively large population of English-speaking Catholics. An advertisement for the sailing of the *Commerce* from Limerick for Baltimore in June 1772 invited settlers to Maryland "where there is liberty of conscience."[129] When John Ewing announced the sailing of his *Charming Molly* the following year he made the same appeal, addressing "Those who chuse to embrace this Opportunity to go to one of the finest and plentiful Countries in America, where all Kinds of Religions are tolerated, either as Passengers, Redemptioners, or Servants."[130]

Nor did Ewing neglect the ease with which newly arrived settlers could travel to the backcountry, especially since his brother was selling land on the South Branch of the Potomac in what is now West Virginia. Thomas Ewing had temporarily returned to Belfast from Baltimore and was offering many small tracts, totalling 10,399 acres, within the Fairfax family's Proprietary of the Northern Neck. His brother pointed out that

Baltimore is much more convenient than any other Port for those who want to go to the back Parts of Pennsylvania,

Maryland, Virginia, or any of the new Settlements on the
Ohio. Those who purchase any of the Lands advertised by
Thomas Ewing had as good embrace this Opportunity.[131]

The Ewings were not the only merchants with an interest in peopling western lands. Robert and Samuel Purviance, Jr. had similar
investments. Even without this inducement, many Ulster folk
chose Baltimore as their own gateway to the backcountry.

If 1773 was the *annus mirabilis* for Ulster emigration to the
American Colonies, it was 1774 that confirmed Baltimore as a
major port of entry for emigrants. Only one ship sailing to
Baltimore advertised for passengers in the *Belfast News Letter* in
1767 and three in 1768. There were four in 1771. Five ships, two
from Londonderry, two from Newry, and one from Belfast were
advertised in 1772 to sail to Baltimore with passengers. In 1773
there were seven and in 1774 a dozen. One of the sailings advertised that year was the *Baltimore Packet*, belonging to David
Gaussan, John Woolsey, and Thomas McCabe. They declared that

> It is needless to say any Thing in Praise of the Province of
> Maryland, as it is well known the Land is equal if not superi-
> or to any in America, and many large Tracts may be got on
> more reasonable Terms than in any other Province there; it
> must also be observed, that any People who intend going to
> the back Part of Pennsylvania will find it to their Account in
> going first to Baltimore, as the Land Carriage is much short-
> er, consequently cheaper, than in any Seaport in
> Pennsylvania.[132]

Within less than a decade Baltimore had grown as a port with
close ties to Ireland, and with significant trade to the West Indies
and southern Europe. Its merchants shipped flaxseed, wheat and
flour to Ulster and brought new settlers from there to Maryland
and the backcountry. In the same short period a small group of
Scotch-Irish Presbyterian became prominent in political affairs.
Charles Steffen found no evidence of hostility to the leadership role
assumed by these Scotch-Irish merchants. It signalled a change in
the economy and society of the upper Chesapeake.

The increase in wheat production, the decline of plantation slavery, and the acceleration of urban development propelled northern Maryland along the same economic and social trajectory as neighbouring Pennsylvania. At the same time the deepening crisis in imperial affairs after 1763 opened the way for a coterie of Scotch-Irish merchants, most with Pennsylvania connections. ... The new merchants flooding into Baltimore town were assimilated rapidly and with remarkably little discord.[133]

They had become the new leaders needed by a town that had trebled in population since they arrived, reaching 6,000 in 1780, and would double in size in the next decade as Baltimore took its place as a major commercial city in the new nation. A new generation of Ulster businessmen, including James Simm, another of Thomas Ewing's nephews, Hugh Thompson, and Robert Oliver, came to Baltimore in 1784 to join the Scotch-Irish merchants who had played an important part in developing Baltimore from a small town on the Chesapeake to a centre of world trade.

Notes

1   *Maryland Gazette*, July 19, 1761.

2   Rev. Patrick Allison, "The Rise and Progress of the Presbyterian Church in Baltimore Town" in Richard D. Fisher, *First Presbyterian Church, Baltimore, Maryland 1761–1895* (Baltimore, 1895), 7–10.

3   Clarence G. Gould, "The Economic Causes of the Rise of Baltimore," *Essays in Colonial History Presented to Charles McLean Andrews* (Freeport, NY, 1966), 227. Geoffrey N. Gilbert, *Baltimore's Flour Trade to the Caribbean 1750–1815* (New York, 1986), 1. Paul G. E. Clemens, *The Atlantic Economy and Colonial Maryland's Eastern Shore* (Ithaca, NY, 1980), 176–9.

4   Paul Kent Walker, "The Baltimore Community and the American Revolution: A Study in Urban Development 1763–1783," Ph.D. dissertation, University of North Carolina (1973), 17–21. Charles G. Steffen, *From Gentlemen to Townsmen: The Gentry of Baltimore County, Maryland 1660–1776* (Lexington, KY, 1993), 160.

5   J. Thomas Scharf, *Chronicles of Baltimore* (Baltimore, 1874), 19–23, 32, 34.

6   *Maryland Gazette*, July 12, 1759, June 19, 1760.

7   Paul G. E. Clemens, "From Tobacco to Grain: Economic Development on Maryland's Eastern Shore 1660–1750," *Journal of Economic History*, 35(1975), 258.

8   Davey and Carsan to Robert Travers, June 5, 1746, to Alexander Auchinleck, December 12, 1746 (Davey and Carsan Letterbook, LC).

9   George Johnston, *History of Cecil County, Maryland* (Elkton, MD, 1881), 271.

10   Doerflinger, *A Vigorous Spirit*, 113–14.

11   Richard K. MacMaster, "Georgetown and the Tobacco Trade, 1751–1783," *Records of the Columbia Historical Society of Washington, D.C. 1966–1968* (Washington, DC, 1969), 1–33.

12   *Maryland Gazette*, April 30, 1767.

13   Robert D. Mitchell, "The Upper Shenandoah Valley of Virginia During the Eighteenth Century: A Study in Historical Geography," Ph.D. dissertation, University of Wisconsin (1969), 371 and fn46 399.

14   Kate Mason Rowland, "Merchants and Mills," *William and Mary Quarterly*, 11(1903), 246.

15   *Maryland Gazette*, January 15, 1767.

16   William Glenholme to William Beath and Co., December 6, 1768 (Orr, Dunlope, and Glenholme Letter Book, HSP).

17   Gilbert, *Baltimore's Flour Trade*, 33, 38–9. Gould, "Rise of Baltimore," 247.

18   *Maryland Journal and Baltimore Advertiser*, March 25, 1785.

19   J. Thomas Scharf, *The Chronicles of Baltimore* (Baltimore, 1874), 49–50.

20   *Maryland Gazette*, July 15, 1762, May 31, 1764, September 27, 1764,

21   *Maryland Gazette*, March 12, 1767.

22   *Maryland Gazette*, July 9, 1761, July 8, 1762.

23   William Eddis, *Letters from America* (London,1792, Cambridge, MA, 1966), 96–8.

24   *Belfast News Letter*, June 30, 1767, August 2, 1768, July 25, 1769.

25   George Bryan, for instance, advertised for freight for the *Earl of Chatham*,

George Woolsey, commander, now lying at Baltimore Town. *Pennsylvania Journal*, November 12, 1767.

26 *Belfast News Letter*, March 3, 1769, March 7, 1769.

27 George Woolsey to Thomas Bateson and Co., January 25, 1775 (Woolsey and Salmon Letterbook. Peter Force Collection, 8D/189, LC).

28 *Belfast News Letter*, June 4, 1771, July 16, 1773, July 27, 1773, *Londonderry Journal*, June 8, 1773.

29 Gould, "Rise of Baltimore," 247–8.

30 Maryland still lagged behind Pennsylvania and New York in the production and export of flour. Gilbert, *Baltimore's Flour Trade*, 4, 31.

31 Walker, "Baltimore Community," 57. Truxes, *Irish-American Trade*, 122–3.

32 *Pennsylvania Chronicle*, February 9, 1767.

33 Johnston, *History of Cecil County*, 273.

34 His father, Justice Samuel Smith from Ballymagorry, near Strabane, Indian trader and one of the original justices of Cumberland County Court, also moved to Baltimore at a later date and died there aged 94 in 1784. *Maryland Journal*, April 9, 1784.

35 Typical of the family connections of these merchants, William Smith was married to another of William Buchanan's sisters. William Smith's mother was a sister to David McClure, who was the father of these McClures and of James Sterrett's wife, also born Mary McClure.

36 Ronald Hoffman, *A Spirit of Dissension: Economics, Politics, and the Revolution in Maryland* (Baltimore, 1973), 63.

37 *Pennsylvania Journal*, July 31, 1766. *Maryland Gazette*, December 11, 1766. Hoffman, *Spirit of Dissension*, 38–41. George W. McCreary, *The Ancient and Honorable Mechanical Company of Baltimore* (Baltimore, 1901), 18–19.

38 LeRoy James Votto, "Social Dynamism in a Boom Town: The Scots-Irish in Baltimore 1760 to 1790," MA thesis, University of Virginia (1969).

39 Cumberland Deeds, 2–A–67 (CCCH).

40 Lancaster Deeds, F–1–387 (LCCH). Barnabas Hughes to Henry Bouquet, March 8, 1760, March 28, 1760, in Louis M. Waddell, ed., *The Papers of Henry Bouquet* (Harrisburg, PA, 1984), V, 490, 502–03.

41 Henry Bouquet to Mrs. Sophia Fesch, October 2, 1762, in Sylvester M. Stevens, ed., *The Papers of Col. Henry Bouquet* (Harrisburg, PA, 1940), 151–3.

42 *Maryland Gazette*, January 21, 1762. Jonathan Plowman and other Baltimore merchants, however, continued to be primarily interested in sending cargoes of tobacco consigned to London and Liverpool firms. *Maryland Gazette*, September 16, 1762.

43 *Maryland Gazette*, March 3, 1763, July 12, 1764.

44 Lancaster Deeds, O–1–368 (LCCH). Fieri Facias Files, November 5, 1764 (LCHS).

45 *Maryland Gazette*, February 21, 1765. Baltimore County Inventories 89:159, 163 (Maryland Hall of Records, Annapolis, MD).

46 *Maryland Gazette*, May 8, 1766, August 21, 1766.

47 John S. Pancake, *Samuel Smith and the Politics of Business* (Tuscaloosa, AL 1972), 1–2.

48 *Pennsylvania Journal*, May 8, 1766. Steffen, *From Gentlemen to Townsmen*, 158. Baltimore County Deeds, 1761–73 (Maryland Hall of Records, Annapolis, MD).

49 *Maryland Gazette*, October 2, 1766. Hoffman, *Spirit of Dissension*, 63.

50 Ewing Family Notes (T2637/5, PRONI). He did not advertise frequently, so the newspapers are not too helpful. He offered a reward in 1766 when a thief broke into "the store of Thomas Ewing in Baltimore Town" using a false key and stole 70 pounds currency. *Maryland Gazette*, April 17, 1766.

51 *Pennsylvania Journal*, March 21, 1765.

52 *Maryland Gazette*, December 11, 1766.

53 In addition to Smith and Buchanan's *Carlisle*, the *Gale* and *Two Brothers* arrived from Baltimore with wheat and flour consigned to John Ewing and the brig *Achsah* brought him flaxseed and flour. *Belfast News Letter*, June 30, 1767, August 2, 1768, July 14, 1769, July 25, 1769, October 17, 1769, April 24, 1770.

54 William Glenholme to Ewing and Brown, April 19, 1768, June 10, 1768, July 16, 1768, October 19, 1768, October 27, 1768 (Orr, Dunlope and Glenholme Letter Book, HSP).

55 Baltimore County Wills, 3, 402–04 (Maryland Hall of Records, Annapolis, MD).

56 "Ship Registers," *PMHB*, 27(1903), 491. *Belfast News Letter*, March 10, 1769, March 8, 1771.

57 *Belfast News Letter*, February 8, 1771, March 1, 1771, March 5, 1771, March 19, 1771.

58 *Belfast News Letter*, July 26, 1771, August 23, 1771, September 13, 1771.

59 Fisher, First Presbyterian Church, 32–3. Henry C. Peden, Jr., *Presbyterian Records of Baltimore City, Maryland, 1765–1840* (Westminster, MD, 1995), 17.

60 *Belfast News Letter*, August 25, 1772, February 28, 1775.

61 *Belfast News Letter*, December 16, 1774.

62 *Maryland Journal and Baltimore Advertiser*, July 9, 1774, July 16, 1774.

63 George Woolsey to George Salmon, November 20, 1774 (Woolsey and Salmon Letterbook, LC).

64 *Maryland Journal and Baltimore Advertiser*, August 9, 1775.

65 Baltimore County Wills, 3, 402–04 (Maryland Hall of Records, Annapolis, MD).

66 *Maryland Gazette*, January 31, 1765, January 15, 1767. *Pennsylvania Gazette*, October 12, 1769. *Pennsylvania Journal*, August 8, 1765, March 5, 1767. Hoffman, *Spirit of Dissension*, 78.

67 *Pennsylvania Journal*, April 26, 1770. *Maryland Gazette*, January 31, 1771, July 25, 1771. *Pennsylvania Gazette*, June 6, 1771. *Maryland Journal and Baltimore Advertiser*, June 4, 1774, May 17, 1775, August 9, 1775.

68 *Maryland Gazette*, September 29, 1768, September 28, 1769, January 4, 1770, May 3, 1770, June 4, 1771. *Pennsylvania Journal*, May 3, 1770.

69 *Belfast News Letter*, March 21, 1769. *Pennsylvania Journal*, August 3, 1769.

70 *Belfast News Letter*, February 12, 1771, April 9, 1771, June 4, 1771, July 19, 1771.

71 *Maryland Gazette*, August 9, 1771.

72   Steffen, *From Gentlemen to Townsmen*, 160.
73   Hoffman, *Spirit of Dissension*, 38–41. George W. McCreary, *The Ancient and Honorable Mechanical Company of Baltimore* (Baltimore, 1901), 18–19.
74   Robert Purviance, *A Narrative of Events which Occurred in Baltimore Town During the Revolutionary War* (Baltimore, 1849), 107.
75   *Maryland Gazette*, December 28, 1769. Hoffman, *Spirit of Dissension*, 86–7.
76   *Maryland Gazette*, February 8, 1770, February 15, 1770.
77   *Maryland Gazette*, April 19, 1770. "The Case of the Good Intent," *Maryland Historical Magazine* 2(1904), 141–50.
78   *Maryland Gazette*, June 14, 1770.
79   *Maryland Gazette*, July 26, 1770, October 11, 1770, November 1, 1770. Lux, a second-generation Baltimore merchant, was in partnership with William Smith. Hoffman, *Spirit of Dissension*, 39.
80   Steffen, *From Gentlemen to Townsmen*, 158.
81   *Belfast News Letter*, January 8, 1773, March 2, 1773, June 11, 1773, June 22, 1773, July 2, 1773, July 6, 1773, August 20, 1773.
82   *Pennsylvania Gazette*, December 5, 1771. *Pennsylvania Journal*, September 25, 1774. *Maryland Journal and Baltimore Advertiser*, November 30, 1774, February 13, 1775, October 4, 1775.
83   Bernard C. Steiner, *Life and Correspondence of James McHenry* (Cleveland, OH, 1907), 1–2.
84   *Maryland Journal and Baltimore Advertiser*, November 6, 1773. Harris and Donaldson to John Mitchell, May 5, 1774, July 29, 1774, Alexander Donaldson to John Mitchell, December 22, 1774, August 8, 1775 (John Mitchell Papers, PSA).
85   *Pennsylvania Journal*, November 12, 1767, September 29, 1768. The *Earl of Chatham* was to carry passengers, but no servants or convicts, according to advertisements in the Dublin newspapers. Audrey Lockhart, *Some Aspects of Emigration from Ireland to the North American Colonies Between 1660 and 1775* (New York, 1976), 199–201.
86   My friend John McCabe traced George Woolsey's family for me. His main sources were Blackwood MS. Pedigrees, I, 42–8 in the Linen Hall Library, Belfast and Woolsey of Clonaugh (T/2595/8, PRONI).
87   Woolsey was at least a part owner of this ship. "Ship Registers," *PMHB*, 28(1904), 351. *Pennsylvania Journal*, November 1, 1770. *Pennsylvania Gazette*, May 2, 1771. Lockhart, *Aspects of Emigration*, 203.
88   George Woolsey to Joseph Wilson, October 28, 1774, to John Mitchell, October 28, 1774 (Woolsey and Salmon Letter Book, LC).
89   *Pennsylvania Journal*, January 1, 1767, March 17, 1768, October 5, 1769, November 8, 1770.
90   John and Mary Darley were the children of Catharine Woolsey's uncle Hugh Darley, a Dublin architect. When he died in 1771, his son John and Catharine's brother George were executors of his will.
91   *Belfast News Letter*, December 11, 1772. *Pennsylvania Journal*, November 24, 1773. *Pennsylvania Gazette*, November 24, 1773. *Maryland Journal and Baltimore Advertiser*, November 26, 1773. *Maryland Gazette*, January 6, 1774. Lockhart, *Aspects of Emigration*, 206.

92 *Belfast News Letter*, March 1, 1774.

93 George Woolsey to David Gaussan, October 30, 1774, George Woolsey to George Salmon, October 31, 1774 (Woolsey and Salmon Letterbook, LC).

94 George Woolsey to John Pringle, October 22, 1774 (Woolsey and Salmon Letterbook, LC).

95 George Woolsey to Thomas Bateson and Co., January 25, 1775 (Woolsey and Salmon Letterbook, LC).

96 *Pennsylvania Journal*, November 9, 1774, November 16, 1774, November 23, 1774.

97 George Woolsey to John Pringle, October 28, 1774 (Woolsey and Salmon Letterbook, LC).

98 George Woolsey to John Mitchell, October 28, 1774 (Woolsey and Salmon Letterbook, LC).

99 George Woolsey to David Gaussan, October 30, 1774 (Woolsey and Salmon Letterbook, LC).

100 George Woolsey to George Salmon, December 5, 1774 (Woolsey and Salmon Letterbook, LC).

101 George Woolsey to George Salmon, December 12, 1774 (Woolsey and Salmon Letterbook, LC).

102 "Memorandum of an Agreement made between Geo. Woolsey & Jno. Lynch both of Baltimore," November 18, 1774. George Woolsey to John Pringle, November 12, 1774, November 18, 1774, November 26, 1774, to David Gaussan, November 20, 1774, to George Salmon, November 20, 1774, to Andrew Thompson, December 12, 1774 (Woolsey and Salmon Letterbook, LC).

103 George Woolsey to John Pringle, November 26, 1774, to George Salmon, December 5, 1774 (Woolsey and Salmon Letterbook, LC). *Maryland Journal and Baltimore Advertiser*, November 30, 1774.

104 George Woolsey to James Forde, to Thomas Matthews & Co., December 8, 1774 (Woolsey and Salmon Letterbook, LC).

105 George Woolsey to Thomas McCabe, December 9, 1774, January 27, 1775 (Woolsey and Salmon Letterbook, LC).

106 George Woolsey to Andrew Thompson, January 28, 1775 (Woolsey and Salmon Letterbook, LC).

107 George Woolsey to John Pringle, December 22, 1774 (Woolsey and Salmon Letterbook, LC). *Maryland Gazette*, December 15, 1774, December 29, 1774.

108 George Woolsey to John Pringle, December 22, 1774, December 24, 1774 (Woolsey and Salmon Letterbook, LC). *Maryland Gazette*, December 29, 1774.

109 George Woolsey to Robinson and Sandith, January 21, 1775, to George Salmon, January 25, 1775, to George Darley, January 27, 1775 (Woolsey and Salmon Letterbook, LC). *Maryland Gazette*, January 5, 1775.

110 George Woolsey to Thomas Bateson and Co., January 25, 1775 (Woolsey and Salmon Letterbook, LC).

111 Samuel Brown to James Hunter, August 30, 1774, in *PMHB*, 28(1902), 104–05.

112 Kenneth Morgan, "The Organization of the Convict Trade to Maryland: Stevenson, Randolph and Cheston, 1768–1775," *William and Mary Quarterly*, 3rd series, 42(1985), 206–07.

113 Farley Grubb, "The Transatlantic Market for British Convict Labor," *Journal of Economic History*, 60(2000), 103–05

114 *Maryland Gazette*, June 26, 1760, August 11, 1763, February 26, 1767, September 13, 1770, February 10, 1774, January 19, 1775.

115 A. Roger Ekirch, "Bound for America: A Profile of British Convicts Transported to the Colonies 1718–1775," *William and Mary Quarterly*, 3rd series, 42(1985), 187. Patrick Fitzgerald, "A Sentence to Sail: The Transportation of Irish Convicts and Vagrants to Colonial America in the Eighteenth Century," in Patrick Fitzgerald and Steve Ickringill, eds., *Atlantic Crossroads: Historical connections between Scotland, Ulster and North America* (Newtownards, 2001), 114–32.

116 *Maryland Gazette*, December 11, 1766, July 30, 1767, November 24, 1768, May 28, 1772. *Belfast News Letter*, April 24, 1770.

117 *Maryland Gazette*, September 28, 1769, May 3, 1770.

118 *Maryland Journal and Baltimore Advertiser*, June 11, 1774, November 30, 1774.

119 *Maryland Journal and Baltimore Advertiser*, July 9, 1774.

120 George Woolsey to John Armstrong, October 30, 1774 (Woolsey and Salmon Letterbook, LC).

121 *Maryland Gazette*, October 20, 1774.

122 George Woolsey to George Salmon, October 31, 1774 (Woolsey and Salmon Letterbook, LC).

123 George Woolsey to George Salmon, December 9, 1774 (Woolsey and Salmon Letterbook, LC).

124 *Maryland Gazette*, December 21, 1774. George Woolsey to George Salmon, January 4, 1775, to William Woolsey, to Robert Lisle, January 12, 1775 (Woolsey and Salmon Letterbook, LC).

125 *Londonderry Journal*, February 23, 1773.

126 *Londonderry Journal*, June 4, 1773.

127 *Maryland Journal and Baltimore Advertiser*, October 16, 1773.

128 *Belfast News Letter*, June 4, 1771.

129 Lockhart, *Aspects of Emigration*, 204.

130 *Belfast News Letter*, July 27, 1773.

131 The detailed description of the Hampshire County, Virginia land is in B*elfast News Letter*, July 13, 1773, the advertisement for the *Charming Molly* is in *Belfast News Letter*, July 27, 1773.

132 *Belfast News Letter*, March 5, 1774.

133 Steffen, *From Gentlemen to Townsmen*, 137.

9

Emigration at High Tide

"They promise fair till they get your money"
The Rev. Joseph Rhea, Presbyterian minister at Fahan, County Donegal, his wife, Elizabeth, their children, Matthew, John, Margaret, William, Elizabeth, Joseph, and Samuel, and his wife's niece, Fanny Dysart, came on board the brig *George*, owned by Samuel Curry of Londonderry, on September 27, 1769 to begin their journey to America. The *George* lay at anchor off Quigley's Point in the Foyle estuary until she was ready to sail. On a fine autumn day, the brig and her passengers rounded Malin Head bound for Philadelphia. Nine other families took passage on the *George* and just five individuals who were not part of a family group. Contrary winds delayed their passage. Cabin passengers, like the minister's family, were drenched on stormy nights as water leaked in. Rhea complained of the food and suffered seasickness. He wrote in frustration:

> I hope in god none of my friends will ever Sail in Sam Curry's brig after this. all the fair promises of these Sycophant owners in Derry signify nothing; they promise fair till they get your money & then their promises vanish into air.

But all on board arrived in good health, after sixty-five days at sea.[1]

They were among 541 Ulster emigrants who landed at Philadelphia that year, a surprisingly small number since Philadelphia and New Castle on the Delaware shared at least half of the ships bringing passengers from ports in the north of Ireland.[2] The number of emigrants leaving Ulster for North American ports rose gradually between 1763 and 1773, reaching a peak in the latter year. On his tour through Ireland, Arthur Young made "many enquiries" at Belfast about the extent of emigration to America "and found that they have for many years had a regular emigration of about 2,000 annually, but in 1772 the decline of the linen manufacture increased the number; and the same cause continuing in 1773 they were at the highest when 4,000 went."[3]

Rhea described an essentially boring, uncomfortable, but otherwise uneventful passage, a typical emigrant experience. Most passengers would find the meagre diet on an Atlantic crossing unappetising and stormy weather made it impossible to prepare food in the camhouse on deck. At such times they had only "bread and butter and grog." As "our Ship goes as the Psalm speaks staggering & reeling like a drunk man," Rhea wrote that "if it was not for the provision we brought with us we wou'd half starve." Near the end of the voyage, with all "hungered by want of meat," he repeated that "had it not been for our own provision we had died with hunger." But the Rheas and other passengers had wisely brought much food with them. On their last day aboard the *George*, Robert Patten reminded the minister that the Rheas had enjoyed "his Rashers and barley" and Rhea "told him of my Potatoes, he eat a barrel & more from me."[4] The *George's* passengers, like others sailing from Londonderry, would have brought a good many other things, including linen to sell. Daniel Clark noted,

> There is an Advantage that Passengers from Derry have which I am afraid will never be allowed in Sligoe viz. that they may bring any article or Quantity of Goods with them they please without let or molestation from any officers and this Indulgence is procured by the Influence of the Merchants there over the Officers, and the desire of the Latter to overlook an affair that conduces much to the Interest of the People of that City.[5]

Most ship-owners promised no dearth of provisions, but some were overly nice in determining how little they need supply and adverse weather could unduly prolong a voyage and cause provisions to run short. The master of an English ship encountered the *Belfast Packet*, owned by the same Robert Wills who sent the *Nancy* to Charleston, on her way to Philadelphia "with about 70 passengers, who had been out about 16 weeks, and were in want of provisions and water, of which Captain Appleton gave them all he could spare." The *Belfast Packet* reached port two weeks later after eighteen weeks at sea, twice as long as *George's* passage.[6] John Gregg, John Campbell and John Ewing of Belfast first advertised the *Earl of Donegall* for Charleston, then dispatched her instead to Philadelphia with passengers early in October. Captain Ferguson was near the Delaware Capes when "on the 16th of December, he met with a gale of wind which laid his vessel on her beam ends, and he was obliged to cut away his mizzen mast before she would right." Sailing with the wind, Ferguson bore away for the West Indies and reached Antigua on January 7, 1769 and refitted there. The passengers reached Philadelphia the last of February, "all well," despite their long ordeal.[7]

Such delays were costly to the merchant, but equally so long stays in port that precluded additional voyages. In the competitive passenger trade, there might not be emigrants waiting for passage when the captain needed to sail from Belfast or Derry or those who booked passage might ask for a delay to settle their affairs in Ireland. Ships in the flaxseed and emigrants cycle had to maintain a fixed schedule, as James Fullton explained to the commander of the Londonderry ship *Rose*:

> My Intention of your Next Voyage if agreeable to the Gentlemen Concerned is For you to Sail with your Ship and what Passengers you Can gett for this place the middle of Next april or first of may at Farthest and no Later Lett the prospect for the West indies for the Ship in order to Return here in time in the fall to Load with Flaxseed. You may assure the gentlemen with me in this Ship That if a Ship is not here Early in the fall on a flaxseed Voyage that its much against the owners interest ... if they Should order you on a Noraway Voyage [or] two and here in the fall for Passengers you are not to Ly Longer than the first or middle of august.[8]

The passenger trade was a competitive business in the 1760s and would-be emigrants found many ships on offer. Fullton, for instance, wrote his Londonderry associates "as there is so many Ships at your place for Philada. that I think you cannot get many Passengers," send *Hibernia* "here as soon as she arrives from Norway" so as not to lose a flaxseed freight.[9] He explained to his business partners in the ship *Hibernia* that "To ly at Derry for Passengers till the middle of Summer and make Only one Voyage in the year will not in my opinion by any means Do" and insisted they "send the Ship from Derry for this Port by the middle of April," which he considered ample time to "get a number of Passengers for this Place." On that supposition, "We Can Probably make a Summer Voyage to Some Port of Europe" with a cargo of iron and lumber to ballast the ship, and with barrel staves for Cork and proceed from there to some port in England.[10]

Ship-owners strove to limit the time their vessels spent in port and wanted them immediately dispatched on another profitable voyage. One general pattern was to send a ship arriving at Belfast or Newry with flaxseed to Norway or the Baltic for lumber and steel, so as to be ready to take passengers to Philadelphia or New York and load with flaxseed. Another common pattern, which Fullton urged on his associates, was to bring out passengers in the Spring, carry lumber and provisions to Cork, and return with passengers in time to take on a flaxseed cargo. Voyages to the West Indies or to southern Europe could be fitted in, but they had to return to New York or Philadelphia before winter, and any delay "would Put the Ship out of the way of a flaxseed freight home in the fall."[11]

From advertisements in the *Belfast News Letter*, it is clear that Philadelphia and New Castle were still the preferred destination for emigrants from Ulster, accounting for half the advertised sailings. In 1766 ship-owners advertised 14 vessels for the Delaware ports, four for Charleston, three for New York and one to Halifax. In 1767 there were 15 passenger ships advertised for New Castle and Philadelphia, nine for Charleston, eight for New York, two for Halifax and one each for Baltimore and Boston. Advertisements in 1768 included eleven for New Castle and Philadelphia, five for New York, three for Baltimore, two for Charleston and one for Savannah. As the demand for passage to America grew in the

1770s, Philadelphia held its lead with nineteen advertised sailings in 1771, seventeen in 1772, and 21 in 1773. It was only in 1773, when the number of emigrants doubled, that shipping for other Colonial ports showed marked increase, with fourteen passenger ships for Charleston and nine for Baltimore.[12]

On both sides of the Atlantic a few firms were prominent in the passenger trade, but there was clearly room for every merchant and ship-owner with an interest in North American commerce. Belfast's share of the passenger trade declined in proportion to other Ulster ports. In 1769, the first year for which we have complete records of passengers disembarking at Philadelphia, and again in 1770, just two ships brought passengers from Belfast, seven from Londonderry, and two from Newry. There were four vessels from Belfast with passengers in 1771, six from Londonderry, and three from Newry.[13]

In Belfast, Gregs and Cunningham and Mussenden, Bateson and Company, later Thomas Bateson and Company, held pride of place.[14] Gregs and Cunningham had their own New York branch and close ties with Torrans and Poaug in Charleston. They advertised for passengers for three ships in 1766 and again in 1767. Bateson had two ships in the passenger trade both years. John Ewing's primary links were with Baltimore, through his brother Thomas Ewing and nephew Samuel Brown. He advertised three ships in 1767, two in partnership with John Gregg and John Campbell.[15] Gilbert Orr, whose connections were to Orr, Dunlope and Glenholme in Philadelphia, and Robert Wills, of Wills and Jackson, also of Philadelphia, each sought passengers for two ships in 1766 and again in 1767.[16] William Burgess and James Henderson also advertised for passengers.

Ships from Londonderry had the lion's share of the traffic with Philadelphia and New Castle on Delaware. In Londonderry Caldwell, Vance and Caldwell was the most important firm in the flaxseed and passenger trade.[17] Caldwell, Vance and Caldwell's ships were usually consigned to William and Andrew Caldwell, so many of the ships arriving at Philadelphia with passengers from Londonderry came to them. They also advertised servants imported from Dublin and Cork. William Caldwell of the Derry firm was the senior partner with his cousin Andrew. James Caldwell, brother of the partners in Derry, arrived in Philadelphia on the *Marquis of Granby* in 1768 to join the Philadelphia firm.[18]

After thirty years in Philadelphia Samuel Carsan was still at the top of his game, with connections to many Derry merchants. His nephew Thomas Barclay and cousin William Mitchell came from Strabane in 1763 and a year later joined the veteran merchant in a new Philadelphia firm. Robert Barclay sold some property near Strabane.

> My reasons for now selling is that my eldest son is settled at Philadelphia in partnership with his uncle Carsan and from his conduct I think wou'd be the better for money; my daughter is lately married and must have money; I have only one son more about 18 years old that I shall soon put into business, and I cannot at present spare so much from my own business as I incline to give my children and I rather chuse to sell than to borrow money, or to be straitened in business.[19]

After 1770 Carsan had a branch in Baltimore with another nephew and namesake. Carsan, Barclay and Mitchell were arguably the most important firm in the flaxseed and passenger trade.[20] As such they drew the custom of Londonderry merchants. James Fullton's long association with James Harvey and Co. came to an abrupt end when Harvey consigned their ship the *Rose* to Carsan, Barclay and Mitchell.[21]

Conyngham and Nesbitt owned ships in the flaxseed trade, but seem to have been more prominent in bringing Irish servants to Philadelphia than other emigrants. They owned the *Culloden* with Robert Alexander and John Knox of Londonderry who naturally dispatched her with passengers to their firm. John Mauleverer, Thomas Beesley and Dickson Cunningham sent their *Marquis of Granby* from Derry with passengers to Conyngham and Nesbitt's care. Like a nabob returning to England from India, Redmond Conyngham and his family sailed on his ship *Hayfield* for Londonderry early in 1766 to enjoy his estates in County Donegal. John Maxwell Nesbitt remained in Philadelphia to carry on the business, with the senior partner still active in Londonderry. David Hayfield Conyngham, Redmond's son, came out in 1768 to begin his apprenticeship with Conyngham and Nesbitt and later became a resident partner.[22]

The list of Londonderry ship-owners with one or more vessels in the passenger trade was a long one, including Robert Alexander, Thomas Beesley, Ninian Boggs, Ephraim Campbell, Samuel Curry, James Harvey, Abraham McCausland, John Mauleverer, James Miller, James Mitchell, Thomas Moore, and James Stirling of Walworth. Boggs and Campbell consigned ships to James Fullton. Harvey, McCausland, Mitchell, Stirling, and most of the others directed their ships to Samuel Carsan and his partners or the Caldwells. Some Londonderry ships were consigned to James Alexander of Philadelphia.[23] James Thompson began as a merchant in Newry, but later settled in Londonderry in partnership with Andrew Gregg. Their ships, except for the *Newry Packet*, also went to the Caldwells.[24]

Newry became more important in the passenger trade by the 1760s with men like George Anderson, William Beath, John Dickson, David Gaussan, Hill Willson, William and John Ogle, John and Hamilton Pringle, Andrew Thompson and Thomas Waring to the fore. The Ogles, proprietors of The American Flour Warehouse, early developed ties with Baltimore. Thompson, who regularly advertised New York and Philadelphia flaxseed, flour and barrel staves, solicited passengers for ships to New York and less frequently Philadelphia with Gaussan and Waring. His brother James Thompson spent several years in New York before settling in Derry in the later 1760s.[25] Another brother Acheson Thompson was a merchant in New York by 1764, importing Irish linens and beef, and one of the founders of the New York Chamber of Commerce in 1768. His colleagues there noted his absence in Ireland at a meeting in 1772. Acheson Thompson was back in Newry advertising for passengers for the *Robert* sailing for New York as co-owner of the ship with his brother Andrew.[26] John Eccles was also active in bringing passengers to New York. He recruited settlers for lands owned by his New York correspondent William Gilliland on Lake Champlain.[27] John Dickson of Newry and Hamilton Pringle of Caledon, County Tyrone dispatched the *Newry Assistance* and the *Newry Packet* with passengers to Philadelphia consigned to John Pringle and his partners Joseph Donaldson and Samuel Fisher.

Fisher, Donaldson and Pringle registered their ownership of the *Newry Packet* in 1766.[28]

Old America hands from the north Antrim towns, the Montgomerys and James McVickar in Larne, George Dunlope in Ballycastle, and John Caldwell, Jr. in Ballymoney were still in the flaxseed and passenger trade. John McNeile and John Tolbert of Ballycastle worked closely with Orr, Dunlope and Glenholme in dispatching ships to and from Philadelphia. John and Charles Galt and Alexander Lawrence in Coleraine had ships carrying emigrants to America, too. The Galts and Lawrence sent the *Providence* to New York and the *Rainbow* to Philadelphia each year with passengers. On the *Providence's* last voyage, she sailed from Portrush August 27, 1768 and two weeks at sea sprang a leak that forced passengers and crew to take to the ship's two boats. Nineteen passengers and crew remained on board. A passing ship picked up the long boat after eight days and took the survivors to Charleston, South Carolina. The others drowned.[29]

William Neilson, who was from Maddybenny, near Coleraine, represented the Galts and Lawrence at New York. David Gaussan, George Anderson and William Beath of Newry addressed their ships to him, too. Neilson was a prominent dry goods merchant, shipping "a large cargo of flaxseed" and importing linens and Irish butter as well as passengers and servants from Coleraine, Newry and Liverpool on his own brig *Conway* and on the *Rainbow*, *Providence*, *Freemason*, *Newry* and *Needham*. He was at home in 1764, about to set off for New York, by way of London, when his brother wrote to a correspondent in New York about prices for flaxseed that season.[30]

Philadelphia Merchants and the Passenger Trade

George Fullerton's first partner, Hector Boyd, was from Ballycastle and a business associate of George Dunlope also of Ballycastle. Boyd and Fullerton imported Irish linens and other dry goods for their store on Walnut Street. Boyd's death in 1763 dissolved their partnership and Fullerton joined George Dunlope's son George Jr. in a new partnership.[31] Fullerton managed the business on his own, freighting flaxseed ships for several merchants in Londonderry and

Belfast as well as George Dunlope and his own partner John
Dunlope in Coleraine. Among other ships, the *Prince George*, "with
about 200 passengers," arrived from Belfast consigned to him. He
sailed for Belfast himself early in 1765 with a cargo of flaxseed and
flour on the *Catherine*.[32] George Fullerton registered the *Catherine*
in 1765 with Philadelphia merchants Thomas and Robert
Montgomery as co-owners. Thomas Montgomery was one of the
most active members of the Presbyterian Committee. The next year
Fullerton and John Campbell and John Gregg of Belfast were
recorded as owners of the *Mary*.[33] He returned to Philadelphia on
the same ship in June, with passengers recruited by George
Dunlope and by Isaac Corry in Newry.[34] Fullerton and
Montgomery sent the *Catherine* to Belfast and then to Bristol in
1766. Thomas Montgomery died in his passage from Philadelphia
and was buried in Belfast. His son Robert carried on the business.[35]

In 1766 George Fullerton married Margaret Blair at First
Presbyterian Church in Philadelphia. She was Captain William
Blair's daughter, Captain James Blair's sister and the sister-in-law of
Belfast merchant William Burgess. In subsequent years Fullerton
was closely associated with Burgess and James Blair and with the
Caldwells, handling freights and passengers for the *Pennsylvania
Farmer*, named in compliment to patriot John Dickinson, the *Earl
of Donegall* and other ships in the flaxseed and emigrant trade.
Fullerton and Blair together owned the *Kitty and Peggy* and shared
ownership of the *Pennsylvania Farmer* with William and Andrew
Caldwell. They took full ownership when William Caldwell of
Londonderry faced bankruptcy in 1772.[36]

George Dunlope and his associates in Belfast, Larne and
Coleraine continued to address ships to Fullerton, but they soon
turned to a Philadelphia firm in which Dunlope and Gilbert Orr of
Belfast had invested without assuming the obligations of a partnership. William Glenholme was one of the new faces in the flaxseed
business in the 1760s. He arrived in Philadelphia in 1764 and
advertised Irish butter for sale made the previous summer. His
father James Glenholme, a Belfast merchant and wool draper, died
in 1739, when William was an infant, but Eleanor Glenholme carried on her husband's business until 1770. She advertised with
Gilbert Orr for passengers for her son's ship *Philadelphia* and for
ships sailing to Charleston and Savannah.[37]

Glenholme, Orr and Company had Manchester checks and Irish linens for sale at their store on Water Street in Philadelphia in 1765. Andrew Orr, Glenholme's partner, was a son of Belfast merchant Gilbert Orr. Andrew Orr was an agent for passage to Philadelphia by William Hogg's *Willey* in 1760 and other ships. In 1764 he advertised for passengers for the brig *Boscawen*, adding that "the said Andrew Orr intends going in said Vessel himself" to Philadelphia. Glenholme was probably on the *Boscawen*, too. She sailed from Belfast in August and arrived at Philadelphia in October.[38]

As her owners Messrs Glenholme and Company and Andrew Orr together registered the newly-built 100-ton ship *Philadelphia* in October 1765. She sailed for Belfast in December, arriving in January with a cargo of flaxseed and flour. Gilbert Orr and Mrs. Glenholme in Belfast and John McAlester in Ballycastle advertised for passengers, redemptioners and servants for her return voyage in April. As the sailing date drew near, they warned no passengers would be taken aboard after April 10 since accepting latecomers too often led to overcrowding and insufficient provisions for the voyage.[39] She returned to Philadelphia, after landing some passengers at New Castle, in June, consigned to Orr, Glenholme and Company, who immediately dispatched her to Cork with provisions.[40] She made a return voyage from Belfast to New Castle and Philadelphia, arriving there in November in time to take on a flaxseed cargo for Belfast. The *Philadelphia* proved to be a fortunate sailer, making the crossing in each direction in a month or less. Advertising for passengers to Philadelphia in February 1767, Gilbert Orr promised "plenty of provisions" and water.[41] On this voyage one of her passengers was George Dunlope, returning to Philadelphia as a partner in Orr, Dunlope and Glenholme.[42]

George Dunlope, Jr., the third partner, was a son of Ballycastle merchant and ship-owner George Dunlope, Sr., who was already prominent in the flaxseed trade. He was in Philadelphia by 1765, finding flaxseed freights for his father's ship the *Prince George*.[43] Andrew Orr remained in Belfast, coordinating the firm's business with his father. The sudden death of George Dunlope, stricken as he walked down a Philadelphia street in December 1767, left William Glenholme to manage the American side alone.[44]

The new firm had commenced business on Dunlope's arrival in June 1767 and immediately loaded the *Philadelphia* with lumber, flour and provisions for Cork and the *Prince George* for Dublin where Andrew Orr was temporarily located, with instructions to return "before the Flaxseed Season comes on." They asked their correspondents at Cork to "procure all the Servts. you can" as well as butter for the return cargo.[45] The *Philadelphia* returned from Cork with servants in ample time to load for Belfast. She returned in August 1768, "all well & the passengers extremely well pleased after a passage of 7 weeks & 4 days & she the only vessel that made so good a passage at the season."[46] Captain McCutcheon brought her back from Cork in December 1768 with no passengers on board and a cargo of Irish beef, stoneware and other articles. Orr, Dunlope and Glenholme sent her to Belfast with flaxseed and flour.[47] *Philadelphia* was thus a model of the ships in the flaxseed trade, bringing passengers from Belfast and returning with flaxseed, with an intervening voyage to Cork with provisions and servants. In July 1769 she brought 92 passengers from Belfast and in December 1769 returned with 15 servants from Cork.[48] If this was the pattern of other crossings, we can assume the *Philadelphia* brought about 100 passengers from Belfast each year and fifteen or twenty servants from Cork. We might assume these were all highly profitable to the firm and, in the long run, they may have been, but Orr, Dunlope and Glenholme had severe cash flow problems as early as 1767, since "the sales of the Servts. and redemptioners would not pay for the disbursements (which amounted to near £400) and the greater part are not paid yet."[49] The expenses incurred by a ship in port could be heavy and required immediate payment. To remedy the shortfall, Glenholme drew bills of exchange on London and Liverpool correspondents.

Like other flaxseed merchants before them, Orr and Glenholme supervised the building of ships for their Ulster clients. They were part owners of the brig *Lord Dungannon*, built at Philadelphia in 1766, with the Belfast merchants James Henderson, James Park, John Campbell, Hugh Donaldson and John Gregg.[50] In 1767 they had the brig *Free Mason* built for William Beath and George Anderson of Newry. Orr, Dunlope and Glenholme were part owners. She made her maiden voyage to Newry with flaxseed in January

1768, followed by the first of several crossings with passengers.[51] A less successful venture involved overseeing construction of the brig *Speedwell*. David Kerr and Co. of London had a quarter share in the brig, as did Orr, Dunlope and Glenholme, Henry McGowan and David McMinn of the tiny North Down port of Donaghadee had respectively a quarter and an eighth interest, with Gilbert Orr holding the other eighth.

Although his letters give few hints of it, Glenholme's business ventures would lead to bankruptcy by the beginning of 1769. Early on Orr had observed "it as a little odd we draw so much on our Friends in London & Liverpool," but Glenholme argued the bills amounted to only half the value of the cargoes he was dispatching. As he explained to one correspondent:

> Our reason for drawing at present was our having four vessels here which we are to load with Flaxseed &c to Ireland and we cannot with any propriety draw on the Gentlemen from whom we have the orders till the goods are shipped.

This habit may have been Glenholme's undoing. The firm stopped payment in February and the next day made over "all their goods" to Benjamin Fuller, Randle Mitchell, John Pringle, James Craig, and John Boyle who acted for his creditors in selling his remaining assets, among them "the famous horse, Northumberland."[52]

Glenholme was not the only merchant in the flaxseed and passenger trade to face bankruptcy, but we should not conclude it was an unprofitable business. The competitive nature of the trade in both passengers and commodities meant sailing close to the wind for many firms. The loss of a ship at sea could be disastrous. James Fullton's *Hibernia*, bound for Bristol with a cargo of iron, ran aground on the Welsh coast in 1768. The iron came from Martick Furnace in Lancaster County, owned by Fullton and James Wallace. Captain William Keith abandoned the wreck and hastened to Bristol, arriving with the news before Henry Cruger had arranged for insurance on ship and cargo. This was a heavy loss for his partners, Ephraim Campbell of Londonderry and his own brother John Fullton of Ramelton, County Donegal as well.[53] Had Keith purchased the salvaged masts and tackle of the ship, Fullton might have bought a hull and "so continue a Vessell in the Trade."[54] Since loss of the *Hibernia*, coupled with Fullton's heavy investment in Martick Forge and Furnace, "has Stripped me of a Great Deal of my Reddy money," he asked his London banker David Harvey to arrange a loan with the ironworks as collateral or to obtain "Fifteen Hundred Pounds Sterling worth of goods," which he listed, on long credit. "I am Satisfied I Can make money of Dry goods if its to be Dun here and in particular at this time When So few is Imported."[55] As it was, James Fullton was reduced to coastal trade, primarily with his cousin Andrew Black in Boston. John Fullton was bankrupt within a few years and came to Lancaster, Pennsylvania with his family to begin anew in 1772.[56] They became part of a surge in emigration in 1772–3 as many sectors of the Ulster economy experienced difficulties.

New England Flaxseed Buyers

Flaxseed grown in New England had the best reputation, but little of it went from seaports in that region directly to markets in Ireland. Even merchants in Boston and Newport shipped flaxseed to correspondents in Philadelphia and New York, the main collection points for American flaxseed, so emigrant ships went there to load for Newry and Belfast.[57] Flaxseed was an important cash crop and, in the buying season, merchants and shopkeepers in neighbouring parts of Massachusetts, Rhode Island, and Connecticut, advertised their readiness to buy any quantity of flaxseed from farmers for cash or goods. Typical of these seed buyers, Samuel and William Chace of Providence, Rhode Island, said they kept "a Vessel constantly going between this Place and New-York; and any Persons desirous of shipping their Seed for the New-York Market, may have it carried" there.[58] Bromfield and Jackson of Newburyport, Massachusetts, sent flaxseed to their friends in Philadelphia, as did Andrew Black in Boston.[59] Samuel Carsan obtained some of his seed each year from a Newport, Rhode Island merchant.[60]

Ulstermen set up as merchants in New England towns as well as in the Pennsylvania backcountry. Archibald Stewart came from Ballintoy on the north Antrim coast, where the Stewarts had been landowners for generations. "Lately arrived from Ireland" at Providence, Rhode Island, in April 1763, Stewart brought with him "A Good Assortment of Linen Cloth, strong and well-coloured, Yard wide and Seven-eighths." He was soon in partnership with Alexander Black, another Ulster emigrant, offering Bohea tea, indigo, cotton wool, Irish linen, silk handkerchiefs, and other goods at their store near the west end of the Great Bridge in Providence. They were primarily interested in the flaxseed trade.

> Said Black and Stewart wants to buy about Two Thousand Bushels of good and well-clean'd FLAX-SEED, for which they will give Goods of different Kinds, or Ready Cash, and those that live out of this Government, may have Silver or Gold for any Quantity of such Seed; and they are determined to give a good Price, and the rising Market, if it should happen.[61]

Among the many flaxseed buyers in Providence through the 1760s, both Black and Stewart and Robert Taylor, also of Ulster origin, advertised "Hard Money for Flaxseed".[62] In 1767 Alexander Black, "a considerable Merchant in this Town," died and Archibald Stewart and Robert Taylor, went into partnership.[63] Three years later Stewart married the widow of Captain James Hutton of Newport.[64] He continued in business in Providence until 1784 when he returned to Londonderry in his own 300-ton ship the *Stewart* with a cargo of Rhode Island flaxseed, barrel staves and timber and invited emigrants to sail with him to Philadelphia on his return to his Rhode Island home.[65]

Seed buyers also came to New England for the season and then returned with a flaxseed cargo to Ireland. John Patrick wanted to buy at least 1,000 bushels of well-cleaned flaxseed to carry with him when he sailed in the autumn. He was still buying in October for ready cash, but warned those with whom he had contracted for flaxseed to deliver it by the 20th of that month.[66] Charles Crouch, "intending to depart hence in about Ten or Twelve Days," was also prepared to pay the highest price for any quantity of flaxseed.[67]

With rising flaxseed prices in the late 1760s and 1770s, country storekeepers were caught between merchants in the larger towns buying for their correspondents in New York or Philadelphia. A storekeeper in Warren, Rhode Island wrote to a Newport merchant:

I bought 20 Casks of flaxseed which I am to pay for this week, or else it will be sold to Providence people, whom [sic] plagues me about getting away what they can from me, as I am confident they will give 7 shillings per bushel for it, before Newport men will have it, as they are collecting for Newyork."[68]

High prices led some New Englanders to ship direct to correspondents in Ireland. The schooner *Lark*, for instance, carried a flaxseed cargo from Newburyport, Massachusetts to William and John Ogle in Newry.[69] Such adventures, however, were few.

"An Almost Total Emigration"

The Rev. Alexander Hewatt observed that the spirit of emigration to America was so strong in "the northern counties of that kingdom" in the 1760s and 1770s as to threaten "almost a total depopulation."[70] By the early 1770s observers in Ulster were inclined to agree. "This prevalent Humour of industrious Protestants withdrawing from this once flourishing Corner of the Kingdom, seems to be encreasing," one writer noted, adding "Their removal is sensibly felt in this Country."[71] Why were they leaving?

Assessing the cause of "the great emigration of the lower kind of people to America," a farmer in County Armagh focused on the anticipation in the winter of 1770 of a great demand in the American market for Irish linen after the non-importation agreements were set aside. With this expectation, "our brown linens rose to an extravagant price" and were quickly followed by "extreme high rents which the unthinking weaver then foolishly imagined the profit of his web would enable him to pay."[72] Weavers and spinners were then caught in a spiralling credit crisis with emigration as their only option.

The British economy was expanding from the mid-1760s with readily available capital and broadening markets and from 1769 experienced a credit boom that reached a dizzy height by 1772. Investment opportunities in India, the West Indies and recently-acquired territories like East Florida vied for capital with manufacturing and turnpikes and canals at home, while long credits underwrote increased exports to America. It all began to unravel with the failure of a London banking house in June 1772.[73] "The breaking of Fordyce & Co. bankers has stagnated business," an American wrote from London. "Every man seems afraid of each other; there has already a number stopped and a continuance of them daily."[74]

There were already warning signs. Orders from the American colonies for British goods, including linens, reached an all-time high in 1771 and temporarily boosted prices. Shortage was promptly succeeded by glut as heavy shipments of goods continued into 1772.[75] Linen drapers were already in trouble. Non-importation agreements disrupted the all-important American market for Scottish and Irish linens. By the end of 1769 there were already indications of a glut and linen prices gradually tumbled bringing lower production and some unemployment. Two years later the British ambassador at the Hague could write that "the linen manufacturers in Ireland and Scotland complain of a stagnation in their business," a situation he ascribed to their flooding colonial markets so that demand soon decreased "and the weavers for the present stand idle."[76] A Belfast merchant commented on the decline of the linen manufacture. It was crucial that "the British plantations take off so much of our cloth." Despite taxes on imports and rebates for linens shipped to English ports, European and Russian linen came as cheap to market as linen woven in Ulster. To remain competitive Irish linen had to be low-priced.[77] Sir William Brownlow, a great landlord in County Armagh, gave a succinct picture of the Irish economy at the close of 1770 in a letter to the Earl of Abercorn:

> The trade of this kingdom is in a very distressed state, the woollen and silk weavers of Dublin starving for want of employment, merchants of note frequently shutting up, and by that means credit at the lowest ebb, our Northern [linen] drapers not able to keep their usual complement of looms at work for want of money, their markets very low, and what they do sell, on four or five months credit instead of one month, bankers afraid to discount, the graziers distressed by an embargo on provisions, corn and meal very dear and a prospect of its being much dearer in the spring, which with the usual wetness of the season will, I fear, produce sickness and famine among the lower people especially in our Northern counties where the harvest could not be saved.[78]

Presbyterian ministers and elders of the Presbytery of Templepatrick in southern County Antrim met late in 1770 and pointed to another social problem, lamenting "the heavy oppression that too many are under from the excessive price of lands."[79] The land system in Ulster was such that only a few individuals actually owned their estates in fee simple. Everyone else, from great landlords to humble cottiers, was a tenant. Some held estates of several thousand acres on long term leases and drew significant income from their holdings, leasing farms to a hundred or more sub-tenants who, in turn, leased part of their land to others and so on. Captain James Erskine noted in 1772 "that over most parts of the county [Antrim] the lands are subset six deep, so that those who actually labour it are squeezed to the utmost."[80]

Some tenants, like Robert Barclay in Strabane, who had "more than 900 years of my lease to come" on property near the town and "a farm in the County of Donegal of about 200 acres forever," held their land on 999-year or perpetual leases.[81] More common were leases for three lives, current so long as at least one of three named individuals was still living. Landlords generally gave long-term leases for bleach greens and beetling mills. To encourage the linen industry some landlords were even willing to lease small holdings on favourable terms to weavers as well as bleachers, but the vast majority rented a cottage and a patch of land from a farmer or farmer-weaver. In 1766 the size of the average family farm in mid-Ulster and the Foyle basin was less than 30 acres and in a few parishes smaller than 12 acres. There still existed a balance between the linen manufacture and agriculture since 30 acres of land could provide a decent living by contemporary standards, but with an increasing rural population more turned to linen weaving to supplement their income and more farms were subdivided.[82]

There was a general tendency in the 1760s for landowners in Ulster to replace poor tenants by solvent ones and to raise rents by letting to the highest bidder. Many of the larger leases on Ulster estates needed to be renewed in 1767–71 and this seemed an appropriate time to raise the annual rent and to demand a substantial fine be paid for the privilege of renewal. Two examples will illustrate how this worked. Arthur Chichester succeeded his uncle in 1757 as 5th Earl of Donegall, inheriting with the title estates of 90,000 acres in County Antrim, including the town of Belfast, and vast holdings in County Donegal and elsewhere. Lord Donegall, who resided in London, began rebuilding his country house at Fisherwick Park in Staffordshire in 1768 and needed money to carry out his project, so his agents advised him to re-lease his Irish estates.[83] Middlemen, the chief tenants who held large estates which they then leased to lesser tenants, followed suit. Clotworthy Upton, one of Lord Donegall's tenants, who resided at Castle Upton at Templepatrick, County Antrim, was one of the first. He advertised his entire estate of near 7,000 acres, divided into 99 holdings, to be let on 21 individual leases which meant all the occupying tenants would have to bid for new leases.[84] Another of Lord Donegall's tenants was Arthur Hill-Trevor, Viscount Dungannon who held an estate of 2,000 acres at Islandmagee, County Antrim at an annual rent of £200, a sum unchanged since the original lease in 1618. Lord Dungannon paid a fine of £18,500 to renew his lease for 99 years at the same rent in 1769.[85] With over 100 tenants of his own, Dungannon advertised all their leases to be re-let to the highest bidder.[86]

Contemporary opinion blamed Lord Donegall and his chief tenants for setting in motion a cycle of rack-renting, but landowners across the province did the same things. The practice was so widespread over the next years that testimonials appeared in the newspapers acknowledging landlords who did *not* raise the rent.[87] The Clothworkers Guild in London, one of the livery companies granted land in County Londonderry at the time of the Plantation of Ulster, leased their entire Proportion from 1669 to the Jackson family of Coleraine. Their latest lease for 51 years expired in 1771 and the Clothworkers advertised their property to be let for 61 years with three lives. Richard Jackson, M.P., a resident landlord, offered to renew his lease and to pay a fine of £20,000, but to keep others from outbidding him he had to raise his agreed fine to £28,000. This was more than he could afford, so he mortgaged the entire estate. He was already in arrears in 1772 both for the annual rent of £600 and the interest on his mortgage. His only recourse was to "raise the rents of his tenants very considerably in consequence of the large fine he had paid." The result was "an almost total emigration" from the districts of Dunboe and Macosquin.[88]

Some middlemen were prominent merchants, since land was

always a worthwhile investment and a mark of status. The Ironmongers auctioned off a lease on their lands around Aghadowey in 1767. William Alexander, a Dublin linen merchant, was the highest bidder, but he was unable to pay the £21,000 fine for renewing the lease and the Ironmongers turned to a director of the East India Company.[89] Thomas Bateson, Belfast merchant and ship-owner, held the Salters' Proportion on a long-term lease from the London livery company and was evidently "the best of land-lords" to his 337 tenants in and around Magherafelt, County Londonderry.[90] His friends and business associates Thomas Greg and Waddell Cunningham had smaller holdings leased from the Earl of Donegall, but bore much of the opprobrium for high rents and evictions. Thomas Greg held nearly 1,400 acres of the Donegall estate in County Antrim and another 3,500 acres in County Donegal. His father John Gregg, one of the first Belfast merchants in the flaxseed trade, bought unexpired leases at auction in 1757 and his son obtained a long-term lease for additional land in 1770, including 600 acres near Ballyclare in County Antrim. Greg removed some undertenants to graze beef cattle on part of his land there, causing much resentment. Cunningham had only two properties of 150 and 370 acres for which he paid a fine of £1,000 to renew his leases. Hercules Heyland of Coleraine and Belfast mer-chants Stewart Banks, Shem Thompson and Alexander Legg, among others, also paid fines to renew leases from the Earl of Donegall.[91]

Landlords across the province raised farmers' rents, not always so drastically, and made them uneasy by requiring them in many cases to bid against others for their lands. Demanding fines from tenants as part of the reassessed value of their holdings added to their resentment.[92] This could not have come at a worse time. A poor harvest in 1769 was followed by two years of short crops and the need to import food. The Earl of Abercorn's agent reported that "The tenants pull up very badly; there is very much complaining, and with reason, of the want of fodder and the poverty of cattle." He quoted the high prices for oatmeal, flaxseed and potatoes which "I never knew so high at this time of the year."[93] But late frosts and heavy rains were not the half of it. James Hamilton reported to Abercorn that:

the badness of our harvests these three years past, that occasioned the extravagant prices of provisions, the sickness that
has raged as long and the low prices of yarn and linen, oweing
no doubt partly to the failures, in the London merchants, have
much distressed this country.[94]

The burden as usual fell heaviest on those least able to bear it. "In
my lifetime I never remember so many beggars as now," Hamilton
wrote, "those who have had little holdings are quite ground down,
with their continual buying [provisions] these three years."[95] A
weaver in County Down wrote "I own the rents have risen greatly
of late years" and "as our rents have risen, the price of everything
that is produced by our land has risen likewise." The market price
of linen, in contrast to provisions, was falling.[96]

The scarcity of money and tightness of credit crippled the linen
industry and made life more difficult. The linen business was
always a cash concern. Buyers and bleachers had stands in the market where weavers brought cloth to sell, brown or unbleached linen.
They received their pay that afternoon, so they could buy more
yarn the same day. Linen weavers had to supplement their supply
of yarn with purchases in the market. Flax was not grown only in
weaving districts and in other parts of the province women spun
tow yarn from their flax as an important cash supplement, often the
only source of cash in the household economy. Jobbers bought up
all the yarn they made and brought it to linen markets to sell. As
prices tumbled, spinners and weavers alike suffered.[97] Tenants of
the Estate of Kilrea in County Londonderry thanked their landlord
Alexander Stewart Esq. of Newtownards, the father of Lord
Castlereagh.

> Besides being indulgent in their Payment of Rent, he has for
> this Season's Sowing given them a Quantity of Flaxseed, and
> Yarn to fill their empty Looms, &c. In short, were it not for
> his Assistance, it would be impossible even for the most indus-
> trious Weaver to make a Livelihood for himself or Family in
> these distressing Times.[98]

"Mercator" urged men of property to let their lands at a moderate rate. With provisions so dear, he argued, labour cost must rise,

and to act otherwise "lays a foundation for so valuable a branch to relinquish the country."[99] One writer claimed that "the North of Ireland has in the last five or six years been drained of one fourth of its trading Cash, and the like Proportion of the Manufacturing People," both through emigration.[100]

Contraction in the linen industry rippled through the economy. Even the most successful linen drapers and bleachers tightened their belts. By the 1760s two or three London firms handled most orders of Irish linen. The Barclays, Dublin Quakers, did a great deal of business with Philadelphia dry goods merchants. David Harvey, a London linen draper and banker to many of the flaxseed merchants in Philadelphia, could give no more than six months credit to American dry goods merchants and "would not break but only sell in lots as put up in Ireland," since he acted on commission for Ulster firms.[101] Bleachers needed cash to purchase brown linens in the market, but they also had to continue to invest in improving their bleach greens to remain competitive. Water-powered wash mills and beetling mills and the introduction of chemical bleaching greatly increased their output, but also caused intense competition among bleachers, so that many weaker firms did not survive.[102] Bankruptcies among linen drapers and bleachers in Dublin, Belfast, and Londonderry were listed in growing numbers in the newspapers.

To this mix of economic motives for emigration was added the sporadic violence of the Hearts of Steel or Steel Boys. They emerged in mainly Presbyterian rural neighbourhoods to defend the rights of lesser tenants against grasping landlords. The first outbreak in July 1769 was in the Templepatrick area of County Antrim, where Clotworthy Upton had made life difficult for his tenants and spread to the Dungannon estates in Islandmagee.[103] Otherwise law abiding farmers and weavers filled the ranks of the Hearts of Steel. They protested evictions by killing and maiming cattle and burning farm buildings. When the leader of the Steel Boys who killed Thomas Greg's cattle was arrested by his business partner Waddell Cunningham and taken to Belfast, more than 500 of them obtained his release and pillaged and burned Cunningham's house.[104] By February 1771 the Earl of Antrim as County Lieutenant could announce that "all Insurrections in this

County have ceased." He was concerned nonetheless that

> A considerable Part of the County is deserted by the
> Inhabitants, who, terrified by their own Apprehensions, have
> fled, forsaken all Kind of Industry, and left their innocent
> Families destitute of Support.[105]

Since they left their families behind, it is unlikely that they fled
as far as America. In a later statement County Antrim magistrates
"determined to make use of the gentlest Means to recall many that
have deserted their Habitations," which suggests they had not gone
far from home.[106] Viscount Townshend, the Lord Lieutenant,
issued a proclamation outlawing the Hearts of Steel, but the movement spread to County Down in 1771 and by 1772 there were
enough outbreaks in other counties for the Irish Parliament to
extend the proclamation to Cos. Armagh, Londonderry, and
Tyrone.[107] Robert Barclay had a letter from his nephew about
widespread activity in County Armagh that he shared with others
in Strabane.[108] Excoriated by some – Presbyterian congregations
distanced themselves from the outlaws and their methods – the
Hearts of Steel were heroes to others.[109] Juries were reluctant to
convict them, although some were sentenced to hang, and moving
trials to Dublin only brought more acquittals. The presence of the
army in the affected districts put an end to armed resistance by May
1772 and at the end of the day there was nothing to do but offer a
general amnesty. Viscount Townshend stated bluntly that excessive
rents were to blame for the disturbances and failure to reduce them
would "compel the wretched tenants to go to America."[110]

Did the Steel Boys contribute to the exodus from Ulster to
America? Captain James Erskine was convinced that a "rigorous
search for the unhappy & deluded offenders" could only result in
"driving 6 or 7,000 manufacturing families out of Ireland."[111]
James Hamilton, Abercorn's agent, thought a rise in the price of
oatmeal was "owing I believe to demand from the countys of Down
and Antrim, where the land was neglected by the Steel Boys, many
of whom quit the country."[112] It was November before an amnesty
was proclaimed. When it was, rumours spread that many on the
passenger ships in Belfast harbour were afraid to come ashore for

fear of prosecution. Shem Thompson, Sovereign of Belfast, went on board the *Elizabeth*, about to sail for Savannah, and read the proclamation offering amnesty, but found no one willing to take advantage of it.[113] Contemporary opinion was convinced, nonetheless, that "numbers of Steel Boys" were "flying to Belfast to take shipping to America."[114]

Whatever individual motivation might be, there can be no question that the number of passengers sailing for the American colonies more than doubled with "an almost total emigration" from some places. In South Carolina they anticipated in 1772 that

> upwards of 15,000 Families intend to remove during the Course of the present Year from Ireland to America; and that, if proper Encouragement is given, 5,000 of them propose to settle in this Province, and to establish a great Linen-Manufactory.[115]

"Those parts of peace and plenty"

Emigration swelled in 1772 and by 1773 the sluice gates were open. The Baltimore *Maryland Journal* claimed that "no less than 3,500" emigrants had left the port of Londonderry only "within one Year." Since ships from Derry accounted for roughly a third of the advertised voyages to America in 1773, this would suggest 9,000 Ulster folk crossed the ocean that year.[116] The *Londonderry Journal* published statistics for the four months August through November 1773 "taken in Philadelphia and the other towns upon the emigrants being landed there." These reports gave a total of 6,522 Irish emigrants, of whom 2,086 arrived at Philadelphia, 1,911 at New York, 966 at Charleston, 717 at Newport, Rhode Island, 516 at Halifax, Nova Scotia, and 326 at New Jersey. Curiously, there are no returns from Baltimore, the advertised destination of several vessels, Savannah, Wilmington, North Carolina, or any Virginia port. With contemporary estimates of the 1773 emigration ranging from 4,000 to 20,000, even a figure for the high season for the passenger trade is helpful in narrowing the possible range.[117]

The emigration season began that year with the sailing of William Burgess's ship from Belfast Lough for Philadelphia:

> Last week, the Friendship, Capt. McCulloch, sailed from this harbour, bound for Philadelphia, with 280 full passengers on board, making upwards of 300 persons, being the first ship with passengers from this place this season.[118]

The newspapers reported the numbers leaving on several ships, reflecting the increased demand for passage to America and the probable overcrowding on some of these vessels. Since they were all bound for New Castle and Philadelphia, it is possible to check their accuracy in reports in the American papers. The brig *Peggy* sailed for Philadelphia with 207 passengers, the brig *Agnes* carried 220 from Belfast and *Minerva* sailed from Newry with near 400. *Betsy* from Newry had 361 passengers on board. The *Needham* also sailed from Newry with near 500 passengers as did the *Robert* with 420.[119] On a single day in June, 1,950 emigrants left from Derry:

> On the 7th of this Month, the four following ships sailed from Londonderry for Philadelphia with the undermentioned number of passengers on board, viz. the *Alexander*, Hunter, 530, the *Hannah*, Mitchell, 520, the *Jupiter*, Ewing, 450, the *Wallworth*, McCausland, 450.[120]

The figures may be an undercounting. The *Pennsylvania Journal* reported the safe arrival of these passengers at New Castle, 513 on *Jupiter*, 630 on *Alexander*, and 580 on *Hannah*. The last two came up the Delaware to Philadelphia landing 550 and 500 passengers respectively.[121]

New York had a share in the 1773 exodus. The *Robert* from Newry, "having onboard upwards of 300 Souls, including Children, Passengers from that Port, who are come to settle in America," arrived at Sandy Hook in July. "We hear about half of them are to be landed at Amboy [in New Jersey], and the Ship to come here with the rest."[122] Contemporary observers certainly had a sense that the movement of people was large, possibly large enough to cripple the linen industry or even depopulate some districts. A meeting of landed gentlemen was reported to discuss means of "preventing the depopulation of their estates by the present great emigrations to America."[123] One correspondent of the *Belfast News Letter* wrote that in 1771 and 1772, "The greatest Part of these Emigrants paid their Passage" and that most of them were "people employed in the Linen Manufacture, or Farmers, and of some Property which they turned into Money and carried with them." The loss of these industrious people was sensibly felt "and it is thought the Number will be considerably larger this year, than ever."[124] Another wrote to the *Londonderry Journal* about the decline of the linen industry, noting that there were fourteen ships at Belfast taking on passengers for America, "most of whom are manufacturers and husbandmen."[125] Noting that this emigration had "already drained the Northern Parts of Ireland of near a third Part of its most useful and industrious Inhabitants," a writer in the *New York Journal* added that "Most of the People being well skilled in the Linen Manufactory, if proper Encouragement is given to them, will be an important acquisition to the British Colonies."[126]

The Rev. John Wesley was in Ulster that summer and added his comments, forthrightly placing blame for the exodus on landlords who increased rents beyond what farmers and weavers could pay. Based on his own experience of Georgia, Wesley thought it would be better to beg in Ireland than to starve in America. He would not have found many to agree with him.[127]

Notes

1   Rev. Joseph Rhea, "My Father The Revd. Joseph Rhea His Journal of his &
    Family's voyage from Ireland Began September 27, 1769," 21 (Rhea Family
    Papers, Tennessee State Library, Nashville). *Pennsylvania Journal*, December
    7, 1769. Richard K. MacMaster, "'For Philadelphia, Boys, Are We Bound':
    the Rev. Joseph Rhea Comes to America in 1769," *Familia*, 22(2006),
    33–50.

2   "Passenger Lists" (Cadwalader Collection, Series III, Box 78, Folder 18. HSP).

3   Arthur Young, *A Tour in Ireland with General Observations on the Present
    State of the Kingdom made in the Years 1776, 1777, and 1778* (Dublin,
    1780), 204.

4   Rhea, "Journal," October 18, 1769, November 27, 1769, December 1, 1769
    (Rhea Family Papers, Tennessee State Library).

5   Daniel Clark to Edward Cochran, December 9, 1761 (Daniel Clark Letter
    Book, HSP).

6   *Pennsylvania Journal*, February 4, 1768, February 18, 1768.

7   *Belfast News Letter*, August 9, 1768, September 20, 1768, March 10, 1769.
    Pennsylvania Journal, March 2, 1769.

8   James Fullton to Joseph McNutt, December 10, 1764 (James Fullton Letter
    Book (typescript), LCHS).

9   James Fullton to John Fullton and Ephraim Campbell, June 30, 1767 (James
    Fullton Letter Book (typescript), LCHS).

10 James Fullton to John Fullton and Ephraim Campbell, December 19, 1766, to
    David Harvey, January 10, 1767 (James Fullton Letter Book (typescript),
    LCHS).

11 James Fullton to John Fullton and Ephraim Campbell, June 1, 1767 (James
    Fullton Letter Book (typescript), LCHS).

12 Figures for 1771–2–3 are summarized from Dickson, *Ulster Emigation*, 238–65.
    Totals for the 1760s were counted by the author from files of the
    Belfast News Letter in the Linen Hall Library, Belfast.

13 "Passenger Lists" (Cadwalader Collection, Series III, Box 78, Folder 18, HSP).

14 When Thomas Greg's son, John Greg, joined the firm in 1765 it became Gregs
    and Cunningham. The New York branch had reorganized in 1761 with
    Hamilton Young and Robert Ross Waddell as the resident partners
    (D/270/6, PRONI). Mussenden, Bateson and Co. reorganized in 1766 as
    Thomas Bateson and Co. The members of the firm were Thomas Bateson
    of Orangefield, Valentine Jones, George Black, John Mathers, and David
    Tomb of Belfast, James Adair of London, Robert Black of Castlehill, and
    John Rainey of Greenville. *Belfast News Letter*, November 4, 1766.

15 This John Gregg (or Greg) was the father of Thomas Greg of Gregs and
    Cunningham and of John Greg of Torrans, Greg and Poaug. *Burke's Landed
    Gentry*, 1972, III, 400.

16 Samuel Jackson, who owned land in Dundonald Parish, County Down,
    handled the American side.

17 The firm took this name when Richard Caldwell became a full partner with
    William Caldwell and Arthur Vance. Catherine Ball to her sister, May 15,
    1769, in John Caldwell, "Memoir," 15 (T/3541/5/3, PRONI).

18   Andrew Caldwell married Jane Mitchell, widow of Captain John Mitchell, in
      1762 at First Presbyterian Church. His stepdaughter Sally Mitchell married
      James Caldwell in 1772. Catherine Ball to her sister, May 15, 1769, John
      Caldwell to James Caldwell, January 1773, in John Caldwell, "Memoir," 15
      and 21 (T/3541/5/3, PRONI). *Pennsylvania Chronicle*, May 8, 1767,
      November 9, 1767. *Pennsylvania Gazette*, December 3, 1767, October 20,
      1768, October 25, 1770. *Pennsylvania Journal*, November 14, 1765, May
      17, 1766, September 25, 1766, October 2, 1766. Andrew Caldwell died in
      1794. Philadelphia Wills, X–51.

19   Robert Barclay to James, Earl of Abercorn, December 30, 1765
      (D/623/A/35/164, PRONI).

20   *Pennsylvania Gazette*, March 10, 1763, August 16, 1764, August 13, 1767.
      Pennsylvania Journal, November 17, 1763, August 9, 1764, August 30,
      1764, February 21, 1765, May 2, 1765, October 17, 1765.

21   James Fullton to James Harvey and Co., February 20, 1767 (James Fullton
      Letter Book (typescript), LCHS). *Pennsylvania Journal*, November 20,
      1766.

22   Conyngham, "Reminiscences," 189–90, 256. *Pennsylvania Journal*, May 1,
      1766, May 22, 1766, October 23, 1766, November 26, 1767, November 2,
      1769.

23   James Fullton to Ninian Boggs, May 22, 1766 (James Fullton Letterbook
      (typescript), LCHS). *Pennsylvania Journal*, May 20, 1766, October 16,
      1766, November 13, 1766, February 6, 1767.

24   *Belfast News Letter*, May 15, 1767, March 1, 1768, February 10, 1769, May 5,
      1769, August 10, 1769. *Pennsylvania Gazette*, October 20, 1768, October
      5, 1769. *Pennsylvania Journal*, October 22, 1767.

25   *Belfast News Letter*, August 1, 1766, June 9, 1767, March 4, 1767, July 17,
      1767, March 22, 1768, June 21, 1768, March 21, 1769, June 20, 1769,
      August 22, 1769, November 7, 1769. Truxes, *Letterbook of Greg and
      Cunningham*, 11.

26   John Austin Stevens, ed., *Colonial Records of the New York Chamber of
      Commerce 1768–84* (New York, 1867, reprinted New York, 1971), 165.
      Belfast News Letter, March 5, 1773, March 15, 1774.

27   *Belfast News Letter*, March 29, 1765, May 6, 1766. Dickson, *Ulster Emigration*,
      174–5. Harrington, *New York Merchant*, 147.

28   *Belfast News Letter*, June 23, 1767, April 22, 1768, January 31, 1769, February
      10, 1769, August 13, 1771. *Pennsylvania Journal*, November 5, 1767, June
      9, 1768. "Ship Registers," *PMHB*, 27(1903), 492.

29   *Belfast News Letter*, July 6, 1764, July 5, 1765, February 4, 1766, May 16, 1766,
      June 23, 1767, July 15, 1768. *South Carolina Gazette*, October 25, 1768.

30   *New York Journal*, February 19, 1767, July 9, 1767, February 4, 1768,
      November 1, 1770. Robert Neilson to Jeremiah Smith, June 18, 1764,
      Proceedings of the Massachusetts Historical Society, 51(1917), 338.
      Harrington, *New York Merchant*, 189.

31   John McMichael and Fullerton administered Boyd's estate. *Belfast News Letter*,
      May 23, 1758, April 26, May 31, 1763. *Pennsylvania Gazette*, November
      27, 1760, January 1, 1761, June 10, 1762. *Pennsylvania Journal*, February
      24, 1763.

32 *Pennsylvania Gazette*, October 13, 1763, November 17, 1763, December 22, 1763, November 15, 1764, December 27, 1764, February 28, 1765, March 7, 1765. *Belfast News Letter*, April 16, 1765.

33 "Ship Registers," *PMHB*, 27(1903), 355, 485.

34 *Belfast News Letter*, April 9, 1765, May 14, 1765, May 28, 1765, June 14, 1765, August 22, 1765.

35 *Belfast News Letter*, April 22, 1766. *Pennsylvania Journal*, March 6, 1766, June 5, 1766.

36 *Pennsylvania Gazette*, November 5, 1767, November 17, 1768, December 14, 1769, November 14, 1771. *Pennsylvania Journal*, September 27, 1770, October 25, 1770, December 29, 1773. "Ship Registers," *PMHB*, 28(1904), 99, 352, 368.

37 *Pennsylvania Journal*, November 1, 1764. *Belfast News Letter*, February 20, 1739, January 17, 1766, July 7, 1769, August 1, 1769, October 10, 1769, January 12, 1770, June 1, 1770.

38 Andrew Orr planned to sail in Spring 1764 on the *Happy Return*, advertising for passengers in April. *Belfast News Letter*, May 20, 1760, May 13, 1763, April 10, 1764, June 29, 1764, July 31, 1764. *Pennsylvania Journal*, October 25, 1764, May 2, 1765.

39 "Ship Registers," *PMHB* 27(1903), 366. *Pennsylvania Journal*, October 24, 1765. *Belfast News Letter*, January 14, 1766, January 17, 1766, March 25, 1766.

40 *Pennsylvania Journal*, June 5, 1766, June 19, 1766.

41 *Belfast News Letter*, February 20, 1767. *Pennsylvania Journal*, November 6, 1766, November 13, 1766, December 25, 1766.

42 William Glenholme to Bigger and Hulbert, July 4, 1767 (Orr, Dunlope and Glenholme Letter Book, HSP).

43 *Pennsylvania Journal*, November 21, 1765.

44 William Glenholme to Gilbert Orr, December 10, 1767, to George Dunlope, December 16, 1767, to Andrew Orr, December 16, 1767, to Samuel Dunlope, December 28, 1767 (Orr, Dunlope and Glenholme Letter Book, HSP).

45 William Glenholme to Andrew Orr, July 6, 1767, July 11, 1767, to Lane, Benson and Vaughan, July 26, 1767 (Orr, Dunlope and Glenholme Letter Book, HSP). *Belfast News Letter*, July 28, 1767.

46 William Glenholme to George Dunlope and Gilbert Orr, August 11, 1768 (Orr, Dunlope and Glenholme Letter Book, HSP). *Pennsylvania Journal*, October 29, 1767, November 12, 1767, August 4, 1768.

47 "Passenger Lists, 1768–1772," December 1, 1768 (Cadwalader Collection, Series III, Box 78, Folder 18, HSP). *Pennsylvania Journal*, December 29, 1768.

48 "Passenger Lists," July 29, 1769, December 18, 1769 (Cadwalader Collection, Series III, Box 78, Folder 18, HSP).

49 William Glenholme to Andrew Orr, November 9, 1767 (Orr, Dunlope and Glenholme Letter Book, HSP).

50 Hugh Donaldson of Belfast, not the Philadelphia merchant of that name, and John Gregg, father of Thomas Greg of Gregs and Cunningham. "Ship Registers," *PMHB*, 27(1903), 491.

51   William Glenholme to William Beath and George Anderson, September 23, 1767, October 5, 1767, January 7, 1768, to Andrew Orr, November 9, 1767, January 7, 1768 (Orr, Dunlope and Glenholme Letter Book, HSP). *Belfast News Letter*, July 12, 1768. "Ship Registers," *PMHB*, 28(1904), 90.

52   William Glenholme to Andrew Orr, November 9, 1767, to Bigger and Hulbert, November 7, 1767 (Orr, Dunlope and Glenholme Letter Book, HSP). Benjamin Fuller, Memorandum, February 28, 1769 (Benjamin Fuller Letter Book, HSP). *Pennsylvania Journal*, March 9, 1769, March 23, 1769.

53   James Fullton to Henry Cruger, March 28, 1768, to Ephraim Campbell and John Fullton, November 26, 1768 (James Fullton Letter Book (typescript), LCHS). *Pennsylvania Journal*, March 24, 1768, May 5, 1768.

54   James Fullton to Ephraim Campbell and John Fullton, November 26, 1768 (James Fullton Letter Book (typescript), LCHS).

55   The non-importation agreement was circulating at this time. James Fullton to David Harvey, March 30, 1768 (James Fullton Letter Book (typescript), LCHS).

56   Details are in John Fullton's lengthy obituary in *Lancaster Intelligencer*, April 5, 1803.

57   Advertisements for ships to Ireland are very rare. "For Belfast, the ship *Catharine*, takes in cargo at Newport, and will be ready to sail by the 12th of January. Benjamin Greene, Newport." *Providence Gazette and Country Journal*, November 8, 1766.

58   *Providence Gazette and Country Journal*, October 8, 1763. Archibald Stewart was born in 1727 and died in 1805. He is buried in St. John's Cemetery, Providence, RI. His brother John (1733–91) married Jane, sole heiress of James Moore of Ballydivity, and changed his name to Stewart-Moore. Charles Clark and Linde Lunney kindly sent me data on the Stewarts and Stewart-Moores of Ballintoy.

59   Jackson and Bromfield to Samuel and Jonathan Smith, October 10, 1766, in Stuart Bruchey, *The Colonial Merchant* (New York, 1966), 186. James Fullton to Andrew Black, December 4, 1770 (Fullton Letter Book (typescript), LCHS).

60   Stocker and Wharton to Christopher Champlin, December 10, 1773, *Massachusetts Historical Society Collections*, 69(1914), 470.

61   *Providence Gazette and Country Journal*, April 23, 1763, May 28, 1763, August 6, 1763.

62   *Providence Gazette and Country Journal*, August 29, 1767, September 5, 1767.

63   *Providence Gazette and Country Journal*, September 19, 1767, November 21, 1767.

64   *Providence Gazette and Country Journal*, February 10, 1770.

65   *Londonderry Journal*, March 23, 1784.

66   *Providence Gazette and Country Journal*, July 28, 1764, September 1, 1764, October 6, 1764.

67   *Providence Gazette and Country Journal*, September 22, 1764, October 20, 1764.

68   John O'Kelly to Christopher Champlin, October 20, 1773, *Massachusetts Historical Society Collections*, 69(1914), 456–7.

69   William and John Ogle to James Hudson, February 13, 1772 in Bruchey, *Colonial Merchant*, 192.

70   Alexander Hewatt, *An Historical Account of the Rise and Progress of the Colonies of South Carolina and Georgia* (London, 1779) in Bartholomew Rivers Carroll, *Historical Collections of South Carolina* (New York, 1836, New York, 1973), I, 488.

71   *Belfast News Letter*, April 6, 1773.

72   A Farmer, *Serious considerations on the present alarming state of agriculture and the linen trade* (Dublin, 1773) in W. H. Crawford, *The Impact of the Domestic Linen Industry in Ulster* (Belfast, 2005), 189–203.

73   Richard B. Sheridan, "The British Credit Crisis of 1772 and the American Colonies," *Journal of Economic History*, 20(1960), 162–6.

74   Joshua Johnson to Johnson, Wallace and Davidson, June 22, 1772, in Jacob M. Price, ed., *Joshua Johnson's Letterbook 1771–1774: Letters from a merchant in London to his partners in Maryland* (London, 1979), 86.

75   Jacob M. Price, *Capital and Credit in British Overseas Trade: The View from the Chesapeake, 1700–1776* (Cambridge, MA, 1980), 130.

76   Henry Hamilton, *An Economic History of Scotland in the Eighteenth Century* (Oxford, 1963), 319.

77   "Mercator," *Belfast News Letter*, March 31, 1772. "A Farmer" made the same point. "Our good friends the English and Americans will never think themselves obliged to take our goods if they are dearer or of an inferior quality to what they can import from other manufacturing countries." Crawford, *Impact of the Domestic Linen Industry*, 197.

78   Sir William Brownlow to James, Earl of Abercorn, January 9, 1771 (D/623/A/39/97, PRONI).

79   *Belfast News Letter*, January 4, 1771.

80   W. A. Maguire, "Lord Donegall and the Hearts of Steel," *Irish Historical Studies*, 21(1979), 372.

81   Robert Barclay to James, Earl of Abercorn, December 30, 1765 (D/623/A/35/164, PRONI).

82   W. H. Crawford, "The Political Economy of Linen: Ulster in the Eighteenth Century," in Ciaran Brady, Mary O'Dowd and Brian Walker, eds., *Ulster, An Illustrated History* (London, 1989), 138–9, 143.

83   Maguire, "Lord Donegall," 360–61.

84   *Belfast News Letter*, November 15, 1768. Maguire, "Lord Donegall," 353–4.

85   James S. Donnelly, "Hearts of Oak, Hearts of Steel," *Studia Hibernica*, 21(1981), 26–7. Donald H. Akenson, *Between Two Revolutions: Islandmagee, Co. Antrim* (Port Credit, ON, 1979), 34.

86   He first advertised the estate as a whole, stressing its fertile soil and convenience to Larne, and then 93 individual holdings. *Belfast News Letter*, January 16, 1770, February 13, 1770.

87   *Belfast News Letter*, April 21, 1772, May 22, 1772, April 30, 1773.

88   "Statement of Negotiations," May 27, 1775 (T/656/73, PRONI). Robert Slade, "Narrative of a Journey to the North of Ireland in 1802" in *A Concise View of the Origin, Constitution and Proceedings of the Irish Society* (London, 1842), ccxii. Richard K. MacMaster, "Richard Jackson: 'An Almost Total Emigration,'" *Journal of Scotch-Irish Studies*, 2(2005), 94–7.

89   William Alexander and his brothers John in Belfast and Robert in Londonderry were all correspondents of Samuel Carsan and other flaxseed exporters. Curl, *Londonderry Plantation*, 358.

90   *Belfast News Letter*, April 21, 1772. Curl, *Londonderry Plantation*, 325.

91   Donnelly, "Hearts of Oak," 29–31, 37. Maguire, "Lord Donegall," 363, 367.

92   Maguire, "Lord Donegall," 362.

93   James Hamilton to James, Earl of Abercorn, April 15, 1770 (D/623/A/39/28, PRONI). Abercorn's agent sold oatmeal at a loss to people on the estate. "The scarcity of [oat]meal is much more than was dreaded, nor could we have subsisted I am persuaded, but for the Scotch, English and Drogheda meal imported into Derry, which chiefly supplies more than thirty miles around it." James Hamilton to James, Earl of Abercorn, July 6, 1770, July 17, 1770 (D/623/A/39/48–50, PRONI).

94   James Hamilton to James, Earl of Abercorn, October 31, 1772 (D/623/A/40/68, PRONI).

95   James Hamilton to James, Earl of Abercorn, July 25, 1772 (D/623/A/40/50, PRONI).

96   "A Presbyterian Linen Weaver, Newry," *Belfast News Letter*, March 10, 1772.

97   "Mercator," *Belfast News Letter*, March 31, 1772. W. H. Crawford, "The Evolution of the Linen Trade in Ulster Before Industrialisation," *Irish Economic and Social History*, 15(1988), 37. Jane Gray, *Spinning the Threads of Uneven Development: Gender and Industrialization in Ireland during the Long Eighteenth Century* (Lanham, MD, 2005), 38–41.

98   *Belfast News Letter*, April 30, 1773.

99   "Mercator," *Belfast News Letter*, March 31, 1772.

100   *Belfast News Letter*, April 6, 1773.

101   Joshua Johnson to Johnson, Wallace and Davidson, July 26, 1771, June 22, 1772, in *Joshua Johnson's Letterbook*, 18, 79. Price, *Capital and Credit*, 110–12.

102   Crawford, "Evolution of Linen Trade," 37. Gray, *Spinning the Threads*, 34.

103   Maguire, "Lord Donegall and the Hearts of Steel," 353–4. Francis Joseph Bigger, *The Ulster Land War of 1770* (Dublin, 1910), 57.

104   Donnelly, "Hearts of Oak," 37–8.

105   *Belfast News Letter*, February 8, 1771.

106   *Belfast News Letter*, February 22, 1771.

107   *Belfast News Letter*, February 15, 1771, June 14, 1771, August 13, 1771, March 13, 1772.

108   Mr. Barclay's nephew in Armagh to Mr. Barclay at Strabane, March 8, 1772 (D/623/A/40/11, PRONI).

109   The columns of the *Belfast News Letter* filled with condemnations of the Hearts of Steel often signed by hundreds. Broughshane and Ballinderry congregations had "none within our Boundaries" and Kilraghts acknowledged "only one." The Presbytery of Route observed that other Presbyterians were the chief victims of their violence. Strabane pointed out that "they have put the harmless inoffensive cattle to agonizing tortures." *Belfast News Letter*, January 3, 1772, March 16, 1772, April 17, 1772, April 24, 1772.

110   Dickson, *Ulster Emigration*, 75.

111   Erskine to John Lees, April 10, 1772, as quoted in Donnelly, "Hearts of Oak," 65.

112   James Hamilton to James, Earl of Abercorn, June 1, 1773 (D/263/A/40/99, PRONI).

113   *Belfast News Letter*, November 10, 1772, November 17, 1772.

114   *Londonderry Journal*, May 17, 1774.

115   *South Carolina Gazette*, March 26, 1772.

116   *Maryland Journal and Baltimore Advertiser*, October 19, 1773.

117   These figures are for emigrants from all of Ireland. *Londonderry Journal*, July 12, 1774.

118   *Belfast News Letter*, March 30, 1773.

119   *Belfast News Letter*, April 30, 1773, May 7, 1773, May 14, 1773, May 21, 1773, September 10, 1773.

120   The *Walworth* sailed for Charleston and arrived there with "about 300 Irish passengers." *South Carolina Gazette*, August 30, 1773. *Belfast News Letter*, June 29, 1773.

121   *Pennsylvania Journal*, August 4, 1773, August 11, 1773. *New York Journal*, August 12, 1773.

122   *New York Journal*, July 15, 1773.

123   *Londonderry Journal*, May 4, 1773.

124   *Belfast News Letter*, April 6, 1773.

125   *Londonderry Journal*, April 16, 1773.

126   *New York Journal*, July 15, 1773.

127   *Londonderry Journal*, June 4, 1773.

10
Patterns of Emigration

HOW MANY PEOPLE LEFT IRELAND IN THESE YEARS or in the whole of the eighteenth century to find new homes or temporary work in North America? Did they come alone or with their families? Were they young or old? For most of the century there are no surviving records, official or otherwise, on either side of the Atlantic, to answer these questions. Scholars have had to make do with educated guesses, extrapolating from the disparate bits of evidence available to them. There are three breaks in the clouds, however, two sets of records of bounty emigrants to South Carolina and an official record of passengers disembarking at Philadelphia between September 1768 and April 1772. While the information from Charleston is easy to interpret, the Philadelphia evidence is complicated by the fact that many emigrant ships sailed to New Castle *and* Philadelphia. With no records of any kind from the Delaware port to complement them, Philadelphia passenger lists raise as many questions as they answer.[1]

There have been many attempts to determine how many people emigrated. Philadelphia merchant James Caldwell wrote his brother John in Ballymoney, County Antrim to say that "I have just gotten the returns of the emigration from the North of Ireland in 1771 and 1772, it exceeds seventeen thousand souls and the influx for 1773 was twelve thousand."[2] Caldwell, as a merchant in the passenger business, was in a position to know, but the figures given appear too generous. From official returns, we know that 1,446 emigrants landed at Philadelphia in 1771. Even if an equal number disembarked at New Castle and the two ports together accounted for half the total emigration that year, all mere suppositions, the estimated total would be in the range of 6,000 emigrants, rather than 8,500 in 1771. Could Caldwell have been right?

He was probably citing an anonymous writer in the *Belfast News Letter* who used an ingenious method in April 1773 to reach his figure. He calculated the number of ships that sailed with passengers from the north of Ireland to North America, and their tonnage, taken from the advertisements published in the *News Letter*. "It may be supposed on a moderate Computation that the Number of Passengers were equal to the Tons," so the 32 ships displacing an aggregate of 8,900 tons would suggest that the number of emigrants in 1771 would be roughly 8,900 and, on the same basis, in 1772 about 8,450 people left Ulster for the American Colonies.[3]

Working on the same assumptions, Sir Edward Newenham MP published in the *Dublin Freeman's Journal* an account of the ships which sailed with passengers from Ulster ports in 1769–74. Between July 25, 1769 and March 25, 1771 seven vessels with passengers sailed from Londonderry, seven from Belfast, four from Newry, two from Larne, and two from Portrush. These 22 ships had an aggregate tonnage of 5,170 and "the number of emigrants is supposed fully to equal the number of tons of shipping" so some 5,000 people left Ulster ports for the Colonies in those eighteen months. Over the next two year period from March 25, 1771 to March 25, 1773 the pace of emigration quickened considerably with fully 62 voyages with passengers for the Colonies and an estimated 17,400 emigrants. The number of vessels, often repeat voyages by the same ship, included 22 from Londonderry, 17 from Belfast, 14 from Newry, seven from Larne, and two from Portrush. Between March 25, 1773 and July 25, 1774, another eighteen months, there were 21 sailings from Londonderry, 19 from Belfast, 20 from Newry, again seven from Larne and one from Portrush. These 68 ships with a combined 20,450 tons would have brought some 20,000 emigrants to North America. Totaling these figures, Sir Edward estimated 43,020 emigrants from Ulster from July 1769 to July 1774.[4] His willingness, in an era of anonymous and pseudonymous journalism, to take ownership of these estimates in the press is an indication that this prominent member of the Dublin Parliament thought they were close to the mark.[5]

In his classic study of Ulster emigration, R. J. Dickson popu-
larised the method of estimating the number of emigrants by the
number of advertisements for ships sailing to American ports in the
Belfast and Londonderry newspapers multiplied by the registered
tonnage of each.[6] Dickson was quite right that with very few exceptions, merchants and shipowners took out newspaper advertisements to secure passengers. Eight of the ten ships arriving at
Philadelphia with passengers from Ulster ports in 1769, for example, advertised in one or more issues of the *Belfast News Letter*. But
there are perils in this method. There is no newspaper advertisement for the brig *Conolly* from Londonderry with 28 passengers
nor the *Elizabeth* which carried just eight passengers from
Londonderry to Philadelphia. On the other hand, William
McCulloch, master of the *Friendship* of 250 tons, advertised for
passengers for New Castle and Philadelphia, but her destination
must have been changed before sailing. William Burgess of Belfast
and William and John Ogle of Newry advertised for passengers,
redemptioners and servants for New Castle and Philadelphia on the
Pennsylvania Farmer, another large ship of 300 tons commanded by
Burgess' brother-in-law, James Blair. She called at Cork and entered
from there with just six passengers. Based on their advertised capacity, these two ships could have brought more than 500 emigrants to
Philadelphia, but in reality only six.

Arthur Young's inquiries on his 1776 tour led him to totals some-
where in the range of 2,000 a year for the 1760s, gradually rising
to a peak of 4,000 or more in 1773.[7] Marianne Wokeck's estimates
of passengers arriving at the port of Philadelphia suggest that
Young's informants may not have been far off the mark. She estimated 1,510 emigrants from Ulster ports in 1766 and close to
1,000 in each succeeding year through 1772. When she added the
neighbouring port of New Castle, Delaware to her calculation, the
numbers rose to 1,961 in 1766 and well over 1,000 a year in subsequent years.[8] Passengers for New York, Baltimore, Charleston,
and Savannah would raise the figures still higher, likely close to the
2,000 a year proposed by Arthur Young and by R. J. Dickson himself for the 1760s.[9] But those were off-peak years.

The number of ships advertised in the *Belfast News Letter*
increased over the decade, roughly doubling in 1773, but those

offering for New Castle and Philadelphia remained about the same, ranging from fifteen to twenty a year. The growing popularity of Baltimore, Charleston, and Savannah as emigrant destinations accounted for the increased demand for shipping, although some of these ships would continue on to Philadelphia and New York to take on a flaxseed freight as they were wont to do. The *Britannia*, for instance, arrived at New York from South Carolina, "where she carried about 200 Irish Protestants to settle in the back Parts of that Province," and sailed a month later for Newry with flaxseed.[10]

The Philadelphia passenger lists, which begin late in 1768 and continue through the first half of 1772, provide solid figures for that period, but bring their own problems. In the last four months of 1768, when the flaxseed business was at its height, nine ships disembarked at least 313 passengers at Philadelphia, but the surviving passenger lists elucidate the difficulty of determining how many emigrants actually crossed the ocean. The pilot boat from New Castle brought 27 passengers from the *Marquis of Granby* to Philadelphia in September. We have no way of knowing how many came ashore at New Castle, so we cannot know how many embarked at Londonderry. Captain William Dysart brought the *Rose* up the Delaware to dock at Philadelphia, consigned to Samuel Carsan and Co. He made out such a complete list of his passengers that a clerk in the Customs House simply noted "see his list" without giving any number for the Philadelphia passengers who came on the *Rose*. Since she entered from New Castle on Delaware, we could not know her full complement of passengers from Londonderry even if Captain Dysart's list survived. The following year *Rose* carried 120 passengers to Philadelphia, so we might expect a number in that range on the missing list. *Newry's Assistance* brought 81 passengers to Philadelphia from Newry, but she, too, entered from New Castle, where some or none of her passengers may have left the ship. Each of these three entries is problematic in its own way and even the total number uncertain.

For the three years for which we have complete lists, the figures still need to be read with caution, but they do show a broad general trend: emigration from Ulster was increasing both in number and as a percentage of arrivals at Philadelphia from Irish ports. In 1769 ships from Londonderry, Belfast and Newry brought 522 passengers and 285 came on ships chiefly from Cork, but also from Sligo, Waterford and Dublin. The figures for 1770 are 651 from ports in Ulster and 284 from other Irish ports. In 1771 the three Ulster ports accounted for 1,305 emigrants arriving at Philadelphia, while only 242 came from other ports in Ireland. The figures for 1772 are too fragmentary to make any further projections. Other general patterns are also apparent. Londonderry dominated the passenger trade, as Cork did the servant trade. In each of the three years seven or eight vessels from Londonderry brought passengers to Philadelphia, two or three from Newry, and one to four from Belfast, with the largest number in 1771.[11]

The only passenger records from the peak years of migration in 1772 and 1773 are the lists of newly-arrived emigrants who qualified for land in South Carolina, lists prepared for meetings of the Governor's Council in December 1772 and January 1773. These settlers are identified as passengers on one of five ships arriving at Charleston. Less complete than some prepared during the years of the South Carolina bounty, they nevertheless provide clues to the flow and composition of emigration in 1772–3.

One group of 1772 emigrants is less easily linked to a ship. At a session of the Council on December 1, 1772 petitions were read from 35 individuals, who "had lately come into this Province with their Respective Familys from Ireland and were desirous to settle and cultivate some vacant lands in the back parts of the Country." Because of "their extreme Poverty" they requested exemption from the usual fees charged for land warrants. Like another group who presented their petitions at a Council session on November 8, 1772, it is tempting to assume they were passengers on the *James and Mary* from Larne. Those who came on this ship were more than satisfied with their treatment on the voyage and 37 of them signed a letter of thanks to her owner James McVickar penned by the Rev. Robert McClintock, one of the passengers. Only one name, William Simpson, appears both on the December 1 list as a land claimant and as a signer of the letter, so identification with the Larne emigrants is at best not proven.[12]

As one would expect, all of these lists confirm that most emigrants from Ulster came "with their Respective Familys" to South Carolina. The Rev. William Martin headed the list of passengers on the *Lord Dunluce* from Larne and all or nearly all of them were his congregants. Next on the list was James McLurkam with a warrant for 300 acres. Thomas, James, Samuel, Mary, Eleanor, Lillias, and Jane McLurkam each received warrants for 100 acres. James and his wife evidently had seven children over the age of sixteen who came with them. Grizell Maybean (Mebane) with children Henry, James, Thomas, and Elizabeth, and John McQuillan with his wife and three grown daughters also represented older parents. The McMasters from Ballymoney, County Antrim were five brothers and their sister. David and James McQuesten, each allowed 400 acres, and David and Elizabeth Morrow, with 550, had younger families, no children over sixteen.[13]

Family groups are readily recognisable in the lists of passengers on the *Hopewell* from Belfast, too. While the *Lord Dunluce* passengers all paid the customary charges for land grants, only ten of *Hopewell's* passengers were able to do so and 53 could not. Did this indicate that this group was significantly poorer than the Covenanters on Rev. William Martin's ship? On the *Pennsylvania Farmer* Rev. John Logue from Broughshane, County Antrim, and 22 other passengers were prepared to pay the requisite fees, but 63 were unable to pay. Surnames found in one group are rarely found in the other, so there may well be economic distinctions among the passengers. Should we conclude that a high percentage of 1772 emigrants exhausted their financial resources by paying their passage? Aboard *Free Mason*, from Newry, a different pattern seems evident. Just seven of the 56 passengers who claimed land were able to pay for their warrants, but John McKnight, who qualified for 350 acres, and John Pressley, who was granted 300, had family members among those unable to pay. Of those who arrived on the *Britannia* from Newry only seven were able to pay and of the remaining 41 claiming land the clerk noted "These are poor people who have severally sworn that they are not worth five pounds sterling." Among those able to pay was William Dunlap and among the poorer people were Mary, Margaret, Robert, William Jr., and Alexander Dunlap, obviously his family. Even the children of a comfortably situated farmer would not be individually worth £5 sterling, so they were telling the simple truth.[14]

Like emigrants travelling to Charleston, passengers for

Philadelphia often crossed the Atlantic in family groups. The percentage of such family units varied greatly from ship to ship, as surviving passenger lists witness. On the brig *George* that brought the Rev. Joseph Rhea and his family to America in 1769, nearly all the passengers (50 out of 54), travelled in family groups, the five servants did not. Of the 95 passengers from Londonderry on the *Newry Packet* in June 1770, 53 were part of extended families and 42 passengers and five servants were travelling alone. More than half her passengers the following year (51 out of 74) were also family units. Families predominated (53 out of 90 passengers) on the *Earl of Donegall* in July 1770. Passengers on the *Newry Assistance*, *Marquis of Granby*, and *Pennsylvania Farmer* were evenly divided. On the majority of ships families comprised less than half of the passengers disembarking at Philadelphia. The proportion dropped notably over the three-year period for which we have records. When the *Rose* arrived from Londonderry in September 1769, 74 of her 120 passengers came with their families; in October 1771 just 35 of Rose's 123 passengers did so. The *Dolphin* brought 98 passengers, of whom just 37 were in family groups, and 15 servants from Newry in May 1771. Of 74 passengers from Derry on the *Walworth* in July 1771 only sixteen came as families as did 43 of the 148 persons arriving on the *Philadelphia* from Belfast the same month. Some ships brought few, if any, for example, only two of 48 passengers on the *Polly* of Belfast in May 1771 and just a few more when she returned with 80 passengers in October.[15] The higher proportion of single passengers, apart from servants, may reflect the lure of Pennsylvania as still the best poor man's country, as an encomium to the captain of the *Philadelphia* in July 1771 was directed to "those of our Friends who design to become Adventurers to this Land of Milk and Honey," as well as the belief that young men would find greater opportunity in the largest city in the Colonies.[16] The greater numbers of passengers each year doubtless meant that some ships were more crowded. The Philadelphia passenger lists indicate a modest increase from year to year, but no strong pattern emerges. *Walworth* of Londonderry landed 47 passengers in 1770 and 84 in 1771. *Phoenix* of Londonderry disembarked 54 passengers in 1769, 85 in 1770, and 115 in 1771. *Jupiter* of Londonderry brought 87 passengers in

1769, 115 in 1770, and 88 in 1771. *Philadelphia* of Belfast carried 92 passengers in 1769, 54 in 1770, and 148 in 1771. This sort of fluctuation from year to year was a common pattern, although some ships, such as the *Rose* of Londonderry had a steady passenger list of 120–23 on each voyage.

The number of passengers reported on emigrant ships in 1772–4 generally were much larger than in earlier years, but in some cases so were the vessels they sailed on. Advertised tonnage is notoriously slippery, as R. J. Dickson pointed out, the same ship claiming far different capacity at different times. Most vessels were in the 250–300 ton range and could comfortably carry up to 300 passengers, but some newer ships in the emigrant trade were larger. Only two advertised vessels claimed 400 tons in 1771, but in 1772 four were of this size, six in 1773, and in 1774 seven as well as two of 450 tons and three advertised as 500 tons. A letter from Londonderry in June 1774 reported "five large ships in this port, ready to sail, each of which will take at least 500 passengers." These evidently included the *Minerva* of 500 tons, and the *Hannah* of 400 tons, the *Ann* of 300 tons, and the *Betty* of 250 tons.[17]

Passengers, Redemptioners and Servants

When emigration was at its height several people in Tullywhisker, a townland in Urney parish in County Tyrone, advertised for a ship to take them to South Carolina. That there were enough potential emigrants in a 517-acre townland that they would consider chartering their own ship is noteworthy, of course, but that they could all pay their passages and had formed ideas of where to go is more interesting. The Tullywhisker folk remind us that tenants had a way to finance their passage and that each new emigrant was preceded by a former neighbor in a chain migration over many years. Tullywhisker is within the Abercorn estate, so we know more about their comings and goings, thanks to James Hamilton's detailed reports as agent. He wrote in 1769 that

> Thomas Mackey of Tullywhisker came and acquainted me, that he intended going to America with his family, and wanted a liberty to dispose of his farm; I told him that if he got a

good tenant to lave in his place that I would inform your
Lordship of it; accordingly he set up his farm to be kented for,
and Thomas Cunningham of Tilnadortans bid highest for
it;[18]

Sale of the lease under Ulster tenant right could easily net enough
to finance emigration. In 1771 Hamilton reported to the Earl that
"Adam Murray of Tillywhisker who pays £3 12s 6d rent intends
going to America, and has agreed to sell his holding to Jeremiah
Alcorn his neighbour at £50."[19] If the sale included not only the
lease and the tenant's improvements, but his crops, farm implements, and livestock, the departing family would have capital to
start afresh in Pennsylvania or South Carolina. Hamilton told of a
son who came home to settle his father's estate:

> John Finlay of Edimore is dead; he left his farm to his son,
> who was then in America, who on his return, gave up the
> mountain part of it which is about a third to his brother-in-
> law for some consideration, and as he resolves going back to
> America, has sold his rights to the remainder to one John
> McNeilans, who is I believe a solvent tenant, at £95;
> McNeilans got the crop, two cows and a horse and some
> things belonging to the farm.[20]

As the pace of emigration speeded up, advertisements appeared in
the newspapers for sales by families soon to depart. William
Johnston, for instance, offered the lease of his farm of 34 acres near
Saintfield, County Down with 24 years left in the lease as he and
his family were leaving for America in May. Most sales, of course,
were never advertised, except by word of mouth among neighbours
who could value each one's holding. And ship owners delayed sailings to allow passengers to "dispose of crops & stock to better
advantage."[21]

Among the passengers from Belfast on the brig *Polly* in October
1771 were Jos. M'Min, a 50-year-old weaver, his 40-year-old wife
Mary, and their three-year-old child. They had "been in this country before" and had "a right to a place in Hopewell township in
Cumberland county," Pennsylvania, but were "obliged to leave it on
account of the Indian war." As redemptioners, they were given

permission to "go in the country to procure money" to pay their passage, but had not returned with the promised cash.[22] The McMins fled their frontier farm and went back to Ulster, but had not prospered. He probably had a cottage with a loom in it and a garden patch as a sub-tenant or cotter on some weaver-farmer's land and, as such, was the most vulnerable to downturns in the linen market. With no tenant right or household goods to sell to finance their passage they pledged that family or friends in Pennsylvania would pay their way. Passenger lists did not identify those who came as redemptioners, but they were numerous enough in these years to generate newspaper advertisements. William and Andrew Caldwell warned a certain Francis Johnston who came over on redemption in the *Jupiter* from Londonderry "and has taken advantage of the liberty given him, to go for a few days into the country, and not yet paid his passage," that they would advertise his description and a reward for taking him up. Other redemptioners on the *Jupiter*, who passed notes and bonds for their passage and neglected to discharge them "may expect their different securities being immediately put into the hands of a lawyer, with proper authority to sue for them."[23] Carsan, Barclay and Mitchell, agents for the *Rose*, also threatened "The people who gave notes to Capt. Dysart, for their passage from Derry" with legal action unless they made immediate payment.[24]

Some family members agreed to go as redemptioners, liable to be sold into indentured servitude, while others in the family paid their passage. Two redemptioners left the *Needham* when she docked at New Castle on Delaware in 1773. William Makee, alias Kee, "left his wife on board, and promised to return after paying a visit to some of his relations at the cross roads, near Philadelphia, who he told Captain Cheevers, would redeem him." He went in company with William Armstrong, who had already paid his passage. Catharine M'Dermot "left the ship, by making use of her sister's receipt, who, in order to deceive, continued on board till the other had concealed herself." Her mother and sister paid their passages, hence the receipt, and the captain had no doubt she was with them.[25]

Almost half of the men and women from Ulster who were indentured as servants by the mayor of Philadelphia in 1771–3 crossed the ocean as redemptioners and found themselves unable to meet their obligations. Redemptioners had in fact entered into a loan transaction, with the cost of their passage and possibly money to buy provisions advanced by the ship-owner, secured by their labour as collateral. They could repay the loan with help from relatives or friends or the ship's captain would indenture them to someone prepared to repay. Although the final result could be the same, servants were in a different category. They made what was really a barter contract, exchanging their future labor for passage to America, while still in their homeland. They were recruited as servants, rather than this being their default position if their prospects in America proved bleak on arrival there. Four of five servants from southern Irish ports indentured at Philadelphia began the voyage as servants.[26]

Not all passenger lists clearly distinguished between passengers and servants, but where they do the number of servants on ships from northern ports is surprisingly small. The *Newry Packet*, coming from Derry in 1770, landed 95 paying passengers and only five servants. The *Jupiter* brought 69 passengers and 19 servants in 1771. Others were in the same proportion. Ships from southern ports, on the other hand, generally had fewer people on board when they reached Philadelphia, but all or nearly all were indentured servants. The 37 persons on the *Myrtilla* from Cork "belong to S. Howell" and the 24 on the brig *Industry* from Dublin "belong to Fisher & Donaldson." The *Elizabeth and Mary* from Cork brought two passengers and 46 servants and the snow *Charlotte* from Waterford carried two passengers and 24 servants.

Most servants came on ships from Cork, Dublin, or Waterford, in that order, but a certain number came from other Irish ports. Agents in every port, most notably Cork, specialised in recruiting servants. Daniel Clark wrote, "My Brother goes home [to Sligo] with Capt. Hamilton, he intends to make a push for servants."[27] Ulster ports were also engaged in the servant trade, but on a smaller scale. Departing emigrants from Ulster often brought servants indentured to them. John Wolfenden, who lived at Lambeg on the road between Belfast and Lisburn, advertised:

> To be sold by publick Cant at the House of John Wolfenden
> in Lambeg, two Leases under the Rt. Hon. The Earl of

Hertford, and all the Household Furniture, cattle, and plowing Utensils, belonging to said John Wolfenden; in whose
Hands said Leases may be seen at or before the Cant, which
will begin on Wednesday the fourth Day of March next, and
to continue until it is sold. 18 February 1767. N.B. Any
young Men that intend going to Philadelphia in America as
Servants, may depend upon having the best of Usage by
applying to said John Wolfenden, who intends going over the
first Opportunity, and his whole Family.

By selling his tenant right in his two leases as well as everything
on his farm, he could afford to pay the passage for his family and
have enough to begin again in America. A number of indentured
servants would provide additional income on arrival.[28] Such advertisements were common. John Donnall, "now at the Glen near
Larne, intends returning to Philadelphia to settle there" and invited others to go with him as servants.[29] John Maxwell, "formerly a
Residenter in America, intends in the month of May to return there
again," and would meet with "Any Persons that design to go as
Servants" in Carrickfergus. John McCullough would spend
Saturdays in Ballymena recruiting "Young Men and Women who
are willing to go to Philadelphia in America" with him.[30]

Although every advertisement for a ship sailing to America was
sure to mention redemptioners and servants, servants comprised
less than a tenth of emigrants from Ulster ports. Most indentured
servants came from southern Irish ports. Servants arrived at
Philadelphia, as already mentioned, in much smaller numbers than
did paying passengers. Samuel Howell landed 60 servants from
Cork in 1768, but the average for ships arriving that year with servants was just 24. Of the eighteen vessels bringing servants to
Philadelphia in 1769, all but five had fewer than twenty on board.
Women and girls were few, even on ships whose consignees advertised them, and it was rare to find two or more servants with the
same surname.[31]

Conyngham and Nesbitt and George Bryan specialised in the servant trade, but a few other firms in the flaxseed trade dealt in servants, too, although generally in a small way. Wills and Jackson
imported "a few servants, all likely lads, from 12 to 20 years of age"
from Belfast and Carsan, Barclay and Mitchell "a few servant Men"

from Cork.[32] Two months later Carsan, Barclay and Mitchell offered "A number of English and Irish Men and Women Servants, Imported in the ship Neptune, [from Belfast] and ship Lecky, David Brown, master, of Londonderry" and the following autumn "a number of young Men and Boys, just imported from [Cork] Ireland in the ship *Walworth*, Edward Boggs, master."[33] Fisher, Donaldson and Pringle brought "A number of healthy likely Indented Servants, Men, Women, and Boys (amongst whom are sundry tradesmen)" on the *Newry Packet*.[34] Fisher, Donaldson and Pringle advertised the twenty-four who came on the *Industry* from Dublin and seventeen on the *Newry Packet* in 1768. The same firm offered "a parcel of healthy servants, men, boys, and girls in the ship *Sally* from Dublin," which landed 37 passengers, and John Pringle alone offered "a few Irish Servants, just arrived from Cork" on the *Newry Assistance*, which brought twenty-three in 1769.[35] All of these ships returned to Ulster ports with flaxseed cargoes. The twenty-three servants in the *Swallow* from Waterford and the nineteen in the *Elizabeth* from Cork were consigned to Carsan, Barclay and Mitchell.[36] Benjamin Fuller imported 21 "healthy Men and Women Servants" in the ship *Sally* from Cork and the brig *Conolly* brought 65 indentured men and women from Dublin to William and Andrew Caldwell in 1770.[37]

The merchants importing servants netted about £10 from each servant sold and close to £400 for the average shipment.[38] Prices also fluctuated according to the season. The mean price for servants in January-February 1772 was £15 and dropped steadily through the spring to only £12 from May through August. It reached £18 in September and held at that level through the winter, dipping again to £11 in March 1773 and slowly rising again to £19 in September 1773.[39]

In 1771-3 six ships from Londonderry brought 765 passengers to Philadelphia of whom 12.9% were servants, five from Newry carried 511 passengers with servants making up 23.2% of the total. Three Belfast ships landed 154 passengers of whom 26.6% were servants.[40] Survival of records of indentures of apprentices, redemptioners and servants processed by the Mayor of Philadelphia in 1771-3 has permitted close analysis of the servant trade there in those years when some 1,300 separate contracts were registered.

Philadelphia's importance as a market for servants drew buyers from as far away as New Hampshire and South Carolina.[41] Germans, who were all redemptioners as were the Scots, accounted for by far the largest number of indentures. Irish servants were half as numerous as Germans and slightly more than those from Ulster in this sample. Of those from Ulster ports who were indentured in Philadelphia half came as redemptioners and half as servants.[42] Most of those who emigrated as servants left from ports in Ireland and only 106 from English ports. The number of men and women who sailed for Philadelphia from Belfast, Derry or Newry as servants and from Cork, Dublin or Waterford in that capacity was nearly the same.[43] During 1771–3 Newry dispatched 216 servants to Philadelphia, Londonderry 173, and Belfast 102. In the same time period 201 servants from Dublin, 178 from Cork, and 136 from Waterford arrived at Philadelphia.[44]

Servants from Ulster were more highly valued in the Colonies than those from Southern Irish ports. The price paid was nearly the same, but they had shorter contracts to work out than those from Cork or Waterford. Female servants invariably had longer to serve than males did. Labour contracts were also subject to seasonal differences with those sold in the spring shorter than those sold in the autumn. Ships with servants reached Philadelphia at all seasons of the year, but the autumn saw the arrival of a great many Germans and a market oversupplied with servants.[45] Servants from Ireland generally came to market in the summer months. In 1771–3 two-thirds were sold in July, August and September and 77.7% from June to September. The autumn, flaxseed season, saw the arrival and sale of the remainder, probably redemptioners, but Germans and Scots also came to market in September and October and rendered Irish servants less saleable.[46]

Unfree labour was largely urban; although many buyers came from the rural counties and the furthest reaches of the backcountry, a clear majority lived in Philadelphia itself.[47] The situation was slightly different for both German and Irish servants with a majority of them located in rural counties of Pennsylvania and neighbouring colonies. Robert Heavner explored the geographical distribution of servants and masters in the 1771–3 records where over 400 locations are mentioned. He found that two-thirds of English and Scottish servants remained in Philadelphia, but only 40.1% of those imported through Rotterdam and 44.3% of those from Irish ports. Among those who went to an urban destination fully a quarter of those from Ireland moved to inland towns like Lancaster, York and Carlisle.[48]

We know less about the young men and women who went out as indentured servants. Grizey M'Colgan went to America "long before the American War" and lived in Hanover Township, Lancaster County, Pennsylvania "in a good way of living ... only I have no land of my own yet." She wrote her sister in Belfast to "advise no boys or girls to come bound as servants to this country, for it is the Devil's own place for either boy or girl to be bound as servants, for they are used like dogs and worse." They should be wary of "a number of villains that follow bringing servants, and tell a thousand lies for their profit." Doubtless other servants could tell a similar tale.[49]

A young woman travelling alone to America was probably encouraged to go out as a servant by some recruiter. Isabella Steel carried with her a certificate:

> That The Bearer Isabella Steel hath lived within the Bounds of this Congregation from her Infancy was born of Creditable Protestant dissenting parents is free of all manner of Publick scandal or Church Censure known to us, and by her good behaviour Honesty and unblemished Character, Justly deserves the Esteem and approbation of all who know her. Certified at Larne in the County of Antrim Ireland this 16th day of July 1773.

It is signed by the minister and two others and witnessed by a notary public. She was to sail for Baltimore, so there are no records of her life before she was married there in 1777 to Thomas Pilkington.[50] There is some evidence that merchants in Ulster either required or provided certificates for servants en route to the American Colonies. Torrans and Poaug, for example, advertised that the servants they had on offer "have Certificates of their good Behaviour from their Infancy," wording suspiciously like Isabella Steel's.[51] Of a runaway servant it was said: "Last fall from Newry came in brief, in the ship *Renown*, with Captain Keith; Certificates in plenty had, Each of them calls him a good Lad; I think of them he is full saucy, One of them signed by Parson Lasley."[52]

Most servants were males, 584 of 840 in the 1771–3 record, and 248 of the 256 females were unmarried, with only eight married couples indentured.[53] Each servant had a different story. Sarah Mahood was one of the 40 passengers on the ship *Newry's Assistance* who came ashore at Philadelphia January 6, 1772. Three weeks later Sarah Mahood from Newry was indentured as a servant before the Mayor of Philadelphia. The man who bought her indenture paid the ship's captain £9. She was to serve three years. The *Jupiter*, consigned to Andrew Caldwell and Joseph Wilson, brought passengers from Londonderry in June 1772. One of them named Catherine McDowd was indentured to Elihu Worrell of Haverford for four years; he paid £14 6s for her time. James and Sarah McCullough came from Belfast on the *Friendship* in May. They were indentured together to Andrew Todd of East Whiteland Township in Chester County at a cost to him of £30. James was bound for seven years and Sarah for four.[54]

Married couples, like the McCulloughs, seem to have been routinely sold together. John Cox and Charles Thomson purchased the time of Thomas and Mary Riordan, husband and wife, who came from Cork on the brig *Pattie*, paying a total of £20, although they were to serve only three years and one year respectively.[55] The employer had built-in safeguards. James and Catherine Dougherty, indentured together, promised "in case Catherine shall bear a child during her servitude, James shall after the expiration of his term pay the master £3 for the loss of time of his wife."[56]

Children could not be indentured without a parent's consent. After crossing the Atlantic with his mother, Peter Brown, all of six years and two months old, went into service:

> With consent of Mother Ann Brown and in consideration of two pounds paid for his passage from Ireland bound an apprentice to William Bonham of Philadelphia & assigns for Eleven years nine months & twenty-nine days to be taught the trade of a Grocer to read in the Bible write a legible hand and cipher as far as the rule of three to be found all necessaries and when free to have two compleat suits of apparel one of which to be new. June 18, 1773.[57]

"Freedom dues," the sum to be paid the servant at the end of his indenture, whether in cash, clothing, tools, or other goods, worked as another safeguard. As one scholar noticed, it functioned as a non-vested pension, a powerful incentive for the servant to work out his full term and a significant savings to the master if he did not.[58] In theory the freedom dues paid to indentured servants at the end of their term readied them for life on their own. In reality they had little more than the clothes on their back. Many shared the experience of Charles M'Cillop (McKillop) who "was brought and landed in this Province of Pennsylvania by Captain William Blair" in 1752. He sailed from Belfast that summer on Blair's ship *Earl of Holderness*. Arrived in Philadelphia he was indentured to Thomas Burney of Drumore Township in Lancaster County "for the space of four whole years." After that, he was a hired man for Richard McClure in Hanover Township in the same county, but eighteen years after coming to Pennsylvania, M'Cillop was certified as a pauper who never "gained any other legal settlement within this Province."[59]

Some servants were acquired by backcountry merchants for later resale. James Wilson of Leacock Township in Lancaster County was a middleman, purchasing a number of indentures to resell the servants in the backcountry. Several of his secondary transactions were recorded by the Philadelphia Mayor as well as the groups of servants he acquired initially.[60] Mary McGill came from Londonderry on the ship *Rose*, landing at Baltimore in August 1775. Before the *Rose* sailed, she was indentured for three years to fellow passenger William Montgomery, in exchange for his paying her passage. Joseph Curry, the ship's captain, and his mate witnessed the transaction. Montgomery, who also lived in Lancaster County, brought her to the county seat, where he sold the remainder of her term of service to attorney John Hubley for £15 10s through Lancaster merchant James Bickham. Hubley noted ruefully on Mary's indenture "absconded from Servitude the 3d Augt. 1776."

Although service for a term of years would seem enough for any man or woman, for some it was the only way to secure a passage back to America. Charles McNeil, a shoemaker by trade, and a runaway servant, spoke "Irish and Dutch well, also some Spanish and Portuguese." He was "well acquainted in this county, this being the second time of his being here, and came last from Londonderry, in the *Jupiter*, Captain Ewing."[61]

Servants from Ulster and from other Irish ports had a much greater propensity to run away than did servants of other nationalities. Of the 90 advertisements for runaway servants in the *Pennsylvania Gazette* in 1771–3, 43 identified the culprit as from Ireland.[62] Runaways, like the servant population as a whole, tended to be young, most often young men, less frequently young women. In these advertisements a distinction is often made between "native Irish" who had "much of the brogue" and servants "from the North of Ireland" who speak "thick in the North country dialect" or "in the Scotch way." The term "Scotch-Irish" is rare. Abraham Holmes, tavernkeeper at the Sign of the Bear in Donegal Township, Lancaster County, for example, advertised "a native Irish servant man, named Maurice Collins" as a runaway. He came from Cork on the brig *Pattie* and was indentured to Holmes in May 1773.[63] John M'Goun in Pequea, Lancaster County, advertised his runaway servant boy in verse: "Likewise John Hunter is his name, He from Antrim, in Ireland, came; Talks much, lies some, inclines to sing, Says he can work at every thing; He's now full eighteen years of age, I think he'll push for Thomas Gage" to enlist in the army.[64] Advertisements occasionally tell us more than the runaway's description. John M'Connell, 20 years old, "born in Belfast, in Ireland, by trade a Taylor," who left his master in Delaware, was "very talkative in Company, and remarkably fond of singing a song, called the Cheating Landlady."[65]

At the end of the day, while we have no precise figures to guide us, we know a good deal about the composition and flow of emigration from Ulster. With obvious exceptions, such as the unfortunate passengers on the *Nancy* or the *General Wolfe*, they arrived in America in good health. The incidence of family groups with parents and children and the youth and general good health of those who came as indentured servants meant that within a few years their numbers would grow by natural increase. Not all of them benefited from Ulster tenant right to finance their family's crossing and arrive in Philadelphia or Baltimore with money to begin a new life, but clearly many did, bringing cash as well as the intangible capital of training and experience as farmers, weavers, or tradesmen of different sorts. Moving to newly-settled regions, they were prepared to grow a new nation.

Notes

1   "Passenger Lists" (Cadwalader Collection, Series III, Box 78, Folder 18, HSP).
2   James Caldwell to John Caldwell, December 1774, in John Caldwell, "Memoir," 24 (T/3541/5/3, PRONI).
3   *Belfast News Letter*, April 6, 1773.
4   *Londonderry Journal*, July 12, 1774.
5   His career as a vocal friend of the American Colonies is traced in James Kelly, *Sir Edward Newenham, M.P. 1734–1814: Defender of the Protestant Constitution* (Dublin, 2003).
6   Dickson, *Ulster Emigration*, 62–4.
7   Young, *Tour in Ireland*, 204.
8   Wokeck, *Trade in Strangers*, 172–3.
9   Dickson found 194 vessels advertised in the *Belfast News Letter* to leave with emigrants to America during this decade, 165 of them for either Philadelphia or New York. He concluded that the number of emigrants who left Ulster in the 1760s "was in the region of 20,000 or slightly higher." Dickson, *Ulster Emigration*, 58.
10 *New York Journal*, October 1, 1767, November 5, 1767.
11 "Passenger Lists" (Cadwalader Collection, Series III, Box 78, Folder 18, HSP).
12 *Belfast News Letter*, December 22, 1772. Janie Revill, *A Compilation of the Original Lists of Protestant Immigrants to South Carolina 1763–1773* (Baltimore, 1968), 118–20.
13 Revill, *Original Lists of Protestant Immigrants*, 121–4
14 Revill, *Original Lists of Protestant Immigrants*, 124–8.
15 "Passenger Lists" (Cadwalader Collection, Series III, Box 78, Folder 18, HSP).
16 *Belfast News Letter*, November 26, 1771.
17 "Letter from Derry, June 14, 1774," *Maryland Gazette*, September 8, 1774. Tonnage figures from Dickson, *Ulster Emigration*, 238–75.
18 James Hamilton to James, Earl of Abercorn, September 17, 1769 (D/623/A/37/159, PRONI).
19 James Hamilton to James, Earl of Abercorn, March 1, 1771 (D/623/A/39/107, PRONI).
20 James Hamilton to James, Earl of Abercorn, June 1765 (D/623/A/36/137, PRONI).
21 *Belfast News Letter*, March 3, 1772, September 1, 1772.
22 He may have been the Josiah McMeen who died in Cumberland County in 1784. Cumberland County Wills, D–1–229, CCCH. *Pennsylvania Gazette*, February 6, 1772.
23 *Pennsylvania Journal*, October 13, 1768, November 21, 1768.
24 *Pennsylvania Journal*, October 27, 1768.
25 *Pennsylvania Journal*, September 8, 1773.
26 Farley Grubb, "Redemptioner Emigration to Pennsylvania: Evidence on Contract Choice and Profitability," *Journal of Economic History*, 46(1986), 408–09. Robert Owen Heavner, "Indentured Servitude: The Philadelphia Market, 1771–1773," *Journal of Economic History*, 38(1978), 701–13.
27 Daniel Clark to Edward Cochran, November 23, 1761 (Daniel Clark Letter Book, HSP).

28   *Belfast News Letter*, February 20, 1767. Wolfenden apparently had substantial holdings. Richard Wolfenden offered leases with unexpired lives, rents and inhabited dwelling houses, conveyed by the Earl of Hertford to John Wolfenden of Lambeg. *Belfast News Letter*, May 2, 1775.

29   *Belfast News Letter*, April 22, 1766.

30   *Belfast News Letter*, March 19, 1771, May 5, 1772.

31   "Passenger Lists" (Cadwalader Collection, Series III, Box 78, Folder 18, HSP).

32   *Pennsylvania Journal*, April 24, 1766.

33   *Pennsylvania Journal*, June 26, 1766, October 8, 1767.

34   *Pennsylvania Journal*, May 26, 1768.

35   *Pennsylvania Journal*, October 6, 1768, December 1, 1768, October 19, 1769, November 9, 1769.

36   *Pennsylvania Journal*, June 29, 1769, October 5, 1769.

37   *Pennsylvania Journal*, May 17, 1770, June 28, 1770.

38   Sharon V. Salinger, *"To Serve Well and Faithfully" Labor and Indentured Servants in Pennsylvania, 1682–1800* (Cambridge, 1987), 76.

39   Robert Owen Heavner, "Economic Aspects of Indentured Servitude in Colonial Pennsylvania," Ph.D. dissertation, Stanford University (1976), 40.

40   Farley Ward Grubb, "Immigration and Servitude in the Colony and Commonwealth of Pennsylvania: A Quantitative and Economic Analysis," Ph.D. dissertation, University of Chicago (1984), p. 175.

41   Farley Ward Grubb, "The Market for Indentured Immigrants: Evidence for the Efficiency of Forward-Labor Contracting in Philadelphia, 1745–1773," *Journal of Economic History*, 45 (1985), 859.

42   Grubb, "Redemptioner Emigration," 408.

43   Grubb, "Market for Indentured Immigrants," 862.

44   Grubb, "Immigration and Servitude," 171.

45   Grubb, "Market for Indentured Immigrants," 866–8.

46   Heavner, "Economic Aspects," 39.

47   Salinger, *To Serve Well*, 67.

48   Heavner, "Economic Aspects," 43.

49   *Londonderry Journal*, June 1, 1784. The letter was signed "your affectionate brother and sister, Neal M'Colgan & Grizey M'Colgan." The M'Colgans, still landless, were in Huntington, Pennsylvania in 1785.

50   I am indebted to her descendant Amma Chancellor Crum for a copy of this document.

51   *South Carolina Gazette and Country Journal*, May 6, 1766.

52   *Pennsylvania Gazette*, September 13, 1775.

53   Grubb, "Market for Indentured Immigrants," 858.

54   "Passenger Lists" (Cadwalader Collection, Series III, Box 78, Folder 18, HSP). *Record of indentures of individuals bound out as apprentices, servants, etc., and of German and other redemptioners in the office of the Mayor of the city of Philadelphia, October 3, 1771, to October 5, 1773, Pennsylvania German Society Proceedings and Addresses*, 16(1907), 58, 86, 100.

55   *Record of indentures*, 88.

56   *Record of indentures*, 261.

57   Heavner, "Economic Aspects," 21.

58   Heavner, "Economic Aspects," 50.
59   Deposition, September 5, 1770. Hubley Papers, MG 2, 2/23. Hanover
      Township Tax Lists (LCHS).
60   *Record of indentures,*104, 164 and *passim.*
61   *Pennsylvania Gazette*, November 10, 1773.
62   Heavner, "Economic Aspects," 78.
63   *Record of Indentures*, 86. *Pennsylvania Gazette*, November 24, 1773.
64   *Pennsylvania Gazette*, October 26, 1774.
65   *Pennsylvania Gazette*, February 9, 1774.

11

Non-Importation, Non-Exportation, and the Flaxseed Trade

"The country's growing rich"

Benjamin Fuller wrote in September 1770 to his friend John Scott, the surviving partner of Scott and McMichael, who was now at home in Armagh, about prices and trends since he left Philadelphia.

> The country's growing rich from the exorbitant prices that the produce of all kinds have borne for some years past. The last crop good, yet flour keeps up at 20 shillings and wheat in proportion. Fear seems to possess all lest the markets to the eastward should fail next spring. I take it that the calamities of poor Poland has been the true cause of enriching this country and whenever that kingdom recovers itself a change will certainly take place here. Luxury has greatly crept in among us – a small family that in your time could have subsisted genteelly on £300 per annum cannot now live in the same manner for £500 per annum.[1]

The years immediately following repeal of the Stamp Act were a time of economic slowdown, but from 1768 recession gave way to a general prosperity and rising expectations. The cost of living had not increased, rather the demand was for more consumer goods and a higher standard of living. The cost of textiles, which made up well over half the goods imported from Britain, had not risen and in many cases dropped through the 1760s and early 1770s, so higher prices for farm produce translated into greater buying power for Americans. Credit, which had been tight, loosened in 1768, reducing the pressure on merchants and shopkeepers. Prices for wheat, flour, and flaxseed kept rising and overseas demand remained high.[2] Political turmoil seemed at an end as well. Abel James, a Philadelphia Quaker merchant, believed that Americans in general, Pennsylvanians in particular, would never give up opposition to taxation by Parliament, "but matters are generally peaceably and Quietly conducted and abundant prosperity seems to attend this new World."[3]

It was an especially good time for merchants and ship-owners in the flaxseed trade. In 1768–72 they sent 233,065 bushels of flaxseed from the Middle Colonies. This was the single most important export to Ireland, earning more than £600,000 for ship-owners. This was greater than the shipping earnings for any other single commodity, except tobacco, and when merchant's profits, insurance and interest are added, more profitable than even the tobacco trade.[4] Higher prices meant higher commissions for the merchants who filled orders for seed and demand in Ulster showed no signs of slacking as prices soared. Flaxseed prices in 1768 ranged from 4/6 a bushel in October at the start of the season to 3/6 at its close.[5] More than 85,000 bushels of flaxseed were exported in 1768 with prices hovering around 4/– a bushel. William Glenholme was afraid these moderate prices caused too much seed to be shipped to Ireland for the market to absorb. The 1769 crop although smaller also sold in that price range, leaving none unsold by the following spring, but flaxseed began a steady upward climb in 1770.[6]

Flaxseed prices were high at the start of the 1770 season and kept rising. James Fullton reported to Hugh Orr in Boston in September that

> The price of flaxseed is not broke yet, But the price I expect will be 5/ to 5/6 to 6/6 and have Even Consulted Some Gentlemen Largely in the Shipping way of that article and they agree with my opinion in the price.[7]

Andrew Black, like Orr, sent New England flaxseed to Philadelphia to enjoy the rising market. Fullton assured him in October that at that moment "Flaxseed 6/ and from the Number of Shipping that's here for that article I make no Doubt but it will be 7/ to 7/6."[8] He was quite right in his estimate. Flaxseed reached

7/– late in November and 8/– in December.[9] Fullton was happy to announce, "I have sold your flaxseed at 7/6 p bushel, and I was the first in the City that got that price."[10] Philadelphia shipped 132,851 bushels of flaxseed in the 1770 season valued at £29,896, more than double the amount and value of the 1769 crop.[11]

The flaxseed crop of 1771 was late in coming to market, as usually happened when prices were rising. It reached 8/3 by December. Only 41,953 bushels went from Philadelphia that year. Philadelphia merchants expected flaxseed to be in great demand by the shipping season in 1772 with prices as high or higher than the previous crop. It reached 10/– a bushel in November and stayed at that level through December. Despite the record prices, Philadelphia shippers sent 73,469 bushels to Ireland that year, far less than in 1770, but at £34,898 worth considerably more than that year's larger shipment.[12] The situation looked even better for the 1773 season, as another Philadelphia seed buyer wrote to a Newport merchant who supplied him with Rhode Island flaxseed:

> We have reason to believe Flaxseed will bear as good a price this year as it did last, for they have none of the old seed left on hand in Ireland; but there is no article comes to this Market so fluctuating as that and therefore there is no forming a Judgment of the price, for we have known a difference of 1/6 to 2/– per bushel in the course of two or three days.[13]

Benjamin Fuller told John Scott of the high prices demanded for flour and wheat when he wrote him in September 1770. "I have not been concerned in any adventure to Ireland in flour, but am afraid too much in Flaxseed." Wheat was quoted at 6/1 a bushel, but, he said, "The farmers are rich and loath to part with it at that, and the millers are afraid to give it, for any large quantity. I think it must be lower, the crop being great and good."[14] His prediction was wrong as prices continued to rise. The prices paid for wheat, flour, and bread rose steadily from 1764 through 1768, but dipped again in 1769, although still above 1764 levels. After that all three began an upward climb that reached a peak in 1772 with the highest prices at any time in the Colonial period. Yorkshireman William Pollard wrote in December 1772, "Our produce has advanced for several years past and is now really very high." He ascribed these record grain prices to "the demand from Lisbon and Cadiz and some other parts of Europe, who formerly had their supplies chiefly from Europe." Prices fell only modestly in 1773 and again in 1774.[15]

These years of prosperity and creeping luxury played out against a background of resistance to efforts to regulate the Atlantic economy from Westminster and to tax a few consumer goods, with "no taxation without representation" as the rallying cry. The generally popular policy of boycotting British goods to secure repeal of the Stamp Act proved successful in 1766. For their own reasons, since credit at home was constricted, British merchants were more reluctant to send goods to America on long-term credit. The call to renew non-importation as a response to the Townshend Revenue Acts of 1767 came at a time when business was stagnant, prices for American produce low, and British merchants were calling in overdue accounts. Merchants in the Colonies hesitated and opted for voluntary agreements to refrain from ordering their usual spring and fall goods. Philadelphia followed the example of Boston and New York in March 1769 and adopted a full-fledged non-importation agreement, the only exceptions being provisions and linens from Ireland.[16] Benjamin Fuller found this exception a hollow concession.

> The late resolutions of the Merchants of this City not to import any Goods from Great Britain until the American Grievances are redress'd, puts it out of my power to order any Linens this year by the way of Liverpool; the bounty is a considerable thing and will more than pay all charges in getting them to this Market.[17]

This second experiment with boycotting British manufactures soon emptied shelves and temporarily raised prices: "The stoppage of Goods from Great Britain has naturally caused a scarcity and an advance in price, it's at present doubled."[18] But it was not in effect long enough, barely eight months, to make a real difference.

The non-importation agreements of the different American Colonies were a dead letter by the late summer of 1770, as one after another broke ranks in response to repeal of all but the tax on tea. "I cannot think the Merchants in general can be so lost to themselves & the Trade of this province," Fuller wrote Scott, "as to sit tamely quiet, while all the provinces round are importing large Quantitys, particularly New York, who has broke through the non-importation agreement & will have goods out this fall." Scott was himself preparing to ship Irish linens to Philadelphia. Fuller approved of his "Linen Scheme."[19] Andrew Caldwell and Joseph Wilson and William West both advertised Irish linens received from Dublin, thus staying within the terms of the agreement.[20] Anticipating non-importation would soon be abandoned, Fuller and his colleagues in the flaxseed trade were ordering linens themselves, now to be sent by way of Liverpool to earn the bounty that would pay shipping costs. He asked his brother Joseph Fuller in Cork to purchase linens in Dublin "for Acct. of Fuller, Fisher, Donaldson & Keith" and have them "sent to Hugh Pringle Liverpool to recover the bounty."[21] He also instructed his brother-in-law Joshua Ashton to send linens from Dublin to William Halliday & Co., Liverpool "and thence to New York c/o Mr. Smith Ramage or to Baltimore c/o Messrs Samuel & Samuel Carsan."[22] Fuller also reminded Joseph that "Woollen goods of most kinds wou'd bring a very considerable profit, provided the Colours be good."[23]

They were not alone in ordering British goods. Randle Mitchell, for instance, left "this province for Ireland" in November 1770 and was in England and Ireland that winter, where he "purchased the goods at the manufacturers himself"[24] The value of imports in 1771 exceeded those of any previous year, stimulating linen drapers in Ulster and Scotland and other British manufacturers to do everything possible to increase production. It did not take long for merchants to complain of the overabundance of goods left unsold in shops and warehouses, but their orders for 1772 were at nearly the same rate, adding to the glut of goods on the American market and the debts incurred by the merchants who had imported them. William Pollard, who represented Yorkshire clothiers in Philadelphia, observed in July 1772:

> Trade was never in such a situation here as at present. The city and country are glutted with every kind of goods and thousands of pounds worth are selling weekly at the different vendues for much less than they cost; and this has been the practice

now for near two years and perhaps may continue for 18 months or two years more, in which time I cannot think but many must fall. And this probably may affect some houses on your side the water, which is the reason I mention it, that you may be on your guard with your London, Liverpool, or Bristol friends.[25]

In retrospect, 1771 marked the peak of a long rise of economic activity. "All the indications of over-trading were present. Indeed, the whole economy was caught up in the optimism of the times."[26] For several years easy credit allowed dry goods merchants in the American Colonies, British iron manufacturers and canal promoters, titled investors in overseas land speculations, and the fabled East India Company to expand their enterprises with no fear of the future. The failure of Fordyce and Company, London bankers, a few days before Pollard warned of the possible effect of the glut of goods in Pennsylvania, brought down the whole house of cards. Before long British merchants were dunning their American customers for immediate payment.[27] Within a few more days, Douglas, Heron and Company, commonly known as the Ayr Bank, also failed with even more dire consequences, particularly for the linen industry.[28]

The resulting credit stringency affected the East India Company in ways that would have unanticipated results. The Bank of England curtailed its regular advances to the Company and called for repayment of long outstanding debts. By July 1772 the Company, "overwhelmed with debt and burdened with the cost of a disastrous war against Hyder Ali," could not meet its obligations to its creditors. Parliament voted a one-time loan of £1.4 million, but could do no more for it financially. Instead, they offered concessions with regard to the export of tea to Ireland and to the American Colonies. The Tea Act, adopted in May 1773, gave the East India Company a drawback or refund of all duties paid on any tea above the quantity of ten million pounds in their warehouses and authorized its direct exportation to Ireland and to the American Colonies under special license. Unwittingly they set the stage for a new round of confrontation.[29]

"The prospect is Dismal"

The credit crisis brought on the failure of firms in the flaxseed trade on both sides of the Atlantic. Too sanguine expectations of the market for British goods ruined many. Walter and Bartles Shee went bankrupt that summer. William West, Thomas Barclay (of Carsan, Barclay and Mitchell), and John Gibson acted for their creditors, while Randle Mitchell, Benjamin Fuller and John Pringle were still endeavouring to settle the affairs of Orr, Dunlope and Glenholme. [30] Randle Mitchell himself announced his intention to close his trade and was soon selling off his assets in different Pennsylvania towns.[31] His brother John was also in difficulties, as Benjamin Fuller wrote to a mutual friend:

> I make no doubt but you will have heard that our friend Jack Mitchell has been obliged to stop, it was an act of his own before his affairs should become desperate, and deserves its merit. He very imprudently greatly over imported himself, in proportion to his original capital.[32]

The Caldwells in Londonderry and in Philadelphia had their own financial problems. William and Richard Caldwell had been selling off some of their ships and other assets to stave off bankruptcy, but they were finished by 1774 and the *Philadelphia* was sold at auction to benefit the creditors.[33] James Caldwell, newly married to Sally Mitchell in September 1773, was doing well in the shipping business and the flaxseed trade. He returned to Derry early in 1775 and arranged for his brother Richard, his family, and his clerk George McConnell, to sail to Dominica to make a fresh start, while James went to Philadelphia to rejoin his family.[34] Samuel Caldwell, another cousin, was still in partnership with James Mease from Strabane. Andrew Caldwell and Joseph Wilson dissolved their partnership in 1773, each continuing in business on his own.[35] Samuel Carsan and his long-time partners Thomas Barclay and William Mitchell had also separated by the 1773 flaxseed shipping season, although they continued to work closely together, for example as agents for the same ships.[36] Samuel Purviance, Sr. continued in business with his son John, but he was retired and living in New Jersey later that year.[37] Hugh Donaldson was in Belfast on a buying trip when he died suddenly in October 1773. His family remained in Philadelphia, so his executors sold his property near Glenarm.[38]

The 1773 flaxseed shipping season was slow in starting, although supplies were good and prices high. One Philadelphia buyer reported to a correspondent in Newport, "We find that Flaxseed is pretty plenty in this part of the Country and those that have taken it in within twenty or thirty Miles of the City having given a Dollar to Eight Shillings." Two weeks later, flaxseed was selling at 9/– to 9/6, "tho no great quantity has yet come to town nor has the Spirit of buying yet caught fast hold of the Purchasers." He decided to hold back the Rhode Island flaxseed, "rather than sell at the price going now which is about 9/3 we will put it in Store a few days," to see if prices would rise, "tho it seems to be the Opinion of many people that it will not be higher this year."[39]

Early in December Thomas Wharton reported "We have the Flaxseed still by us as 9/6 or 9/7 is the highest we have been offered, and it is now rather slack as considerable quantitys are in Town for sale." He added that Sam Carsan had already received his customary cargo of Rhode Island flaxseed. With a good supply on hand, the market price slipped. "Seed has been sold within a few days as low as 8/6 some parcels of very good at 9/ and there is a great deal in the Town unsold." By the end of December it was over.

> Our Navigation is now interrupted by the Ice so that there is little expectation of any more Seed coming to Market this Season, but the quantity already shipt from hence will exceed the quantity exported last year, near 2000 hhds it is expected.[40]

Speculators, like Stocker and Wharton, had to scramble to find anyone able to take their flaxseed. Stocker and Wharton found a buyer for Champlin's seed or at least someone willing to take it on consignment. Samuel Jackson and his partner John Bayard took it off their hands. "We had agreed with Bayard, Jackson & Co., Owners of the Snow *Dickinson* to ship the Seed in that Vessel, or they to give the price of 8/9 per bushel if you had rather sell than ship it." The plan was "for the Vessel first to go to the Harbour of Loughsweilly," where it was "addressed to Mr. Redman

Conyngham of the House of Conyngham and Nisbitt of this city, and of equal credit to any on the Continent." The snow *Dickinson* cleared for Letterkenny, County Donegal at the end of February.[41]

"Allow poor Ireland some Flaxseed"

Passage of the Tea Act was noted in the Philadelphia papers without comment, but the announcement that 600 chests of tea would soon be on their way to the Colonies caused a furore. Ships carrying East India Company tea sailed from England in the first weeks of autumn. They had scarcely put to sea when a meeting of Philadelphia merchants passed resolutions condemning the duty on tea as "a tax on the Americans, or levying contributions on them without their consent" and the East India Company scheme as "a violent attack on the liberties of America."[42] Benjamin Fuller wrote:

> The East India Company's attempt to send Tea to America has made a great bustle among us, and you may depend on what I say, that if it comes here, it will not be suffered to be landed, on any terms whatsoever, but a repeal of the Duty.[43]

Several prominent Philadelphia merchants, notably Thomas Wharton and the firm of Abel James and Henry Drinker, had readily agreed to act as agents for the East India Company, but they were pressured to resign their charge.[44] In Philadelphia, as in New York, Charleston, and Boston, there was little to do but await the tea ships. The arrival of a ship from London caused a stir early in December, until it was ascertained that her cargo included no chests of tea. When the tea ship *Polly* finally came up the Delaware on Christmas Day, Thomas Wharton and other merchants found a proper supply of necessaries and fresh provisions, advanced cash to Captain Ayres to meet other expenses and dispatched the ship back to London with all her cargo still on board.[45] The speed with which the Philadelphia consignees declined delivery of their goods and provided Ayres with whatever he needed defused the crisis and sent the *Polly* on its way before ice closed the port. In contrast, a lengthy impasse in Boston was only ended when radicals, thinly disguised as Mohawks, boarded the tea ships and threw the tea into the harbour. This wanton destruction of private property alienated many Americans, others rallied to the Bostonians.[46]

The draconian measures adopted by the British Parliament in response to the Boston Tea Party did more to unify Americans than any radical could have hoped. Closing the port of Boston and placing Massachusetts under martial law caused outrage in Ulster as in the Colonies. Back in Belfast Samuel Brown remained a faithful friend of America. He wrote to a business associate in Philadelphia:

> The people in America must be in great confusion now on Acct of the Boston Port Bill. I sincerely wish the Americans may make a steady firm & unanimous stand for their Libertys, & get the better of a corrupt Tyranical Ministry.

Brown was particularly unhappy with the generous provisions of the Quebec Act, passed the same day, which he saw as "establishing Popery in Canada." With talk of renewed non-importation and even non-exportation in the air, Brown was concerned for Ireland's dependence on the flaxseed trade, adding "I hope if you come to Resolutions not to export goods, you will allow poor Ireland some Flaxseed, or they wont be able to pay their passages to go to you."[47]

Ulster Presbyterians had their own version of taxation without representation. Church of Ireland vestries had substantial civil duties, including levying taxes (cess) for construction of roads and other local improvements. The Irish Parliament decided in 1774 that only Anglicans could vote in vestry elections, depriving dissenters of their traditional rights. This grievance gave them greater empathy with their cousins across the Atlantic.[48] A letter from Derry published in the *Maryland Gazette* reported its effect on emigration:

> You cannot conceive the ferment the Presbyterians are in on account of the late act. Multitudes are daily arriving here to go to America. There are five large ships in this port, ready to sail, each of which will take at least 500 passengers which will amount to 2,500 souls of the most industrious people in the kingdom.[49]

News of Parliament's action did not reach the American Colonies until May and was met by a still-divided business community. Paul Revere carried an appeal from Boston to each of the Colonies to stand with them by cutting off both importation from and exportation to Great Britain and the West Indies. "Some of our warm politicians talk of again entering into a non-importation agreement," Thomas Wharton wrote, "but this I am satisfied they cannot effect, as our merchants are dissatisfied with the former conduct of the Bostonians."[50] Philadelphia dry goods merchants did not want to again go the non-importation route that led to nowhere. The radicals, led by Charles Thomson from Maghera, County Londonderry, wanted to take an immediate stand by adopting resolves. A general meeting two days later allowed Thomson to put the radical case for non-importation and non-exportation, but John Dickinson, Thomas Wharton and Joseph Reed successfully argued against any precipitate action and Philadelphia refused Boston's invitation. Instead, they proposed each city and county choose delegates to a general meeting to deal with the crisis. They did appoint Thomas Barclay, John Maxwell Nesbitt and others to a committee to correspond with the other Colonies.[51] Dickinson sent a report of the Philadelphia action to Dr. John Stevenson and Samuel Purviance, Jr. in Baltimore.[52] Purviance and William Lux led the Sons of Liberty in Baltimore and Sam Adams sent them Boston's plea to adopt strong measures in responding to the Intolerable Acts. Baltimore did not go beyond appointing Purviance and William Buchanan to correspond with Annapolis merchants on the eve of their meeting.[53]

A meeting at Annapolis, Maryland, on May 25, 1774 proposed non-importation and non-exportation as well as a moratorium on law suits by creditors in Great Britain. Unanimity was essential, they knew from experience, if such a policy were to succeed. The tobacco colonies would have to agree to halt exportation as well as importation and this would mean the destruction of their economy. They waited on Virginia's decision. A week later delegates to a Baltimore County meeting, including Samuel Purviance, Jr., called for a general meeting of all Maryland counties at Annapolis to decide on a course of action. They did name a committee of correspondence, among them Purviance, Buchanan, John Smith,

William Spear, and William Smith. As he had as a member of the Presbyterian Committee, Samuel Purviance, Jr. proved a committee in himself, firing off letters to Alexandria, Norfolk and Portsmouth, Virginia.[54]

The Virginia House of Burgesses had been prorogued by the governor, but those delegates who still remained in Williamsburg met at the Raleigh Tavern to adopt resolves calling for election of delegates to a provincial meeting in August and for a general meeting later of delegates from all the Colonies.[55] What was initially put forward by conservatives as an alternative to precipitous action by their more radical brethren turned out to be by far the more radical course. If a merchant chose to cancel his orders for fall goods from Liverpool and Manchester, that was surely his prerogative. He broke no laws. To call for an elected assembly to set policy for the colony or for all the colonies, without reference to governor or council, was sailing close to the wind of revolution.

Samuel and Robert Purviance wrote to a friend in Boston bringing him up to date on the situation in Maryland since the Baltimore County meeting:

> We transmitted you a copy of the resolution entered into by the people of this county. Since which, similar resolves have been adopted, in several other counties, and a general congress of the whole province, is to be held the 22nd inst. at Annapolis, to consider in a united manner, the case of our suffering brethren of Boston; all parts of this province discover the most forward zeal in the cause – and we sincerely wish Philadelphia was equally disposed to embark in the matter.[56]

Philadelphia conservatives had brushed aside demands for non-importation and shifted the initiative to Governor Penn to call a session of the Pennsylvania Assembly to deal with the crisis and await a general congress of all the American Colonies. For different reasons, Penn summoned a special session. It was understood it would select delegates to a Continental Congress. The Philadelphia committee then invited county committees to send delegates to a meeting in Philadelphia in July to instruct those delegates in how they should vote. Pennsylvania was now on board. Charles

Thomson wrote Purviance that "Our counties are in motion, Lancaster and Chester have met."[57]

With the port of Boston closed, many people there who depended on commerce for their livelihood were in distress. William Buchanan and Samuel Purviance, Jr. were prepared to help them.

> A proposal has been made by some gentlemen of Chestertown, in this colony, to open a subscription for support of the poor inhabitants of your town, who may be most immediately distressed by the stagnation of business. Some of us have had the same object in contemplation, and determine to propose it to the general congress of deputies for this province, which, we doubt not, will be generally adopted.[58]

Purviance then took charge of the collection of relief goods for Boston.

> Samuel and Robert Purviance, Baltimore Town, will receive into their stores at this place, and the charge of shipping off, (without any expence), all contributions made in any kind of provisions or grain, for the relief of the distressed inhabitants of Boston, either by the people of this, or any county in the province of Maryland, or the western counties of Pennsylvania.[59]

From New Hampshire to Georgia county meetings and provincial congresses adopted resolutions calling on their delegates to the upcoming Continental Congress to vote for non-importation and non-exportation and advocating any number of plans for greater self-sufficiency at home. On September 5, 1774 the delegates assembled in Philadelphia to begin their deliberations. Their meeting cast a pall of uncertainty over the flaxseed season then about to begin.

Stocker and Wharton were certain flaxseed "will bear as good a price here as it did the last year," since in Pennsylvania and Maryland "the Crop falls short of the last year." They were hopeful that it could still be shipped to the Irish market, but were in the dark as to what action might be taken.

> We can expect no kind of information from the Delegates in
> Congress as they are sworn to Secresy ... We however can
> hardly think that a Non Exportation can take place to Ireland,
> unless it becomes general, that is an intire Suspension of
> Trade.[60]

The initial reports confirmed their optimism. A resolution in
Congress in September was merely to "Request merchants and others in the several Colonies, not to send to Great Britain any orders
for goods, and to direct the execution of orders already sent to be
delayed or suspended."[61] The final action taken by the Continental
Congress in October did not exempt Ireland, but at least they postponed non-exportation for a year.

> Flaxseed is not prohibited to be sent to Ireland, so that we
> hope you have made tolerable progress in the purchase of that
> article. ... Unless the Acts of Parliament be repealed by the
> 10th of September next a Non Exportation is then to take
> place to Great Britain, Ireland and the West Indies[62]

The Continental Congress adopted a resolution on October 22,
1774:

> That from and after the first day of December next, we will
> not import into British America from Great Britain, or
> Ireland, any goods, wares, or merchandise whatsoever. The
> earnest desire we have not to injure our fellow-subjects in
> Great Britain, Ireland, or the West Indies, induces us to sus-
> pend a non-exportation, until the tenth day of September
> 1775.[63]

Despite earlier uncertainty, flaxseed prices started high and continued to rise through the buying season. "It is selling here in small
parcels at 11/6, and have no doubt of its obtaining 12/ and
upwards for any tolerable quantitys," Stocker and Wharton wrote
their Rhode Island supplier.[64] Flaxseed was quoted at 12/– a bushel
the first week of November, 13/– a week later, 13/6 the following
week and remained above 13/– during December.[65] Benjamin
Fuller shipped flaxseed to his brother in Cork and other Irish correspondents. Fuller wrote his brother-in-law James Doyle that "the

market is now over – the Crop was very Short and the Average price about £5 Currency pr hhd."[66] Stocker and Wharton were fearful prices might have been too high that season.

> We are not so sanguine in our expectations from the Irish market as you are. They can be supplied from Holland at about 70/ to 80/ [per hogshead], and will no doubt when they find there is a scarcity in America send to Holland for what they may want. If they have not time to do this we think it will be high – tho not so much as you expect.[67]

The delay in implementing non-exportation allowed another year's crop of tobacco, hemp and indigo to be shipped to the British Isles. In September 1775, as the deadline loomed, Glasgow and Whitehaven factors hastened to get the last hogsheads of Maryland or Virginia tobacco on shipboard so the vessels could clear customs in time. There was no such mad rush for the flaxseed crop which would not come to market that early. With the sailing of the last of the flaxseed ships in January 1775 for Newry and Londonderry the trade that had bridged the Atlantic for so many years came to an end – at least for the present.

Notes

1   Benjamin Fuller to John Scott, September 5, 1770 (Benjamin Fuller Letter
    Book, HSP).

2   Marc Egnal, *New World Economies: The Growth of the Thirteen Colonies
    and Early Canada* (Oxford, 1998), 63–6, 76. On the 1766–8 slump,
    Bezanson *et al.*, *Prices in Colonial Pennsylvania*, 308.

3   Abel James to ----, September 22, 1772, (Abel James Letter Book, HSP, as
    quoted in Jensen, *Maritime Commerce*, 196.

4   Gary M. Walton and James F. Shepherd, *The Economic Rise of Early America*
    (Cambridge, 1979), 82–3.

5   *Pennsylvania Journal*, October 20, 1768, November 3, 1768, November 17,
    1768, December 1, 1768, December 15, 1768, January 5, 1769, February
    9, 1769, March 2, 1769.

6   William Glenholme to Lane, Benson and Vaughan, January 2, 1769 (HSP).
    Prices in 1769 ranged from 4/- to 4/6. *Pennsylvania Journal*, October 19,
    1769, November 2, 1769, November 16, 1769, November 23, 1769,
    December 14, 1769, December 28, 1769, March 8, 1770. Bezanson *et al*,
    Prices in Colonial Pennsylvania, 71–2.

7   James Fullton to Hugh Orr, September 25, 1770 (Fullton Letter Book
    (typescript), LCHS).

8   James Fullton to Andrew Black, October 23, 1770 (Fullton Letter Book
    (typescript), LCHS).

9   *Pennsylvania Journal*, October 18, 1770, October 25, 1770, November 8,
    1770, November 22, 1770, December 6, 1770, December 13, 1770,
    December 20, 1770, December 27, 1770.

10 James Fullton to Andrew Black, December 4, 1770 (Fullton Letter Book
    (typescript), LCHS).

11 Jensen, *Maritime Commerce*, 296.

12 Bezanson estimated 110,000 bushels in 1771. Jensen's much lower figure is
    drawn from the Customs House records in PRO. Bezanson *et al.*, *Prices in
    Colonial Pennsylvania*, 72. Jensen, *Maritime Commerce*, 296.

13 Stocker and Wharton to Christopher Champlin, August 6, 1773,
    Massachusetts Historical Society Collections, 69(1914), 449.

14 Benjamin Fuller to John Scott, September 5, 1770 (Benjamin Fuller Letter
    Book, HSP).

15 Bezanson *et al.*, *Prices in Colonial Pennsylvania*, 44–9. Egnal, *New World
    Economies*, 63.

16 Jensen, *Maritime Commerce*, 179–80.

17 Benjamin Fuller to Joseph Fuller, April 28, 1769 (Benjamin Fuller Letter Book,
    HSP).

18 Benjamin Fuller to John Scott, December 12, 1769 (Benjamin Fuller Letter
    Book, HSP).

19 Benjamin Fuller to John Scott, September 5, 1770 (Benjamin Fuller Letter
    Book, HSP)

20 *Pennsylvania Chronicle*, December 10, 1770, January 2, 1771.

21 His associates are Samuel Fisher and Joseph Donaldson, Philadelphia

merchants, and Captain William Keith. Benjamin Fuller to Joseph Fuller, June 9, 1770 (Benjamin Fuller Letter Book, HSP).

22   Benjamin Fuller to Joshua Ashton, June 12, 1770 (Benjamin Fuller Letter Book, HSP).

23   Benjamin Fuller to Joseph Fuller, June 25, 1770 (Benjamin Fuller Letter Book, HSP).

24   *Pennsylvania Gazette*, October 18, 1770, December 27, 1770. *Pennsylvania Chronicle*, May 13, 1771.

25   William Pollard to John Woolmer, July 1, 1772 (William Pollard Letter Book, HSP). Bezanson *et al*, *Prices in Colonial Pennsylvania*, 284–6.

26   Henry Hamilton, "The Failure of the Ayr Bank," *Economic History Review*, 8(1956), 410.

27   Richard B. Sheridan, "The British Credit Crisis of 1772 and the American Colonies," *Journal of Economic History*, 20(1960), 162–6.

28   Hamilton, "Ayr Bank," 413–14. Douglas, Heron and Co. had branches in Dumfries and Edinburgh and, before the crash, sold Scotch linens and English woollens in their Philadelphia store. *Pennsylvania Chronicle*, October 7, 1771.

29   Sheridan, "Credit Crisis," 172. Gipson, *Coming of the Revolution*, 217–8.

30   *Pennsylvania Journal*, August 4, 1773, August 11, 1773.

31   *Pennsylvania Journal*, September 22, 1773, November 10, 1773.

32   Fuller advised Stocker, who was then in England, to remain there as he, too, faced bankruptcy at home. Benjamin Fuller to Anthony Stocker, November 15, 1773 (Benjamin Fuller Letter Book, HSP).

33   *Londonderry Journal*, April 29, 1774, June 10, 1774.

34   Richard Caldwell died in Dominica in 1779. James Caldwell died in Philadelphia in 1783. John Caldwell, "Memoir," 21, 26 (typescript, PRONI). *Pennsylvania Journal*, August 18, 1773.

35   Joseph Wilson, another Caldwell cousin, was later U.S. Consul at Dublin, dying there in 1809. *Pennsylvania Journal*, August 11, 1773.

36   *Pennsylvania Journal*, August 25, 1773, November 17, 1773.

37   *Pennsylvania Journal*, September 1, 1773, September 29, 1773, November 17, 1773.

38   *Belfast News Letter*, September 16, 1774. *Pennsylvania Journal*, December 22, 1773.

39   Stocker and Wharton to Christopher Champlin, November 4, 1773, November 20, 1773, November 23, 1773, *Massachusetts Historical Society Collections*, 69(1914), 459, 461, 464. Flaxseed was quoted at 8/– a bushel in October and early November, rising rapidly to 9/6 later in November and December. *Pennsylvania Journal*, October 27, 1773, November 5, 1773, November 24, 1773, December 1, 1773.

40   Stocker and Wharton to Christopher Champlin, December 10, 1773, December 17, 1773, December 30, 1773, *Massachusetts Historical Society Collections*, 69(1914), 471–5.

41   Stocker and Wharton to Christopher Champlin, January 18, 1774, February 9, 1774, *Massachusetts Historical Society Collections*, 69(1914), 477, 482. *Pennsylvania Gazette*, March 2, 1774.

42   *Pennsylvania Gazette*, July 14, 1773, September 29, 1773, October 20, 1773.

43   Benjamin Fuller to Anthony Stocker, November 15, 1773 (Benjamin Fuller
      Letter Book, HSP).

44   Frederick D. Stone, "How the Landing of Tea Was Opposed in Philadelphia,"
      PMHB, 15(1891), 385–94.

45   *Pennsylvania Gazette*, December 8, 1773, December 29, 1773. *Pennsylvania
      Journal*, December 8, 1773, December 29, 1773. Thomas Wharton to
      Thomas Walpole, December 29, 1773, to Samuel Wharton, January 1,
      1774, in *PMHB*, 33(1909), 321–4.

46   Gipson, *Coming of the Revolution*, 220.

47   Samuel Brown to James Hunter, August 30, 1774, in *PMHB*, 28(1902), 104–05.

48   Vincent Morley, *Irish Opinion and the American Revolution, 1760–1783*
      (Cambridge, 2002), 83.

49   "A Letter from Derry, in Ireland, June 14, 1774," in *Maryland Gazette*,
      September 8, 1774.

50   Thomas Wharton to Samuel Wharton, May 17, 1774, *PMHB*, 33(1909), 335.

51   Thomas Wharton to Thomas Walpole, May 31, 1774, *PMHB*, 33(1909),
      336–9. *Pennsylvania Gazette*, May 18, 1774, May 25, 1774. Purviance,
      Narrative, 115.

52   Purviance, *Narrative*, 112.

53   Purviance, *Narrative*, 115.

54   This last provision was repudiated by a long list of participants in the meeting.
      Maryland Gazette, June 2, 1774, June 9, 1774. *Pennsylvania Gazette*, June 8,
      1774. Purviance, *Narrative*, 12–13, 117–9, 130–32.

55   Kate Mason Rowland, *The Life of George Mason 1725-1792* (New York, Russell
      & Russel, 1964), vol. 1, 167-71.

56   Samuel and Robert Purviance to Jeremiah Lee, June 11, 1774, in Purviance,
      Narrative, 148–9.

57   Charles Thomson to Samuel Purviance, Jr., June 24, 1774, in Purviance,
      Narrative, 159–61.

58   William Buchanan and Samuel Purviance, Jr. to the Boston Committee, June
      13, 1774, in Purviance, *Narrative*, 149–50.

59   *Pennsylvania Gazette*, August 3, 1774. *Pennsylvania Journal*, August 10, 1774.

60   Stocker and Wharton to Christopher Champlin, September 8, 1774,
      Massachusetts Historical Society Collections, 69(1914), 512.

61   *Maryland Gazette*, September 29, 1774.

62   Stocker and Wharton to Christopher Champlin, October 25, 1774,
      Massachusetts Historical Society Collections, 69(1914), 517.

63   Worthington C. Ford, ed., *Journals of the Continental Congress* (Washington,
      1904,) I, 75.

64   Stocker and Wharton to Christopher Champlin, November 4, 1774,
      Massachusetts Historical Society Collections, 69(1914), 520.

65   *Pennsylvania Journal*, November 9, 1774, November 16, 1774, November 23,
      1774, December 7, 1774.

66   Benjamin Fuller to James Doyle, December 23, 1774. Benjamin Fuller to
      Joseph Fuller, February 2, 1775 (Benjamin Fuller Letter Book, HSP).

67   Stocker and Wharton to Christopher Champlin, December 5, 1774,
      Massachusetts Historical Society Collections, 69(1914), 522.

Bibliography

Manuscripts

Abercorn Papers, D623, PRONI.

John Cameron Ledger 1767–70, Wistar Papers, HSP.

Conolly Papers, T2825, PRONI.

John Caldwell, "Particulars of History of a North County Irish Family," T/3541/5/3, PRONI.

Daniel Clark Letter Book 1759–62, HSP.

Davey and Carsan Letterbook, LC.

John Elder Papers, Historical Society of Dauphin County, Harrisburg, PA.

Benjamin Fuller Letter Book 1762–74, HSP.

James Fullton Letter Book, LCHS.

James Fullton Papers, HSYC.

Grubb Papes, HSP.

Hubley Papers, LCHS.

Lutwidge Letter Book, Cumbria Record Office, Whitehaven, England.

McAllister Papers, MG–81, PSA.

William McCord Papers, MG–2, PSA.

Minutes of the Corporation for the Relief of Poor and Distressed Presbyterian Ministers, PHS.

John Mitchell Papers, MG–92, PSA.

[John Montgomery], "Leger 3 1765–1771," Joseph Kent Collection, MS 092–31, Virginia Polytechnic Institute and University, Blacksburg, VA.

Murray of Broughton Papers, D/2860, PRONI.

Mussenden Papers, D/354, PRONI.

Naval Officers Returns, Port of New York, CO/5/114/111, PRO, Reel 46, British MSS., Manuscript Division, LC.

Orr, Dunlope and Glenholme Letter Book, HSP.

"Passenger Lists," Cadwalader Collection, Series III, Box 78, Folder 18, HSP.

William Pollard Letter Book 1772–74, HSP.

Preston Papers, 1QQ2, Draper Collection, Historical Society of Wisconsin, Madison, WI.

Rhea Family Papers, Tennessee State Library, Nashville, TN.

Shippen Papers, HSP.

Woolsey and Salmon Letterbook, Peter Force Collection, 8D/189, LC.

Paul Zantzinger Ledger, MG–2, PSA.

Dissertations and Unpublished Papers

Laura L. Becker, "The American Revolution as a Community Experience: A Case Study of Reading, Pennsylvania," Ph.D. dissertation, University of Pennsylvania (1978).

Paul Erb Doutrich, "The Evolution of an Early American Town: Yorktown, Pennsylvania 1740–1790," Ph.D. dissertation, University of Kentucky (1985).

Marc Egnal, "The Pennsylvania Economy, 1748–1762: An Analysis of Short-Run Fluctuations in the Context of Long-Run Changes in the Atlantic Trading Community," Ph.D. dissertation, University of Wisconsin (1974).

Norman E. Gamble, "The Business Community and Trade of Belfast 1767–1800," Ph.D. dissertation, University of Dublin (1978).

Farley Ward Grubb, "Immigration and Servitude in the Colony and Commonwealth of Pennsylvania: A Quantitative and Economic Analysis," Ph.D. dissertation, University of Chicago (1984).

Robert Owen Heavner, "Economic Aspects of Indentured Servitude in Colonial Pennsylvania," Ph.D. dissertation, Stanford University (1976).

John W. McConaghy, "Thomas Greer of Dungannon 1724–1808 Quaker Linen Merchant," Ph.D. dissertation, Queens University Belfast (1979).

Robert D. Mitchell, "The Upper Shenandoah Valley of Virginia During the Eighteenth Century: A Study in Historical Geography," Ph.D. dissertation, University of Wisconsin (1969).

Michelle M. Mormul, "Circle of Linen and Flaxseed Trade across the North Atlantic, 1765 to 1815," unpublished paper presented at the Fourth Scotch-Irish Identity Symposium, Philadelphia, June 30, 2007.

Robert F. Oaks, "Philadelphia Merchants and the American Revolution 1765–1776," Ph.D. dissertation, University of Southern California (1970).

Judith Anne Ridner, "A Handsomely Improved Place: Economic, Social, and Gender Role Development in a Backcountry Town, Carlisle, Pennsylvania, 1750–1815," Ph.D. dissertation, College of William and Mary (1994).

Emily Moberg Robinson, "The Covenanter Diaspora: Presbyterian Rebellion in the Atlantic World," unpublished paper presented at the Irish Atlantic conference, College of Charleston, Charleston, SC, March 1, 2007.

LeRoy James Votto, "Social Dynamism in a Boom Town: The Scots-Irish in Baltimore 1760 to 1790," MA thesis, University of Virginia (1969).

Paul Kent Walker, "The Baltimore Community and the American Revolution: A Study in Urban Development 1763–1783," Ph.D. dissertation, University of North Carolina (1973).

Books

Jean Agnew, *Belfast Merchant Families in the Seventeenth Century*. Dublin: Four Courts Press, 1996.

Donald H. Akenson, *Between Two Revolutions: Islandmagee, Co. Antrim*. Hamden, CN: Archon Books, 1979.

John Richard Alden, *General Gage in America*. Baton Rouge, LA: Louisiana State University Press, 1948.

Charles M. Andrews, *The Colonial Period of American History*. New Haven, CN: Yale University Press, 1938, 1964.

Maurice W. Armstrong, Lefferts A. Loetscher, and Charles A. Anderson, eds., *The Presbyterian Enterprise: Sources of American Presbyterian History*. Philadelphia: Presbyterian Historical Society, 1956.

Bernard Bailyn, *Atlantic History: Concept and Contours*. Cambridge, MA: Harvard University Press, 2005.

Carl L. Becker, *The History of Political Parties in the Province of New York, 1760–1776*. Madison, WI: , 1960.

J. V. Beckett, *Coal and Tobacco: The Lowthers and the Economic Development of West Cumberland*. Cambridge: Cambridge University Press, 1981.

Anne Bezanson, Robert D. Gray and Miriam Hussey, *Prices in Colonial Pennsylvania*. Philadelphia: University of Pennsylvania Press, 1935.

Francis Joseph Bigger, *The Ulster Land War of 1770*. Dublin: Sealy, Bryers and Walker, 1910.

Tyler Blethen and Curtis Wood, eds., *Ulster and North America: Transatlantic Perspectives on the Scotch-Irish*. Tuscaloosa, AL: University of Alabama Press, 1997.

T. H. Breen, *The Marketplace of Revolution: How Consumer Politics Shaped American Independence*. New York: Oxford University Press, 2004.

John Brewer and Roy Porter, eds., *Consumption and the World of Goods*. London: Routledge, 1994.

Maurice Bric, *Ireland, Philadelphia and the Re-invention of America, 1760-1800*. Dublin: Four Courts Press, 2008.

Carl Bridenbaugh, ed., *Gentleman's Progress: The Itinerarium of Dr. Alexander Hamilton, 1744*. Chapel Hill, NC: University of North Carolina Press, 1948.

Carl Bridenbaugh, *Mitre and Sceptre: Transatlantic Faiths, Ideas, Personalities and Politics 1689–1775*. Oxford and New York: Oxford University Press, 1962.

Stuart Bruchey, *The Colonial Merchant*. New York: Harcourt, Brace and World, 1966.

Edmund Burke, *An Account of the European Settlements in America*. London: R. and J. Dodsley, 1757.

John H. Campbell, *History of the Friendly Sons of St. Patrick*. Philadelphia: The Hibernian Society, 1892.

Batholomew Rivers Carroll, *Historical Collections of South Carolina*. New York, 1836, reprinted New York: Arno Press, 1973.

Cary Carson, Ronald Hoffman and Peter J. Albert, eds., *Of Consuming Interest: The Style of Life in the Eighteenth Century*. Charlottesville, VA: University Press of Virginia, 1994.

J. D. Chambers and J. E. Mingay, *The Agricultural Revolution 1750–1880*. London: Batsford, 1966.

Paul G. E. Clemens, *The Atlantic Economy and Colonial Maryland's Eastern Shore*. Ithaca, NY: Cornell University Press, 1980.

L. E. Cochran, *Scottish Trade with Ireland in the Eighteenth Century*. Edinburgh: J. Donald, 1985.

Linda Colley, *Britons: Forging the Nation 1707–1837*. London: Pimlico, 2003.

Brenda Collins and Philip Ollerenshaw, eds., *The European Linen Industry in Historical Perspective*. Oxford: Oxford University Press, 2003.

W. H. Crawford, *Domestic Industry in Ireland: The Experience of the Linen Industry*. Dublin: Gill and Macmillan, 1972.

W. H. Crawford, *The Impact of the Domestic Linen Industry in Ulster*. Belfast: Ulster Historical Foundation, 2005.

David Cressy, *Coming Over: Migration and Communication between England and New England in the Seventeenth Century*. Cambridge: Cambridge University Press, 1987.

L. M. Cullen, *An Economic History of Ireland Since 1660*. London: Batsford, 1972.

Hubertis Cummings, *Scots Breed and Susquehanna*. Pittsburgh: University of Pittsburgh Press, 1964.

James Stevens Curl, *The Londonderry Plantation 1609–1914*. Chichester, Sussex: Phillimore, 1986.

Robert L. D. Davidson, *War Comes to Quaker Pennsylvania 1682–1756*. New York: Columbia University Press, 1957.

R. J. Dickson, *Ulster Emigration to Colonial America 1718–1775*. London, 1966, reprinted Belfast: Ulster Historical Foundation, 1996.

Thomas M. Doerflinger, *A Vigorous Spirit of Enterprise: Merchants and Economic Development in Revolutionary Philadelphia*. Chapel Hill, NC: University of North Carolina Press, 1986.

Wayland F. Dunaway, *The Scotch-Irish of Colonial Pennsylvania*. Chapel Hill, NC: University of North Carolina Press, 1944.

John R. Dunbar, ed., *The Paxton Papers*. The Hague: M. Nijhoff, 1957.

William Eddis, *Letters from America*. London, 1792, reprinted Cambridge, MA: Harvard University Press, 1966.

Marc Egnal, *New World Economies: The Growth of the Thirteen Colonies and Early Canada*. Oxford: Oxford University Press, 1998.

P. Beryl Eustace and Olive C. Goodbody, *Quaker Records Dublin Abstracts of Wills*. Dublin: Irish Manuscripts Commission, 1953.

Richard D. Fisher, *First Presbyterian Church, Baltimore, Maryland 1761–1895*. Baltimore: First Presbyterian Church, 1895.

Patrick Fitzgerald and Steve Ickringill, eds., *Atlantic Crossroads: Historical connections between Scotland, Ulster and North America*. Newtownards: Colourpoint Books, 2001.

Henry Jones Ford, *The Scotch-Irish in America*. Princeton, NJ: Princeton University Press, 1915.

Joseph S. Foster, *In Pursuit of Equal Liberty: George Bryan and the Revolution in Pennsylvania*. University Park, PA: Pennsylvania State University Press, 1994.

Peter Francis, *A Pottery by the Lagan*. Belfast: Institute of Irish Studies, Queen's University Belfast, 2001.

John H. Gebbie, ed., *An Introduction to the Abercorn Letters*. Omagh, County Tyrone: Strule Press, 1972.

John Gibson, ed., *History of York County, Pennsylvania*. Chicago: F. A. Battey, 1886.

Geoffrey N. Gilbert, *Baltimore's Flour Trade to the Caribbean 1750–1815*. New York and London: Garland, 1986.

Conrad Gill, *The Rise of the Irish Linen Industry*. Oxford: Clarendon Press, 1925.

Lawrence H. Gipson, *The Coming of the Revolution 1763–1775*. New York: Harper, 1954.

Joyce D. Goodfriend, *Before the Melting Pot: Society and Culture in Colonial New York City 1664–1730*. Princeton, NJ: Princeton University Press, 1992.

Clarence G. Gould, "The Economic Causes of the Rise of Baltimore," *Essays in Colonial History Presented to Charles McLean Andrews*. Freeport, NY: Books for Libraries Press, 1966.

Jane Gray, *Spinning the Threads of Uneven Development: Gender and Industrialization in Ireland during the Long Eighteenth Century*. Lanham, MD: Lexington Books, 2005.

Patrick Griffin, *The People With No Name: Ireland's Ulster Scots, America's Scots Irish, and the Creation of a British Atlantic World 1689–1764*. Princeton, NJ: Princeton University Press, 2001.

Philip M. Hamer, ed., *The Papers of Henry Laurens*. Columbia SC: University of South Carolina Press, 1968–80.

Henry Hamilton, A*n Economic History of Scotland in the Eighteenth Century*. Oxford: Oxford University Press, 1963.

David Hancock, *Citizens of the World: London merchants and the integration of the British Atlantic community, 1735–1785*. Cambridge: Cambridge University Press, 1995.

Virginia D. Harrington, *The New York Merchant on the Eve of the Revolution*. New York: Columbia University Press, 1935.

Daniel Hay, *Whitehaven, A Short History*. Whitehaven: Whitehaven Borough Council, 1966.

Alexander Hewatt, *An Historical Account of the Rise and Progress of the Colonies of South Carolina and Georgia*. London: A. Donaldson, 1779 reprinted Spartanburg, SC: Reprint Company, 1962.

Ronald Hoffman, *A Spirit of Dissension: Economics, Politics, and the Revolution in Maryland*. Baltimore: The Johns Hopkins University Press, 1973.

Warren R. Hofstra, ed., *Cultures in Conflict: the Seven Years' War in North America*. Lanham, MD: Rowman and Littlefield, 2007.

Adrienne D. Hood, *The Weaver's Craft: Cloth, Commerce and Industry in Early Pennsylvania*. Philadelphia: University of Pennsylvania Press, 2003.

Richard J. Hooker, ed., *The Carolina Backcountry on the Eve of the Revolution: The Journal and Other Writings of Charles Woodmason, Anglican Itinerant*. Chapel Hill, NC: University of North Carolina Press, 1953.

W. G. Hoskins, *Industry, Trade and People in Exeter 1688–1800*. Manchester: Manchester University Press, 1935.

George Howe, *History of the Presbyterian Church in South Carolina*. Columbia, SC: Duffie and Chapman, 1870.

George Howe, *The Scotch-Irish and Their First Settlements on the Tyger River and Other Neighboring Precincts in South Carolina*. Columbia, SC: Southern Guardian Press, 1861.

William A. Hunter, *Forts on the Pennsylvania Frontier 1753–1758*. Harrisburg, PA: Pennsylvania Historical and Museum Commission, 1960.

James H. Hutson, *Pennsylvania Politics 1746–1770*. Princeton, NJ: Princeton University Press, 1972.

Owen S. Ireland, *Religion, Ethnicity and Politics: Ratifying the Constitution in Pennsylvania*. University Park, PA: Pennsylvania State University Press, 1995.

Alfred P. James, ed., *Writings of General John Forbes Relating to his Service in North America*. Menasha, WI: The Collegiate Press, 1938.

Francis Jennings, *Empire of Fortune: Crowns, colonies, and tribes in the Seven Years War in America*. New York: Norton, 1988.

Arthur L. Jensen, *The Maritime Commerce of Colonial Philadelphia*. Madison, WI: State Historical Society of Wisconsin, 1963.

George Johnston, *History of Cecil County, Maryland*. Elkton, MD: The Author, 1881.

George Lloyd Johnson, Jr., *The Frontier in the Colonial South: South Carolina Backcountry 1736–1800*. Westport, CN: Greenwood Press, 1997.

Guy S. Klett, ed., *Journals of Charles Beatty 1762–1769*. University Park, PA: Pennsylvania State University Press, 1962.

Burton A. Konkle, *George Bryan and the Constitution of Pennsylvania*. Philadelphia: G. H. Campbell, 1922.

James T. Lemon, *The Best Poor Man's Country: A Geographical Study of Early Southeastern Pennsylvania*. Baltimore: The Johns Hopkins University Press, 1971.

James Weston Livingood, *The Philadelphia-Baltimore Trade Rivalry 1780–1860*. Harrisburg, PA: Pennsylvania Historical and Museum Commission, 1947.

Audrey Lockhart, *Some Aspects of Emigration from Ireland to the North American Colonies Between 1660 and 1775*. New York: Arno Press, 1976.

Alexander Mackie, *Facile Princeps: The Story of the Beginning of Life Insurance in America*. Lancaster PA: Lancaster Press, 1956.

I. H. McCauley, *Historical Sketch of Franklin County*. Chambersburg, PA: D. F. Pursel, 1878.

George W. McCreary, *The Ancient and Honorable Mechanical Company of Baltimore*. Baltimore: Kohn and Pollock, 1901.

John McCusker and Kenneth Morgan, eds., *The Early Modern Atlantic Economy*. Cambridge: Cambridge University Press, 2000.

William L. McDowell, ed., *Documents Relating to Indian Affairs 1754–1765*. Columbia, SC: South Carolina Archives Department, 1970.

Neil McKendrick, John Brewer and J. H. Plumb, *The Birth of a Consumer Society:*

The Commercialization of Eighteenth-Century England. Bloomington, IN: Indiana University Press, 1982.

Felix McKillop, *Glenarm: A Local History*. Glenarm, 1987.

Jackson Turner Main, *The Social Structure of Revolutionary America*. Princeton, NJ: Princeton University Press, 1965.

Ann Smart Martin, *Buying into the World of Goods: Early Consumers in Backcountry Virginia*. Baltimore: The Johns Hopkins University Press, 2008.

Cathy Matson, *Merchants and Empire: Trading in Colonial New York*. Baltimore: The Johns Hopkins University Press, 1998.

Robert L. Meriwether, *The Expansion of South Carolina, 1729–1765*. Kingsport TN: Southern Publishers, 1940.

Harry Roy Merrens, *Colonial North Carolina in the Eighteenth Century*. Chapel Hill, NC: University of North Carolina Press, 1964.

Jane T. Merritt, *At the Crossroads: Indians and Empires on a Mid-Atlantic Frontier 1700–1763*. Chapel Hill, NC: University of North Carolina Press, 2003.

Kerby A. Miller, Arnold Schrier, Bruce D. Boling and David N. Doyle, eds., *Irish Immigrants in the Land of Canaan: Letters and Memoirs from Colonial and Revolutionary America, 1675–1815*. New York: Oxford University Press, 2004.

Peter N. Moore, *World of Toil and Strife: Community Transformation in Backcountry South Carolina, 1750–1805*. Columbia, SC: University of South Carolina Press, 2007.

Edmund S. and Helen M. Morgan, *The Stamp Act Crisis*. Chapel Hill, NC: University of North Carolina Press, 1953, reprinted New York: Collier Books, 1963.

Edmund S. Morgan, *Prologue to Revolution*. Chapel Hill, NC: University of North Carolina Press, 1959.

Vincent Morley, *Irish Opinion and the American Revolution, 1760–1783*. Cambridge: Cambridge University Press, 2002.

Richard C. Morris, ed., *Select Cases of the Mayor's Court of New York City 1674–1784*. Washington, DC: The American Historical Association, 1935.

Bobby Gilmer Moss, ed., *Journal of Capt. Alexander Chesney, Adjutant to Major Patrick Ferguson*. Blacksburg, SC: Scotia-Hibernia Press, 2002.

Michael J. O'Brien, *In Old New York: The Irish Dead in Trinity and St. Paul's Churchyards*. New York: American Irish Historical Society, 1928.

Denis O'Hearn, *The Atlantic economy, Britain, the United States and Ireland* Manchester: Manchester University Press, 2001.

John S. Pancake, *Samuel Smith and the Politics of Business*. Tuscaloosa, AL: University of Alabama Press, 1972.

Howard H. Peckham, *Pontiac and the Indian Uprising*. Princeton, NJ: Princeton University Press, 1947.

Henry C. Peden, Jr., *Presbyterian Records of Baltimore City, Maryland, 1765–1840*. Westminster, MD: Family Line Publications, 1995.

John D. Post, *Food Shortage, Climactic Variability, and Epidemic Disease in Preindustrial Europe: The Mortality Peak in the Early 1740s*. Ithaca, NY: Cornell University Press, 1985.

Jacob M. Price, ed., *Joshua Johnson's Letterbook 1771–1774: Letters from a merchant in London to his partners in Maryland.* London: London Record Society, 1979.

Jacob M. Price, *Capital and Credit in British Overseas Trade: The View from the Chesapeake, 1700–1776.* Cambridge, MA: Harvard University Press, 1980.

Robert Purviance, *A Narrative of Events Which Occurred in Baltimore Town During the Revolutionary War.* Baltimore: J. Robinson, 1849.

G. D. Ramsay, *The English Woollen Industry, 1500–1750.* London: Macmillan, 1982.

Record of indentures of individuals bound out as apprentices, servants, etc., and of German and other redemptioners in the office of the Mayor of the city of Philadelphia, October 3, 1771, to October 5, 1773, Pennsylvania German Society Proceedings and Addresses, 16(1907), reprinted Baltimore: Genealogical Publishing Co., 1973.

Janie Revill, *A Compilation of the Original Lists of Protestant Immigrants to South Carolina, 1763–1773.* Columbia SC: The State Company, 1939, reprinted Baltimore: Genealogical Publishing Company, 1968.

Hannah Benner Roach, *Colonial Philadelphians.* Philadelphia: Genealogical Society of Pennsylvania, 1999.

Charles Rhoads Roberts, *History of Lehigh County, Pennsylvania.* Allentown, PA: Lehigh Valley Publishing Company, 1914.

Priscilla H. Roberts and James N. Tull, *Adam Hoops, Thomas Barclay, and the House in Morrisville Known as Summerseat, 1764–1791, Transactions of the American Philosophical Society Held at Philadelphia for Promoting Useful Knowledge, Volume 90, Pt. 5.* Philadelphia: American Philosophical Society, 2000.

Alan Rogers, *A Twice-Born Village Muff (Eglinton) Co. Londonderry.* Londonderry: The University of Ulster, 1984.

Philip S. Robinson, *The Plantation of Ulster: British settlement in an Irish landscape, 1600–1670.* New York: St. Martin's Press, 1984.

Sharon V. Salinger, *"To Serve Well and Faithfully": Labor and Indentured Servants in Pennsylvania, 1682–1800.* Cambridge: Cambridge University Press, 1987.

J. Thomas Scharf, *Chronicles of Baltimore.* Baltimore: Turnbull Brothers, 1874.

Merri Lou Scribner Schaumann, *A History and Genealogy of Carlisle, Cumberland County, Pennsylvania, 1751–1835.* Carlisle, PA: The Author, 1995.

Leila Sellers, *Charleston Business on the Eve of the American Revolution.* Chapel Hill NC: University of North Carolina Press, 1934.

Carole Shammas, *The Pre-Industrial Consumer in England and America.* Oxford and New York: Oxford University Press, 1990.

Robert Simpson, *The Annals of Derry.* Londonderry, 1847, reprinted Limavady: Northwest Books, 1987.

John Smail, *Merchants, Markets and Manufacture: The English Wool Textile Industry in the Eighteenth Century.* London: Macmillan, 1999.

Warren B. Smith, *White Servitude in Colonial South Carolina.* Columbia, SC: University of South Carolina Press, 1961.

Charles G. Steffen, *From Gentlemen to Townsmen: The Gentry of Baltimore County,*

Maryland 1660–1776. Lexington, KY: University of Kentucky Press, 1993.

Bernard C. Steiner, *Life and Correspondence of James McHenry.* Cleveland OH: Burrows Brothers, 1907.

Jean Stephenson, *Scotch-Irish Migration to South Carolina, 1772: Rev. William Martin and his Five Shiploads of Settlers.* Washington, DC: The Author, 1971.

John Austin Stevens, ed., *Colonial Records of the New York Chamber of Commerce 1768–1784.* New York: J. F. Trow, 1867, reprinted New York: B. Franklin, 1971.

Sylvester K. Stevens, Donald H. Kent, Louis M. Waddell, eds., *The Papers of Henry Bouquet.* Harrisburg, PA: Pennsylvania Historical and Museum Commission, 1951–80.

Theodore G. Tappert and John W. Doberstein, eds., *The Journals of Henry Melchior Muhlenberg.* Philadelphia: Evangelical Lutheran Ministerium, 1942–4.

Theodore Thayer, *Israel Pemberton, King of the Quakers.* Philadelphia: Historical Society of Pennsylvania, 1943.

Joseph S. Tiedemann, *Reluctant Revolutionaries: New York City and the Road to Independence 1763–1776.* Ithaca, NY: Cornell University Press, 1997.

Thomas M. Truxes, *Irish-American Trade 1660–1783.* Cambridge: Cambridge University Press, 1988.

Thomas M. Truxes, ed., *Letterbook of Greg and Cunningham, 1756–57: Merchants of New York and Belfast.* Oxford: Oxford University Press, 2001.

Albert T. Volwiler, *George Croghan and the Westward Movement 1741–1782.* Cleveland, OH: Arthur H. Clark, 1926.

Nicholas B. Wainwright, *George Croghan Wilderness Diplomat.* Chapel Hill, NC: University of North Carolina Press, 1959.

Gary M. Walton and James F. Shepherd, *The Economic Rise of Early America.* Cambridge: Cambridge University Press, 1979.

Matthew C. Ward, *Breaking the Backcountry: The Seven Years' War in Virginia and Pennsylvania, 1754–1765.* Pittsburgh, PA: University of Pittsburgh Press, 2003.

Philip L. White, *The Beekmans of New York in Politics and Commerce 1647–1877.* New York: New York Historical Society, 1956.

Philip L. White, ed., *The Beekman Mercantile Papers.* New York: New York Historical Society, 1956.

John Wily, *A Treatise on the Propagation of Sheep, the Manufacture of Wool, and the Cultivation and Manufacture of Flax, with Directions for making several Utensils for the Business.* Williamsburg, VA, 1765.

Marianne Wokeck, *Trade in Strangers: The Beginnings of Mass Migration to North America.* State College, PA: Pennsylvania State University Press, 1999.

Jerome Wood, Jr., *Conestoga Crossroads: Lancaster, Pennsylvania 1730–1790.* Harrisburg, PA: Pennsylvania Historical and Museum Commission, 1979.

Arthur Young, *A Tour in Ireland with General Observations on the Present State of the Kingdom made in the Years 1776, 1777, and 1778.* Dublin: George Bonham, 1780.

Articles

Walter S. Barker, "Flax: The Fiber and the Seed, A Study in Agricultural Contrasts," *Quarterly Journal of Economics*, 31(1917), 500–29.

Wayne L. Bockleman and Owen S. Ireland, "The Internal Revolution in Pennsylvania: An Ethnic-Religious Interpretation," *Pennsylvania History*, 41(1974), 125–60.

T. H. Breen, "The meaning of things: interpreting the consumer economy in the eighteenth century," in John Brewer and Roy Porter, eds., *Consumption and the World of Goods* (London, 1993), 249–60.

T. H. Breen, "An Empire of Goods: The Anglicization of Colonial America, 1690–1776," in Stanley Katz, John Murrin and Denis Greenberg, eds., *Colonial America: Essays in Politics and Social Development* (New York, 1993), 367–97.

Paul G. E. Clemens, "From Tobacco to Grain: Economic Development on Maryland's Eastern Shore 1660–1750," *Journal of Economic History*, 35(1975), 256–9.

W. H. Crawford, "The Evolution of the Linen Trade in Ulster Before Industrialisation," *Irish Economic and Social History*, 15(1988), 32–53.

W. H. Crawford, "The Political Economy of Linen: Ulster in the Eighteenth Century," in Ciaran Brady, Mary O'Dowd and Brian Walker, eds., *Ulster, An Illustrated History* (London, 1989), 134–57.

L. M. Cullen, "Merchant Communities Overseas, the Navigation Acts, and Irish and Scottish Responses," in L. M. Cullen and T. C. Smout, eds., *Comparative Aspects of Scottish and Irish Economic and Social History* (Edinburgh, 1976), 165–76.

David Dickson, "The Place of Dublin in the Eighteenth-Century Irish Economy" in T. M. Devine and L. M. Cullen, eds., *Ireland and Scotland 1600–1850 Parallels and Contrasts in Economic and Social Development* (Edinburgh, 1983), 177–92.

Thomas M. Doerflinger, "Commercial Specialization in Philadelphia's Merchant Community, 1750–1791," *Business History Review*, 57(1983), 20–49.

Thomas M. Doerflinger, "Farmers and Dry Goods in the Philadelphia Market Area, 1750–1800," in Ronald Hoffman et al., eds., *The Economy of Early America: The Revolutionary Period, 1763–1790* (Charlottesville, VA, 1988), 166–95.

James S. Donnelly, "Hearts of Oak, Hearts of Steel," *Studia Hibernica*, 21(1981), 7–73.

A. Roger Ekirch, "Bound for America: A Profile of British Convicts Transported to the Colonies 1718–1775," *William and Mary Quarterly*, 3rd series, 42(1985), 184–200.

John E. Engle and Eugene K. Engle, "A Letter from Immigrant Ulrich Engel to Switzerland in 1755," *Pennsylvania Mennonite Heritage*, 16(July 1993), 11–18.

E. E. R. Evans, "The 'Strange Humours' That Drove the Scotch-Irish to America, 1729," *William and Mary Quarterly*, 3rd series, 12(1955), 113–23.

Patrick Fitzgerald, "A Sentence to Sail: The Transportation of Irish Convicts and Vagrants to Colonial America in the Eighteenth Century," in Patrick Fitzgerald and Steve Ickringill, eds., *Atlantic Crossroads: Historical connections between Scotland, Ulster and North America* (Newtownards, 2001), 114–32.

E. R. R. Green, "Queensborough Township: Scotch-Irish Emigration and the Expansion of Georgia, 1763–1776," *William and Mary Quarterly*, 3rd series, 17(April 1960), 183–99.

Mary K. Geiter and W. A. Speck, "Anticipating America: American mentality before the Revolution," in David Englander, ed., *Britain and America: Studies in Comparative History 1760–1970* (New Haven, CT, 1997), 26–47.

H. D. Gribbon, "The Irish Linen Board 1711–1828," in L. M. Cullen and T. C. Smout, *Comparative Aspects of Scottish and Irish Economic History* (Edinburgh, 1977), 77–87.

Farley Grubb, "The Market for Indentured Immigrants: Evidence for the Efficiency of Forward-Labor Contracting in Philadelphia, 1745–1773," *Journal of Economic History*, 45 (1985), 855–68.

Farley Grubb, "Redemptioner Emigration to Pennsylvania: Evidence on Contract Choice and Profitability," *Journal of Economic History*, 46(1986), 407–18.

Farley Grubb, "British Immigration to Philadelphia: The Reconstruction of Ship Passenger Lists from May 1772 to October 1773," *Pennsylvania History*, 55(1988), 118–41.

Farley Grubb, "The Transatlantic Market for British Convict Labor," *Journal of Economic History*, 60(2000), 94–122.

Henry Hamilton, "The Failure of the Ayr Bank," *Economic History Review*, 8(1956), 405–17.

Horace Edwin Hayden, ed., "The Reminiscences of David Hayfield Conyngham 1750–1834 of the Revolutionary House of Conyngham and Nesbitt, Philadelphia, Pa.," *Wyoming Historical and Genealogical Society Proceedings*, 8(1903), 181–291.

Jo N. Hays, "Overlapping Hinterlands: York, Philadelphia, and Baltimore 1800–1850," *Pennsylvania Magazine of History and Biography*, 116(1992), 295–321.

Robert Owen Heavner, "Indentured Servitude: The Philadelphia Market, 1771–1773," *Journal of Economic History*, 38(1978), 701–13.

Adrienne D. Hood, "Flax Seed, Fibre and Cloth: Pennsylvania's Domestic Linen Manufacture and Its Irish Connection, 1700–1830," in Brenda Collins and Philip Ollerenshaw, eds., *The European Linen Industry in Historical Perspective* (Oxford, 2003), 139–58.

Craig W. Horle, "William West," *Lawmaking and Legislators in Pennsylvania: A Biographical Dictionary* (Philadelphia, 1997), 2 (1710–1756), 1055–64.

James H. Hutson, "The Campaign to Make Pennsylvania a Royal Province, 1764–1770," *Pennsylvania Magazine of History and Biography*, 94(1970), 427–63, 95(1971), 28–49.

Owen S. Ireland, "The Ethnic-Religious Dimension of Pennsylvania Politics,
    1778–1779," *William and Mary Quarterly*, 3rd series, 30(1973), 423–48

Jimmy Irvine, "Drumnasole," *The Glynns*, 11(1983), 1–6.

Francis G. James, "Irish Colonial Trade in the Eighteenth Century," *William and
    Mary Quarterly*, 3rd series, 20(1963), 574–84.

Graeme Kirkham, "Ulster Emigration to North America, 1680–1720" in Tyler
    Blethen and Curtis Wood, eds., *Ulster and North America: Transatlantic
    Perspectives on the Scotch-Irish* (Tuscaloosa, AL, 1997), 76–97.

Ned C. Landsman, "Ethnicity and National Origin Among British Settlers in the
    Philadelphia Region," *Proceedings of the American Philosophical Society*,
    (133)1989, 170–77.

Audrey Lockhart, "Quakers and Emigration from Ireland to the North American
    Colonies," *Quaker History*, 77(1988), 83–6.

Richard K. MacMaster, "Instructions to a Tobacco Factor, 1725," *Maryland
    Historical Magazine*, 63(1968), 172–8.

Richard K. MacMaster, "Georgetown and the Tobacco Trade, 1751–1783,"
    *Records of the Columbia Historical Society of Washington, D.C.
    1966–1968* (Washington, DC, 1969), 1–33.

Richard K. MacMaster, "Emigrants to New England from the Conolly Estates,
    1718," *Journal of Scotch-Irish Studies*, 1(2000), 18–23.

Richard K. MacMaster, "James Fullton, A Philadelphia Merchant and His
    Customers," *Familia* 17(2001), 23–34.

Richard K. MacMaster, "The Voyage of the Nancy 1767," *Familia*, 19(2003),
    64–73.

Richard K. MacMaster, "'For Philadelphia, Boys, Are We Bound': the Rev. Joseph
    Rhea Comes to America in 1769," *Familia*, 22(2006), 33–50.

W. A. Maguire, "Lord Donegall and the Hearts of Steel," *Irish Historical Studies*,
    21(1979), 351–76.

Joseph McClenachan, "A Controversial Cleric: The Reverend William
    McClenachan," *Journal of Scotch-Irish Studies*, 1(2003), 80–103.

Kenneth Morgan, "The Organization of the Convict Trade to Maryland:
    Stevenson, Randolph and Cheston, 1768–1775," *William and Mary
    Quarterly*, 3rd series, 42(1985), 201–27.

Michael P. Morris, "Profits and Philanthrophy: The Ulster Immigration Schemes
    of George Galphin and John Rea," *Journal of Scotch-Irish Studies*, 1(2002),
    1–11.

James Myers, "The Rev. Thomas Barton's Authorship of the Conduct of the
    Paxton Men," *Pennsylvania Magazine of History and Biography*, 118(1994),
    3–34.

R. C. Nash, "Irish Atlantic Trade in the Seventeenth and Eighteenth Century,"
    William and Mary Quarterly, 3rd series, 42(1985), 329–56.

George W. Neible, comp., "Servants and Apprentices Bound and Assigned Before
    James Hamilton, Mayor of Philadelphia, 1745," *Pennsylvania Magazine of
    History and Biography*, XXX (1906), 348–52, 427–36, XXXI (1907),
    83–102, 195–206, 351–67, 461–73, XXXII (1908), 88–103, 237–49,
    351–70.

Michael J. O'Brien, "Some Interesting Shipping Statistics of the Eighteenth Century," *Journal of the American Irish Historical Society*, 13(1914), 191–201.

R. Nicholas Olsberg, "Ship Registers in the South Carolina Archives 1734–1780," *South Carolina Historical Magazine*, 74(1973), 219.

Herbert L. Osgood, ed., "The Society of Dissenters founded at New York in 1769," *American Historical Review*, 6(1901), 498–507.

Judith Ridner, "Relying on the 'Saucy' Men of the Backcountry: Middlemen and the Fur Trade in Pennsylvania," *Pennsylvania Magazine of History and Biography*, 129(2005), 133–62.

Marvin F. Russell, "Thomas Barton and Pennsylvania's Colonial Frontier," *Pennsylvania History*, 46(1979), 313–34.

Robert A. Selig, "Emigration, Fraud, Humanitarianism, and the Founding of Londonderry, South Carolina, 1763–1765," *Eighteenth-Century Studies*, 23(1989) 1–23.

A. G. Seyfert, "The Wallace Family and the Wallace Store of East Earl," *Journal of the Lancaster County Historical Society*, 28(1924), 20–29.

Carole Shammas, "Changes in English and Anglo-American consumption from 1550 to 1800," in John Brewer and Roy Porter, eds., *Consumption and the World of Goods* (London, 1993), 177–205.

Richard B. Sheridan, "The British Credit Crisis of 1772 and the American Colonies," *Journal of Economic History*, 20(1960), 162–6.

Robert Slade, "Narrative of a Journey to the North of Ireland in 1802" in *A Concise View of the Origin, Constitution and Proceedings of the Irish Society* (London, 1842), cci–ccxvi.

Henry A. M. Smith, "Wragg of South Carolina," *South Carolina Historical Magazine*, 19(1918), 122–3.

Frederick D. Stone, "How the Landing of Tea Was Opposed in Philadelphia," *Pennsylvania Magazine of History and Biography*, 15(1891), 385–94.

William M. Swaim, "The Evolution of Ten Pre-1745 Presbyterian Societies in the Cumberland Valley," *Cumberland County History*, 2(1985), 3–30.

Daniel B. Thorp, "Doing Business in the Backcountry: Retail Trade in Colonial Rowan County, North Carolina," *William and Mary Quarterly*, 3rd ser., 48 (1991), 387–408.

Thomas M. Truxes, "Connecticut in the Irish-American Flaxseed Trade, 1750–1775," *Eire-Ireland*, 12(1977), 34–62.

Diane Wenger, "Delivering the Goods: The Country Storekeeper and Inland Commerce in the Mid-Atlantic," *Pennsylvania Magazine of History and Biography*, 129 (2005), 45–72.

J. E. Williams, "Whitehaven in the Eighteenth Century," *Economic History Review*, 8(1956), 393–404.

Index